LUTHER'S WORKS

LUTHER'S WORKS

VOLUME 18

LECTURES ON THE MINOR PROPHETS

I

Hosea, Joel, Amos
Obadiah, Micah, Nahum
Zephaniah, Haggai, Malachi

HILTON C. OSWALD
Editor

CONCORDIA PUBLISHING HOUSE · SAINT LOUIS

ISBN 978-0-5700-6418-3

9 780570 064183

RELIGION / Christianity / Lutheran

151760

Library of Congress Catalog Card No. 55-9893

ISBN: 978-0-570-06418-3

MANUFACTURED IN THE UNITED STATES OF AMERICA

Library of Congress Cataloging in Publication Data (Revised)

Luther, Martin, 1483-1546.
Works.

Vols. edited by H. C. Oswald.
Vols. 31- edited by H. J. Grimm and others.
General editor: H. T. Lehmann.
Vols. 31- have imprint: Philadelphia, Fortress Press (formerly Muhlenberg Press)
Includes bibliographical references.
— — — — — — — Companion volume. BR350.E5 1955 suppl.
1. Theology — Collected works — 16th century. 2. Lutheran Church — Collected works. 3. Bible — Commentaries. 4. Bible — Criticism, interpretation, etc. — History — 16th century. I. Pelikan, Jaroslav, 1923- ed. II. Oswald, Hilton C., ed. III. Lehmann Helmut T., ed. IV Title: Luther the expositor.
BR330.E5 1955 208 55-9893
ISBN 13: 978-0-570-06418-3 ISBN 10: 0-570-06418-X

8 9 10 11 12 13 14 15 16 17 32 31 30 29 28 27 26 25 24 23

Contents

General Introduction

THE first editions of Luther's collected works appeared in the sixteenth century, and so did the first efforts to make him "speak English." In America serious attempts in these directions were made for the first time in the nineteenth century. The Saint Louis edition of Luther was the first endeavor on American soil to publish a collected edition of his works, and the Henkel Press in Newmarket, Virginia, was the first to publish some of Luther's writings in an English translation. During the first decade of the twentieth century, J. N. Lenker produced translations of Luther's sermons and commentaries in thirteen volumes. A few years later the first of the six volumes in the Philadelphia (or Holman) edition of the *Works of Martin Luther* appeared. Miscellaneous other works were published at one time or another. But a growing recognition of the need for more of Luther's works in English has resulted in this American edition of Luther's works.

The edition is intended primarily for the reader whose knowledge of late medieval Latin and sixteenth-century German is too small to permit him to work with Luther in the original languages. Those who can, will continue to read Luther in his original words as these have been assembled in the monumental Weimar edition (*D. Martin Luthers Werke.* Kritische Gesamtausgabe; Weimar, 1883 ff.). Its texts and helps have formed a basis for this edition, though in certain places we have felt constrained to depart from its readings and findings. We have tried throughout to translate Luther as he thought translating should be done. That is, we have striven for faithfulness on the basis of the best lexicographical materials available. But where literal accuracy and clarity have conflicted, it is clarity that we have preferred, so that sometimes paraphrase seemed more faithful than literal fidelity. We have proceeded in a similar way in the matter of Bible versions, translating

Luther's translations. Where this could be done by the use of an existing English version—King James, Douay, or Revised Standard—we have done so. Where it could not, we have supplied our own. To indicate this in each specific instance would have been pedantic; to adopt a uniform procedure would have been artificial—especially in view of Luther's own inconsistency in this regard. In each volume the translator will be responsible primarily for matters of text and language, while the responsibility of the editor will extend principally to the historical and theological matters reflected in the introductions and notes.

Although the edition as planned will include fifty-five volumes, Luther's writings are not being translated in their entirety. Nor should they be. As he was the first to insist, much of what he wrote and said was not that important. Thus the edition is a selection of works that have proved their importance for the faith, life, and history of the Christian church. The first thirty volumes contain Luther's expositions of various Biblical books, while the remaining volumes include what are usually called his "Reformation writings" and other occasional pieces. The final volume of the set will be an index volume; in addition to an index of quotations, proper names, and topics, and a list of corrections and changes, it will contain a glossary of many of the technical terms that recur in Luther's works and that cannot be defined each time they appear. Obviously Luther cannot be forced into any neat set of rubrics. He can provide his reader with bits of autobiography or with political observations as he expounds a psalm, and he can speak tenderly about the meaning of the faith in the midst of polemics against his opponents. It is the hope of publishers, editors, and translators that through this edition the message of Luther's faith will speak more clearly to the modern church.

JAROSLAV PELIKAN
HELMUT LEHMANN

Introduction to Volume 18

When Luther's lectures on the minor prophets were first published (in the Wittenberg edition, Latin Vols. IV and V, 1552 and 1554), only a few of the lectures printed (Nahum, Zephaniah, Malachi) represented recensions based on original manuscripts, and those originals were not identified. It is possible that manuscript materials were not readily available to the editors at the time, but there is also an apparent preference among them for the revisions of Luther's lectures provided by Veit Dietrich, for Luther's own German editions of his previous Latin lectures, and even for Latin retranslations of previous German translations of the original Latin versions. In Vol. VIII of the German section of the Wittenberg edition (1556) the Haggai lectures are even represented by a version provided by Melanchthon, with the explanation "because no commentary of Luther's on this prophet was available."

Contrary to what one might expect, the situation was much better when the great 19th-century editions of Luther's works were published. When Johannes Linke prepared Vols. XXIV–XXVIII in the *Exegetica opera* series of the Erlangen edition (1884–86), he was able to base his texts on various 16th-century manuscripts. The Weimar edition carried this work forward, and in 1889 Gustav Koffmane was able to publish in Vol. XIII not only various parallel manuscript texts of the lectures on the full roster of the minor prophets but also a convincing discussion of the intricate relations among the manuscripts. A few of the manuscripts may briefly be described here.

Preeminent is the manuscript of these lectures preserved in the library of the *Gymnasium* in Altenburg. It consists of 501 quarto pages containing the lectures on 10 of the minor prophets (Joel–

Zechariah). Corrections and notes entered by Luther's friend George Spalatin establish its date as before 1545, the death date of Spalatin. The manuscript is too deliberate, critical, and careful to represent notes taken down in the lecture hall. It shows a good deal of editorial activity and seems to have been prepared for someone on order, perhaps on the basis of more than one earlier manuscript. This eventual owner is even addressed, it seems, in various asides in marginal notes, and for his benefit an unusually large number of references to the Hebrew text and to Luther's earlier works seem to have been added. Dr. Linke suggests that Caspar Cruciger may have been the compiler. Dr. Koffmane conjectures that George Rörer may have been the compiler and Spalatin the recipient of this manuscript.

A second source for the text of the lectures on the minor prophets is a group of manuscripts associated with Zwickau in Saxony. These were discovered and made available to the Erlangen editor by George Buchwald, later one of the editors of the Weimar edition of Luther's works. In general, these Zwickau manuscripts are true student notebooks.

A further source is a Halle manuscript. This is the only manuscript containing all 12 minor prophets, although Zechariah is incomplete. It is evidently an effort to copy all the lectures from various sources.

Beside these manuscript texts, a number of early printed versions of the lectures on the minor prophets became available. Luther himself issued German versions of his commentaries on Jonah and Habakkuk (*Luther's Works*, Vol. 19) and on Zechariah (*Luther's Works*, Vol. 20). In Basel, Thomas Wolff in 1526 published the lectures on Hosea but in an incomplete version. Veit Dietrich published a version of the lectures on Joel, Amos, and Obadiah in 1536, one on Micah in 1542, one on Hosea in 1545, and a second version of Joel in 1547. These were hardly representative of Luther's work, however, for Dietrich felt free not only to modify Luther's statements but occasionally even to turn them into their opposites. Luther withheld his approval of Dietrich's earlier ventures in this field, but Dietrich was discouraged only temporarily. Besides, there was hardly anything like a feeling for copyright protection in those days.

For some time it was assumed that Luther lectured more than

once on the minor prophets. That supposition helped to explain how some of Dietrich's statements could disagree with those contained in earlier texts. Luther had obviously said something different the second time! But the editor of the Weimar text fails to find either time or warrant for a second series of lectures on the minor prophets. He argues that Luther was too busy with other lectures in the years following, was much more in demand for other work too, and was himself physically less able to take on additional lectures. Besides, while there is abundant evidence for the first series of lectures on the minor prophets, there is none for a second series. Not even Dietrich, who could well have used a reference to a second series to defend his changes in Luther's exegesis, gives any hint that he is reporting on a second series.

A number of incidental dates in the manuscripts help us determine the time of these lectures. Additional information is recorded in letters of the time or may be inferred from Luther's own statements in the lectures. Luther began to lecture on the minor prophets about March 1524. From a letter of Spalatin's we learn that Joel was being commented on in July, and the Altenburg text records August 9 as the day on which Luther finished Joel. After a pause, Luther lectured on Amos from December until the end of January 1525. Obadiah was concluded February 1. Jonah must have followed soon. The Altenburg text adds "in the month of March" to both Jonah and Micah. By April 7 Luther had finished Micah. Then business took him away from Wittenberg, and he probably did not resume these lectures until after his marriage, which occurred June 13, 1525. The Altenburg text introduces Nahum with "the commentary of Luther the newlywed." Completing this July 4, Luther went on to lecture on Habakkuk from July 18 until August 2. Zephaniah was begun August 14, and Haggai September 11. After another pause, Zechariah was begun near the end of the year and completed in the first months of 1526. It is hard to imagine that the text of the lectures on Malachi, which the Wittenberg edition presents, was delivered at some later time. It fits well into the circumstances of 1526 and was probably completed early in the year, immediately after Zechariah.

In presenting these lectures in English, we have followed the Weimar edition as well as the St. Louis edition in rejecting the thought of producing a conflation of the various texts, a single composite version. Unlike those editions, however, we have not presented all the texts but have chosen to translate only one manuscript, the Altenburg text. But to complete the series, we have added the Hosea lectures on the basis of the Zwickau text and the Malachi lectures on the basis of the Wittenberg text.

In his exegesis Luther has here reached a new level of independence and maturity. He no longer follows but more often rejects the thoughts of commentators like Jerome and Lyra. He feels more free than before to fault the Vulgate text on the basis of references to the original Hebrew text. Thus he freed himself of patristic and scholastic shackles, and the old fourfold interpretations hardly come in for mention any longer. The prophets think and speak in the direction of the New Testament.

H. O.

LECTURES ON HOSEA

The Zwickau Text

Translated by
RICHARD J. DINDA

CHAPTER ONE
THE WORD OF THE LORD

IT is well known that it is the custom of the Hebrews and the prophets to begin books with titles. God always announces repentance before His wrath comes, as one may see in the case of Jonah to the people of Nineveh and in the case of Christ to the Jews.

This prophet, however, begins the Word ridiculously at the very time when the kingdom of Israel, rich and fat, was flourishing greatly under Jeroboam. The result was that the people thought Hosea was mad. Furthermore, the words "Take to yourself a wife, etc." (v. 2) are very foolish among a people so learned and wise. There is no doubt that they considered him a fool and a heretic. This, however, is the nature of the Word, that it deals in apparent foolishness with the very wise. Another characteristic of the Word is the cross that he could not escape. It seems that he is fighting alone against all the prophets and even Moses. Moses says that Israel is the people of God, but Hosea denies that God is the God of Israel. Moses promises a God who is kindly disposed; Hosea says that the sin of Israel is unforgivable. Therefore the priests and lawyers had to declare that he was a heretic.

The aged prophet seems to have been still alive in the captivity that he foretold.

Here people stir up big questions on account of that harlotry, whether the prophet committed fornication by the dispensation of God or took a harlot as wife. What some people say does not satisfy me, not even the words of Jerome.[1] By their names the sons signify below what sort of people the Israelites are going to

[1] Jerome, *Commentaria in Osee prophetam, Patrologia, Series Latina,* XXV, 823: "The prophet did not lose his chastity because he was joined to a harlot, but the harlot gained a chastity she did not have previously; especially because Hosea did what he did not for the sake of excess, not because of lust or his own will, but because he obeyed the will of God."

be. I think we must say the same thing about the harlot, because she was called a "wife of harlotry" to signify that the people now were committing harlotry and would do the same by forsaking God in the future. So also the sons born of her are called "sons of harlotry." Do not take this to mean, then, that harlotry is charged to the wife, that is, do not take this in the active sense, but understand that the wife has allowed herself, her sons, and her husband to be so named because of the people and against the people, as if she were saying: "I am called a harlot and my husband is called a whoremonger because you are harlots and whoremongers." Oh, how great a cross they suffered with those insulting names for the sake of the Word of God! He prophesies not only with words but with things which the senses feel.

2. *First.* More accurately, "The first time, when the Lord began to speak through Hosea."

For the land commits great harlotry. He is speaking in common terminology. The true seed that purifies our souls is the Word of God. When you depart from this, you commit harlotry. He transfers a simile of the flesh to the spiritual realm. Committing harlotry means practicing idolatry. Idolatry is the genuine trust in works; harlotry is to sin with unfaithfulness against the First Commandment. Properly, harlotry is to act against the First Commandment in the name of God, that is, to do without faith what you imagine you are doing to worship God.

4. *Jezreel.* At one time this was a great city of the kingdom.[2] We must take note to understand the account in simplest terms, from which alone one may realize how great a faith this prophet had. You see, Jehu had turned to wickedness after he had done well. This began under Zechariah, the great-great-grandson of Jehu,[3] and the affliction of the kingdom lasted all the way to the captivity.

5. *And on that day.* Here he is prophesying the word of faith which ought to have warned those who were penitent. He foretells destruction, and God gives a blessing. He is therefore a heretic. Let him be burned! But yet the Word of God lives.

[2] Cf. 1 Kings 21:1.

[3] Cf. 2 Kings 15:8-11.

4. *The house of Jehu.* We do not know whether to take this actively or passively. Histories do not help either to tell whether that house poured out blood or allowed its blood to be shed. Jehu was a good king. Yet neither he nor any other kings of Israel abandoned the golden calves and their worship, without which they believed their kingdom could not stand. Therefore let the meaning be this: Jehu poured out his blood because of the calves in Jezreel.[4] This prophecy was incredible, that the kingdom was going to be taken away because of the wicked kings, for God had promised the kingdom to Jehu. People could not believe this until they began to feel it. Yet you say, "Did not God give the kingdom to Jeroboam himself?" I answer, "This is true, but always with the added condition, 'If you do My will.'" The kingdom of Judah is the kingdom of David which came to Christ forever. The kingdom of Israel, however, was carried off to the Assyrians and was never restored.

6. *Not Pitied.* The names should have remained in Hebrew. That is, he was indicating a people whose God would have no pity. Earlier He says that He would destroy the kingdom; here, that He would never restore it. Ps. 28:5: "You will break them down and build them up no more." Therefore He is not speaking here about the mercy of the Gospel, about which He will speak later; rather, He says that He will not restore the kingdom. What follows speaks about the eternal kingdom: "I will have pity on the house of Judah." This was to remain until Christ, who established it forever. But in this fact, that ten tribes were carried off and the Assyrians could not carry away two, very clearly seems to lie the efficacy of the power of God and of His Word. This is something which He says clearly in this way:

7. *I will not deliver.* All the prophets look forward to the kingdom of Christ with wonderfully sweet words. Also note that it has to be true that Israel would never return, and yet Israel would be one kingdom with Judah.

8. *When she had weaned.* Perhaps it is a mystery that, so far as external worship is concerned, the entire people is to be aban-

[4] The Latin spelling of Israel and Jezreel is somewhat confusing, especially since Jezreel may stand for Israel by metonymy. We have translated "Israel" for *Israhel* and *Israel* and "Jezreel" for *Iesrahel* and *Iesrael.*

doned, not only Israel when it has grown to manhood. The third child, then, connects the prophecy of the temporal kingdom with that of the eternal kingdom. "I will no longer foster the synagog. I will lift up another people. If My former people joins this one, it will be saved. If it does not, it will not be My people." This people has to be rejected and a new one taken up, so that all the prophecies which seem contrary or which appear here may be true. He says that this will not be His people, and yet:

10. *The number of the people in Israel will be.* You see here what Paul says in Rom. 1:2: "The Gospel . . . promised . . . through His prophets." Note the explanation of this passage in Paul, Rom. 9:26. The kingdom of Judah was never destroyed but was transformed into a better one. The kingdom of Christ is the preservation of the kingdom of Judah.

The number will be. We have a similar statement in Isaiah.[5] History bears witness that at the time of Christ this people had multiplied and become countless. Their own region was filled, and there were Jews in almost every city of the Gentiles, including even Rome.

In the place. This place is neither Jezreel[6] nor Judah but a place where up to now there was no people of God, that is, there the kingdom of God, the victory over sin, death, and hell, will be preached. Otherwise they could not be called the people of God in a place that was Gentile rather than Jewish. There will be another people of God, not fixed to a place or to external things.

11. *One head.* We necessarily take this to mean the kingdom of Christ. After the division of the kingdom after Solomon, they never had one head, that is, a temporal king. These truths will not stand at the same time: that they will be completely rejected and that they will be the people and children of God, unless you understand that corporal things have been cast down and spiritual ones lifted up.

And they will go up. He does not place this kingdom on earth. Rather, it will be lifted up from the earth from day to day, from earthly things to heavenly. Know what things are on high!

[5] Cf. Is. 10:22.

[6] Cf. n. 4 above.

For great. I believe that this was added to obscure the prophecy for those who do not believe so that it is not seen until it is fulfilled, as are all the prophecies.

For great will be the day. It will be a great day when God will illumine the hearts of men that they may be the sons of God. No longer will Jezreel be terrestrial but celestial. It will not be led back physically. This is how he often signifies neither a carnal Israel or Zion but a spiritual one. We seldom find names among the Hebrews that do not end in a name of God, EL or IA, as Michael, Isaiah, Jeremiah. So also Jerusalem is "the vision of peace," that is, where one may see peace and an abundance of all things. So also Jezreel is "the seed of God," because all things abounded there. Whatever "the seed of God" may be, it is known as the place from which the children of God come, as Luke 8:11 tells us.

CHAPTER TWO

I UNDERSTAND that the entire chapter is addressed to those who have obtained mercy—both Gentiles and Jews. The rejected sister I take to mean the unbelieving Jews, so that this is the word of the apostles and Christians which the prophet orders them to speak to their brothers. It is the word of the Gospel. The synagog is the mother of the church. "You, my mother, are not the wife of God, my Father." The Gospel condemns the works of the Law and the confidence of the mother. Whatever the mother uses as an excuse for her wickedness is useless. She is a harlot.

2. *Plead,* that is, condemn those who say that they will believe as the fathers do. Their confidence is wickedness; their traditions are against the Word of God. Paul writes (Rom. 9:8): "Not the children of the flesh, etc."

Breasts. These are the wicked teachers who, like a mother's breasts, feed the people. But they are the sons of a wicked mother, who has conceived them in adultery.

3. *Lest I strip her.* "I shall take away the priesthood, the kingdom, the Law, yes, everything earthly." These things have come to pass, as we see.

The day she was born. This is when she had neither kingdom nor priesthood.

In a wilderness. This is where there is no teacher, no prophet, no Word of God. We read in Is. 5:6: "I shall also command the clouds that they rain no rain upon it." Christ says: "The kingdom will be taken away from you" (Matt. 21:43).

With thirst. Cf. John 7:37. All this is warning if they do not turn back.

5. *I will go.* We do not take this to mean the harlotry after the

coming of Christ. The Hebrew language is rich. Sometimes it says with one word what we can barely express with many words, and sometimes it expresses with many words what it could have said with two, as here.

Who give me my water. Scripture rebukes wicked teachers, belly-worshipers, who teach wicked things that bring them profit. This is what he is saying here. The papists used to live in plenty, but today preachers of the Gospel are in need. A wife cannot support the latter, but many prostitutes used to support the former. So at one time there were among the Jews men who once were so wicked. What do I have to do with the Law and the doctrine of the Law? Let other things give us our bread, etc. This is what the common crowd and the princes say to Jeremiah: "Let us pour out libations to the queen of heaven" (cf. Jer. 44:17). Take a look also at the account of the Maccabees (1 Macc. 1:11). The belly cannot rely on God. If you listen to it, you will go off into adultery. The "lovers" were the Gentiles—the Assyrians, Moabites, etc., whose friendship they could not have without getting involved with their gods. Wicked doctrine is fed richly; devout doctrine must suffer need. "Virtue is praised and yet freezes." [1]

6. *I shall hedge up her way.* She herself said, "I shall go," but she did not get what she wanted. She wanted to be safe from the Assyrians, Ammonites, etc. She wanted to associate with their gods, but she was tripped up, just as the king himself said, "I shall sacrifice to the gods of Syria, etc." (cf. 2 Chron. 28:23).

Here the Lord stops until they should say, as one reads in the Book of Judges (cf. Judg. 6:6): "Lord, help me!"

7. *Better than now,* "because then I had only tribulation in the flesh. Here both flesh and spirit have been cast down."

8. *She did not know.* She did not know the hand of the giver. The wicked say and confess that they serve the true God. What good things they have they say they have from that God whom they serve and worship. "I am a monk. I serve God with vows and ceremonies. Because of this, He will give me eternal life." But who tells you that you thus are worshiping the true God, when He has not commanded these things? Therefore you have made up

[1] Cf. Juvenal, *Satires,* I, 73: *Probitas laudatur et alget.*

for yourself some god who wants these things, although there is no true God who requires this or who wants to give eternal life because of this. What then are you worshiping except an idol of your own heart, whom you think the righteousness of your works pleases? Those, therefore, who most of all maintain that they know the hand of the giver do not know it most of all. All Scripture urges this, that one truly know the true God. Where that knowing does not exist, there harlotry and false knowledge of God cannot but be. From this also comes outward idolatry. Those Gentiles or wicked Jews were not saying that they were worshiping demons but God. "That Baal of yours is the god who brought us out of Egypt; those golden calves are gods, etc." The wicked do not hear: "Trust in God and you will be saved," but "Go into a monastery and do this or that." The people, too, want to be misled. They assign everything they get to the wicked worship of a god.

Baal. This word is properly used of the husband and lord of a wife and a house. Those worship Baal who dream that a life that serves God with faith and love is imperfect but a life that serves with chastity, poverty, and obedience is perfect.

9. *I will take back.* "I will destroy the grain and other things with damages from heaven and earth. I will force them to return to Me. They glory in the works and ceremonies with which their priests abound and foster wickedness, as if they were next to God, whose gifts fatten them. These I will take away." If the pope's belly were in need today, there would not be so many papists.

10. *In the sight of her lovers.* They have been struck down by the very foes to whom they have gone over. Misled by seducers, they will be confounded.

12. *These are my hire.* Scripture repeats this with hatred.[2]

Her. Rather, "them."

Beasts. The opposing Gentiles.

13. *With her ring.*[3] This is a metaphor taken from maidens or wives. "Ring" is a wicked word among the wicked, a pious word of God among the devout.

[2] I. e., in the parallel statement following: "Which my lovers have given me."

[3] I. e., "earring."

When she burned incense, that is, when she prayed, for incense signifies prayer in Scripture.

14. *Therefore.* As I have said, these are all words that have been put into the mouth of the apostles. Also, the preceding words in the future tense should rather be in the subjunctive.

I will allure her. "Through My apostles I will teach you a sweet doctrine that is different from the Law."

Into the wilderness. "I shall not entice her into a land which is at the moment in flower, that is, where one may see carnal things."

15. *Vinedressers,*[4] or vineyards. Here[5] there will be a need for faith and for the father to draw her with the gentle words of the Gospel. Otherwise, who will guess that there are vinedressers, or vineyards—that is, an abundance—in the wilderness?

14. *I shall speak to her heart.* This is a Hebrew phrase meaning "to speak tenderly." Cf. Is. 40:2.

15. *In the same place,* that is, in the wilderness.

The Valley of Achor. See Joshua 7:24: Achor, that is, "the valley of confusion." The Valley of Achor seems to have gone into a proverb among the Hebrews so that it is called the "valley of Achor" when someone is oppressed with evils. This is the same as when we talk about a "valley of grief" or "of tears." He says, "I shall speak to her, and I shall turn her wretchedness into good hope."

Hope. One should rather read "expectation" or "patience." The sense, rather, seems to be: "I shall give her the Valley of Achor, that is, the cross and stirring up of evils, so that there through patience she may be prepared for Me as My wife." The Valley of Achor will be better for her than the riches of Baal.

And she will sing. This is the praise of God in the New Testament, because we have been freed from death and from all tribulations.

16. *And it will come to pass.* He is speaking about the New Testament and the preaching of the Gospel. Those who do not know what the Gospel is will not understand these things.

[4] The Vulgate has *vinitores,* but the Hebrew כֶּרֶם means "vineyard."

[5] We have read *hic* for *hoc,* as in the Erlangen edition.

In that day. That obviously will be "when I shall have allured her and brought her into the wilderness, when I shall have changed a carnal kingdom into a spiritual one, etc."

My Baal, that is, "My spouse [will no longer call Me so]." [6] "I shall take away that worship and confidence by which she believes that because of her works I am a husband separated from her, etc. I shall take away every alien confidence, every perverse idea, and I shall reveal Myself truly." Notice, here, that outward worship was not shown to wood, stone, etc., but to God. You see, God here says clearly that they called Him "Baal."

Baal and Baals. A husband or married people used these names indiscriminately.[7] Ahab and Jezebel were both very wise according to the flesh. Compared with them our princes are blockheads. Ahead of the other rulers they established an external worship of God. They hired priests to establish this worship according to the Law of Moses. Jehu, therefore, had to have very brilliant light from God when he destroyed those things.

17. *I will remove from her mouth.* That is, "I will show them this grace, that they no longer teach the figments of their imagination, but My truth." This certainly is a great promise, etc.

18. *And I will make a covenant.* That is, "I will see to it that nothing harms her." Even the beasts will be in harmony with us, and all things will be under our feet. This is not an external covenant. The believer has everything. If I say to this mountain, etc.,[8] if I say to a beast, "Come," it will come, etc. All things are ours. All things serve our salvation. See Is. 2:4. A psalm (Ps. 46:9) speaks about taking away warfare, etc. We take these things to refer to the kingdom of the Christians among themselves. We read in Rom. 5:1: "Since we are justified by faith, etc." If we have peace with God, we have it even if the devil and the whole realm of sin and hell are unwilling.

In confidence. Rather "in safety," as follows.[9]

[6] The Basel text has *Non appellabit me amplius Baali coniunx mea.*

[7] I. e., for male and female.

[8] Cf. Matt. 17:20.

[9] The Basel text here adds: "'I will make them lie down.' When the prophets describe the reign of Christ, they make it a quiet, tranquil, and peaceful

19. *And I will betroth.* These are wonderful words. He does not say, "I will make a covenant," as He said to the fathers, but, "I will betroth." There is on earth no love more ardent than that between a groom and his betrothed. The groom gives his bride not a gift but himself, the deepest love of his heart and all his property. He goes ahead of his bride; he seeks her out, etc.

In righteousness. This is the righteousness *(iustitia)* which justifies us.

In justice. This is the justice *(iudicium)* by which we condemn all that is our own and also our errors, and by which we have dominion over all things, so that even sin cannot accuse us after that righteousness.

In mercy, that is, in grace or kindness. In Greek this is χάρις. Consequently, he is endowed with grace, that is, he has obtained mercy. Also for the Greeks ἐλεημοσύνη is [10] kindness [11] done for a neighbor.

And in compassion. "Imperfection will stay with you, but I will not count it against you. I will bear with your weaknesses. I will help and comfort you."

20. *I will betroth you to Me in faithfulness.* Hebrew is a rich language. It often repeats the same thing. Therefore he is explaining himself here: Will this be a physical betrothal? Will it be a carnal righteousness? No. The wedding and the kingdom rather will be matters of faith. In the gospel we hear (Matt. 22:2): "The king gave a marriage feast for his son." In Hebrew it is: "in truth." [12] This, however, is the same thing, except that the Jews today—as even some of our own people—like to engage in battles of words. This also used to happen at the time of the apostles. Oppose all

kingdom. Therefore the evangelists write that the highest peace on earth reigned when Christ was born, and so they signified that for a Christian — one who belongs to the kingdom of Christ — all things are quiet and tranquil and peaceful, and he fears neither death nor sin nor hell, obviously because he knows that nothing can harm him but everything must be only for his good." Cf. W, XIII, 11, n. 2.

[10] For *et* we have read *est.*

[11] *Beneficium.* The Basel text adds: "Properly, *misericordia* is what Paul calls χάρις, the Latins *beneficium,* and the Germans *Gottesgüte.* Cf. W, XIII,11, n. 5.

[12] *In veritate.* Cf. *Luther's Works,* 19, p. 198 and n. 5.

these things to works. She becomes a bride through righteousness, justice, mercy, pity, faith, and not through works.

And you will know the Lord. This is the progress of faith from day to day—a progress which Paul invokes on us everywhere.

21. *And it will come to pass.* Paul, too, takes this from Isaiah (cf. Is. 49:8) when he speaks of "the acceptable time, etc." (2 Cor. 6:2). We also have this in "before they call, I shall answer" (Is. 65: 24). It is the glory of Christians that when we cry out in need we are heard, and the Spirit "intercedes for us" (Rom. 8:26). "Ask, and you will receive, etc." (John 16:24). Let us pray for the Word, against heretics, against Satan, for the necessities of this life, etc.

I will answer. "You will not pray in vain." We must take the simple meanings here, lest we mistreat Scripture. "Jezreel will desire grain, oil, etc. The grain will want to be there. The earth will hear the desire for grain. The earth will want rain from heaven. Heaven will want it from Me. All creatures will serve the faithful, and I will serve the faithful in all creatures." Moreover, if it be the will of God, according to 1 Peter 1:6, that we suffer need, yet God will still not abandon us so that His creatures will not serve us, etc.

22. *And they will answer Jezreel.* This is added to obscure the prophecy, as I mentioned earlier.[13] Just as the churches are named after Jerusalem, so she is named after the metropolis Jezreel, as I also said earlier.[14]

I will hear (v. 21) would have been more clear as: "I will answer, they will answer, etc."

23. *And I will sow her,* "that she be My land." You see that the Lord is alluding to the name of Jezreel. It is as if He were saying: "She will be for Me the true Jezreel, 'the seed, or sowing, of God,' that is, in her the true Word of God will be." You are very safe then in following that allegory of the name. Even the Lord uses it to interpret the church. Besides, He said earlier, "I shall have mercy not on Jezreel but on the house of Judah."[15] Therefore

[13] Cf. p. 7 above.

[14] Cf. p. 4 above.

[15] Cf. p. 5 above.

Jezreel here is a spiritual thing, just as at the end of the preceding chapter. From both peoples [16] the church was gathered which had not yet received mercy before. When Christ said: "He who believes and is baptized will be saved" (Mark 16:16), what else is that than to say to believers: "You are My people"?

[16] I. e., from the physical and the spiritual Jezreel.

CHAPTER THREE

We have heard the prophecy about Christ. Throughout the rest of the book the prophet speaks against the hypocrites of his time and against the wicked, with the exception of the prophecy in chapter 4, where he treats prophecies of coming events.

1. *And the Lord said, etc.* He is explaining what precedes. It is a figurative speech up to "For the children of Israel shall dwell many days," where he explains himself. Some take this to mean the Babylonian captivity; others, the Roman captivity. It is clear that we must not understand it as a reference to the former, because he is not speaking about the children of Judah, who were in that captivity. I have taught that we must understand this as being about the captivity he had spoken of earlier. It was in that captivity that the Israelites were carried off and were never brought back except in a spiritual sense. The Jews will return to Christ. As Paul indicates, this took place through the Gospel (cf. Rom. 11:25 f.), and it seems to me that our text has to do with that idea. Do not let it bother you that one and the same concept is indicated by various figures. After all, this is the custom of the prophets, just as Jeremiah signifies the same thing with bonds and a cup (cf. Jer. 27:2; 25:15). To this seems to pertain what he says:

Go again, etc. The Lord is again offering him a genuine adulteress, but he does not lie with her.

Love. "Woo her." The Lord explains how.

Even as the Lord loves. Yet she is an adulteress who puts her trust in strange gods.

Grapeskins (vinacia). I do not know what these mean. They do have something to do with wine. I think this means what is left after the grapes have been pressed. These leavings are thrown to the pigs. They fall away from the truth and go over to traditions and belly-doctrines. They have the appearance of grapes, but the juice has been squeezed out. That is, they are food for pigs. Others take this to mean jugs for wine, so that this figure also holds: They are empty jugs and love the appearance thereof, but they despise the real wine, etc.

2. *And I bought her.* More accurately, "I contracted for her," that is, "I entered into an agreement with her. I agreed with her for a price that she wait for me and abstain from her adultery and from another marriage.

Homer, a Hebrew word (חֹמֶר) meaning only a peck. This word appears also in the gospel.[1]

4. *Many days.* He explains the figure.

Will dwell. Better: "will remain."

The children of Israel. He is therefore not speaking about the captivity of Judah. Besides, the phrase "without king" does not fit Judah. Also, he is not speaking about the ephod which God instituted. That was in Jerusalem. Rather he is speaking about king, sacrifice, and ephod that were turned away in Israel, and not according to God. To this pertains the fact that he says "teraphim." These properly mean images, as one reads about the idols of Rachel (cf. Gen. 31:34). This also does not fit Judah. Images to the Israelites mean golden calves or other things about which one does not read that they were established by God. He is saying, then, "All the things which you have now set up for your religious worship will be destroyed."

5. *And afterward.* You understand that this necessarily happened after the Assyrian captivity. However, you do not read of another return of Israel except the one that took place through Christ.

And David. It is clear that we understand this to be about the return, through the Gospel, to Christ, the Son of David, etc. He does not say, "They will return to their own king of Israel, to their own sacrifices, etc." Rather, "They will return to the king of Judah, to David."

[1] Cf. Luke 16:7: "A hundred measures of wheat."

To. Rather, "into the presence of."

In the last days. That is, "in the following days." They are deceived who are ignorant of the figurative language of Scripture and who take such things to refer to the last day of the world.

And to His goodness. These are very clear words. They obviously refer to spiritual matters. Paul says, "Do not let your good be spoken of as evil" (Rom. 14:16). This "goodness" is the Gospel. For joy they will come in fear to this goodness. Under the Law they also came in fear, but to the evil; here they come in fear to the good. The expression "come in fear" cuts off the security of the flesh, etc. Note that he is saying that he has given the harlot temporal good, just as God also gives this to hypocrites, but he also describes the measure. In spiritual matters there is no measure. It is only called "goodness." So much for chapter 3.

CHAPTER FOUR

In this chapter the prophet begins to rebuke manifest sins, the fruits of unbelief, now that he has treated faith. The prophet is certain that he is preaching the Word of the Lord, etc.

1. *A controversy.* In clearer words, the Lord is holding something against the inhabitants of the earth.

Kindness. A good deed, whether God shows this to men or men show it to men.

Truth. Paul often translates this as "faith." אֱמֶת (how God is true) is active. אֱמוּנָה is passive, when God pours truth into our hearts. "The righteous shall live by faith" (Rom. 1:17), that is, he will live in the truth which he has received, by which he is made true; that is, the truth by which he himself clings to divine truth. *There is no truth.* "There is no faithfulness on earth." Truth belongs to a few; faith belongs to many.[1]

Kindness. This is friendship. No one does good for another.

Knowledge (scientia). "Knowing" *(notitia)* would be better. Passively, this is "learning to know" *(cognitio).* This is how Is. 11:9 has it: "For the earth is full of the knowledge *(scientia)* of the Lord." See also Is. 53:11. To know *(cognoscere)* God as God, to know that we receive every good thing from Him—that is learning to know *(cognitio)* God.

2. *They have broken all bounds,* that is, they roam freely and abound everywhere.

Murder follows murder. There is bloodshed upon bloodshed,

[1] The editor of the St. Louis edition of Luther's works translates *Treue ist bei wenigen, Untreue bei vielen,* assuming that *mala fides* is meant in the second clause. He feels that this emendation is necessary because the sentence is otherwise "untrue, and certainly not consistent with Luther's views." Cf. St. Louis Edition, VI, 964, n. 2.

that is, the charge or outcry about shedding blood or avenging it, etc.

3. *Therefore.* This is the punishment.

The land will mourn. This is metaphorical speech. It means: "It will be made a wilderness. It will be reduced to great poverty." The land will take on a pitiful look; it will suffer miserably.

All who dwell in it will languish. He is speaking about vengeance on earth. That is, the land will be impoverished, weakened. The cattle will waste away either because the animals fail to bear offspring or because they perish from disease. The dominion of men will be broken.

Will be gathered together. Better, "they will be taken away," snatched away, so that no fish, no animals, no birds will be in the land. In Hebrew "to end" is used. In the psalm (Ps. 26:9) we read: "Sweep me not away with sinners."

4. *Yet, etc.* "Yet let no one contend." Better would be, "Let no one bring charges." "Don't tell them!" This is the way it reads in Isaiah (Is. 30:10): "Speak to us smooth things."

Because. The prophet answers. They are the kind of people who accuse the denouncer and accuser in return. They throw your word back into your own mouth.

5. *By day . . . by night,* that is, in a short time. "Today or tomorrow you will fall, and there will be no help for you."

The prophet. He takes this to mean the son who will stumble, etc. He will not just mourn. There is no help for him who will not listen.[2]

I have made your mother to be silent. "I have restrained your mother." [This means I have forced her] to be silent, to keep still. Vergil speaks of the silent shadows, the quiet places.[3] This means to reduce her to nothing. What is stilled can never be stirred up again. By "mother" he means the synagog.

6. *For lack of knowledge,* that is, because of ignorance. Because

[2] The modern German version of Luther's proverb is *Wem nicht zu raten ist, dem ist auch nicht zu helfen.*

[3] *Aeneid,* VI, 264—265.

the people do not want to be accused, because they want no argument, they will be silent before men.

Because you, etc. Understand it this way: "As you rejected knowledge, etc." He is saying, as it were: "You refuse to learn from God, and yet you boast about your priesthood, etc. I shall take away from you your teacher and pupil. I shall cause you to not know Me. I shall hand you over to judgment." The priesthood of God is where there is a true knowledge of God. Here we have a warning about both the present and the future punishment.

7. *According to their number, etc.* This is a Hebrew expression meaning they committed as many sins as there were people. We read in Jer. 2:28: "They have as many sects as they have villages and cities." So also we, etc.

Their glory. This is what he calls their idol and their worship, which [they say] was established by the true God, etc. We read in the psalm (Ps. 106:20): "They exchanged His glory, etc." This is what we glory and trust in. "This great show of the sects I will reduce to nothing." This is the way it happens with the papacy, whose glory has been changed into shame. It is as if He were saying: "This is getting to be too much for Me."

8. *The sins, etc.* They boast of their own glory and become fat in it. They feed very well on the sins of the people, etc.[4] They are enriched, they are well fed, because the people live in wickedness. Note the ugly interpretation of the papists: "The more the people bestowed, the more we devoured."

They lift up their soul. We read in the psalm (cf. Ps. 25:1; 86:4; 143:8) "To Thee I lift up, etc." This means to hold in suspense, to gaze open-mouthed, to marvel, etc. Paul says (Titus 1:14): "Instead of giving heed to Jewish myths," that is, they hold the people in suspense and make them pay attention to their sins and unrighteousness, because those people believe that these are righteous acts and deeds. Such is the worship of the priests.

[4] Luther repeats this sentence in German, but for *nähren* ("feed") the text mistakenly has *mehren* ("increase"). The Basel text adds the following explanation for "feed on the sins of My people": "They have set up a cult that is nothing but sin, from which they themselves lead a splendid existence; they have enough through this perverted worship. The people bring their offerings to feed those who serve and maintain this worship." Cf. W, XIII, 17, n. 4.

9. *And it will be.* Now follows the revenge. This was and still is like a proverb: "They're all alike to Me." "I will take away both the people and the priesthood. I'll get after them."

For their ways . . . for their thoughts, that is, for their pursuits. Thus they will dine and eat and not be filled; they will play the harlot and not multiply. They will have no one to succeed them. They will vanish. This is a better way to understand what follows:

10. *They shall eat, etc.* that is, "I will reduce you to indigence, poverty, and hunger; I will reduce you to penury. It is as if He were saying: "Now you are feeding on the sins of the people, you fatten yourselves on these, etc. I will see to it that you have neither the crumbs nor the crusts of these, etc." They cannot commit sexual sins as much as they wish, etc. This will leave only the desire for wickedness, and yet they cannot put it into practice, etc.

11. *Harlotry, wine, and drunkenness take away understanding.* I think this is said proverbially about all the people throughout every region. He says, as it were: "It is a true statement that harlotry, wine, and drunkenness make fools, etc." See our popes and monks! What is more dull, more stupid than they? They are interested in their belly alone, like true guzzlers. The Hebrew reads "wine and sweet wine."

12. *So that My people ask their wood and that their staff gives them oracles.* This is better.[5] We read in the Law (Deut. 18:11) not to ask the dead, etc. It is as if He were saying: "Aren't they mad fools? They go for advice to a god of wood, and a wooden staff gives them advice, etc." They are looking for an answer. He speaks with deprecation and contempt: "their wood!" Note the passage in Is. 44:9. Note also the clothing and food in which we trust. Nothing has dulled us except that harlotry of the spirit, wealth, wine and sweet wine, etc.—the abundance of things, etc. We ourselves make these statues in which we trust. Now tell me, are we wiser than they, etc.? I do not think that the prophet here speaks of divining rods, divination with a rod, but simply about idols which are made of wood that grew in their gardens and out of which they could make staffs.

[5] I. e., better than the Vulgate reading, which has an indicative mood. The Weimar text does not set v. 12 off in the usual manner as we have done here.

For the spirit of harlotry has led them astray. This is the way you should read, that is, "This very wind causes them to err, etc." This is the way Paul writes to the Ephesians (cf. Eph. 4:14). Instead of "spirit," "wind" is a better word, because there is no constancy there. From carnal harlotry he has taken a metaphor for spiritual harlotry.

13. *On the tops, etc.* For "they made offerings" he read "they make offerings,"[6] that is, "they run to idols," namely, on the mountains and hills. This is the way they are charged also by Jeremiah (cf. Jer. 2:24). He is rebuking their desires and good works, which they themselves have chosen. This is why He says later (Hos. 6:6): "I want mercy and not sacrifice, etc." Instead of "they made offerings" read "they burned incense." These names of trees are uncertain, except the first, etc.[7]

Because their shade is good, that is, it is pleasant. They used to look for green and delightful places to titillate their senses also, etc. In place of "your brides" stands *daughters-in-law.*[8] This is punishment. Amid the harlotry with idols they have served their bellies. As a consequence, carnal lust and harlotry follow, etc., as we now see in the clergy.

Therefore your daughters will play the harlot. This is because I will send them away, etc.[9]

14. *I will not punish, etc.* "I will see to it that all this goes unpunished," just as it is happening now. What is the reason? This is the punishment of God, etc. For we do not have prudent princes, etc.

The men went aside, etc. Better, "they were scattered, separated in different places," here a whoremonger, there a whoremonger, "because you have been scattered among many whores, etc." To be with harlots or whores is better than being

6 That is, Luther read *accendunt* for *accendebant*. This is presumably an entry by the copyist.

7 The Basel text adds: "Terebinth. Translators have a way of saying terebinth when they don't know what kind of tree is meant. I think that it was either the oak or the beech."

8 That is, in the Hebrew text.

9 The Weimar text makes this a part of v. 14.

With cult prostitutes. Jerome takes these to mean eunuchs, but I do not believe Jerome here. It is as if he were saying: "Just as you consort with harlots or whores, so also your daughters will consort, etc."

And a people . . . shall come to ruin. This will be the punishment: "I will strike the people with blindness."

15. *Though you play the harlot.* He turns his address to the tribe of Judah: "You who have the true kingdom, the true priesthood, and the true temple, see that you do not play the harlot. This will happen if you do the things which follow." It is as if he were saying: "Stay in your temple." For "Bethaven" Jerome does well in reading "Bethel," since we read nothing of a cult being established in Bethaven. Ordinarily there were cults in those places where God did something unusual with the patriarchs, etc. Bethaven means "house of iniquity."

And swear not, "As the Lord lives," that is, "Do not take the name of the Lord in vain," because He is not in these places, etc.[10] Although God is everywhere, yet He does not want you to worship Him the way you have begun. Therefore, "Swear not, etc."

16. *Israel departs,* bolts, like a stubborn cow, a young heifer. She is untamed; she does not walk on the straight and royal way. "Untamed" is better than "stubborn." She does not stay on the path but goes off on her own ways.

The Lord will now feed them, etc. Make it rhyme![11] "Feeding a lamb" does not have the bad connotation Jerome gives it with considerable violence, etc. We cannot take it to mean the Assyrian captivity. It is as if he were saying: "If you will remain in your ways, the Lord will feed you in joyful pastures like lambs."

17. *Ephraim is joined to idols.* Don't look to Ephraim. Keep away from him, because he is joined to idols. He has made a pact with Israel.

18. *Their band of drunkards is set apart.* Better: "Let their

[10] The Halle text adds: "Only the devil is."

[11] Luther invokes the German proverb *Reim dich, oder ich fress dich!* ("Make it rhyme, or I'll devour you!") This is used to indicate that force is sometimes used to make things agree in problematic situations. The "force" here would be Jerome's reading "not" for "now" and interpreting accordingly.

band be set apart." It is as if He were saying: "Keep away and let their feast in connection with the worship of idols be off limits for you. Let them eat and drink; you stay away."

They give themselves to harlotry. Let them be. Let them fornicate as they wish. Better: "Let them give themselves to harlotry, and let them love shame, etc." "Shields" *(clipei)* [12] is a name for the "big shots" among the people. God is also called "Shield," or "Buckler" (2 Sam. 22:31; Prov. 2:7).

Let them love, that is, "Let them be eager for the [shame] of their protectors or for their protectors." Let them vie with one another in bringing shame upon themselves.

19. *A wind has wrapped them.* Here Jerome has made a mistake. "Their altars will be put to shame." The Septuagint, then, is better. Instead of "Spirit," "wind" is a better reading.

In the wings of Israel. The wind has gathered them in its wings. That is, they are caught up by the wind like a bird that is picked up by its force. They sail along, propelled by the force of their harlotry, etc. This is figurative speech. The wings of Israel were their priests and kings, whom he called "shields," etc. He means that confederation of prophets, kings, and people. But yet their altars will turn to sin and shame. Even now you also see that alliance of clergy and people. They are all linked together.

[12] In the Hebrew text.

CHAPTER FIVE

In chapter 5 he will treat a single cult. This prophet did not write everything at the same time, nor did he preach all in the same year. The Assyrian captivity took place while Hosea was still living. He prophesied over a long period of time, 40 years or more. If you keep this in mind, it is easier to understand the prophecy.

1. *Hear this, etc.*, that is, "so shall it not be among you." This is a marvelous sermon. It requires attentive listeners. This account is not given in any of the Books of Kings, etc. They appear to have initiated a program to establish a new idolatrous cult for placating God against the king of the Assyrians, who was now in their land, etc. They wanted to act pious, when they should have been keeping the Law and Word of God and should not have begun a new cult, etc. When the prophet noticed this, he was led, etc. This sermon of the prophet is filled with spirit and boldness. It is a censuring sermon.

For you have been a snare at Mizpah. This has to be the proper name for a place, but none of the interpreters saw this. Isn't that a temptation? Mizpah is a well-known place, a very famous city, etc. You read it this way: "For you have been a snare at Mizpah and a net spread upon Tabor." We must make a guess at this account, because no one has written it, etc. Where an outstanding thing takes place, we erect an idol. The Jews, or Israelites, did the same thing, etc. "Because Samuel anointed Saul in Mizpah, we will set up a new cult there." Concerning famous Mt. Tabor, see Judg. 4. They established a cult there. The prophet says, "You have become a snare and a scandal to all the people in setting up a new cult." It is as if he were saying: "It was not enough to have initiated a cult on the mountaintops; you are now beginning a new one, etc."

2. *And the sacrificial victims.* The prophet is speaking with very hateful language. Because of his indignation, he calls it slaughter, or a butcher shop. He does not deign to speak of sacrificial victims, etc. The Hebrew text has, "Having been turned away, you laid deep." [1] He means the disguise and mask with which they used to deceive or meant to deceive the people and the true prophets, etc. Note: If the popes were eager for a reformation, they would thus "lay deep," etc. "Woe to those who hide deep," says Isaiah (Is. 29:15).

And having been turned away, you have made the sacrificial victims lie deep, that is, "you have hidden your sacrificial victims under the very beautiful disguise of your reformation, etc., and you believe that you are deceiving us. This will not happen, nor will you deceive God, etc." Consequently, God says:

And I. It is as if He were saying: "You will set a snare for the people, but I will be the Avenger. You will not conceal this from Me."

3. *For now, O Ephraim, you have played the harlot.* They are making it even worse.

4. *Their thoughts.* Better: "their interests." They remain among their idols and are not eager to return to God.

5. *And the pride of Israel will testify.* He is prophesying a future evil. That is, conscience will finally assert itself, and it will shame Israel. Distress brings understanding.[2] "I have this coming. I have well deserved this." Ephraim is the tribe, the region.

Judah also will stumble. By synecdoche we must take this to mean: not all of Judah, but a large part thereof, will stumble.[3] Earlier, in the first chapter, he said it would not stumble, etc.

6. *But they do not find Him.* We must read this "with their flocks," as he says, and not "with their offerings." They are only sheep and oxen, etc.

[1] *Aversi profundastis* for the Hebrew text שֵׂטִים הֶעְמִיקוּ.

[2] Is. 28:19.

[3] We have read *ruet* for *ruit,* as the text seems to require.

He has withdrawn from them, from the false prophets, because of the false teachings and the wickedness.[4]

7. *Alien children.* These are idolatrous children. It displeases the Lord very much that they bring up their children not in the fear of God but in idolatry and in ignorance of God, etc.

With their parts. Better: "With their fields."

The new moon. He gives a definite time for an indefinite one. It is as if he were saying: "It is a matter of a certain time of the month, then it will devour them." Those "parts" are properly called the distributions of their inheritances, as if to say: "The king of Assyria will take away both your citizens and your possessions in one month, etc."

8. *Blow the horns in Gibeah, etc.* Here the prophet is obscure. From the geography of the Holy Land you know that Benjamin lies in the middle between the tribes of Israel and Judah. Among the cities of Benjamin are numbered these two cities: Ramah and Gibeah. See Joshua about Bethaven, etc. (Joshua 7:2). I don't know whether the prophet wants to be understood so here, etc., but it seems to me that he is speaking here about the total and general destruction of the people of Israel as well as of Judah. There should have been a new chapter beginning here if he wanted this to be in harmony.[5] The prophet has before his eyes that the Assyrians and Babylonians are going to destroy the people of Israel and finally harrass them into captivity, until, in their vexation, they come to their senses and seek the face of God, etc. So he is passing from the temporal kingdom of Israel to the spiritual kingdom of Christ.

Bethaven, which is behind your back, O Benjamin! That is, Bethaven lies behind you, within the confines of Judah. It is as if he were saying: "Issue the call to arms; you will need it!" He begins with a magnificent gathering of the people, as if he were

[4] The Basel text adds: "*They have dealt faithlessly with the Lord.* It is as if He were saying: 'It wasn't enough that they went away from Me and set up a wicked cult, but they also forced their children and boys to become idolaters." Here you see what an awful sin it is when you do not train your sons in the law of the Lord and in His fear.' "

[5] The syntax of the last three words of this sentence, *usque consonare vellet,* is obscure.

going to announce something great, namely: "Your death, or destruction, and the establishment of Christ's kingdom!" The people used to get the signal for battle with horns or trumpets.

9. *Ephraim will become a desolation.* This is the conclusion. "It's all over! You may cry out, whistle, etc., but it will all be over soon. There will be no return. It's all over, all over!"

Among the tribes of Israel. "I declare" instead of "I have shown."

What is sure, that is, the certainty. "I want to prove that My words will be true. I will show that My prophets have spoken the truth. They will realize from experience that I am honest in My words. I will finally have the truth."

10. *The princes of Judah have become, etc.* Now He is speaking about Judah.

Like water, that is, very abundantly.

Who remove the landmark, that is, who move it. See the passage in Deuteronomy (Deut. 19:14), which says that widows' [6] landmarks should not be removed. You must not move your boundary out and the neighbor's in. Judah and Israel used to disagree with mortal hatred, and they fought bitterly. Judah wanted Israel to be destroyed completely. The reason was that there were boundaries which now the one, now the other, took, etc. Even today our princes battle over land and people.

I will pour out. "They, too, must be put away." This is one and the same final statement about Judah and Israel, etc.

11. *Ephraim has suffered oppression.* It seems that we must take this to mean a people set up in captivity and what they suffered there. He now involves both peoples. It is certain that they were ill-treated as foreigners. One must endure oppression. Ephraim is exposed to the oppression of all men.

Crushed, that is, "broken." This means that no man passes judgment on his judgment. Even if he has a just cause, he must be crushed, as it happens now in the case of paupers, even in just causes.

[6] Deut. 19:14 speaks of the "neighbor's landmark."

For he began to go, etc. "Because he began to go after a command." That is the way the Jews take it. Meanwhile, I am sticking with Jerome, who reads "go after vanity." The sense is: he suffers oppression and does not have the execution of his case and judgment, because they follow their own uncleanness and vanity. "After a command of men" is harsh, but "vanity" is better. They will become heathen.

12. *Therefore, I, etc.* "Like a moth I consume those daily who daily become Gentiles, etc."

13. *When Ephraim saw.* We feel the punishments but rarely the blame. Ephraim sees his sickness but does not feel his vanity. He does not know from where to get help for his pain. Instead of "chain" *(vinculum)*, "pain" *(dolor)* would be better.

Then Ephraim went, etc. Ephraim sees his wretchedness and joins himself to the king of Assyria, saying: "Gracious lord, I shall do what you wish." We must take a guess here. The king of Assyria is called King Jareb, either from the city or from the fortress, etc. He sent envoys for help, when we [would send for] an avenger. It is as if He were saying: "Even he will not be able to cure you. I will gnaw away at you and eat you, and you will experience no help, etc."

14. *For I will be.* It is as if He were saying: "Punishment is Mine. I, who otherwise am a gentle and merciful Savior, with you will be a lion and a young lion. I will punish you with My attack."

I, even I, will rend. The "I" is thus repeated in the Hebrew.

15. *I will return again,* that is, "I was with you. You had My prophets, My Law, and all things, etc. I will now depart from you. You will not have My prophets until Christ comes—neither in the captivity nor after it. I will abandon you." Then traditions began to hold sway.

Until you fail. "You will be condemned and judged for a long time; that is, until you feel your sins and guilt. Then your own sin will drive you to seek My face." The things that follow now are about the kingdom of Christ. He now passes over from the captivity to the kingdom of Christ, etc.

CHAPTER SIX

1. *They will rise up early.*[1] "They were looking for Me early." He-sought-Me-early[2] is a unique word. "These people will come to Me only in distress." "Early" means quickly and with haste. Those who get up early are anxious to come.

For He has torn. Read it this way: "Because He tears to pieces and heals, etc." This is where the kingdom of Christ begins. The Law does not teach this, but the knowledge of the new doctrine does. The Law does not teach one to turn to a God who strikes but to flee an angry God, etc.

2. *He will revive us.* He is speaking about Christ's resurrection. So it is permitted to stand, and we will receive it. Paul glories about this passage when he says that Christ was to rise on the third day (cf. 1 Cor. 15:4). This is so magnificent that it cannot refer to the temporal kingdom of Judah. He does not say, "He will rise up after, etc.," but, "He will revive." His resurrection will accomplish this, etc.

In His sight, etc. To live, but to live a true life.

3. *We will know.* The knowledge will be here.

We will follow, "pursue," "chase after." This is not the interest of the Law and of the synagog but of a new people. We have "pursue peace" in the psalm (Ps. 34:14). We shall press on that we may know the Lord more and more.

His going forth is as sure as growing light, better: "as dawn"; or "like the dawn, whose rising is ready." We have in 2 Sam. 23:4:

[1] In the Vulgate this last sentence of chapter 5 is taken as a part of chapter 6.

[2] Luther coins the Latin word *manicabat* (from *mane,* "in the morning") to translate the Hebrew word used.

"He dawns on them like the morning light, etc." We also read in the psalm (Ps. 19:5): "Like a strong man it runs its course with joy." He wants to say: "The knowledge of Him will rise up through the Gospel like a dawn which is not held back." His coming, that is, Christ's coming, is like the dawn, which progresses. Its rising is established and directed. It is sure, and it makes headway.

And He will come, etc. This is just too great! This happens through the handing down of the Gospel, by which we know God.

Like the timely showers, better, "morning showers." We can understand this in no other way except about the preaching of the Gospel. The Word of the Gospel is the evening rain, because it is the Word of the cross. It is the morning shower because it is the Word of comfort and re-creation. This would be the mystery of the evening and morning rains.

4. *What shall I do with you, etc.* He is still connecting those two tribes. It is as if he were saying: "I preach the Gospel to you, otherwise you do not become godly. If I do not preach, you remain as you were, etc."

Your mercy, that is, "the blessing which was promised to you and which has now been revealed."

A morning cloud. The sun clears this away. This is the dew which the sun dries. It is as if He were saying: "You allow grace to be preached to you in vain. It is yours, but you are not aware of it."

5. *I have hewn,* "I have shaped," [3] namely, through the prophets. It is as if He were saying: "What I have done through the prophets has to do with the fact that I judge you to have been killed and about to be hewn, so that I may reduce you to size. This I do to teach you that you are sinners and to cause you to come to your senses. Nothing, however, has been accomplished."

Judgments. These are laws or doctrines. It is as if he were saying: "He wanted to do this through the prophets, so that your judgments, which you ought to receive from the prophets, ought

[3] Luther uses the German verb *hobeln,* "to plane," perhaps not without reference to some proverb like *Wo gehobelt wird, da fallen Spähne* ("Where planing goes on, shavings must fall").

to break out like the sun, etc." Thus we have it in Isaiah (Is. 40:5) that His judgment would be declared throughout the entire world.

6. *For I desire steadfast love and not, etc.* With one word He abrogates all the ceremonies, as Isaiah also did (cf. Is. 1:11). This can be taken for the steadfast love bestowed [on us by God] and on that to be bestowed [on our fellowmen by us].[4]

Knowledge. Better would be "awareness."[5]

7. *But they, etc.* "They let it go by. They do as their father did. He transgressed the covenant he had received. Thus they have transgressed My covenant; that is, because they do not believe. They have dealt faithlessly by playing the harlot with their idols."

8. *Gilead, etc.* This is a difficult passage; it has also been corrupted. That translation[6] is worthless; "tracked with blood" should rather be "lying in wait for blood," and the "society or band of priests is like the jaws of thieves."[7] Also "on the way from" is left over. Gilead is not a city but the name of an entire region. The prophet uses this name as a title for the whole synagog. He is speaking about the kingdom and the priesthood. See Jer. 21 or 22.[8] It is the more important part of the people—the kings and the priests—whom the prophets call Gilead. There those are gathered among whom is the testimony, namely, of ruling and teaching—the throng of the testimony, those who ought to teach others. He means the priests, etc.

Idol. Read "evil" instead. He accuses the princes of shedding blood, and thus He assigns this work. Consequently "lying in wait for blood" is better, as it now follows.

[4] The Basel text adds: "The steadfast love is first of all that which has been given, that which we have received, that is, from God, and with which He has blessed us; in the second place it is that which I owe to my neighbor. Therefore the meaning is: 'I have done this through My prophets, who have slain you, in order to erect a reign of steadfast love, so that I may bless you all with My steadfast love without your sacrifices and works.'"

[5] The Weimar text has this line after v. 7.

[6] In the Vulgate.

[7] That is, so it should read in v. 9. Instead of the Vulgate's *particeps sacerdotum* we should read *societas vel foedus sacerdotum est quasi fauces latronum.*

[8] Cf. Jer. 22:6.

9. *And as, etc.* See what Jerome says here.[9] We have the same thing in Jeremiah (cf. Jer. 23:9 ff.). Therefore *Shechem, etc.* Between Shechem and Jerusalem there was, I believe, a grove and forest in which thieves used to hide. The Gospel of Christ confirms this in Luke about the man left half dead (Luke 10:30). The sense is taken from a simile about thieves and the way they act, etc. "Such are My priests, who follow perverse pursuits, etc." We have drawn this text to the time after the resurrection of Christ, when the apostles suffered many things for Christ's sake at the hands of persecutors. It is only a simile. The Christians were killed as they tried to go to the true God.

Thieves. Instead, read "soldiers." The Hebrew expression means "properly girded for war, etc." Elsewhere they are the "raiders of Syria" (cf. 2 Kings 6:23). They are footsoldiers. He says "jaws," which intend to devour and which would violently take up the Christians, etc.

11. *But for you also, O Judah.* This passage is very obscure, were we to follow the interpretation of Jerome.[10] We take it to mean the leading back from the new spiritual captivity, etc. "But for you, also, O Judah," that is, "You will have the glory of the Gospel and will convert many to yourself, etc."

[9] Jerome, *Commentaria in Osee prophetam, Patrologia, Series Latina,* XXV, 871: "The priests of Bethel . . . would station robbers [between Shechem and Jerusalem] who were to waylay travelers [to Jerusalem], so that people might prefer to worship the golden calves in Dan and Bethaven rather than God in the temple at Jerusalem."

[10] Jerome, *Commentaria in Osee prophetam, Patrologia, Series Latina,* XXV 872: "Judah, that is, the church, is told that through its sins it is getting ready its own harvest, or vintage, since the time of judgment is approaching."

CHAPTER SEVEN

THIS is also an obscure chapter. Briefly, its sense is this: It seems to make this point, that, when the prophet has now reproved the king and the people and perhaps brought them to repentance, the false prophets come into the picture. They stir up the people against the good prophet. They cause the Word to be useless, as also happens now. After this, he hits on the picture of baking. He becomes a miller or a baker. He says, as it were: "With your doctrines you will cause the people to stir up God to anger and to become an Ephraim on whom the Assyrian may chew, etc."

1. *When I would heal,* namely, "from idolatry through My prophets." He has all but cured His dear little nation, but the princes of Samaria precipitate a new catastrophe, spread a new falsehood. They instruct the people how they should behave toward their lord and how they should seek peace from the Assyrian. "No one, however, teaches the people to have faith in Me, etc."

And the thief, etc. It seems to me that the prophet here is referring to the wicked teachers. They change themselves into an angel of light, etc. They go in as thieves and come out as murderers. He even accuses them of theft and robbery. I can speak about our own priests in this way. They come in as thieves; they go out as robbers. They admonish us to give against the Turk, etc. He is not speaking about foes, who enter in in any way, etc. Wicked doctrines destroy both in conscience and in substance. "They do not even think that I have all their evils before My eyes." They act smug and publish their lies, etc., just as if the Lord were dead and did not once see them, etc.

2. *Let them not by chance say in their hearts, etc.* We must

delete the "by chance," that is: "They do not ever consider that I remember all their evil works."

Now their deeds encompass, etc. Around and around again, that is, "Everywhere such pursuits exist among them, and I have them before My eyes." With those beautiful lies they bedaub the mouths of the kings and people, as is seen in the case of indulgences, etc. They all have names, titles, and pretenses for putting down the Turks and freeing the brethren. This is falsehood.

3. *By their wickedness, etc.* That is, that the king might not be sorry for his sins and turn back to repent, the evil prophets turn him away, etc. They comfort such people; they make them stubborn, so that the kings do not recognize their sin. The princes, too, are a source of derision. These people make the princes glad. The princes are happy to listen to them, etc. This takes place so that it may become clear that the Word is protected by the power of God and that it stands by its own power, lest they boast that they preserve it with their own virtue.

4. *They are all, etc.* This is a difficult text.

By a cook. Better would be "a baker." Let us see if we can hit it. That is, everyone—princes and people—are opposed. They commit adultery; that is, in a spiritual sense.

Like. This is a simile.

An oven. An oven kindled by a baker is the simile for their adultery, etc. Wicked teachers kindle this oven, that is, they prepare and inflame the heart of this people to stick to their foolish falsehood which they themselves have set forth against the prophet Hosea.

It has rested. Understand it thus: The baker has stopped kneading the mixed dough until it should be leavened.

5. *On the day of our king the princes became sick with the heat of wine.* Note the manner and form of preparing for baking, etc. The entire simile is one of the baker. He is speaking about bread to eat rather than royal bread, etc. He speaks about the common bread, bread to eat, not luxury bread, etc. The wicked teachers are the baker.

The heart is the oven. It is heated up to commit adultery with you. The kneading is living in such a way that the heart is inflamed by false doctrine. To let the dough rest and rise is to await the king of Assyria, until the whole population is taken in by the falsehood and false persuasions. That is, the people believe you and live this way until they are completely leavened. "A little while" does not appear in the Hebrew. That inflammation causes you to be swollen and proud, etc.

The day of our king, etc. He is saying in substance: "You are doing this baking on the solemn day of the king. That is, you have done all these things on the day of our king, when the princes became sick with the heat of the wine, namely, when they were inflamed by you."

That he (namely, the king) may stretch out his hand with mockers, that is, with the false prophets who mislead the people.

6. *All night he slept, etc.*, that is, "My (obviously, false) prophets are not as secure as the baker who has mixed the dough."

In the morning, that is, in the following time when all have been persuaded, etc. The meaning is clear, etc. The king of Assyria is to devour the cake and the bread.

7. *All of them are hot as an oven, etc.* "Hosea, that liar there, said that we would perish. That means nothing."

Their judges. These are the men who pass judgment correctly. They have to take it on the chin.

All their kings. It is as if he were saying: "Isn't it a shame that all the kings fall? They cry out well under My name but not to Me, etc."

8. *Ephraim.* This is the application of the simile. Ephraim is mixed among the peoples. Everyone devours him, and he is scattered in all directions. "Food" would be better than "cake," that is, Ephraim has become the food of all peoples, especially of the king of Assyria.

Which is not turned, that is, the situation does not change, etc. He is always being devoured.

9. *Aliens devour his strength,* that is, whatever he could accomplish with his strength, etc. On his wine, land, and grain other people feed.

And he knows it not. We should read: "He is not aware of it," that is, he is near his own destruction. He is done for; he has had his day.

10. *The pride of Israel is humbled in its face.* We have the same expression above: "And the pride of Israel testifies to its face."[1] Both can stand. "Will testify" pleases me more. To say one thing after another, to speak alternately, this is the Hebrew expression. One humiliation will follow after another, etc.

Yet they do not return, etc. The prophets did all things for the First Commandment and for faith, etc. The prophets note, as now, that the greatest sin is unbelief.

Nor seek Him, for all this. Although Israel was being torn to bits and its wickedness was witnessed to before its face, yet it did not return to the Lord, etc. Take note of wicked King Ahaz. The more he was struck, the more he multiplied his altars, etc. So it is also in the case of our men, etc. We have increased sin with sin when we wanted to avert and pray away our misfortunes.

11. *Ephraim is like a dove, etc.*, that is, easily misled, easily persuaded, without guile. He is misled by false prophets and passes no judgment on their doctrines. Look, this is the reason for the whole sin. We are still like a dove who believes easily. We believe men, but not God, etc. He adds "without sense"; in other circumstances this would be a praiseworthy persuasion. In this way our bishops have taken away our sense. They have removed judgment from us and have kept it for themselves. A well-meaning, silly people is Ephraim.

Calling to Egypt. This obviously is at the advice of the wicked prophets and under the guidance of their own unbelief and wickedness. But why are they not calling the Lord? You see, this is the way the false prophets have persuaded them, etc. That is, they have confidence in human advice, and this is against the First Commandment, etc.

[1] The same Hebrew expression occurs also in Hos. 5:5, where the Vulgate translates *Et respondebit arrogantia Israel in facie eius.* In the present passage the Vulgate reads *Et humiliabitur superbia Israel in facie eius.* Luther is commenting on the Latin verbs used to translate the Hebrew עָנָה, "to respond as a witness" or "to sing responsively."

12. *And as they go, etc.* All of these things have been spoken with figurative language. "Just let them go, since they will sit smugly and seem to rule. I shall drag them down, etc." A bird is caught unexpectedly, etc. "I shall suddenly bring down upon them the king of the Assyrians. I shall lead them to a place from which they cannot escape."

I will chastise them according to the report[2] *of their congregation.* These are exaggerations and repetitions of the same prophecy. He prophesies against the return of the people in almost the entire fourth chapter.

13. *To stray* is to be away from God, to worship God with a worship other than the true one. "So long as that sin of idolatry remains, I shall destroy them. I am the Redemption of Israel. I do redeem that people and I often have redeemed them. They really ought to stand out because of Me, but they deceive Me and fail Me, etc." This is the way the Holy Spirit is forced to be the author of many things in councils, etc.

14. *They have not cried out.* "I should be the God who should lead them back and on whom they should call, etc., but they flee in another direction, etc." "You do wail well to Me, but you do not cry out, namely, in your heart, etc. There is no faith. You cry out through your works and interests—which is pure howling tumult, *Geplärr, Getümmel,* when the Holy Word of God is chanted without involving the heart." Only the prophetic Spirit sees this, etc.

For grain, etc. Note that this passage is also well known because of its application to the Sacrament of the Altar;[3] but look at their righteousness, etc.

[2] The Basel text adds: "This word 'report' can be taken in an active or a passive sense. Jerome takes it in the active sense, so that the meaning is: 'I will chastise them because they prefer to hear one another rather than Me.' For they would say, 'Why shouldn't we do thus and so? The king, the prince, the priest, and the whole crowd do so.' God answers: 'I will chastise those who hear as well as those who teach.' But the meaning may be passive: 'I will chastise them according to what has been heard, that is, according to My words, with which I have threatened them,' so that the meaning would be: 'I said through the prophets that they would come to grief, and so it will be. I will alter nothing in My decision, since they are making no change in their life.' "

[3] The Basel text adds: "This passage has been twisted by the sophists to apply to the Sacrament of the Altar; whatever mentions wine and bread they immediately apply thus."

They kept thinking. I want this to be the word for gathering grain, etc. That is, their interest runs only to seeking temporal things. "Their wicked, unbelieving cry does not seek My glory, but their own belly, that they may flourish in the land." In Ps. 4:7 we read: "When their grain and wine abound." They become great, etc., when they have plenty to eat and drink. "But I rejoice in my heart, etc."[4] "They worship their belly as god, and they desert Me."

They have strayed, that is, "They turn away from Me."[5] Better would be: "They flee from Me."

15. *And although I trained.* These are amplifications of the same unbelief. I do this and ought to do it, but they train themselves with new doctrines and laws. They look for Pharaoh and other kings—human help.

They devised evil against Me. What they plan against the prophet they also plan against God. They do nothing but condemn the teaching of the prophet and establish their own, etc. "I am ready to train them, redeem and protect them, but they are ready to teach themselves, etc. They reject Me."

16. *They have turned away.* They are turning away.

Without the yoke, or free. That is, "They turn away of their own volition, so that they are not under My control, so that they do not endure My Word. Consequently, they are the children of Belial, unruly children. They do not want to be subjected to My advice and to Me in faith."

A *treacherous bow.* This is a phrase of Scripture. It occurs quite frequently in the prophets that the Lord calls His people[6] a bow, as in the psalm (Ps. 7:13). We are the bow of the Lord when we walk in His Word as if wearing weapons. When He does battle through us against the faithless and wicked, then we are called His bow. It fights using His Word. Consequently, we are both bow and arrow. "They become a false bow against Me. I ought

[4] The Weimar text treats this clause as if it were a part of the Hosea text commented on, but it is in fact a part of the quotation of Ps. 4:7.

[5] We have read *a me* for *me.*

[6] For *in populum* we have read *populum.* This agrees with the reading *populus appelletur arcus* in the Basel text.

to be battling against wickedness through them, but they turn their interests against piety. They are a deceitful bow. You see, they have the appearance of being fighters for piety, but with that appearance they fight against piety, etc. They are a deceitful weapon. I ought to be using it against impiety, but with their good appearance they turn against piety."

Their princes will fall, etc. "Obviously, then, because they allow Me to cry out in vain and because they fight against goodness, not only the people will fall, but also the elect, the kings, etc."

Because of the insolence, that is, because of the anger of their tongue. Relate this to God; that is, because of that evil which their tongue brings upon them, etc. That is, their own wicked tongue is the wrath of God, etc. Or, the wrath of the princes is against their own people, etc.

This shall be their derision. This will turn into mockery, as in the psalm (Ps. 79:4). Those who have not set their hope on God are squires who would put their trust in Egypt, etc. Everywhere they will be mocked. Here the sense of Jerome does not please me, etc.[7] The prophet preached this to bring the people to faith and to draw them away from their empty worship, etc. This hopeless sham creates hypocrites.

[7] The Basel text says that Jerome interpreted this "derision" as referring to the sin in Egypt.

CHAPTER EIGHT

HERE again the Spirit is encouraging the prophet to press on and continue, because the people lived in wickedness and put on a great appearance of worship.

1. *To your lips.* In Isaiah (Is. 58:1) we have this expression, "Lift up your voice like a trumpet, etc." "Run! Fire! Cry out! Cry out! The more you are hindered, cry out the more!"

Like an eagle. I don't know what this is. What Jerome says is cold, distorted, violent.[1] If it could hold water, I would take it this way: "Be a trumpet and cry out over the people like an eagle over the house of the Lord." I don't know what it is. I'll let it go at that.

They have broken. They did this by worshiping idols. It reads (v. 2) "they cry."[2]

2. *Israel,* that is, "we, Your people, etc." The Lord allegorizes their words, etc.

3. *Israel has spurned.* "Why is it that they thus call on Me merely with words? But what are they doing? They are spurning the good things. They are rejecting what I teach. They repudiate it. They are a far way from listening. Those are lies. So cry out loudly against that sham, etc."

4. *Princes have been set up* is better.[3] "Princes have emerged, and I don't know about it; one king always strangles the other." See 2 Kings 15:10 ff. Among the five kings, none died a bloodless

[1] Jerome, *Commentaria in Osee prophetam, Patrologia, Series Latina,* XXV, 883: "The sense is: 'Nebuchadnezzar with his entire army will come so suddenly, so quickly, that he will be like an eagle swooping down upon its prey; and he will come to no other place than to Jerusalem, where the temple of God is, in order to overturn and destroy it.' "

[2] Present tense instead of the Vulgate's future tense.

[3] I. e., *principes facti sunt* is better than the Vulgate translation *principes exstiterunt* ("princes have risen").

death. This has to do with the last kings who killed each other. "I am God. I am King of this people, and they are setting up themselves as kings and princes. Should I not know about this?"

With their silver and gold, etc., that is, they look for a way to go into ruin.

5. *Your calf has been spurned, O Samaria.* I believe He is calling Bethaven the "calf." Note what we said earlier about Jezreel, the city of Israel. Samaria was the seat of the kingdom where both states were. I do not think that they have set up a new calf.

Has been spurned. He is prophesying that the kingdom will be destroyed. That worship, all Samaria, both kings and people—all of it is headed for the gallows. The word "calf" is a depreciation.[4] He does not dignify it with the name of a god, as if to say: "This god will share your fate. This god will have to pay for it."

Be cleansed, that is, become innocent, blameless. "When will the time come when they will be faultless and without charge (Ps. 19:13: 'I shall be innocent of a great transgression') so that they have a good and blameless reputation? They force Me to be angry and to destroy them, because their wickedness wants to go on forever."

6. *He,*[5] namely, their god whom they have invented for themselves. This god did not make Israel, but Israel made him. He is a creature, not a creator. Consequently, the creature must perish with its creator. The work of our hands is called an idol. Whatever we set up in that divine worship which we have fabricated and thought up is the work of our hands, etc. Free will creates nothing but an idol, because it wants control in divine matters. God wants to fashion, not to be fashioned, that is, be born of a god. Here, however, he says, "Israel created that god."

A workman. He makes himself clear. He speaks of those interests with words of contempt. He notes their interest and heart and accuses them, namely, for their confidence in that worship which

[4] For the Latin *tapinosis*, cf. *Luther's Works*, 26, p. 362, n. 5.

[5] The Weimar text did not recognize this word as part of the Vulgate text *Quia ex Israel et ipse est.*

they are developing. Where this trust is, there is their god, their treasure, their heart, etc. This is the way it is with the hood, the fasts, etc. of the monks. He calls this worship "god." Gold was their worship. Therefore gold is their god.

For the calf of Samaria will be spider webs. "For, etc.," he[6] reads differently. The Hebrew is שְׁבָבִ, to become שְׁבָבִ, like bits and pieces cut off of timbers. It is refuse. The god of Samaria is שְׁבָבִ. He becomes refuse. He will be reduced to nothing.

7. *For they sow the wind, etc.* "For, etc.," he reads differently.[7] This is figurative language. Both sowing and harvesting require calm weather. They are sowing the wind. They will also reap the whirlwind, or storm. This was perhaps a very common proverb among the people. We can say the same thing proverbially about our own monks: they sow the wind, they harvest the whirlwind. The fruit of their labor is fear and trembling of the conscience. This is fools' work with a useless reward or fruit. They honor God badly and worship Him badly. Therefore, they will be compensated badly. This means: "Your hope will be deceived. You hope to worship God and receive blessing from Him in return etc., but you will be destroyed."

The standing grain. קָמָה. "Standing heads" would be better. That is, whatever fruit you hope for will perish. This, too, is metaphor. We can also understand it without metaphor. This is better—that the king of Assyria will come and take away whatever you have sown, etc. This beautiful metaphor serves us, etc.

8. *Israel is swallowed up.* That is, the king of Assyria will come. He will destroy and devour everything, etc. This is a prophetic statement of that which is going to happen.

As an unclean vessel. Like a chamber pot, a vessel which we dignify with no respect. The Hebrew indicates "a vessel of reproach," and this is better. That is how Paul writes to Timothy (2 Tim. 2:20).

[6] Luther. His Latin translation read *Ideo in frustra comminuetur vitulus Samariae.*

[7] These words conspicuously repeat the comment in v. 6. Perhaps the copyist inserted one of these statements by mistake. But both can be defended. Here Luther's Latin translation reads *quoniam* for the Vulgate's *quia.*

9. *For they have gone up, etc.*, that is, they have been led and forced to go up.

A wild ass. Among the other characteristics, this is rather well known, that he walks alone, as Job says,[8] and loves the wilderness, far from slavery to men. Wild asses are also known for their thirst. He is describing the customs of the people and says in addition: "Junker Ephraim is not My hereditary ass. Rather, he wants to be free. He does not want My law to restrain him. When I have been rejected and am not considered their God, they go about alone, and I leave them without pasture, etc."

Ephraim has given gifts to his lovers. That is, he pays them wages. "They desert Me and make themselves gods for themselves. They ally themselves with the heathen. They give them money enough. They think that they will stand firm and endure, etc. They want to arm themselves with their own money."

10. *But also with a fee.* That is not in the text, but this is: "also among the heathen."[9] "Lovers" (v. 9) he calls their allies with whom they carried on their idolatrous worship.

I will soon gather them up. "I will really join them together as often as they conspire together. I will make them one cake for the Assyrian to eat."

And they will rest. This word means to be in the anguish of childbirth. We have this often in the Psalms: "He confounds the hinds."[10] Paul says the same thing in Rom. 8:22. For a while they will still be upset by the taxation and persecution of the princes, obviously, until the king of Assyria will have come. That is, they will be oppressed. First let them suck you dry by taxation, wear you out and tax you to death; then I will take them away, etc., life and limb. This is the way it happens also to us.

11. *Because Ephraim has multiplied altars for sinning.* Read it this way: "Ephraim uses altars for sinning." The more I preach,

[8] Cf. Job 24:5; 39:6.

[9] In the Hebrew.

[10] With the editor of the St. Louis edition of Luther's works, VI, 995, we have read *cervas* for the Weimar editor's *terras* and the Erlangen edition's *cerras* to agree with Ps. 29:9.

the more they build altars. "Not only do you erect sinful altars, but you also sin." So it happens, etc.

12. *Were I to write for him.* This is also obscure. Read it thus: "If I write My law for him very often," that is, if I give it to him all written—yet I accomplish nothing. Rather, he regards it as a strange thing.

13. *They will offer sacrifice, etc.* See Jeremiah 7. "Don't bother Me with your sacrifices. Let them bring their sacrifice to Me. Let them sacrifice their meat and eat it." But this does not please the Lord. This business of sacrifices means nothing to the Lord, but that they hear His voice, etc.

For He will remember. He will remember that they turn to Egypt, namely, for help, and abandon their God and trust in their own fleshly arm.

14. *For Israel has forgotten his Maker.* That is the way I read this.

And Judah, etc. We should read it as Judah, not Judas.

Palaces. These are royal dwellings, temples, etc. The Hebrew means they build beautiful palaces, etc. They strive to stand by their own strength, etc. "But I will take away both the temple and them—the one with the other."

CHAPTER NINE

HERE we have a new chapter. The prophet persists in his warning of the coming captivity as he takes away from them all their self-confidence. Note the five kings—Shallum, etc., who killed each other, etc.[1] The prophet is assailing the security in which they were standing after they had made peace with the king of the Assyrians and with the king of Egypt, etc. No nation changes its God. See also Jeremiah (Jer. 2:11). This is also present in the histories of Rome. Only piety changes; wickedness persists. It is as if he were saying: "You alone have played the harlot against your God. Other peoples do not do this."

1. *Rejoice not, O Israel, with exultation, like the heathen, etc.* That is the way I read it.

A harlot's hire. See above, chapter 2.[2] "You hoped for pay."

You have loved, etc. The Latin, and also our way of speaking, calls for "you would like, etc." "To love," "to have affection for," is what the Hebrew calls it. "But your hope will fail you," for

2. *The threshing floor, etc.* Elsewhere (Hab. 3:17) we have: "The produce of the olive will fail." It gives less than was hoped for. This is what he means when he says: "The winevat will fail, etc." "God will curse your grain." The harvest will not be like the hope.

3. *Ephraim has returned.* "But Ephraim will be resident,

[1] Cf. Hos. 8:4 above.

[2] Hos. 2:12 is obviously referred to, but this reference does not yield any additional explanation. The Basel text for the present passage has: " 'Hire,' as in chapter 2 above, means abundance and wealth of temporal things, that is, 'You hoped for a wealth of reward for your worship . . . but your hope will fail and disappoint you. Your olive press will fall short of your expectations and yield less than you hoped for; even if all should be there in abundance, it will slip right through your fingers, and you will not know where it is going.' "

etc.," is better. "These will be your reward, for which you hoped on your threshing floor and in all your winevats."

And among the Assyrians. He is saying, as it were: "It will come to this: not only will you not have much, but all of your substance will be defiled."

4. *They will not pour libations.* He is describing what is going to happen in the Assyrian captivity. The libation, drink offering, probably is wine. They will not pour out wine for the Lord, that is, they will not pour libations and make offerings. That is, "We will shall eat polluted food," and there will be no place there for making sacrifice, because they are not in the land of the Lord. In a land that is not the Lord's all things that are pleasing to God, that He commands, stop. He is placing the captivity before their eyes. This is the summary.

Their sacrifices, etc. Look this up in Deuteronomy (Deut. 26:11-14). No one was allowed to make an offering in grief. He demands happiness and banquets as sacrifice, etc. The sacrifice is defiled if it is made in grief or on behalf of the dead.

Mourners' bread. This is so because it is quickly defiled by the very grief and pain. The Lord hates the sad sacrifices of such people, namely, of mourners (better than "of them"). They may of course eat of that bread which will be their food, but it will not be an acceptable sacrifice to the Lord, etc.

5. *What will you do, etc.?* He is saying: "Nothing." מוֹעֵד are special times of the year, such as Pentecost, Easter, Christmas. These are different from feast days. The moon is the source and mother of those times. In Galatians (Gal. 4:10) Paul translates this as "seasons." We have the same word in Gen. 1:14. On the feast day of the Lord, such as Pentecost and Easter.

6. *Egypt, etc.* They will be there, but they will dare to do none of these things there, etc.

Thorns. This is the thistle, the sticker.

Desirable silver. These are beautiful or precious things made of their silver, etc. "So far are you from being able to make your sacrifices and hold your feasts there, etc."

7. *The days of punishment have come, etc.* This means there will be a day of reckoning.

Know, O Israel. This passage is obscure—our translators, still more obscure. I explain it as follows: "Know then, when those days have come, etc., you will realize," that is, then the Israelites will know, "what a mad and stupid prophet I have been."

8. *A watchman*, that is, "you will recognize [in me]." This is how we must read this.[3] "You condemn My prophets, devout and holy men. They have to be fools in your sight, because you hate them." These are words which the people speak in insulting fashion against the prophets. It is as if he were saying: "At that time, I, too, will behave insolently. Then you will see what kind of fool I really was." What the Jews are saying here is not pleasant, because they now have false prophets as a punishment. Against these Hosea makes his prophecy. "This 'foolish prophet' (v. 7) refers to me, for I am compelled to play the fool." "Because of your iniquity" belongs to "fool," not to the verb "to realize." "Because of your sin, I have to be a fool." "Prophet," too, may be an insulting word. The word is ambiguous: a term of honor, which is rare; and an insult, as we have it here now. Thus [they call him] an insane or furious man of wind, a man who deals in irresponsible nonsense. As Vergil says "a windy tongue,"[4] so a man can be called windy. Thus what follows (v. 8), "a watchman, etc." (everything in the active voice), has a good connotation in Scripture, as we see it in Ezek. 3:17. In Greek this is a bishop, a superintendent, a watchman, an overseer.

Snare. "This is the one whom you consider a snare because of your great hatred, because I was a snare for you in all your ways, etc." He is speaking here about the punishment, not about the blame. Also we read prophet as an objective rather than a subjective form.[5]

[3] Luther means to say that we ought to read *speculatorem* for the Vulgate's *speculator* and make it the object of the verb *cognoscetis*. Luther is still expounding verse 7, but he has borrowed a word from v. 8 to point out the contrast between the popular view and the truth concerning the position of the prophet.

[4] *Aeneid,* XI, 390.

[5] *Prophetam, non propheta.*

His ways, that is, the prophet's.

Madness. You hate the prophet.

In the house of their God, that is, of the people's God. Here is a summary: "On the day of your visitation you will realize who I was, etc."

9. *They have deeply corrupted themselves.* Or read it this way: "They have so completely destroyed themselves," as if to say: "You have been such rebels that you have resisted the devout prophet. He was worthy of your affection, but you hate him. He wanted to explain to you, but you call him a snare, etc."

As in the days of Gibeah. Note the account of the Levite's woman who was ravished, etc., in Judges 19. This is deep corruption, where there is not just weakness or mistake, but where there is pure evil. The prophets cite the histories, as Isaiah (Is. 13:19) does that of Sodom. The people of Gibeah defended their sin, etc.

Therefore He will remember, etc. Now He will come. It is as if he were saying: "Look at the example. God allowed a very great victory over Israel. Why did He permit it? That the people of Gibeah might become stubborn and proud and be inflated, etc."

10. *Like grapes, etc.* He compares the children with their fathers. He repeats the ancient account and says in substance: "Human nature will always be the same; [6] if the mother is a harlot, so is the daughter; and a goat will never leave the garden of his own accord." The firstfruits were the best loved because of their rarity. They are called the "firstborn." Firstfruits are to be offered to the Lord as the finest fruits. Jacob told Reuben, "You are my firstfruit, my might, etc." (Gen. 49:3).

They came, namely, the fathers. "That was My first people." See the account in Num. 25.

Shame. "Shame" is what Scripture calls the idol, the heathen, and the glory of idolatry, etc. We are shamed by that very idol before God, because we shame Him, etc.

And consecrated themselves to shame. This is how I read it,

[6] The German proverb is *Art lässt von Art nicht.*

etc.[7] The glory in which we glory is the shame that shames us before God, because we shame God.

11. *Ephraim flew away like a bird.* Here he is beginning to speak about the plague of sterility among men, that they are not multiplying as they had up to this time. The glory of Ephraim, which came from birth, from pregnancy, from conception, flew away like a bird. This is the way I construe this. In the Hebrew manner of speaking, "their" is superfluous. He does not deny all childbearing, but the abundance of people in His kingdom. After all, after they were scattered, they did have children in the captivity. Note the prophecy of Jacob about Ephraim (cf. Gen. 48:19; 49:22). The generation of offspring will be reduced to barrenness. Things turned out well for this people in conception, in pregnancy, in birth. We must take this to mean warnings and promises to happen only to a part. The punishments would occur this way too. We must understand this as synecdoche. "I will even kill the children you have already reared and nursed, but yet I will not kill them all" (v. 12). He always leaves a part. The great part He kills, etc.

12. *But woe to them.* This is a great bone of contention. It looks as though it might signify the incarnation of Christ, as Lyra says, but I don't know. Paul of Burgos[8] follows this idea too. It seems forced to me. This is my interpretation: "I will kill his offspring. They will be most unfortunate in their offspring and also in the fact that I will completely depart from them. I will send them away into all the other kingdoms. I will not be with them. I will let that remnant[9] which I have not killed live most wretchedly and unhappily. We see this in the Jews.

13. *Ephraim's sons, as I have seen.* He declares Himself more broadly in the destruction of the offspring.

[7] Perhaps Luther means to indicate that by reading the reflexive active verb *abalienaverunt se* instead of the Vulgate's passive *abalienati sunt* he has opportunity to indicate where the fault lies.

[8] A Spanish Jew (c. 1351—1435) who was baptized in 1390 and became a Christian bishop, apologist, and exegete. He is often mentioned together with Nicholas of Lyra because his exegetical comments on Bible texts *(Additiones)* were published together with Lyra's interpretation *(Postilla)* and were meant to be an amplification or a correction of Lyra's work.

[9] To *in eo* we have added the word *residuo,* which is used in the parallel passage of the Basel text.

Tyre was founded on beauty. Better than "on beauty" would be "on homes or habitations." Tyre had been filled with people, etc., and with very fertile wives who had filled their homes. A fertile wife with her offspring is called "the splendor of the home." Note what we read in the psalm (Ps. 68:12), "divide the spoil at home"; also (Ps. 128:3), "a fruitful vine."

As I have seen. "At that time, when I saw it." For "was founded" read "was planted." However, this glory was preserved for this, that Ephraim is led out and brings his children to the executioner.

14. *Give them, O Lord.* He concludes that loss of glory. Instead of "drying" read "dry." That is, he will not be in power.

15. *Every evil of theirs.* "All their wickedness is in Gilgal." This is the place they selected because of Samuel, etc., as above. There there is every evil of theirs, because of which He hates them. As a result, he says, "Because of their evil pursuits, etc."

I will not add that I love them, etc. He will no longer love them forever. It's all over for them. There is no longer a hope that this kingdom will flourish again. John uses this figure of speech in Luke 3:9: "The ax is laid to the root, etc."

16. *Fruit.* That is, the kingdom will no longer return to its prior status and administration. Its princes will be tyrants, etc.

The beloved, that is, their children, in whom will be their great hope, etc. "If ever they have recovered an outstanding man in whom they may place their hope of restoring the kingdom, this will not happen. I will kill him, etc."

17. *Among the nations.* Among the heathen; that is, among the Assyrians, in an uncertain home, as even now, etc.

This entire ninth chapter sets before their eyes that captivity as it applies to individual persons; they will be limited in their offspring, etc.

CHAPTER TEN

THE meaning is obscure, although the words are not. A curious prophet, this. He still seems to be speaking about the captivity, etc. Although there may be those who seem to live otherwise and make a false pretense of repentance, they do not intend with true zeal to better themselves, etc.; they are like the bishop of Rome now. When a fool wants to avoid his faults, he runs in the opposite direction.

1. *Luxuriant.* The Hebrew reads "wasted."[1] I would gladly agree that it remain "luxuriant,"[2] and one may not understand this as an antiphrasis,[3] etc. "Luxuriant," that is, widely spread and multiplied in the land. It is as if he were saying: "The vine is splendid but useless. It is displeasing to God. As widely as it is spread, so widely does it have a people, etc."

The more his fruit increased, the more altars he built. Jeremiah says, "The more his cities increased" (cf. Jer. 2:28). We had the same thing earlier, "because of your great iniquity" (Hos. 9:7). They did this to take care of the matter by multiplying their worship.

Richness. This is goodness. Wherever there was good land, they put up a priests' establishment. We have "well-established statues" in the Hebrew; "well cared for," as now; where the fat lands are, there are institutions and monasteries.

2. *They will perish, etc.* Now they will sin. They will be culpable, caught in their wickedness. The word[4] means to be guilty.

[1] The Hebrew בָּקַק has both meanings, "be luxuriant" and "to empty."

[2] The Latin translation in the Vulgate has *frondosa* ("leafy"), which may suggest a display of healthy growth that wastes its strength in appearance but fails to bear fruit.

[3] A rhetorical device in which words are used to mean their opposites.

[4] That is, the Hebrew word אָשַׁם.

Instead of "He [will break down their images]" I would read "this," namely, the fact that their heart is false. Either reading is a good one. "He" is obviously the Lord.

Their images, that is, their altars. This has been translated: [5] "He will destroy their images."

3. *For now they will say;* rather, "they are saying: 'We feel as if we had no king.'" Behold the outward appearance of the true worship of God! In their idols they worshiped the true God, as in Jerusalem. Hosea wrote this chapter at the time of the last king, [the last] of those under whom he prophesied.

4. *They utter mere words; with empty oaths.* In Hebrew, "words of an empty oath." It is as if he were saying: "All right, now you are pious and saintly people," as if to say: "All things are in vain. Those are words of an empty oath, because you are still going on in your empty works, etc. You are not laying hold on faith; you are depending on your own strength." "Make a covenant!" would be better.[6]

Like poisonous weeds. This is poison, gall. "With falsehood" is extra.[7] This is pure metaphor, [expressed] by a figure of speech. "You will reap nothing from it. You sow a false covenant and an empty oath, but heartache will spring up for you wherever you will be.

5. *Calves.* He is explaining himself. I am pleased to see Lyra read it thus: "The inhabitants of Samaria fear for the calves of Bethaven." This is the way it should be read.

And its idolatrous priests. Read it thus: "In which its idolatrous priests would generally exult[8] over its glory." This is the meaning: "We shall implore God in Bethaven merely that the calves remain." The people of Samaria are very fearful that their calf will be taken away, etc., because they hear that the calves also will be taken away from Samaria. This is similar in every way to what we

[5] That is, in the Vulgate.

[6] Luther suggests substituting the imperative *ferite* for the Vulgate's future indicative *ferietis.*

[7] That is, the equivalent of *cum mendacio* is not found in the Hebrew text. But our Vulgate text does not have it either.

[8] We have read *exultare* for *exaltare,* as the context seems to require.

said about the Turks when they made stables out of the temples, etc. Nevertheless, in the meantime, etc. It is with contempt and insult that he calls them "young cows" and "calves." "O Lord, we want to be pious too," because the king is not able to help. The idolatrous priests were religious men, monks, who lived a more devoted and more restricted life in their worship, etc., than the rest. The standard of perfection, the observants,[9] who had been assigned to it to worship. He does not dignify them with a priestly name, as we speak of the discalced,[10] the Augustinians, the Paulinians,[11] the observants.

6. *Yea, the thing itself, etc.* "The thing itself" obviously is the calf of Samaria; better: "a gift for King Jareb." [12] That is, even the calf itself is going to be carried away to Assyria as a gift for King Jareb, etc. They feared for the young cows or calves, that they would be taken to Assyria, etc.

Ephraim will be put to shame and Israel will be ashamed in his will. Read "of his counsel" for "in his will." He means here those dogmas and persuasions with which they lead one away to their own counsel. He[13] will be ashamed—obviously, after he sees that his own plans have been to no avail, etc.

7. *Perish, etc.*, that is, everything will be reduced to a desert. For things destroyed and reduced to nothing, the Hebrews use דום or דָּמָה, which he here translates "made him perish." "His king of Samaria has fallen silent" is better; or "he has become silent," or "he has been reduced to nothing," so that he does not realize that this has happened. There is nothing more fleeting than a blister on the water, a bubble. Therefore it will all be over soon for Samaria, as in the case of a bubble "on the surface of the water." [14]

[9] Cf. *Luther's Works,* 10, p. 75, n. 66.

[10] Prominent among the discalced, or "barefoot," orders at Luther's time were the Franciscans, the Carmelites, the Capuchins, and the Augustinians.

[11] An order of originally Hungarian monks that adapted the Augustinian rule in addition to their own strict observance.

[12] The Vulgate translates *regi ultori,* "the king who avenges." Luther considers the translation "King Jareb" better. Cf. p. 30 above.

[13] We have read *confundetur,* as in the Vulgate, for *confundentur.*

[14] The words *super faciem aquae* are marked as Biblical quotation in the Weimar text; here the quotation is part of the commentary.

8. *Will be destroyed.* Better would be "will be laid waste,"[15] or "will be ruined."

The high places of the idol. These are like the foundations that we had. They placed their altars on any hill. These are called the high places, the foundations. Instead of "of the idol,"[16] "of iniquity" reads better; that is, the high places of their wicked worship, which brings no comfort but afflicts the more, etc.

The sin. Namely, whatever sin there is.

And they will say to the mountains. Christ quotes this in the gospel (cf. Luke 23:30). This was a common statement among the Jewish people. Here it has a general sense which is applied to any future captivity or devastation. We apply it to the coming judgment; Christ applies it to the final captivity of the Jews; Hosea, to the Assyrian captivity.

9. *From the days of Gibeah, etc.* Here he has altered the text.[17] This is another exordium with which the prophet attacks this people. He intends to encourage them to bring better fruit. It is as if he were saying: "What should they do? This is an old villainy, etc." See above (Hos. 9:9) concerning the sin of Gibeah. This is the first place in which he describes what the people have done. What they did seemed right to them. The city is Dan, in which they made the first idol. Take note of Micah, etc.[18] This sin was born on Mount Ephraim and then was spread to the tribe of Dan. Here the prophet is saying, as it were: "It's an old sin; they have lived in it a long time, etc." It is the ancient leprosy. There they stand and cannot move, etc. They stand in the way of sinners, etc., as in Ps. 1:1. Instead of "over," it is "because of."[19]

[15] *Vastabuntur,* obviously meant to be explanatory of the text *disperdentur,* is printed in the Weimar edition as if it were quoted Biblical text. We have translated under the supposition that Luther said *Disperdentur, sic melius: vastabuntur vel delebuntur.*

[16] As in the Vulgate.

[17] That is, Luther has altered the text. The student who took down Luther's dictation points out that for the Vulgate's *peccavit* Luther substituted the second person singular *peccasti* to read "You have sinned, O Israel."

[18] Judg. 17:1.

[19] That is, in the phrase *super filios iniquitatis,* "on account of the wayward people."

Shall not war overtake them? I read this as mimetic, imitative. He is saying, as it were: "We will not experience the same" as in Gibeah, etc. "Would God really punish people so?" "We have struck a treaty, etc.," says Is. 28:15.[20] "It will not overtake them, etc.," as we read in Micah 2:6. But the prophets say, "Evil will come." They say, "It will not, it will not." Or we may take it as a statement, as if He were saying: "I will not seize them like the Benjamites, but I will punish them severely."

10. *In My desire.* "Not according to their wishes, etc. I will vent My spleen on them. I will not punish them as then, etc."

For their double iniquity. He understands this as two calves and two idols, etc.

11. *Ephraim was a heifer trained.* This is an obscure passage. "My Ephraim is a calf, for it likes to be on the threshing floor at threshing time." Every interest of theirs is toward seeking their own; their interest is in eating and drinking. Ephraim is trained to seek its own gain. The first sin is that they mislead the people with false doctrine; the second, that their belly is their concern, etc. Once they have taken good care of the belly, the rest follows. After all, the soul is dead and is not fed with the Word. True piety does the contrary; it does not permit the soul to go hungry, no matter how the body is cared for. The most irksome work lies in the wicked life; yet these people do it gladly, etc., because they are accustomed to it. It is as if he were saying: "No heifer can be forced to love threshing, only that heifer Ephraim, namely, because it wants to eat and drink, etc."

On the beauty, Or "goodness." A strong ox has a durable neck. That is, "I will climb up on his fine neck. I will tire him out. I will transfer them from that vexation of wickedness to another."

I will mount Ephraim. "I will do this the way a rider mounts a horse or chariot. That is, I will saddle them with the Assyrian captivity."

Judah will plow. When the kingdom of Israel will have been removed, there will be nothing in the land except Judah.

20 The Weimar editor suggests Is. 8:12, but that seems unsuitable. Luther did not specify chapter and verse.

12. *Sow.* An exhortation follows to make them reflect on righteousness and truth. "Sow righteousness; reap mercy!" That is, "You will receive mercy, etc." So Paul has it: As a man's work is, so shall his reward be.[21] He is saying, as it were: "Come to your senses!"

In view of mercy, that is, "according to mercy."[22] I take it this way: "Sow, then, on behalf of[23] righteousness and reap on behalf of mercy. Do good, and good will be done to you in return."

That He may come, etc. He has related this to Christ, etc. Paul says it this way (1 Thess. 5:23): "At the coming of our Lord Jesus Christ," as we await the coming of the great day, etc. Also: "Be like men waiting for their master to come, etc." (Luke 12:36). This title is not given to any prophet. No one taught righteousness except Christ in public, etc. Whoever does a good work in order to get something (and not freely) from God, he plows wickedness, he reaps iniquity and eats the bread of falsehood (v. 13).

13. *Because he trusted,* etc. See Jer. 2:33, 35.

14. *As Shalman destroyed, etc.* Again, a difficult text. "Just as in a peaceful house there is destruction in the day of the ambush of war." That is how I read this. That is, this is what happens to him who sits in his home at peace when suddenly the enemy rushes in and destroys everything: mother, daughters, etc. Yet, I rather believe that this refers to an episode of history that is not recorded. After all, Betharbel, Shalman, etc., are proper names. So also Luke 13 at the beginning touches on unwritten episodes of history with a few words, etc. He says, as a parallel to this episode, that the Israelites are going to be destroyed.

[21] E. g., 1 Cor. 3:8, 14; 2 Cor. 9:6; Gal. 6:7; 1 Tim. 5:18.

[22] We follow the editor of the St. Louis edition of Luther's works (St. L., V, 1008) in supposing that *in ore viae* and *iuxta viam* should be read *in ore misericordiae* and *iuxta misericordiam,* in which the word *misericordia* was probably abbreviated and then misread *via.*

[23] Luther explains the expression *in ore iustitiae* with *pro iustitia.*

CHAPTER ELEVEN

In the morning,[1] or "as in the morning." "At dawn" would be preferred.

The sense of this chapter is this: Idolatry is the chronic evil of that people; they were fashioned as sinners from the very womb, etc. Isaiah writes (Is. 48:8): "From birth you were called a rebel" because they are evil. "You have never stopped being naughty." Stephen speaks this way in Acts (Acts 7:51).

In the dawn the king of Israel is completely cut off, or: "Silent, the king kept silent in the dawn." That is, this was sudden, etc. That is, "I have magnified this people, so that all peoples admire this kingdom." This is a rebuke for the kindnesses received and given in the delivery out of Egypt, and a reminder thereof. That is, "From the very beginning, when they were young, I loved them very much; I always blessed them. My love went ahead of them, etc. They went wherever they were called. They ought to have followed Me, but whenever a new teacher came up, they would follow him, etc." Paul reports in Acts (cf. Acts 13:18): "He tolerated[2] their bad habits for 40 years."

4. *With the cords of men, etc.* that is, "I shall capture them with the kindnesses, etc., with which men are caught."

With the bands of love, that is, with light yokes. This is the way Christ says it (Matt. 11:30): "My yoke is easy, My burden is light." But that yoke did not please them. In fact, they looked for other gods, etc.

I have eased, That is, "I have lifted the yoke that kept pressing on their jaws; I have always eased them from the yoke they were suffering, etc."

[1] Other texts add this sentence to the end of chapter 10.

[2] We have read *toleravit* for *toleravi.* The Vulgate has *sustinuit.*

That he may be fed. Better, "That I might feed him."

5. *He will not return.* Again this is a warning.[3] "This is what I have done for them, etc. Therefore they will not return to Egypt." He reads: "They[4] will not return." This "not returning to Egypt" is this: the Lord wants to subject this people to the king of Assyria, and Egypt's assistance will not help them, etc.

6. *The sword has raged.* The king of Assyria captured many cities, especially of the tribe of Naphthali.

The elect. This is "bars" in the Hebrew. It is the custom of the Hebrew language to call princes bars, mountains, fortresses, walls.

And will devour, that is, it will eat away at their counsels. That is, they will fall in their own counsels; that is, because of their own counsels, etc. Their counsels will be very bad for those who take their advice.

7. *And My people.* Take this to refer to a spiritual return. It began with Christ when the Gospel was sent throughout the world. That is, "they will be in suspense, they will be put off, until I shall have returned, etc."

Moreover, a yoke. This passage is especially obscure. He is speaking about a physical yoke that will never be taken off.

8. *How, etc.* It is as if he were saying: "I shall not protect you. I shall not free you. How shall I give you up? How shall I deal with you? In Jeremiah we have a reference about Sodom (Jer. 49: 18).[5] Not a handful would remain. Thus nothing will be carried away; that is, this kingdom will be completely destroyed.

My heart recoils. That is, it has been changed. He promises great mercy. It grieved the Lord according to the multitude of His mercy when He went too far. This is called repenting. He is saying, as it were, "That My people have been so afflicted grieves Me."

[3] With the Erlangen edition, we have read *comminatio* for the Weimar editon's *comminutio*.

[4] The student means to say that Luther diverges from the Vulgate's singular form *non revertetur* to read in the plural *non revertentur*.

[5] The Weimar editor suggests Jer. 23:14.

9. *I shall not execute, etc.* "I shall not follow the entire path of My wrath."

I am God, and not a human being. The Hebrew reads, "and not a man." He is saying, as it were, "I strike down and I heal. Man wants to uproot everything, but not I." This is a wonderful promise of the mercy of God: "I want My reputation for mercy to remain safe. I also want people to flee to Me for refuge." Satan wants no one to remain a Christian. In the midst of death God promises mercy. "If I oppress you, you should flee for refuge to Me. Stay here." By nature man wants to run away when God oppresses him. "To Me! To Me in distress!" We had this "in distress" earlier in Chapter 6:1.

The Holy One. You see, He Himself sanctifies and justifies. Note: to enter and go out into the midst of men is to spend one's life with them.

And I shall not come, that is, "I shall not spend My time in the cities." He gives a description of His coming kingdom in a few words: It will not be a physical but a spiritual kingdom. It will be free in the Spirit. It will not have cities. The kingdom of God is not something for us to observe (Luke 17:20).

10. *He will roar like a lion.* That is, they will follow that Lord who will speak out as with the roar of a lion. We have the same thing in Amos (1:2): "The Lord will roar, etc.," that is, "the Gospel will be preached with a great, lion-like roaring and with a loud voice, etc." This is the Lion of the tribe of Judah, who will roar for His elect cubs against the wicked foes, etc. As He roars, "the sons of the sea will be afraid," that is, they will flee. That is the flight which takes place in a camp when a hue and cry is made. Stampede! The word [6] means both fear and flight.

Sons of the sea. So we also say "strength of the sea"; that is, the very strong wind that has its abode near the sea. This sea here means the sea which the Jews called the "western sea." That means the people who live near the Mediterranean Sea will not resist Him but will obey Him.

11. *They will fly away.* This is the same word as "they will

[6] The Hebrew word חָרַד.

be afraid." They will flee to the Lord who is striking them. Not only the Jews but also "the sons of the sea"—the Assyrians and Egyptians—will follow the Lord at His roaring, etc. This is one of the passages cited by Paul in Rom. 1:16.

And I will return them. That is, "I will gather them into the church, into the many mansions that are in the home of My Father." He also promises them gifts, etc. This is a summary of the preaching of the Gospel, etc.

CHAPTER TWELVE

Ephraim has encompassed Me, etc. Here[1] a new sermon begins.

Hosea did not prophesy in only one year. Here he is calling Ephraim forth to zeal by comparing them with the tribe of Judah, etc. "Shame on you. Look at them; they are pious people." He is using a Hebrew phrase when he says: "Has encompassed me with lies." It means deceitfully, fraudulently. In the same way "with wisdom" is wisely; "with intellect" is prudently; "with bravery" is bravely. "To encompass" is: "You go about in the city"; not around the walls, but here and there, back and forth, in the city. The wicked walk about the city, etc. When scoundrels, who are without the Spirit, come into power in the spiritual area, they exercise an ugly influence.

Moreover, Judah still rules with God and with the faithful saints, that is, "with sacred things." That is how I read this.[2] Judah rules in the presence of God, that is, Judah rules and governs the people with the Word of God. He is looking forward to the time of Hezekiah. Earlier He found fault with Judah.[3]

With the saints. That is, the Levitical order and everything else is safe in Judah. What Lyra says, however, pleases me: "'With the saints,' that is, with God." The Hebrew often addresses the Divinity in the plural. Thus in Joshua (24:19) with God we see "holy" in the plural;[4] and in the prophet (cf. Jer. 10:10), "living" in the plural.[5] "With the faithful Saints," that is, the One in whom they believed.

[1] In our reckoning, this is v. 12 of chapter 11.

[2] For the Vulgate's *Judas autem testis descendit cum deo, et cum sanctis fidelis,* Luther has *Iuda autem adhuc dominatur cum deo et cum sanctis fidelibus.*

[3] Cf. Hos. 5:5, 10.

[4] The Hebrew is אֱלֹהִים קְדֹשִׁים הוּא.

[5] The Hebrew is אֱלֹהִים חַיִּים.

1. *Ephraim herds the wind and pursues Eurus.*[6] This is the southeast or south wind. He is using a special name for a general one. By wind he means empty pursuits. The apostle speaks about beating the air (cf. 1 Cor. 9:26). It is as if he were saying: "Ephraim attempts many things, but all things are vain." To work in vain is "to herd the wind," so that the damage returns to the person working, etc. "He pursues" means he attends to it with excessive zeal.

All day long. He is explaining Himself, that is: "They resolve to take over the government by making a treaty with the Egyptians; they have abandoned Me, and they are dealing with treacherous means. Everything is useless."

Falsehood. We must not relate this to worship but to vanity.

Oil, that is, gifts. As the principal things, He mentions wine and oil. They are the chief products of that land. Judah rules with the holy[7] and faithful God.[8] The Lord, therefore, passes judgment in favor of Judah. He won the case for Judah. He did this against King Sennacherib.

2. *And the Lord will visit Jacob.* He will visit them with punishment.

According to his ways. That is, they have been wicked, and wicked people will destroy them.

3. *In the womb . . . he strove.* He wrestled with God. This passage has been corrupted.[9]

4. *He wrestled with the angel and prevailed.* The account in Gen. 32 is well known. Actually Jacob fought that harsh and

[6] The Vulgate has *aestum,* "the hot wind," for which Luther read *eurum,* "east wind."

[7] Luther uses the plural *sanctis* but follows with the singular *fideli.* Cf. n. 4 above.

[8] This comment belongs to v. 2.

[9] The Weimar text has a colon at this point and thus indicates that the "corruption" lies in the words quoted next. It is more likely that the "corruption" seen by Luther in the Vulgate text lies in the words not fully quoted at the head of this paragraph: *et in fortitudine sua directus est cum angelo.* We have accordingly taken the words that follow the Weimar edition's colon as text from v. 4. Cf. St. Louis edition, VI, 1016, n. 1.

lofty battle against God.[10] The conscience feels the force of sin and at the same time the force of divine wrath, which is intolerable. At that time Jacob was in agony because the Lord wanted to kill him, etc., when neither Satan nor a creature seemed to fight, but God. From the sword the conscience goes over to divine wrath, when He threatens with the spear. Before Jacob was born, he was a conqueror, but the sort of conqueror who had beaten a man. After he had been born and when he lived, he overcame God and the angel, etc.

He wept and sought his favor. He said: "I will not let You go unless You bless me." (Gen. 32:26) He "found Him" twice at Bethel, as we see in Genesis.[11]

5. *Memorial.* This is what we call name, or glory. This is the story, but what does it mean? What is the connection of the text? In their preaching the prophets have the custom of teaching what happened in the past. From that they compose consolation or rebuke for present situations. It is as if he were saying: "Ephraim now is surrounding Me with his lies. The Lord will render to him as he deserves. Yet they ought to look to Him and worship Him as the God whom their fathers, or his father, worshiped, etc. If you want to worship God correctly at Bethel, do what your father did. What did he do? 'In the womb, etc.' This was divine election. God worked in him. There is no reason for you to glory in your self-chosen worship. If you want to be genuine followers of Jacob, do what Jacob did, etc. You do not supplant, but you are supplanted. Also, he wrestled with God. This is an example of very great faith. You, however, do not cling to the promises of God as Jacob did."

In his manhood (v. 3). The text provides the connection. This was not his own manhood but a divine manhood given him by God. With such manhood we overcome an angry God. Even though we have our own manhood, it is like chaff against the wind. Divine wrath is unbearable. How much less, then, can anyone fight against Him, etc.? Third, in Bethel they worship God. This is a certainty; but how do they do this? What happened earlier in

10 Cf. *Luther's Works,* 6, pp. 125—128.

11 Cf. Gen. 35.

Bethel? The Lord spoke, etc. They had to look to His Word. God requires faith in His Word. He respects no place, no time.

6. *So you, by the help of the Lord your God, return. Hold fast to mercy and justice, etc.* He is applying and explaining the story. "You will return when you hold fast to mercy and justice and hope in God, not when you flee to Egypt, etc. You are absolute liars when you abandon God and look for strange gods to worship, etc. "Mercy" is the name of the gift we receive from God or give to a neighbor—benefaction.

Justice. This is the custom and practice "according to the justice of daughters" (cf. Ex. 21:9). We read in Deuteronomy (1:17) not to be partial in judgment. This also means the responsibility of ruling and of administering justice. In Ps. 1 we read that the wicked will hold no office; they will not be kings and administrators, etc. He is also speaking about the execution of justice or of the law. That is, "You ought to be generous. You ought to make all your goods common to all men. You ought to harbor ill thoughts about no man. You ought to condemn what should be condemned, approve what should be approved, etc. You ought to be of real service to your neighbor. There is no need for you to carry oil to Egypt, but trust in Him, etc."

7. *Canaan.* The Hebrew reads more properly "a merchant," a businessman. In the last chapter of Proverbs (Prov. 31:24) we have: "She delivers girdles to the Canaanite;" that is, to the merchant. You are like a merchant, etc. I construe it this way: You are indeed a merchant. In your hand you carry a set of lying scales. You love to trick and harm. This, therefore, is a simile. It is not that Ephraim was such a merchant. After all, he is speaking about faith. Consequently, you should take this to mean false doctrine which deceives and destroys souls and turns them away from God. The Hebrew word און signifies pain at times and virtues at other times. It even means might, as in the blessing of Jacob for Reuben (Gen. 49:3). Consequently, it does not mean idol here. It means filled with grain, wine, oil, etc. When they served the true God, they were poor people and cast down; but if they were involved in wickedness, they became wealthy. This is the way it is today in the case of the priests. Wicked doctrine makes the teachers as well as the people rich. It is Satan who does this, although God

does at times take away food in order to strengthen faith, etc. But these people do not want to hope, they want to be sure and to have plenty.

9. *As in the days of the feast.* These were the feast days appointed for preaching so that the people might hear the Law. This is looking toward the coming of Christ, just as we always consider the Last Day as if it were very present. This is the way the prophets considered the incarnation of Christ. This means: "There will come a time for you to again assemble and hear what you used to hear on feast days, namely, the Word of God."

10. *And I spoke.* "I shall explain everything that is going to happen. I shall speak, etc."

I shall multiply, etc. "I shall make another prophecy. Before you hear it. You will go into Assyria with another prophecy. I shall reveal My Word, and I myself shall teach it, as we have in Joel 2 and Is. 54:13.[12] God will teach all men. This is looking toward the coming Christ.

In the hand of the prophets. That is, "whoever will listen to the prophet at that time will listen to Me. The prophets will be like Me, and I will be like the prophets. They will speak as gods, and I will speak as a man among them." This is a prophecy about the coming of the Spirit, who will be given through Christ.

11. *If there is an idol in Gilead, etc.* We must become accustomed to the state of mind and to the figurative language of the prophets. In their preaching the prophets relate everything to the coming Christ, etc. They do not seem to harmonize well, but we must consider their state of mind. He is remaining with his exhortation and shaking up of the people, etc. "If in Gilead." He seems to be touching on an episode of history which has not been recorded. It seems that Gilead and Gilgal made comparisons between themselves, like Observants and Franciscans. The one wanted to have a greater name than the other. Gilead is the region across the Jordan; Gilgal is on this side of the Jordan. It is as if he were saying: "You are just as godly as the people in Gilead; they stink in comparison with you." He translates אָוֶן as "idol." [13] It is rather "in-

[12] The original has Jer. 31.

[13] In the Vulgate.

iquity." If one is godly, they all are. "If they are wicked in Gilead, you in Gilgal are vain, because you sacrifice great bulls, etc."

Even their altars, that is, will be. "Your altars, about which you boast in Gilead, will be like furrows of the field, overturned."

12. *Jacob fled.* He sets forth another example.

He did service for a wife, "on account of," or "on behalf of."

13. *By a prophet,* that is, through a prophet. This does not seem to hang together. Again he sets an example of a father against those wicked sons. Instead of "he did service," read "he took care of," namely, cattle, or a treaty and compact. It is as if he were saying: "That good father of yours could serve men in Syria. These youngsters cannot serve Me. He was an exile, yet he could and did do this and still served his God. Those of you who now have an abundance of all things and who live in a fat kingdom are his degenerate sons, etc. They do not serve Me; they abandon Me, etc. Because they do this, they provoke Me to send them tribulations."

14. *Bitterness.* This is what the Jews call disobedience or rebellion. Their interest is nothing except to embitter the Lord; that is, to provoke Him. Therefore, blood, or misfortune will descend on their heads. We have this in the Book of Kings (2 Sam. 3:28-29),[14] where David says, "Let the judgment be upon you who have deserved it. I am innocent." That is, "Let them carry the burden themselves." Guilt is declared. "Disgrace will come upon them, and ridicule to boot. Their sins have brought on bloodshed."

Reproach. "The reproach with which he reproached Me. He shames Me with his idols. Shame will come upon him."

[14] The Vulgate counts four Books of Kings, our 1 and 2 Samuel being 1 and 2 Kings, and our 1 and 2 Kings being 3 and 4 Kings.

CHAPTER THIRTEEN

He again begins a new sermon. He preached those sermons in different years and at different times. It is as if he were saying: "And now there is a new game." The prophets kept rebuking every worship of theirs. They were always establishing new cults, just as we build new altars and temples, etc.

2. *And now.* They keep adding to it.

Of silver. He says, as it were: "What splendid saints they are! They make a god out of their own silver." He says with disparagement and contempt: "Of your silver and your gold."

1. *When Ephraim spoke horror; he was exalted in Israel, etc.* I think we must make "horror" the object of the word "spoke,"[1] as if he were saying: "Ephraim has been having its way long enough with its preaching, etc." Also, "Through Baal he has set up a strange worship [and has died]." I believe that he is speaking about spiritual death. This is a recapitulation and repetition of their past evils, as we say, "Up to now you have done this and this. Now you have added something else, etc." These are horrible things they have said and done, etc.

As if, etc. He means those who are making a likeness of the idols. In Hebrew, "to work with difficulty," as in "who eat the bread of anxious toil" (Ps. 127:2). "Of idols" is in Hebrew "of trials."[2] אָוֶן properly means grief, *Mühe*. They turn only to idolatrous wickedness. You see, their idols bring grief, etc., trouble, because "there is no peace for the wicked."[3] Those who are work-

[1] In the Vulgate *horror* is the subject of *invasit Israel.*

[2] Luther treats the Hebrew word עֲצַבִּים ("idols"), which occurs in this text, as identical with עֲצָבִים ("anxious toil"), which the Vulgate in Ps. 127:2 translates *dolorum.*

[3] Is. 48:22; 57:21.

ing are people afflicted with the wretched pursuit of idols. He is referring to the painstaking craftsmen of idols, etc.

They say to these, that is, they speak to these images by prophesying and crying out. Instead of "worshiping," we have "kissing," as in Ps. 2:11. We have the same thing in Job [31:27] and in the Book of Kings (1 Kings 19:18): "They did not bend their knees, etc." A kiss is a sign of adoration. It means the custom and ritual of adoration.

Men. First they sacrificed calves; now they sacrifice men. This is a new thing. They were offering their children. The prophet is saying "men" out of spite, although they are little children, etc. It is horrible to hear this. What he is saying here is a horror.

3. *Therefore they will be like the morning mist*. We have considered these words earlier (Hos. 6:4). "They will be," that is, they will pass over like the morning cloud which the sun dissipates. This is how your worship, your security, and boasting will turn out. He is describing the pleasant feeling they have from that worship, but that will quickly pass and be changed.

Like the dust. This is chaff, as in Ps. 1:4. It is "husk" in Hebrew —a beautiful simile.

From a smokehole. Chimney. Smoke must go where the wind takes it, etc. The chaff from grain follows the same pattern.

4. *I am the Lord your God*. The prophet brings this in to lead the people back to the worship of the one true God. "This way, this way!" This is a complete condemnation of every worship which God has not established. "There is no salvation outside of Me. I have saved you. I can still save you. But it helps not at all, etc. They have their fill. As they have an abundance of things, so also do they enjoy that abundance. Thus they rage proudly against Me and the prophets whom I send. In this way, they hold in contempt the God who wants them to worship Him in faith and fear, etc."

6. *They were filled and their heart was lifted up*. They dare to do everything—whatever comes to mind.

7-8. *And I will be . . . I will tear open their breast*. He is saying: "I will cut their hearts to pieces with My sword." A poniard, or dagger, or sword is what the Hebrew word means. They have done the same thing as we have done with the Turks. First we prayed and made our supplications. Then we looked for human assistance, etc. The Turk, however, keeps on attacking.

There, namely, in Assyria.

Their heart. Not that of everyone. This is synecdoche. "Many will go into captivity. In Me they will have a very harsh foe, etc. They will lie unburied. They will be laid low without mercy. No one will take their side."

9. *I will be your ruin.* Here He begins His reviling. "Your loss has been effected. Your own devices accomplish nothing. I will make you see that people must flee to Me for refuge."

10. *Where is your king?* "The king in whom you kept trusting."

In your cities. Better would be "among the enemies whom you have," as if to say: "He would not be able to defend you against a single one."

Give me. It is as if he were saying: "We cannot trust in God. We must have a king whom we can trust, etc." They have always misused their kings.

11. *I will give you.* He is saying this proverbially, as it were. The sense is this: "I will give you; that is, I am able to give you a king, that you may suffer under the king, and suffer very much when you lose him."

12. *The iniquity of Ephraim is bound up.* Here he is concluding this warning. These things are tied together; they have made a compact. They cannot be set free from their iniquity. They justify their sin. They cannot bear the fact that their sin is considered sin. This is what our own priests are doing. "My Ephraim has put his sin into a sack and is hiding it."

13. *The pangs of childbirth will come for him*, that is, they cannot escape. They must suffer. Where there is no confession, there is no healing.

He is an unwise son. "He is a foolish child, a silly son." He is speaking like a father.

14. *I will free them from the hand of Sheol.* "Sometime I will take death away." Immediately He comes to think of Christ. "Death

and hell" is a very common expression among Hebrews. Jerome catches the sense well and truly here. Hell is the name for every place to which the soul went. When the soul is separated from the body, the result is called death. "I will redeem them from the hand of hell, and I will free them from death."

I will be your death. Death here is that plague which certainly kills, etc. That is, "I, the Christ, through My resurrection shall work from day to day to kill you. I shall be your pestilence, O death, and your sting, O hell." When God struck down the cattle in Exodus (Ex. 9:3), it is called דֶּבֶר, which means plague. "Death, I will be your poison; hell, I will be your plague." He is referring to the kingdom of Christ. They[4] have translated "sting" *(morsus)* as in Deuteronomy (Deut. 28:21)[5] and in the psalm (Ps. 91:6): "From the devil's attack at noonday, etc." Here it is not "sting" but a wasting pestilential fever. "O hell, I will be your devil." The Hebrew word also signifies Satan, who strikes and afflicts one with a sharp fever, etc. Paul translates the sense of the prophet freely: Death will be overcome and swallowed up; hell will be destroyed (cf. 1 Cor. 15:54-55). That is what this means. The apostles were not superstitious in their words. In fact, this is something which Paul even censures.[6] Paul's translation is not that of the Septuagint. Christ swallowed up death and hell for those who believe. He is speaking about the act of Christ, about what Christ did. How this was dispensed will follow. Few people achieve this victory. The failure is in us; we do not arrive at it. Christ has taken away every evil.

Compassion. It is as if he were saying: "Not every man will gain this victory." This is the way Paul speaks: "I am deeply grieved" (cf. Rom. 9:2).

Is hid. That is, there will be cause for sadness.

15. *He.* Better would be "this."

Among brothers. That is, some will seize the victory, some will not. He means not only the act but also the fruit, because some are going to believe, and some are not, etc.

[4] The translators of the Vulgate.

[5] But here the Vulgate has *pestilentiam.*

[6] Cf. 1 Tim. 6:4.

The Lord will bring a searing wind. This is the east wind, *Eurus.* When it blew, the Red Sea dried up. Paul alludes to this when he calls sin "the sting of death" (1 Cor. 15:56).

It will make his spring desolate. Here he is calling sin a spring, etc. "The searing wind" is the Holy Spirit, who will blow into our hearts and dry up the springs of death, the source, with this medicine. He is going to give us the Holy Spirit into our heart. He will dry up the fountains, that is, sin. Instead of "make desolate," it is "parch." That is, He will move from an external kingdom to a spiritual kingdom.

CHAPTER FOURTEEN

THIS is the prophet's farewell. He is coming to the conclusion. It would be better to take everything in the indicative.[1]

1. *She has embittered her God,*[2] that is, she is disobedient to her God. This will be the end. Obviously, he is making a prophecy about the kingdom of Christ.

Return, O Israel. This kingdom of Ephraim has fallen into ruin. Therefore, take your place in another kingdom. There will be a new ritual; it will deal not with cattle and sheep but with words and a confession.

2. *Take words with you.* There is no other sacrifice in the New Testament except the sacrifice of praise. We should flee for refuge not to our own works but to grace and mercy. The confession of sin and a thirst for grace will be the voice of the new people.[3]

Accept that which is good. That is, "Take the good thing, that You may give us something to distribute among ourselves." He is saying, as it were, "Put aside our wrath and iniquity from Your hand. Take a good thing to give us." These are the proper bulls; that is, thanksgivings and the preaching of the Gospel. This is what the sacrifices of the Old Testament signify. Paul says (Rom. 15:16): "I sanctify," that is, "I treat the Gospel in priestly fashion, that it may become an offering, etc."

The bulls. These are the words of preaching. In Heb. 13:15[4] we hear of "the fruit of lips." It appears that he read "fruits" instead of "bulls" in the Hebrew. We also read about those bulls at the end of Psalm 51 (Ps. 51:21).

[1] Not in the subjunctive, as in the Vulgate.

[2] In our reckoning, this is in Hos. 13:16.

[3] Cf. p. 296, n. 16, below.

[4] The original has "Heb. 11."

Return, etc. Get away from your confidence, and you will wait for Christ.

3. *We will not ride upon horses.* "We have no confidence in our own strength." Isaiah (Is. 30:15) says "in quietness and trust."

We will say no more. "We will no longer worship with that type of worship, etc."

In Thee, that is, "through Thee." "Through You the orphan will still come to mercy, that is, that wretched people will find mercy through You."

4. *I will heal, etc.* The promise follows. "I will heal their conversion, that is, to those who are converted of that people, that is, who are going to be converted, I will reveal My love, so that they see that they have not earned it but everything to the contrary. Israel will be destroyed, yet I will be 'as the dew,' that is, I will be preached as sweet rain." That is how we read it in Micah (5:7). No one knows how that word regarding Christ descends by the miraculous work of the Holy Spirit.

5. *Lily,* or rose. "Ephraim will be destroyed, yet I will have mercy on him." That is, it will be a handsome people, but of a rosy color before God.

6. *His shoots will go out.* That is, they will be diffused, spread broadly, namely, throughout the entire world. He is speaking according to a very pleasant metaphor.

The olive. "It will praise You like the olive." That is, the Christian people will be a people of mercy and of grace. The olive is praised for its oil.

Soft. Better would be "gentle." [5]

Fragrance. It will have a pleasant odor, etc. This is the reputation with which Christian people are fragrant. As Paul says, "We are the aroma of Christ" (2 Cor. 2:15).

7. *Beneath his shadows.* This is the shadow of the olive or of Lebanon. Those who are under the shade of Lebanon will return. Those who are not will turn away. That refers to the church.

[5] "Soft" is not in the Vulgate text. The St. Louis edition assumes the reading to be *Mollis populus blandus* ("a mild, gentle people") and adds it to the preceding paragraph.

They will live with grain and increase as a vine. He takes this to mean the preaching of the Gospel. The wine must be the finest wine. My idea is that this is the Gospel. If you wish to relate this to the Sacrament of the Altar, you can. It is a beautiful promise about the kingdom and grace of Christ.

8. *O Ephraim, etc.* The Spirit will glory then, because Ephraim no longer will have his idols.

Green. An evergreen. With this he signifies that the kingdom and word of Christ stands firm in persecution and prosperity.

From Me. Not from you! This is a prophecy of mercy—a rejection of everything that belongs to us. "I am the vine, you are the branches, etc." (John 15:5).

9. *Whoever is wise, let him understand these things. Whoever is discerning, let him know them.* That is, there are few of these people. These are outstanding promises. But who understands them? People stick to their own parades; but who will succeed? The church blushes with shame. They will be terrified by the cross.

The ways are right. However, they will appear heretical and will be condemned.

Liars. These are transgressors. Here you have a picture of how the Gospel should function: the poor will be improved by it; others who are in the parade will be offended because of it, etc.

So far Luther on Hosea, etc.

LECTURES ON JOEL

The Altenburg Text

Translated by
RICHARD J. DINDA

All the prophets have one and the same message, for this is their one aim: they are all looking toward the coming of Christ or to the coming kingdom of Christ. All their prophecies look to this, and we must relate them to nothing else. Although they may mix in various accounts of things present or of things to come, yet all things pertain to this point, that they are declaring the coming kingdom of Christ. So every time the prophets announced something bad or something good, they intended one to look at the kingdom of Christ. One may see the same thing here in the prophet Joel, who is the first to treat the most destructive pest brought upon the people of Judah. He took up this subject to terrify the Jews and to call back to repentance those whom he had frightened, so that they might thus wait for the coming Christ (about whose kingdom he will speak in considerable detail below). In regard, then, to the first chapter of this prophet, the meaning I take is this—that in the first chapter he is not prophesying but, as I said, is simply recounting the current history of that catastrophe and the destruction of the crops and of all the fruits of the earth—something he had seen.

In the second chapter, however, he appears to begin his prophecy. It is about a different kind of grasshoppers—about the Babylonians. Thus a summary of the first chapter (and he treats nothing else in it) is this, that he terrifies the Jews by placing that plague before their eyes—a plague which the Lord had inflicted—that, thus frightened, they may repent and learn to know themselves.

Because, however, it is the nature of the world to despise and laugh at the Word of God (after all, we have seen that the same thing has happened and is happening still today), no doubt the same thing happened to Joel, too. The world never changes its character. Its prince is Satan. It is his impulse which leads it into every evil. It is, you see, the kingdom of darkness which cannot but hate the light. John 1:5. Thus it despises and persecutes the heralds of the Word of God. It calls them fools, and finally it even kills them as worthless men. Paul calls Christians the περίψημα ("offscouring") of the world (1 Cor. 4:13). Here there is no reason to hope for better things.

There is no sufficient agreement as to when Joel prophesied. You see, he makes no mention of times and kings, which the other prophets generally state in the beginning of their prophecy. It seems clear to me that he is an old prophet. Thus I think he prophesied before Isaiah, Hosea, and the rest, namely, when the kingdom of the Jews still flourished and was established in great peace. Then, I think, he saw this great plague about which he is speaking here. By the way, that order of the prophets and, in fact, of the other books of Scripture which has been approved by Jerome and others is of no value. They are clearly in error when they think that the prophets followed each other in the way they have been arranged.[1] Some think that he prophesied under Hosea, but this does not seem likely to me.

[1] That is, in the Bible.

CHAPTER ONE

2. *Hear this, you aged men.* He gave the sermon of this chapter not just in one place but often and in many places. After all, he is addressing all the inhabitants of the land.

3. [*Tell your children*] *of it.* This is a common Hebraism of Scripture which even the author of the Epistle to the Hebrews used when he said, "Of the angels He says, etc.," that is, "About the angels He says" (Heb. 1:7). So here, "of it," that is, "about it," which the Greeks generally express with the preposition περί.

4. *What the caterpillar left.* He is simply giving an account of the plague which he saw, in which all the produce—grains, fruit, and grapes—was consumed. This plague certainly was a very harmful plague, for it brought both hunger and disease at the same time.

Furthermore, there is no agreement nor do I dare make any definite assertion as to what sort of insects these are which he mentions here and which ate and destroyed everything. You see, so great is the variety of Hebrew interpreters[1] that one can gather nothing certain from them.

But concerning the caterpillar we are sure, for there is agreement about this word. The Hebrew word גָּזָם is equivalent to the Latin *eruca* and to the German *Raupe*. But the word which follows is "locust," for which the Hebrew word is אַרְבֶּה, and this they translate very inconsistently. Some translate it as *bruchus* ("wingless locust"), and others as *locusta* ("locust"). These creatures are unknown to us, for our land is unfamiliar with them. I would gladly translate this *bruchus* as *die grosse Raupe* ("large caterpillar"), but I would not dare. It is certain that we have neither locusts nor the *bruchus*, unless, as I said, we may wish to interpret them as those huge caterpillars.

[1] The text merely says "the Hebrews."

Blight. In German we generally call blight *Brand,* or *Meltau,* but this is not the same thing here. No, the prophet is here indicating the name of a creature about whose name the Hebrew grammarians argue strangely, so that we may make no certain decision about it. We are sure that these were four kinds of creatures of different types which ate up and destroyed the crops and all the fruits of trees and vines.

5. *Awake, you drunkards, and weep.* This is what I said before; The prophet is calling them to repent with this account of the destruction of the crops and fruits. But when he says, "Awake, you drunkards," he is not saying that they are drunk now, nor is he charging them with drunkenness at this time. He rather intends this and says in sum: "Wake up, you people who are accustomed to luxurious and splendid living, you who are accustomed to having an abundance of all things so that you are drunk from that abundance, wake up now! Weep, mourn, repent! Look at God's work and be terrified. Consider what is going to happen to you!"

You who drink wine in sweetness. More accurately this reads: "You who drink new wine freely," when it is still fresh and sweet. It is as if he were saying: "You who are accustomed to these luxuries, weep! You will lack them. You will suffer hunger and need. You will suffer shortages. Indeed, you see that everything has been destroyed, and the wine disappears from your mouth."

6. *For a nation has come up. Ascendit* ("has come up") we must read as a completed past tense. Here Joel appears to poetize, as Vergil also does in *Georgics,* IV, 21 ff. Vergil attributes to bees a wondrous instinct to follow their leaders. He imagines that others keep watch, etc. So here, Joel is imagining that some of those animals about which he has spoken are coming up as if they have drawn up battle lines. He says, as it were: "Those creatures are going to bring such evils as some powerful king barely would have brought." The sense, then, is this: the "cutting locust," the "swarming locust," the "hopping locust," and the "destroying locust" come as if with an army. Since theologians did not follow this simple sense of the text, they have, in their usual fashion, prattled all sorts of nonsense about peoples who are coming. Thus Jerome troubles himself much but uselessly here.

Its teeth are lion's teeth. Because the Hebrew language is very verbose, it is accustomed to repeat the same thing often—something one can see very well here, if nowhere else. Those who read sacred literature must especially know this. Thus here we have a repetition of the previous statement about the power and about the multitude of those beastly creatures. It is as if he were saying: "So great is their number that one cannot know it. So many evils do they bring in that lions, however fierce, could scarcely have brought in so many."

7. *It has laid waste my vines.* Here the prophet is putting on and assuming the person of each and every Israelite who laments about that disaster and destruction of his fruits and vines. Therefore this passage stands as an argument that the prophet has used these creatures as types of countless heathen. You see, the Assyrians (these they interpret as a powerful and innumerable people), or finally any enemies, would destroy not only vines or fields but cities and their inhabitants as well. But he makes no mention of this here. He only says that the vines and fruits were eaten. This he attributes to those creatures.

And has stripped the bark from my fig tree. This is poorly translated. In Hebrew it reads: "and splintered my fig trees." I simply take vines and fig trees here for the natural vines and fig trees which those creatures stripped and destroyed. I do not take them to refer to people as some interpret them.

It has stripped off its bark and despoiled it. This is a pure repetition of the same statement. This is the way with the Hebrew language, that it uses very many words. "It has despoiled," obviously, of its fruit and foliage, as Vergil in the same way lets winter strip the forest of its honor.[2]

Their branches are made white, that is, they are bare, devoid of foliage.

8. *Lament like a virgin.* He brings in a simile by which he amplifies his subject. He says, as it were: "Just as a girl who loves her betrothed and loses him weeps very bitterly and laments her dead betrothed, whom she had loved (you see, the love between a bride and her betrothed is very strong), so also you, lament and mourn!" Thus he is inviting them to repent as if to say: "Lament with very

[2] Vergil, *Georgics* II, 404: *Frigidus et silvis Aquilo decussit honorem,* but Horace, *Epodes,* II, 5—6, seems closer: *December . . . silvis honorem decutit.*

loud wailing, louder than all other wailing." In addition, for "of her puberty" [3] we read more accurately "of her youth."

9. *The cereal offering* [*and the drink offering*] *are cut off.* He amplifies their misery and hardship and says, as it were: "This plague not only has to do with the destruction of crops, trees, and vines. Libations will also fail. This glory of yours, for which you are renowned beyond all nations of the earth, that divine worship established through the Word of God will suffer harm. The priests will be unable to sacrifice or offer drink offerings, because the crops have been thus consumed." You see, they used to give the first-fruits and tithes of all their crops to the Lord, according to the command of the Law, Deut. 26. This was a sacrifice in which solid things, such as grain and cereal, would be offered. They would make their drink offerings out of liquids—oil, wine, etc.

10. *The area is laid waste,* [*the soil mourns*]. Read this from the Hebrew this way: "The fields are laid waste, the ground mourns, because the grain is destroyed, the wine is poured away, the oil languishes." He is giving the reason why the cereal and drink offerings are going to be cut off. He says that the fields are laid waste, all the grain and wine have been destroyed, etc. In this text we see obviously poetic figures of speech. After all, poets say that the meadows and grasses laugh. That is, they are productive. Here, on the contrary, he says that the earth mourns, the wine is poured away, etc.

The wine is poured away. This is a new expression in this prophet. He speaks this way frequently. In German we accurately imitate this manner of speaking in the expression *Der Wein steht schändlich.* Solomon also used this expression often in Proverbs when he speaks about a foolish son and a quarreling wife—*ein schändlich Weib* (cf. Prov. 19:13).

The oil languishes, that is, it does not produce fruit.

11. *The farmers have been confounded.* I feel sorry for them.

For the wheat, the wine, and the barley. According to the Hebrew this reads: "For the wheat and the barley," for "wine" does not appear in the Hebrew text. That is, the farmers see that there

[3] The Latin text has *super virum pubertatis suae.*

will be no harvest. Because all the crops of the earth have been devoured, they see that nothing remains except grief and sorrow.

12. *The vineyard withers*, more accurately, "the vine withers." This is the same repetition of the current disaster.

Gladness fails. You see that this is a characteristic expression on the part of the prophet, because he is speaking about confusion.[4] Gladness, that is, that over which they ought to be glad, has totally perished and has been destroyed.

13. *Gird on [sackcloth].* This is another repetition of the same calamity to provoke them to repent. But what we read as "are withheld from the house of God" is in the Hebrew "are forbidden, etc."

14. *Sanctify a fast.* This is a Hebrew expression that occurs frequently in Scripture.

15. *For [the day of the Lord] is near.* Here he seems to touch on the prophecy which we will see in the second and following chapters, as if to say: "You see the present evil, the terrible disaster. Beyond any doubt this means that another evil is going to come upon you."

The day of the Lord. Obviously another day will come on which the Lord will come to visit, just as Peter also calls it a "day of inspection," or a "day of visitation" (cf. 1 Peter 2:12).

As destruction from the Almighty. That is, when the day comes, its character will be such that it is going to bring destruction with it. "You will not be able to stop it. Therefore, repent!"

16. *Is not [the food cut off] before your eyes?* He is again setting forth the present evil so that they do not forget the visitation which is yet to come, as if to say: "I am telling you, He will visit you. Therefore come to your senses!"

17. *Your cattle shrivel.* It is remarkable how far apart the interpreters are on this passage. In the Hebrew it reads this way: "Your seeds shrivel in the dust, your storehouses are desolate, etc." The silly talk about cattle is worthless. To me the sense seems to be

[4] Throughout this section of the Biblical text the Latin verb *confundo* is used repeatedly. It has been translated "is poured away" (v. 10), "have been confounded" (v. 11), "withers" (v. 12), and now "fails."

this: "Your storehouses are desolate" means "whatever was going to be put there and kept there for use the next year or in any emergency—all that was destroyed." You see, the Hebrew calls "storehouses" whatever is put in bins or granaries. In German we call this *Vorrat*. And "your seeds shrivel" means "not only have those things perished which would be your daily food, but not even seeds will be left for you. All these will shrivel away. There will be no reason to hope that you will receive anything or even save something to sow.

The threshing floors, or granaries. He says, as it were: "There will be no need to build threshing floors. Nothing edible will return to you. That pest, then, will consume everything, so that not even the seeds will be left to you."

18. *Why do the animals groan?* According to the Hebrew this reads: "How the beasts groan!" That is, we must pity them. The oxen and flocks lack pasturage on which to feed.

And the flocks of sheep. According to the Hebrew: "Even the flocks of sheep [5] are forsaken."

19. *Unto Thee, O Lord, I cry.* These are words of sympathy. In the German we can render them accurately this way: *Ach Herr, lass dich's erbarmen; ach Herr Gott, wie geht es zu!* [6]

The beauties of the wilderness. The meaning of this word [7] changes strangely in sacred literature. *Speciosum* ("that which is beautiful") is used for habitations, huts, and cottages. Here we must render this word as habitations.

Fire. Here I think fire is taken metaphorically. Thus the meaning is: "Your habitations have been made so empty that you would think they had been gutted by fire." Yet, here I want everyone to use his own judgment.

The flame. I also take this in a metaphorical sense. He says, as it were: "All your trees have died in such a way that you would think the flame had burned them." Thus neither men nor beasts have any hope left for finding food.

[5] We have read *ovium* for *omnium*.

[6] "O Lord, have mercy; O Lord God, what awful things are happening!"

[7] The Hebrew word נְאוֹת, for which the Vulgate had *speciosa*.

20. *But even the beasts of the field* [*cry to Thee*], that is: "Even the wild animals cry out and growl as they look for water to quench their thirst." This, you see, is the same word [8] that is also used in the Psalms (cf. Ps. 42:2).

Because all the water brooks are dried up. They cannot find drink. They, too, must perish. Thus in this first chapter the prophet Joel describes very simply that punishment and plague inflicted on the land by those creatures, as we have heard.

[8] The Hebrew word עָרַג ("crave").

CHAPTER TWO

In the first chapter the prophet busied himself with recalling that small plague of caterpillars and locusts. From that he wanted to make some inferences regarding that real and total plague which threatens all Israel. This is what he does in the second chapter. But he speaks in generalities. He does not name either the Assyrians or the Egyptians when he describes a hostile army which is to come up against Israel to indicate that a great calamity will occur. In His management of the world, God has always acted in miraculous fashion and in His own way, and He still does so today. We think that human ingenuity manages and administers everything. Yet, whatever happens is His divine will. So also here the prophet interprets the coming disaster as the work of the Lord, not the work of their enemies. He also says that those foes would prevail not because of their own strength or power but because of the power of the Lord. He says that the Lord will utter His voice before His army and will so terrify Israel by revealing their consciousness of sin that Israel will be unable to stand firm or keep from being afraid of a falling leaf (cf. Lev. 26:36).

Clearly we are experiencing the same thing in our time in the case of the Turks. We are not unaware of the great increase of their kingdom and power in a few years. Almost everywhere they come out as successful victors while our armies succumb. They certainly will finally overcome us, for they are very evidently the scourge of God.[1] Therefore, just as we are accustomed to preach about the

[1] The papal bull *Exsurge Domine* of June 15, 1520, listed among its 41 "poisonous, offensive, and misleading" statements on Luther's previous writings the following: "To carry on war against the Turks is to fight against God, who visits our iniquities upon us through them." In December 1520 Luther defended his statement in part by saying: "If God were not against us and did not have the Turks as the rod for our iniquity, our luck against the Turks would have come out altogether better." Cf. W, VII, 140. Also see *Luther's Works,* 31, pp. 91—92; 46, p. 162.

coming of the Turks, the prophet did the same thing in this chapter. The people of Israel were living in the midst of enemies. They were a source of great hatred to the nations which lived around them—Amorites, Moabites, Hagarenes, etc. They were always at odds with these nations. Especially hostile to them at that time was the king of the Assyrians. The Assyrian state was under control of a monarchy. Looking at this, the prophets warned the people that either the Assyrians or Babylonians would come at some time to destroy all Israel.

Jerome and other interpreters of the prophets disturb themselves strangely over the coherence of the text. You see, they are not looking at the entire activity, at the whole picture, the way the Holy Spirit clearly has embraced the entire people and the entire kingdom of Christ. Therefore those who will be intelligent should include at the same time both the kingdom of Israel and the kingdom of Christ in the picture together. Then the text will hold together very well.

Therefore in the second chapter he prophesies a genuine and substantial plague which is going to destroy the entire people of Israel. He warns them and calls them to repentance, as we shall see in the context, when we unfold the two parts of the chapter. It is as if he were saying: "Beware! Watch out for yourselves! Repent! Come to your senses! The Lord will visit you. This will all go to pieces sometime!"

1. *Blow the trumpet in Zion,* [*howl on My holy mountain*]. Where we read "howl," you will more accurately read from the Hebrew as "shout," or "cry out."

In Numbers [cf. chap. 10] Moses has described the trumpet calls—what sort of calls ought to be sounded when the chiefs of the people had to be called together, when the people had to assemble, when war or peace was being indicated. We, too, have certain trumpet calls when the enemy is near or when fire rages in the city, etc. The prophet, therefore, is ordering that the trumpets sound to call together the entire people, as if to say: "Cry out, cry out, summon all the people, ring all the bells!" We have the same custom that the entire population may hear that destruction threatens. "Let us hold back the enemy, let us repent, etc.," as he also adds:

Let all the inhabitants of the earth tremble! We say: "Let them all be stirred up, that is, let them all draw near." The trumpet sounds for all.

For the day of the Lord is coming. The prophets do not call only the final Day of Judgment "the day of the Lord." They also give this name to any day of visitation, just as Peter calls it a day ἐπισκοπῆς, "of visitation" (1 Peter 2:12). You see, the Lord comes in His time. He destroys those whom He wants to destroy, those at whom He used to close His eyes for a time. This, then, he calls "the day of the Lord." This is a day when the Lord visits us either in grace or in anger.

It is near. According to the Hebrew this is "it is close by." All the prophetic warnings sound this way—as if those things which they predict were at the door, just as Peter also foretold that the Day of Judgment would come in a short time. But here the forbearance of God is inviting us to repentance. Here are commended to us the prayers of righteous men.

2. *A day of darkness and gloom.* Here we have another construction. We should not connect it with the preceding as it has been connected in our books.[2] It is as if he were saying: "Surely at some time a hostile people will attack us. They are going to destroy everything so that we will be allowed no escape." We must also take note of the phraseology of Scripture. The successful outcome of affairs, when things turn out well, Scripture calls "light" and "peace." On the other hand, it calls it "darkness" when things turn out badly. This is the way Solomon expresses himself in Prov. 31:18.[3] "Her lamp does not go out at night." Also, these are poetic means of speaking—means familiar to poets. So he calls tragic times—a day of adversity and tribulation—"a day of darkness and gloom, a day of clouds and thick darkness."

Like the morning spreading over the mountains. This is a simile with which he points out the power of the coming army of their enemies. One cannot hold back the dawn. There is no one who can escape it. "Such," he says, "will be the character of the multitude of the enemy to come that we will be unable to escape its hand, just as the mountains cannot escape the light of the rising sun. That

[2] In the Vulgate.

[3] The Weimar text has "Prov. 28."

light comes over them, declares itself and shows itself." This is how it is with us when the Turk approaches. The Greeks used to think that they were safe and that no evil would befall them. Then suddenly the Turk came and made them subject to him. This is what Paul says (1 Thess. 5:3): "When people say, 'There is peace and security,' then sudden destruction will come upon them." Our people today, too, point out the same thing very well. To comfort themselves, they say, "It will not happen to us. Our opposing foe will be able to accomplish nothing, because the Lord is with us." That's fine. The Lord is at hand for the righteous. He protects them. He pulls them out of trouble. But not so for the wicked!

3. *Fire devours before them, and behind them a flame burns.* Jerome wants to apply this passage to the caterpillars and locusts, but that is a mistake, for it ought to be applied to the Assyrians or to that nation which is going to destroy Israel—as very clear texts later on will declare. As I said in the first chapter,[4] that we have to take "fire" in a metaphorical sense, so also here. It is as if he were saying: "As fire consumes, devours, and reduces everything to ashes, so also those people who are going to come against you will ruin and destroy everything completely."

The land is like the garden of Eden before them. We have the same word in Genesis,[5] when Moses describes the paradise of pleasure. Here he compares the destruction to come with the flowering earth, as if to say: "Were you to compare the destruction which follows with your present abundance, all things now would seem to be in flower, all things would appear to abound. However, everything has been prepared for fire and destruction. There will be nothing left. Everything will be ruined and destroyed." We, too, in the same way build beautifully and heap up many things which others are going to destroy. So also the fortress at Babylon was at first a splendid and magnificent edifice, but the Lord later destroyed it. So, too, the kingdom of Israel perished, so that afterward one could never repair the damage. It never rose up again. It never became as glorious as it was before. It was never built so beautifully. It never again had such forces or such wealth. To put it

[4] Cf. p. 86 above.

[5] Cf. Gen. 2:8.

briefly, it remained without glory. This is what the Lord does with all the kingdoms that He wants to ruin and destroy. This is what happened to Rome, Corinth, Milan, Jerusalem, etc. We all know how greatly these cities flourished and what wealth they had. When the Lord, however, had once destroyed them, they could never repair the damage afterward. This is what the prophet says, "but after them a desolate wilderness."

4. *Their appearance is like the appearance of horses.* With all of this he describes the courage of those who are to come—that they are going to run about swiftly and fight bravely.

5. *As with the rumbling of chariots they leap on the tops of the mountains.* That is, those whom one cannot resist will come out victorious everywhere. He expressly states, "They leap." This expression also appears in the Psalm [114:4]: "The mountains skipped like rams, the hills like lambs." It is as if the prophet were saying: "They will be far from fearing your power or resistance, because they are going to rejoice and be glad when they attack and destroy you. They will kick up their heels [6] for joy." That is what this properly stands for.

Like the crackling of a flame of fire devouring the stubble. This means: just as fire quickly consumes the stubble, and consumes it in such a way that nothing is left, so you will be the prey for Assyria or the Babylonians.

6. *Before them peoples are in anguish.* Peoples will be in travail before them. That is: "Not only you will perish, but also all the remaining areas will be devastated along with you at the hands of that kingdom of the Assyrians." All these will be in travail, that is, they will suffer, they will be in anguish. Scripture often uses this expression. It is taken from the pain of women in childbirth. When they suffer in labor, they do not know, because of the pain, whether they are going to die or live. They would gladly flee the pain, but they cannot escape. Paul uses it in this way in Rom. 8:22: "We know that the whole creation has been groaning in travail together until now." We also read it often in the Psalms. It means suffering and anguish in perils from which one may not escape, for one knows no way to escape them.

[6] Luther uses the German expression *sie werden lecken.*

All faces are made as black as a pot. It is not completely clear to me what this means. Almost the same figure of speech is used in the prophet Nahum 2:10: "The faces of all of them are like a black pot." The meaning of the person who translated it[7] in this way is this, that people became so sad and worn out with grief that they went about gloomy and worn with grief, just as dark clothes are usually an indication of mourning. However, I do not approve of this idea because the Hebrew does not read that way. You see, the Hebrew reads as follows: "All faces will be gathered together in a pot." Here too, I would want this passage to be understood this way. This is the sense I get—as if the prophet were saying: "They have broken my people like meat in a pot." This idea, which also appears in Moses,[8] means chopping meat into pieces. We must not trust the Jews in this matter. They no longer have the Hebrew language pure among themselves. Therefore the sense of Jerome pleases them. "They will be gathered together into a pot"—they will be hacked to pieces, as meat is generally cut into pieces and thrown into a pot. They will be chopped up as in a kettle, as Micah 3:3 says, that is, they will be unable to escape the might of their foe. You see, it is absolutely certain that the word "gather together"[9] is used in the Hebrew here. We read it this way: "They will be gathered together or forced into a pot." There will be heaps of them.[10] This, then, will be a metaphor that he takes from meat cut up and thrown into a pot. There is a quite similar phrase also in Is. 3:6: "A man will take hold of his brother in his father's house, etc."; Is. 3:8 "Jerusalem has stumbled, and Judah has fallen, etc."

7. *They run like giants.* We certainly must not take this to mean locusts, as Jerome wants it to be understood. Many other passages in this prophet will indicate this. The sense is this: "Those enemies are very brave and aggressive. They will fight against you without fear, etc."

The men march in their own ways. According to the Hebrew

[7] In the Vulgate.

[8] Cf. Lev. 1:6, 12.

[9] The Hebrew word is קָבַץ.

[10] The Weimar editor suggests that in the expression *Es wird in Haufen gehen* the word *Haufen* may be equal to *Hafen* and so mean "receptacle," or "pot." But the usual meaning of *Haufen* seems quite suitable.

read it this way: "Each will march in his own way." You see, the word "men" in Hebrew at times signifies a universal affirmative. That is, it means "anyone," as follows immediately (v. 8): "Each does not force his own brother." The sense, then, is this: "They will march in their own ways," that is, "they will break through, and there will be no one to resist them."

And they will not swerve, that is, "they will not fail."

9. *But they break through the windows.* This is strange, if it has been translated this way correctly. The Septuagint translators have translated "javelin" for "window." I translate it this way: "They will fall down before the javelin and will not be wounded," as if to say: "God will give success to the attack of your enemies so that, even if javelins are aimed at them, they can fall down, and the javelins will neither touch nor wound them. You will bend the bow against them in vain, because they will easily be able to avoid the javelins you will hurl at them."

10. *The earth quakes before them.* This text sounds as if the prophet were speaking about the Last Judgment, but he is not. The meaning of the prophet here is this, as if he were saying: "The earth will tremble. The stars will withhold their beauty." He has said all this because of the state of mind of those who are frightened. You see, to those who are about to die and who have thus been sitting in anguish, all things seem black, tragic, adverse, hostile. On the other hand, to those who are joyful, all things are pleasant—even those things which under other conditions are not very pleasant. They can rejoice even over filth or some other useless thing. The prophet is speaking, then, in this state of mind, because, even if the sun is most pleasant and the stars are shining very brightly, yet all things will seem very upset.

11. *And the Lord utters His voice.* "All this," he says, "is going to happen, not because those enemies can accomplish that much, not because they have so much strength, but because this is the will of the Lord, because the Lord will terrify us with His voice and we shall not be able to stand firm. Such great evils will overrun us, not because they are powerful, but because we are sinners." This is especially horrifying and terrible in any adversity, when God terrifies us by making us aware of our sins. For people so frightened every courage and confidence fails, so that even a falling

leaf terrifies us, as I mentioned at the beginning of this chapter. Otherwise, if every devil were to fall upon a righteous man, they would still accomplish nothing against him. His conscience is safe before God if he knows that God still intends good for him, that God will not desert him, etc. But when the Lord utters His voice, when He takes away our courage, He has an easy time fighting against us. Here no man will be able to stand firm.

For the day of the Lord is great. "This is not the day of your adversaries, but it is the day of the Lord. Although the Assyrians may think that they are accomplishing such things with their own strength, this is the might of the Lord." This is the custom of the prophets when they describe catastrophes of this kind. They remove everything from man and from the power of man and attribute it to God and to the power of God. You see, God acts in this way: He utters His voice. With it He terrifies the consciences of those whom He wishes to destroy. Those who have been so terrified must succumb, however great their strength and armor, etc. The Lord does the same thing in every victory of His.

Up to this point the prophet has been setting forth the disaster with which he wanted to call them to repentance, so that they might come to their senses and prevent the coming disaster. Now the second part of the chapter follows.

12. *Return to Me in all your heart.* Up to now we have been listening to God's severe threat about the coming persecution and disaster. Now He adds His plan and comforts them, if He can possibly avert or at least postpone this disaster. It was not averted but postponed. We also see the same thing in the case of Abraham, who prayed so earnestly for the salvation of the Sodomites that he also postponed the judgment of God. However, he accomplished nothing. They refused to repent. Finally, then, the wrath of God came upon them, and they all perished to a man. Therefore the prophet here is prescribing the method by which one can resist this evil. Finally, however, when the people did not persevere, there followed the judgment of God of which he here had warned them.

In all your heart. This is a Hebraism, that is, "with all your heart." The "in" is unnecessary. He is clearly saying, "with your whole heart, without pretending but truly, without any hypocrisy." He aptly touches hypocrisy and that servile worship of God of hypocrites about which we read in Ps. 78:34: [11] "When He slew them, they sought for Him and returned, etc." Their heart was not right with Him. You see, in time of persecution, hypocrites pretend penitence but not with a right or whole heart.

With fasting and weeping. Do these externals also accomplish something for the matter, or is not true repentance of the heart alone enough? Certainly the latter is true, but we judge a tree by its fruit. To be sure, this demands fasting, weeping, mourning, etc., but he first sets down "with your whole heart," as if to say: "Unless these come from a right heart, they are hypocrisy. They accomplish nothing." A genuine conversion, however, is later indicated by those external signs. The Holy Spirit has beautifully described conversion in such a way that the heart first repents truly, not spuriously. Finally, it also shows faith [12] outwardly by those works. If that faith should not be present, everything else becomes nothing, as the prophet clearly adds:

13. *Rend your hearts and not, etc.* He purposely makes this addition to condemn hypocrisy. It was a custom of the Jews to tear their clothing when they were afflicted or mourning over something. This is something one sees everywhere in sacred literature. With it writers would show a great and violent disturbance of the heart. But yet, from the long use of this practice, it had degenerated into hypocrisy, as genuflection, so-called processions, and very many other things have become pure hypocrisy among us. Thus he wants them to rend their hearts, not only their clothes. He says, as it were: "At times you are accustomed to rend your clothes hypocritically and not your hearts."

Return to the Lord. It is as if he were saying: "This will be the means—where you have come with your whole heart, with a true heart, then you are returning to the Lord. Otherwise, it will not happen."

For He is kindly-disposed and merciful. "Kindly-disposed" is what we more accurately call "gracious, favoring, *gnädig.*" "Merciful": the Hebrew word רַחוּם properly signifies *barmherzig,* one who

[11] The original text has "Ps. 77."

[12] We have read *fidem* for *fidei.*

is compassionate, that is, one who sympathizes with us because of our fall.

Abounding in steadfast love. More accurately, this is "abounding in kindness." He abounds in helping all men. All these we also find in the Psalm (Ps. 103:8): "The Lord is merciful and gracious, slow to anger and abounding in steadfast love, etc."

Preeminent over evil. It is not clear to me what this says in the Latin. In the Hebrew it reads as follows: "He easily repents of evil," namely, that which He intended. He quickly discontinues the misfortune He intended to inflict. This is a familiar phrase, occurring here and there in the prophets, as in Jeremiah (Jer. 18:8): "If that nation . . . turns from its evil, I shall repent of the evil that I intended to do to it." This repentance is often attributed to God, namely, when He changes His mind about an evil He had intended to inflict. The sense is as if you would say: "He is easily moved to forgive." These are promises that are very beautiful, very rich, very broad. They are held forth by the Holy Spirit for this purpose, that in a time of the wrath and anger of the Lord the feeble heart or conscience which is looking for consolation should run to them and remember them. After all, it is wonderful to see here the plan of the Holy Spirit, who up to now has been heaping up and enlarging the threat in order to send them back to the goodness and mercy of God, indicating by this that the wrath and anger of God work toward salvation, so that sinners who have thus been terrified by the threats and judgment of God come to their senses and accept and recognize God as their merciful Father. In this way, you see, He terrifies sinners in such a way that they lift up their hearts in hope and in the mercy of God. This is the custom of all the prophets—they first terrify with very violent and bitter threats, but they immediately add very great, very sweet promises about the mercy and goodness of God. The effect of each word (that is, of threats and promises), however, is different in the righteous from what it is among the wicked. You see, the wicked use neither threats nor promises correctly. When they hear threats, they do not think the threats apply to them. This is the way they support their own hypocrisy. Thus they remain obdurate in their wickedness, which they nevertheless think is the epitome of righteousness. Therefore such broad promises, which require nothing but broken and contrite hearts, are also not effective in them. And because this does not happen in the wicked through threats, neither are promises effective in them. The righteous, on the other hand, use them correctly, for they are bruised and cast down by the angry threats of God; they bear divine judgment; they recognize their sin and their damnation. So, when they hear these promises, they turn to the mercy of God. In this way their consciences again are lifted up and become peaceful. The wicked are hard-hearted anvils; unmoved by all of this, they never act differently. So we entertain only vain hopes today that they will act differently. This, however, is the custom of God Almighty, that He takes His faithful to hell before He brings them back. Finally, however, after condemning and terrifying them, He brings them back and comforts them. Today we see the same thing clearly among our own wicked people. So long as we have been receiving the holy Gospel of our great God through the grace of Christ, our princes have been doing nothing else than oppose themselves to God with their stiff necks. When we preach that the judgment and vengeance of God are going to come, they laugh at us. In fact, they want to be charged with absolutely no wickedness. They pretend that they stand squarely on the Gospel. Because they are so blind, no threats stir them. In the meantime, God is postponing His judgment, which already for a long time He has intended for them. I say, He is postponing it for the sake of some pious people, lest they also perish along with the wicked and this become the disgrace of the Gospel. When these pious people have been removed, then those despisers will feel the vengeful wrath of God upon themselves. This is what Isaiah says (Is. 57:1): "Devout men are taken away, while no one understands." You see, this is a hidden plan of the Lord—why He gradually gathers the devout to the fathers. But at last we understand it, etc.

We must most certainly take note of this passage of the prophet. This one is among the most significant. God cannot refrain from saving His devout people, whom He terrifies with His judgment. He does not, however, allow them to lose hope. You see, immediate consolation follows. Also, it is because of the righteous alone that He adds the comfort. One may see the same thing in all the prophets—that they first threaten very terrible things, but afterwards they add the sweetest consolations. When consciences have been terrified and shocked, the word of threat has performed its function. Therefore the heart must be lifted up immediately, so that after it has been upset and terrified, it may embrace the mercy and goodness of God. When this happens, that person's bones again become strong.

14. *Who knows whether He will not turn and repent?* He is speaking in the fashion of a terrified conscience which finally, after being afflicted, is barely encouraged and begins to breathe again for hope and for the goodness of God. But this has not been translated well enough. In German we say it this way: *Wer weiss, er möcht sich umwenden* and repent of the evil. That is, He ceases from the evil which He had intended. He does not continue to want evil for us, etc.

And leave a blessing behind Him. That is, "He will not be so angry that He will show no remnants of His mercy." Certainly it happens in contrite consciences that they desire some shred of the merciful goodness of God. This is what we see in the woman of Canaan, about whom the Gospel speaks.[13] This is how the contrite and humble conscience comforts itself. Those people who have experienced this know and understand such things. Therefore the prophet has used especially elegant and appropriate words. We must lament the fact, however, that this has been translated so vaguely in our books. You see, it reads as follows in the Hebrew: "He will leave some remnants of His blessing later (that is, after while), so that clearly it is not pure wrathful indignation in Him, but He will also show a sample of His goodness and mercy. Here we see what sort of thing the conscience is. It tenaciously guards the hope it has about God so that even in the greatest desperation, in the greatest tribulation and anguish, it grasps for the goodness of God, it still hopes for good things from God. Especially does it perceive the wrath of God upon all creatures. Yet it does not despair. It still believes that there is a bit of mercy and reconciliation left for it. This we must particularly note. You see, this passage is a very common word for service in every temptation. Therefore this passage ought to be recommended to us so that we can use it in any sort of temptation at all. He immediately adds:

[13] Matt. 15:27.

A cereal offering and a drink offering for the Lord your God. This connects with what has gone before in this way: God will not be so forgetful of His goodness that He will not leave some remnant thereof behind—namely, "a cereal offering and a drink offering for the Lord your God," that is, that we shall still sacrifice cereal and drink offerings to the Lord, we shall still serve Him and declare His wondrous works, etc. This is the same thing which we read in the Psalm (Ps. 42:5): "Why are you cast down, O my soul, and why are you disquieted within me? Hope in God, for I shall still praise Him, etc." Also, we read elsewhere (Ps. 118:17): "I shall not die, but I shall live and recount the deeds of the Lord." Again, we read in Ps. 6:2-5: "Be gracious to me, O Lord, for I am languishing. . . . deliver me for the sake of Thy steadfast love, for in death there is no remembrance of Thee; in Sheol who can give Thee praise?" But these, nevertheless, all are fluctuations between hope and despair. The sense, then, is this: "He will have mercy on us. He will take back His wrath. The Lord will look on us with kindness. Let us just repent. He will not reject us. Let us just lay hold of His goodness. There will be some shred of His mercy left. He will not be angry forever, etc.

15. *Blow the trumpet in Zion; sanctify a fast.* Now the prophet himself is speaking. He prescribes the manner of speaking and tells them how they ought to be converted. Thus everywhere we see that faithful Teacher, the Holy Spirit, who still does not wish our damnation, for He is also prescribing to us the manner in which we should pray and come to our senses. This surely is a great comfort.

Let the bridegroom leave his room. For the most part he is explaining what he meant with the fast—not so much an abstinence from foods, but that they should abstain and hold themselves back from all pleasures and delights. For this he wants to call the old and the young, in short, the entire people, that he may remind them all. Note also the great love in the prophet. He still wanted the salvation of the people.

17. *Between the vestibule and the altar let the priests, the ministers of the Lord, weep and say.* This is how he teaches them to pray.

Spare Thy people, O Lord. Here the text provides sufficient evidence to confirm my feeling which I expressed at the beginning of the chapter: that the prophet is not speaking about locusts but about the hostile army of either the Assyrians or Babylonians—an army that was going to devastate and destroy all Israel, etc.

Thy heritage, that is, "Your people Israel."

The nations, that is, "the heathen." Yet he does not detail this.

Why should they say among the peoples: Where is their God? This is how the prophets always urge on the Lord—through His own personal glory. Surely this is a strong and powerful prayer before God. It is as if he were saying: "What is finally going to happen, O Lord, if You will have destroyed all of us? The matter will bring You into disgrace. Your glory will be in peril, for this affair will provide the unbelieving nations with an opportunity to blaspheme against Your people and against Your holy Word. If we should all perish, the shame would be Yours." He certainly is pressing God hard with this prayer. This is something Moses knew, too. In similar fashion he objected to the Lord, who intended to destroy Israel. He said it was a matter of His glory—that it would be imperiled if He would thus destroy the very people He had chosen for Himself and had declared His own very clearly with many signs and miracles. For Moses speaks as follows in Ex. 32:12: "Why should the Egyptians say, 'With evil intent did He bring them forth, to slay them in the mountains and to consume them from the face of the earth'? etc." Undoubtedly today for the sake of His own glory He also spares us who hold His Gospel in contempt. Otherwise He would have punished us long ago already. This is not a common question but a very difficult one. It also gave so much trouble to the apostle Paul that four chapters were scarcely enough for him to treat it, as we see in Romans. Yet he explained the matter quite coldly and not completely satisfactorily. Finally he thinks he has resolved it and says, "Surely, God has not rejected His people altogether, for I myself am an Israelite, etc." A remarkable solution! Therefore we will not be able to match him in solving the problem. God smites His people, and yet He does it in such a way that the heathen may not say, "Where is their God?" Still He saves only the tiniest remnant of His people. This is the way Paul argues.

18. *The Lord became jealous for His land.* All of what follows now we must read in the subjunctive or optative mood, just as we had to do in Hosea. Thus the meaning will be: [14] "If you will have thus humbled yourselves and will have turned back to the Lord with your whole heart and will have prayed, "Spare Thy people, O Lord" (v. 17), then what I am saying will turn out to be true." But he is speaking in the past tense as if the Lord will already have done this. Yet he means that it is going to happen. It is as if he were saying: "Were you to pray this way and turn back [to the Lord], the Lord would become jealous for His land. He would spare His people. He would answer and say, etc." This is how he admonishes them of the truth of God, as if to say: "You would finally learn from experience that the Lord has become reasonable and wants what is good for you, etc., when He sends you grain and wine and oil, etc." (v. 19).

20. *And him who is from the north* [*I will put far away from you*]. They have also taken this text to refer to the locusts, but that is poor interpretation. After all, He is speaking about a king who is coming. He says that He will keep him from being able to hurt them, provided they come to their senses. He says, as it were: "If you live a godly life, I will certainly restrain the Assyrian."

[*And drive him*] *into a parched and desolate land.* This bothers Jerome very much. As I have said, my idea is that we must take this as subjunctive. Jerome explains it as a simple indicative and brings out the account of the killing of Sennacherib and of the 185,000 soldiers whom the angel killed in the camp of the Assyrians, according to Is. 37. But what account are you going to give me in regard to the "stench and foul smell" which the prophet Joel immediately adds here? But, because we are ignorant of the customary usage of the Hebrew language and because we cannot find that out from the grammarians—and there are many such things in other languages, too—we have to guess. At the time these things were said, the Jews understood them well. In my judgment, then, the meaning is as follows. It is as if he were saying: "Nevertheless, have faith. Regain your courage. Just recover your senses, and I shall bring it to pass that the Assyrian will not overwhelm you. You see, he is in My hand. I will be sure to hurl him wherever

[14] With the Erlangen edition we have read *erit* for *erat*.

I wish, so that one piece will rot here, another there." We shall also understand what follows in the same way.

His front into the eastern sea. He calls the Dead Sea "the one that is before him." The Mediterranean Sea he calls "the one that is behind," or "the western one." The kingdom of Judah lay between the two. The meaning, then, is this: "If you will have returned to Me, I will restrain the Assyrian. I will destroy him in such a way that I will throw one part into the Dead Sea and the other part into the Great Sea. Thus he will decay and be consumed in the land." This appears to me to be the very simple meaning.

For he has acted proudly. If I were allowed to hebraize here, I would gladly relate this to the Lord rather than to the Assyrian. In the Hebrew it reads as follows: "since he has done great things." After all, this is exactly the same wording as that which follows immediately in the next verse, where our translator has also rendered it, "for the Lord has done great things." We also have the same expression in Ps. 126:3: "The Lord has done great things for us." Thus the sense would be: "The Lord will rage grandly. He will perform a valiant act here."

21. *Fear not, O land.* It is as if he were saying: "If you will have repented and turned back to the Lord, the Lord will do great things for you. An opposing army will be able to accomplish nothing against you. The Lord will restore every loss. You again will abound with all supplies of wine, oil, cattle." All of this the locusts had devoured earlier. So he also adds:

22. *Fear not, you beasts of the field.* Just as he earlier threatened land, people, and beasts with destruction and devastation, so now again he comforts them all in order and says that it will not come to pass that they will die, provided they repent; that all things will bear rich fruit, etc.

The pastures of the wilderness. This is the same expression we had earlier in the first chapter (Joel 1:19), when the fire ate the "habitations of the wilderness," that is, huts and cottages. Just as he said earlier that the huts were consumed by fire, so he now says that they are going to bud, the timber will again produce its fruit, provided that they come to their senses.

The fig tree and the vine have given their full yield. The Hebrew method of speaking is: "They have given their power," that is, their abilities. This means: The trees will give and produce that which is in their power. This expression is also used in Ps. 78:51.[15] In short, he means that they will again receive a plentiful abundance of the fruit of all things. He means that effective power and energy in trees.

23. *[Be glad,] O sons of Zion, etc.* We must read "sons," not "daughters."

For He has given you a teacher for your vindication. This Hebrew expression causes a great variety among translators. You see, מוֹרֶה means both "teacher" and "rain" to the Jews. This is something one may see here in a single verse of Joel, where the same word is translated both as "teacher" *(doctorem)* and as "rain" *(imbrem).* Therefore, we, too, shall not take it to mean "teacher" but "rain." Therefore we shall translate it as follows: "For He will mercifully give you rain." The following word "vindication" which we have here is aptly rendered with the word "clemency," or "mercy," just as it is also translated in the psalm (Ps. 24:5): "He will receive blessing from the Lord and mercy from the God of his salvation." So here we shall take this in an adverbial sense: "He will mercifully give you rain."

He will let the late and early rain pour down for you. In sacred literature these two rains are well known. Both, you see, are very necessary. It is as if he were saying: "The Lord will give you the rains by turns. He will give the early rain that the seeds may grow and the latter rain lest the crops be eaten up and wither away for excessive aridity, etc." You see, these certainly are rains of divine mercy, obviously so that there may not be too much wetness of the land or excessive dryness.

24. *The threshing floors will be full of grain.* We see that this translator has varied his words, for he has been translating now in the past, now in the future, so that our policy mentioned earlier is still in effect—that we must read all these words in the subjunctive.[16] But all these explanations are full of promise.

25. *I will restore to you the years which the swarming locust has*

[15] This passage contains a synonym only, *primitiae* ("first issue").

[16] Cf. p. 102 above.

eaten, that is, "the Lord will plentifully restore to you everything that the locusts devoured and destroyed. He will repair the loss you took, and He will do this abundantly."

My great army. Here we have the same word which we earlier translated "full yield" (v. 22). I take it in the objective case, although I do not worry how you take it, provided you get the correct sense to which the prophet wants to apply it here. Now, he speaks as follows, "I will restore to you My power, that is, I will send My very rich ability among you so that you will have a plentiful supply of all things. This will be 'My great army,'" so that we apply "army" not to the locusts but to divine blessing. Jerome was having hallucinations because he did not do this but applied it to the locusts.

26. *And My people will never again be put to shame*. All the prophets are accustomed to use this manner of speaking. Moses used it, too. The words sound as if that generation of the Jews would last and be glorious forever. This, however, is not the meaning. You see, "forever" or "to eternity" among the Jews means an indefinite time. The meaning is exactly this, as if he were to say, "And My people will never be put to shame again." We often see the same expression in Scripture. It is used also in the Book of Kings [17] and here and there elsewhere.

27. *There is none else*. What we read here we must read according to the Hebrew: "There is no other one beyond Me." Up to now he has prophesied about that temporal destruction of the people: that everything would collapse if they did not repent, just as they did not repent; that God would restore everything if they did repent; that they would abound with a rich supply of all things. In this way the prophet shows the mercy and goodness of God, who prefers the life and conversion of the sinner to his death.

28. *And it will come to pass afterward that I will pour out My Spirit*. Here the real prophecy begins, which we must clearly separate from what has gone before. Peter has treated this in Acts 2:17 ff. First we must speak about the transition of the prophet. If readers of the prophets do not understand it, it offends them very much. You see, it is the custom of the prophets that when they

[17] Cf. 2 Kings 6:23.

have declared that prophecy for which they had been sent, they put aside what has taken place after the revelation of their prophecy and immediately go on to prophesy about Christ. Although all the prophets were sent to announce some temporal punishment, yet they would always connect something about Christ to it too. Here the prophet Joel did the same thing. He quickly passes across from the Jews to the future people of Christ, and he meanwhile skips everything that took place after the declaration of the prophecy about the destruction of all Israel. So he clearly is beginning a new prophecy here. Thus when he says "afterwards," we must not apply this to destruction at the hands of the Assyrians. Rather, it is the custom of the prophets at this point to omit certain events that have taken place and to go on to announce other things that are going to happen much later. After all, that revelation of the Holy Spirit about which the prophet speaks here occurred long afterwards.

I will pour out My Spirit on all flesh. The Holy Spirit is poured out in two ways: by manifest vision or revelation and by secret inspiration. Here, then, he is speaking about the Holy Spirit as He is manifestly poured out and revealed with obvious signs. He is no longer speaking here about the old synagog of the Jews and about the people of the synagog, for whom certain kings and princes had been established by God, for whom a definite order of Levites had been established by Moses—an order whose duty it was to teach. There there was a certain respect for persons. The prophet says that it will be much different in the case of that new people. Here there will be no respect for persons, for to each will be given the authority to teach and preach, neither through man nor by man but divinely by God. There will not be some order—as there was in that old people—of those who alone had the power of priestly function. Instead, the Holy Spirit will be poured out on all flesh. All will be teachers and priests of God. Therefore it was especially necessary for this kingdom, so clearly different from that earlier one—to be established and confirmed by obvious signs and by an open revelation, or outpouring, of the Spirit, for certainly that secret revelation of the Spirit was also in the synagog. The passages which we read here and there in the prophets and in the writings of the apostles square with this and must be applied to it. For instance, Jeremiah says (Jer. 31:33-34): "I will put My law within them, and I will write it upon their hearts; and I will be their God, and they shall be My people . . . for they shall all know Me from the least of them to the greatest." Also Is. 54:13: "All your sons shall be taught by the Lord." John 6:45: "They shall all be θεοδίδακτοι ("taught by God"), etc." This was fulfilled on the Day of Pentecost. When the Gospel had been revealed, therefore, and made well known by the apostles to all the territories of the earth —for thus it had been prophesied in the Psalms—these signs ceased. You see, there is now no doubt about the verity of the Gospel, which was confirmed by such clear and visible signs at a time when there was a need for it, when the preaching of it was still a new thing. We, therefore, must no longer look for signs to confirm the Word, which has already before been clearly confirmed and shown to the world. Signs which God gives He gives not for the sake of one person but for the usefulness of many people, as the apostle Paul says in Corinthians (1 Cor. 12:7): "To each is given the manifestation of the Spirit for the common good." You have no need for the manifestation of the Spirit, but others do. Therefore what our prophets cook up for themselves about their signs in our day is worthless. This prophecy of Joel, then, is a prophecy about the public revelation of the Holy Spirit. After all, the Holy Spirit has always been in the devout from the beginning of the world, which no one can deny, but He has not been publicly manifested.

On all flesh. To be sure, that pouring out of the Spirit is made on all flesh, but the gift itself is not the same, for the whole world saw that manifestation of the Holy Spirit in the apostles when they taught and preached the Gospel. But the gift did not come to all. You see, Isaiah speaks in the same way and says (cf. Is. 49:26): "All flesh shall see the Salvation of our God." Simeon also says in his song (Luke 2:31): "Which Thou hast prepared in the presence of all people." This means: Christ has been prepared, revealed, and placed to be seen by all flesh. Thus in the New Testament the Holy Spirit has been poured into the hearts of the godly, yet He has also been declared openly by very obvious signs to confirm the Word. Therefore it is nothing that our prophets are looking for support for their own error from this text when they say that they have the Holy Spirit and that it is necessary that a person feel the Holy Spirit, although they themselves have not yet given evidence of the Spirit. To such we must respond in this way: "It is not enough to have the Spirit poured in. Indeed, this benefits you alone. But you must show and openly give evidence of that manifestation and outpouring of the Spirit in order that all flesh may see it." Because they cannot do this, just as our prophets never can, let them with us remain students of Holy Scripture. We now have no revelation of the Holy Spirit other than Holy Scripture. They must not establish some new kind of doctrine which they pretend to establish by the authority of the Holy Spirit. After all, if Christ is going to establish a new kind of preaching, He will not do this in darkness nor in the heart of one or another person. Rather, He will declare it with an open sign, lest anyone be able to have doubts about it. This is something obvious in the spread of that new kingdom about which he prophesies here. Peter also glories about it when he says (1 Peter 1:12): "Through the Holy Spirit sent from heaven, etc."

Your sons [*and your daughters*] *shall prophesy.* This is what I said earlier. In this kingdom there will not be some difference of persons. There will not only be prophets, priests, and Levites as before, but sons as well as daughters will prophesy and teach without difference. Here he sets down three kinds of divine illumination: first, prophecy. This occurs when the mystery of Christ or the grace shown to the world through Christ is preached in clear detail, as when Jeremiah says (Jer. 31:33): "I will put My law within them." Also, when Paul or the other apostles are manifestly interpreting Scripture, this interpretation is prophecy. Secondly, there are dreams, when certain images are represented. These, nevertheless, one understands when the Spirit interprets them so that those who have seen them have no doubts that the dreams come from God. Third are visions—certain apparitions, as when Joel saw the locusts, caterpillars, and jumbo caterpillars or when Isaiah saw the glory of the Lord above the temple, etc.

29. *But also upon menservants and maidservants.* The pronoun "My" [18] does not appear in the Hebrew. The sense is as if he were saying: "There is a difference now between menservants and maidservants. This, however, I will cause to cease, for there will be both menservant prophets and maidservant prophets." This is a very obvious passage against that ghostly papist priesthood, in

[18] The Vulgate reads *super servos meos et ancillas.*

which they do not want just anyone to be priests but where there is a respect of persons. Christ says that all His faithful people are going to be priests. After all, what else does a priesthood require except the declaration of the works of and Word of God? No one can deny here that this is being given to every Christian. Indeed, Christ says without any discrimination of persons that He will give His Holy Spirit to both sons and daughters, menservants and maidservants, etc.

30. *And I will give portents in the heavens.* That is, "I will give My Spirit in such a way that I shall confirm this with very clear and very firm witnesses—namely, signs, so that no one may be able to doubt." We shall detain our prophets for a long time with this text. We shall not trust their spirit unless they themselves also show clear signs and wonders to confirm the presence of the Spirit. This is something that will never happen. God, therefore, has given those signs both in the heavens and on earth to declare that kingdom of His to the world, as all creatures bear witness about it. You see, God is not playing around or acting in darkness to spread some new word. In the matter of publishing the Law we know with what great and terrible signs and portents He confirmed it—fire, smoke, thunder, hail, the mighty blast of trumpets, etc. All this—as well as these things about which he prophesies here—occurred to make consciences certain so that they could by no means doubt but rather became absolutely certain that this was the Word of God which [19] they were hearing. Thus the meaning is as if he were saying: "Heaven and earth shall be moved when the Gospel rises, so that every creature may bear witness that these are God's words." This is something that God will not do for the false prophets. Certainly God will not bear witness against His own Word, which He once before revealed to the world with such magnificence as well as with various signs.

Blood and fire and a column of smoke. I do not know for certain when all those signs occurred, nor do I know for sure whether it was written that they all did occur.

Fire. No doubt this was when fire came down from heaven and cloven tongues, as it were, of fire appeared on the apostles on the

[19] We have read *quod* for *de quo*.

Day of Pentecost, as Luke writes in Acts (Acts 2:3). It is likely that there was also smoke there, a sign by which the Holy Spirit not only here but also later declared Himself clearly, as we see in Acts 10:44: "The Holy Spirit fell on all who heard the Word." No one denies that this took place visibly. Indeed, there follows immediately "And the believers from among the circumcised . . . were amazed" (Acts 10:45). So it is very likely that the Holy Spirit also at that time revealed Himself by fire, just as Peter says, "Who have received the Holy Spirit just as we have" (Acts 10:47).

Blood. I do not know if he is speaking in this way and is taking "blood" here the way he takes it in the following verse, for I would gladly interpret "blood" here as "redness." The Hebrew word allows this. That is what we have in Gen. 49:11: "He washes . . . his vesture in the blood of grapes"; and in Deut. 32:14: "And of the blood of the grape they drank wine." They are talking about the redness of the choicest grapes. I think he means this here too (although I am not completely sure). After all, it seems to me to be too bold, too distorted, that we should want to establish that this sign indicates the blood of Christ and of the martyrs shed on the ground—as some people do. Whoever wants to relate these signs to the final Day of Judgment will do this without any resistance from me. Christ also prophesied about the signs preceding Judgment Day in Luke 19. On the other hand, I would simply want this to be applied to the time the Holy Spirit was sent—namely, that all these signs accompanied the Holy Spirit sent on the Day of Pentecost, and that that great day was the day the Gospel was revealed. You see, we know that at the time of Christ's Passion the sun was hidden and that perhaps many other signs occurred which the evangelists, nevertheless, did not write about.

31. *The moon to blood.* This is Hebrew phraseology, that is, "the moon has become bloody," and "it has become like blood." In Rev. 6:12 we have a similar manner of speaking: "The sun became black as sackcloth, the full moon became like blood." You see, the Hebrew uses substantives instead of adjectives.

The terrible day of the Lord. What we read here would be read more accurately according to the Hebrew as the "fearful" or "awesome" day. In Scripture God is often called "terrible" in this sense. When Jacob says in Genesis (Gen. 28:17): "How awesome is this place," the same word is used as the translator here has rendered "terrible."

32. *And it shall come to pass that all who call on the name of the Lord shall be delivered.* This is the passage which impels me to want all the signs to be taken to mean the day the Gospel is revealed. That certainly is a great and awesome day! But haven't the devout been calling on the name of the Lord since the beginning of the world? Yes, indeed! But again we must relate this to a manifest revelation. Christ has always been the same; the faith of the devout has always been the same. They have drunk of the "supernatural Rock," as Paul says in 1 Cor. 10:4. Yet what has now become open in the time of the revealed Gospel had been hidden under the Law, fear, and that ministry. The apostle Paul has treated this passage with sufficient reverence in Romans 10:13 ff. In this passage we have the sum of our salvation. We must understand it simply, just the way the words sound, without adding any strange glosses. "He shall be delivered," that is, redeemed from sin, death, and hell. He will pass from the misery of this life to eternal life. This deliverance is derived from no other source except from the Holy Spirit poured out on all flesh, and He sees to it that people call on the name of the Lord. In short, what he is saying here is the same as what Paul emphasizes everywhere—that man is justified by faith, without the works of the Law. You see, "to call on the name" is to believe, as Paul has interpreted it with very beautiful steps in Romans 10:14: "How are men to call upon Him in whom they have not believed? And how are they to believe, etc." With these steps he has very beautifully included the entire progression of our salvation. You see, first people must be sent to announce the Gospel. Hearing follows this sending, faith follows hearing, calling on the name of the Lord follows faith, and salvation follows this invocation. Thus the Christian kingdom is nothing else than the kingdom of faith in the Word of God—namely, that salvation comes to us not by our own strength, not by our own merits or righteousnesses, but out of the gracious mercy of God, who, as Paul says in Romans (Rom. 5:10), loved us even when we were still His enemies, who sent His Holy Spirit into our heart to be the effective Cause of our calling on the name of the Lord, in whom alone we must be saved, etc. He clearly said, "The name of the Lord." To be sure, in this life we cannot see the Lord face to face. Instead

we have the kingdom of faith here until we die. Then we are going to know the Lord face to face, etc. To summarize all this: Our salvation consists solely of the mercy of God which we call for and desire. The Psalms are full of passages of this sort: "Deliver me for the sake of Thy steadfast love." (Ps. 6:4); and "Forgive our sins for Thy name's sake" (Ps. 79:9).

For in Mount Zion and in Jerusalem there shall be salvation, that is, the basis for salvation will be there. This is what Isaiah says (Is. 2:3): "Out of Zion shall go forth the Law, and the Word of the Lord from Jerusalem." Also Christ says in the last chapter of Luke (Luke 26:46-47): "Thus it is written that the Christ should suffer and on the third day rise from the dead, and that repentance and forgiveness of sins should be preached in His name to all nations, beginning from Jerusalem, etc." So here, too, there is one passage which holds that the Gospel would come first out of Jerusalem—the Gospel which, along with many other things, Christ certainly disclosed to His disciples. See here the marvelous goodness of God, who still wanted to make our consciences certain so they could by no means entertain doubts about the Word of God. Thus also in the first spreading of the Gospel, He used a special place, special persons, and even special outward signs. At that time this was especially necessary so that the obvious signs and places and persons could show and bear witness of the first spreading of the Gospel. To such a degree is God at enmity with inconstant spirits,[20] who produce all such uncertain things. But now that the Gospel has been openly revealed, it is no longer bound to any persons or places, as immediately follows:

And among the survivors shall be those whom the Lord will have called. It is as if he were saying: "To be sure, in Jerusalem will be the beginning of salvation. The Gospel of salvation will be preached there first. It will not, however, remain only there. It will reach even the nations and will be preached everywhere throughout the world. Afterwards there will be no distinction either of places or of persons."

[20] Luther uses the German expression: *So ist Gott den fliegenden Geistern feind.*

CHAPTER THREE

I AM not sure to what we should apply this chapter—to what follows or to what precedes. In my judgment, I apply it to the kingdom of Christ. I believe it is an explanation of the verses preceding—namely, how the situation will develop in the world so that the kingdom of Christ is spread more widely. Let me summarize. As I said in the beginning, this is one of the oldest prophets. He prophesied at a time when things were going very well for the Jews. He also saw the very bitter hatreds and persecutions of the Idumeans, Palestinians, Moabites, and other nations against the Israelites, a people whom God had chosen to be His. This we read in sacred history. Therefore the prophet speaks in this way; "Yes! Let the wicked nations rage and set themselves against the people of God. There will come a time—yes, there will be a time—when the enemies of the people of God will lose all that confidence of theirs. I will again avenge terribly that insult they have brought upon My people. This, nevertheless, I will do in such a way that My revenge will be a salutary thing. You see, I am going to send them the Word of the Gospel. In this way they will acknowledge their error and their sin. I will make those who previously had been My great enemies My friends." In this way he applies the present raging of the foes to the day of Christ about which he is prophesying.

1. *When I have returned the captivity of Judah.* He foresaw that the Jews would be captured. We must apply these ideas, then, to the kingdom of Christ. It is as if he were saying: "When I redeem My people Judah from the true captivity of death—that is, of sin and hell; when I have risen from the dead and have given the Holy Spirit."

2. *Then I will gather all the nations.* This is something which never happened physically. Also, how could this take place, that

He gather all nations into that very small place? After all, the valley of Jehoshaphat, which lies between Jerusalem and the Mount of Olives, is so narrow that it holds scarcely a few people. Thus I cannot agree with those who apply this passage to the Day of Judgment: namely, that the Lord will sit for His judgment in the valley of Jehoshaphat and there will judge all nations. When we press these people about the narrowness of the site, they apply it to that entire area which surrounds Jerusalem. No matter how eloquently they say this thing, they are still in error, for the whole world—to say nothing of Judea—will barely be able to hold that countless host of all men who have lived since the beginning of the world. Indeed, as Paul says, some will be on earth and others will be flying in the clouds (cf. 1 Thess. 4:17). Forced, then, by this absurdity, we must apply this passage to a mystery, for it does not fit literally. We shall take it to mean the preaching of the Gospel which gathers all nations and calls them to judgment, which declares to them their error and passes the judgment that they are damned, and which shows them Christ, their Salvation. This has happened and does happen daily from the time when the Holy Spirit, about whom he spoke earlier in chapter 2,[1] was sent from heaven so that the nations which were summoned to judgment might recognize their sin and pray for forgiveness. You see, the word "Jehoshaphat" certainly is not a common noun but a proper noun. The prophet, then, is misusing the proper noun and is making it a common noun, just as Hosea did when he took the name of the city Gilead for the synagog (Hos. 6:8). To summarize: The prophet is speaking about the summoning of all nations to the church of God by the Gospel.

And I will enter into judgment with them. He is making a transition from the present evil to the coming revenge, as if to say: "There will come a time when I am going to sit in judgment. Then they will not escape. I shall judge them, too. I will find them out all right, much as I may now close My eyes to their great cruelty with which they rage violently against My people." He takes, then, the entire number of the nations and of all the peoples. Yet he takes this also to mean that portion of the adversaries of God's people.

[1] Chapter 2:28-29.

3. *They have given a boy for a harlot and have sold a girl, etc.* What occurs to the mind of Jerome is strange; here again, as is his custom, he talks nonsense about the nations. The Hebrew word זוֹנָה means a prostitute and a female shopkeeper, or hostess. Consequently, some, not without reason, consider that the harlot Rahab was a shopkeeper.[2] It is very likely that those spies who were sent by the Israelites had sought some decent lodgings. Therefore, since we have the same word here, which means both prostitute and shopkeeper, we can also take it to have a double meaning. The sense seems to me clearly to be: they have set up a boy like a harlot or like a shopkeeper and [have sold] a girl for wine, that is, that she be a servant at wine just as they used the lad as a servant in the inn. This sense pleases me more than that we apply it to lust. Indeed, the people they had carried off they used as slaves and maidservants.

4. *What are you to Me, O Tyre and Sidon?* The sense is the same as I mentioned earlier. He again recounts the present evil to postpone the vengeance to the time when the Gospel would be revealed, as if to say: "You have violently assailed My people. If you have taken anything from them, you have taken it from Me, such as the gold and silver vessels of the temple and the other things. I shall requite your deed upon your own head." Not that the Jews should hope for some physical revenge on their foes, as wretched men today still boast. The meaning, then, is this: "Also what would you do to Me, O Palestinians and your regions? Will you direct your revenge at Me, if you do take revenge?" It is as if He were saying: "Just go ahead. You will have to smart for that." [3]

Swiftly. Obviously this will be when the Gospel comes. "Then I will make those who now are enemies friends, and thus I will be avenged on you."

5. *My rich treasures.* In the Hebrew this reads: "My good rich treasures," that is, the gold and silver vessels of the temple.

[2] Veit Dietrich's footnote to this assertion is: "But the New Testament twice [Heb. 11:31 and James 2:25] calls her a harlot." Cf. St. Louis edition, VI, 1467, n. 3.

[3] This proverbial expression from Terence, *Eunuchus*, 381, *in me cudetur faba* ("the bean is made to strike me") is interpreted by Jerome's teacher, the grammarian Aelius Donatus, to mean *in me malum recidet* ("the evil comes back to plague me").

You have taken away. Clearly, when the people were taken captive, the neighboring nations were delighted over the calamity of the Jews because they were taken away as captives. This is something the sacred accounts tell us. It is also described in the psalm (Ps. 137:7): "Raze it! Raze it! Down to its foundations!" Thus I apply all these things to Christ and not to the Babylonian captivity, as Jerome and others do. Otherwise, we shall never be able to make an explanation according to the consequences, nor will these things otherwise fit together.

7. *But now I will stir them up from the place.* We must apply all this to the revelation of the Gospel. After all, had the prophet described some simple skirmish or revenge, he would not have used so many very effective words. As we see here, he does enlarge the situation. We must, therefore, take that "stirring up" to mean the preaching of the Gospel, which came not only to the Jews but to the entire world.

8. *I will sell . . . in the hands of the sons* [*of Judah*]. That Hebrew idiom [4] is rendered in Latin with the preposition *per* and among the Germans with the word *durch,* since the Hebrew language does not have an equivalent for the preposition "through." This is the way it is everywhere in the prophets, the Word of the Lord "in the hand of Isaiah" (cf. Is. 20:2), that is, by the hand of Isaiah; what the Lord had Isaiah preach, etc. Here "in the hands" means "by the hands," that is, through the sons of Judah. This is what happened through the apostles, who announced the Gospel as they went traveling to all nations.

They will sell them to the Sabeans. The region of Sabea is farther away from Jerusalem than Greece is from Palestine. This is Arabia, for history has three Arabias: Petraea, the desert, and the fruitful area. In Arabia Petraea are the Idumeans, the Ammonites, the Ishmaelites, etc. Surely the region of Petraea is very large. The city of Petra is located in it. The fruitful part faces toward India, near the upper coast of the Red Sea. The Hebrew calls this "Sheba." The account of the queen of Sheba is in the Books of Kings (1 Kings 10:1) and also in the gospel (Matt. 12:42). Therefore, by synecdoche (which is a familiar figure of speech with the prophets) he calls them Arabs in place of all the distant

[4] "In the hands of."

nations. Thus he means a spiritual selling, because they were brought back and made Christians throughout the world.

For the Lord has spoken. He adds this to confirm his prophecy. It is as if he were saying: "All these things will not fail because it has not been a man who has predicted such things. Rather, the Lord has spoken, and He cannot lie."

9. *Proclaim this among the nations.* "This" is clearly the things we have mentioned. "Cry out loud and clear." But this happens through the Gospel, which is the proclaiming voice. This entire passage and everything that follows is filled with metaphors, just as all the prophets are filled with metaphors. This is something we see also in this verse of the psalm (Ps. 118:22): "The stone which the builders rejected has become the head of the corner." This passage we must take to mean Christ, since Christ and all the apostles thus interpret it: He is the One in whom the Gentiles as well as the Jews must become unified, in whom alone salvation lies. However, that the builders rejected Him—that is, that the scribes and Pharisees rejected Him—not even the slightest word seems to indicate this meaning. Isaiah also speaks in this way (Is. 28:16): "Behold, I am laying in Zion for a foundation . . . a cornerstone, etc." This passage, too, was spoken about Christ; yet the words plainly do not seem to have the same idea. Rather, that which follows explains the metaphor:"He who believes will not be confounded." This one statement adds light to the entire metaphor. It is worthwhile observing this in the prophets, who are accustomed to use so many metaphors for this purpose, that they either obscure their prophecy or exercise their ingenuity. We see the same thing here in Joel, too. After all, the sense of this passage is as if he were saying: "You who are preaching the Gospel, go on and declare it. Make it known to all nations. Gird yourselves for war. Stir up the strong. Let all the men who want to fight rise up and go. Let all who are fit for war come nigh."

10. *Beat your plowshares into swords.* These are pure metaphors. You see, this is how the prophet abounds in the Spirit. This is how he builds up this spiritual battle. There would have been no need for him to declare this in the case of a physical battle. To summarize: Take the Word and fight bravely. The plowshare and pruning hook are instruments of peace; spears and

swords, instruments of war. The meaning, then, is this: "Those very instruments which you used for peace before you now must accommodate to war and battle." This is what Christ says: "Let him who has two mantles sell the one and buy himself a sword" (cf. Luke 22:36). Isaiah has exactly the opposite, for he says in chapter 2:4: "They shall beat their swords into plowshares and their spears into pruning hooks." Yet both are speaking correctly. You see, Isaiah is speaking about the physical and spiritual peace which began under Christ, but Joel is speaking about the spiritual battle of the Word of the Gospel.

Let the weak say: I am a warrior. This properly pertains to Christians, so that we certainly cannot take it to mean a physical battle. After all, as Paul says (cf. Rom. 5:3): "We rejoice in our sufferings." Although Christians may be weak, helpless, and cast down, they nevertheless are very powerful. This is something Paul teaches very beautifully everywhere: "Having nothing, yet possessing all things," in 2 Cor. 6:10; also: "We have become . . . as the refuse of the world, the περίψημα ("offscouring") of all things. To the present hour we hunger and thirst, we are ill-clad and buffeted, etc.," in 1 Cor. 4:13, 11. Christ also said regarding Himself (Luke 9:58): "The Son of Man has nowhere to lay His head." Outstanding soldiers, indeed, who will thus suffer all miseries; also, wondrous war, indeed, and clearly against every example of the entire world—one in which the soldiers are weak, that is, powerless; where they suffer many things and are cast down! But Paul explains this military service when he says, "The weapons of our warfare are not worldly, etc." (1 Cor. 10:4).

11. *Hasten and come, all you nations* [. . . *the Lord will bring down your warriors*]. "Your warriors" are your powerful men. You see, the Gospel will stir up all the peoples of all the earth. Yet the prophet is speaking as if to the people of Palestine alone when he says "Your warriors." Yet, by synecdoche, he includes along with Palestinians all the nations that exist. All these He kills with the Spirit of His mouth. He makes them subject to Himself through the Gospel.

12. *Let the nations bestir themselves and come up* [*to the valley of Jehoshaphat*]. The prophet explains himself in greater detail. It is impossible, as I have said earlier, for all nations to be able to

be gathered in the valley of Jehoshaphat, however large it may be, which it is not. Rather, we must take this to mean the church in which all men will be gathered under the Word of God. You see, just as the sun illumines the entire world with its rays, so are all men gathered together under the Word of God, so that though not all believe the Word, it is nevertheless declared to the wicked as well as to the devout. For the latter it is the power of God to salvation, for the former it is judgment.

To judge. I apply all this to the day when the Gospel will have been revealed and to the entire time of the new Zion, and not to the day of final judgment.

13. *Put in the sickle, for the harvest is ripe.* These are pure exhortations to declare the Word with zeal and diligence. Moreover, this is all metaphor. It is as if he were saying: "Begin to preach. Strive energetically. Indeed, the harvest is now ready. The suitable time has come." This is what Christ says, too, John 4:35: "Lift up your eyes and see how the fields are already white for harvest, etc."

Go in and tread, for the winepresses are full, the vats overflow. This, you see, we read accurately according to the Hebrew. The explanation of all this follows.

For their wickedness is great. Here he has explained clearly what he meant with "winepresses," the "harvest," and the "threshing floor"—namely, the whole world, in which the grapes are pressed and wine abounds. This is the way Isaiah has used this (Is. 63:3): "I have trodden the winepress alone, and from the peoples no one was with me, etc." Thus through the Word He crushed all nations under His power, whether they were unwilling or willing. The unwilling ones are judged and condemned. After the willing ones have been judged, they come to their senses. They acknowledge His grace, and, once they have acknowledged His grace, they are saved. Indeed, faith is nothing else than the genuine recognition of the goodness and mercy of God or of the face of God, as the prophets say. In these passages, then, we have the pure preaching of the virtue and power of the Word of God.

14. *Peoples, peoples, in the valley of decision!* The Hebrew הָמוֹן means a "great multitude." Here the prophet has used the

plural, as if to say: "Many throngs of peoples." Throngs, throngs—wherever you may turn, you see throngs. Therefore, we certainly cannot take this to mean solely the Jewish people, since he has described all things with such detailed and very clear words. I have already mentioned this earlier. He calls the valley of Jehoshaphat the "valley of decision." This Hebrew expression [5] is the one which Paul translates in Rom. 9:28 as follows: "The Lord will execute His sentence upon the earth with rigor and dispatch." This properly means "to set a certain limit, to abridge"—we say "to sum it up." Thus here it means in a defined, certain, limited valley. This is what our translator has rendered poorly as "of decision." You see, the Latin word *concisum* does not mean defined, certain, or abridged but cut and recut into many pieces. Daniel, too, used this word in describing the Antichrist (Dan. 7:12) [6]: "For the times of life have been established for him for a season and a time." This valley, then, is the church of Christ, as I have said earlier.

15. *The sun and the moon are darkened.* This we also explained earlier in the second chapter. You see, the prophets have the custom of describing a situation in such a way that to those whom the Lord terrifies and wants to deliver into the hands of their foes not only the heaven and earth but the stars and all creatures appear to be opposed. We read this also in the Book of Judges about Sisera: "From heaven fought the stars, from their courses they fought against Sisera, etc." (Judges 5:20), for it seems to the wicked that all creatures resist them. This means: Because of the great fighting, the limitless slaughter and attacking, smoke rises, and not even the sky can be seen. This is something which those know, too, who have once experienced that serious warfare. It seems to those who are vanquished that all creatures oppose them. The fear of death, set before their eyes, also causes this. But here the prophet is taking a metaphor from physical carnage to show the magnitude and violence of the spiritual warfare to which Paul alludes in Rom. 1:18: "The wrath of God is revealed from heaven against all ungodliness and wickedness of men."

[5] חָרוּץ.

[6] The Weimar editor suggests Dan. 12:9, where the Hebrew word חָרוּץ is indeed used, but in a different sense. The Vulgate translation here quoted establishes Dan. 7:12 as the text referred to, even though the Hebrew word is not used there.

16. *And the Lord will roar from Zion.* This is an explanation of everything he so beautifully said earlier about that conflict. Here he is describing the weapons of that war, but he is saying: "There will be nothing of iron, there will be no weapons in this war. Rather, the Lord will bring this battle to pass solely by His Word." We certainly cannot take this passage to mean an external battle, but we must take it to mean a spiritual one. He says, as it were: "Such will be this assault that the Lord will roar from heaven as He sends His Holy Spirit. That is, He will terrify all nations with His Word which He is going to publish and which He will cause to come first of all from Jerusalem." This is what He said earlier at the end of Chapter 2—that salvation will be on Mount Zion and in Jerusalem. Take a look at what we said there.

And the heavens and the earth will shake. Haggai also speaks this way in his second chapter (Hag. 2:6): "Once again in a little while, I shall shake the heavens and the earth and the sea and the dry land, etc." You see, when Christ was born, the angels appeared and were heard to announce that Christ was born, and all creatures, the stars and the sky bore witness of His birth.

The Lord will be the Hope of His people. Here again the prophet is explaining clearly what sort of a war that is going to be, namely, a spiritual one: that Christ is going to rule among His people, that is, among the faithful who are going to believe in Him. Thus He will be the Surety of His people, for this is more correctly rendered with the word "Surety." In His kingdom, then, all human powers, all weaponry, will cease, All things will be done in faith. "And then," the Lord says, "you will know that I am your God, who dwell in Zion" (v. 17).

17. *And Jerusalem shall be holy, etc.* This promise has never been fulfilled physically. It has, however, been fulfilled this way through Christ or through the kingdom of Christ. Jerusalem was called holy not for the reason that men who lived there were holy, but because of the holy Word of God which ruled there. After Christ had again been taken up into heaven, they corrupted and ignored that Word. That holiness, consequently, ceased. We must, then, certainly take this to mean the spiritual Jerusalem, the church of Christ which the Word sanctifies and cleanses.

18. *And it will come to pass in that day that the mountains*

shall drip sweet wine. So it is in Hebrew.[7] You see again that these are pure metaphors. He is speaking about the sort of kingdom of Christ that, when it will have begun, the sweetest wine will be on the mountains. That is, in all places will be preached the sweetest promise of the Gospel, which is as sweet as sweet wine.

And the hills shall flow with milk. This is the same thing. With both of these the strong and the weak are refreshed. It will accommodate itself to the abilities of all men, as the apostle Paul also interprets milk in 1 Cor. 3:2. He means, then, the sweetness of the Word.

And all the stream bed, etc. He means the abundance of the Word, or the course of the Word of God.

And a fountain shall come forth from the house of the Lord and water, etc. In the Hebrew it reads this way: "And it will water the valley of Shittim." Shittim is the place across the Jordan where the children of Israel lived after the death of Moses. It is toward the east, away from the Dead Sea. The meaning, then, is this: From the house of the Lord and toward the east will spring up a beautiful fountain (it faces the site of the temple and the temple door). It will flow beyond the borders of Israel all the way to the Gentiles. With this figure he signifies the course of the Gospel throughout the earth. You see, by synecdoche, he means by Shittim all the nations outside Judea in the entire world. It is as if he were saying: "So great will be the abundance of the Word of God that it will be preached not only to the Jews but to all the Gentiles," as all the prophets also say.

19. *Egypt will become a desolation.* Here we have the epilog, in which he recapitulates the results of that war which he has described in such great detail with such beautiful language. He says, as it were: "When all this will happen, Egypt will be desolate, and Edom a desert. But this will be a strange devastation—through sweet wine, milk, and a fountain. Will there not rather be need here for weapons and a great army of soldiers?" As I have said, we must take everything in a spiritual sense, for he means the power and efficacy of the Word of God. This is the way Jacob also de-

[7] That is, "sweet wine" (*mustum*) instead of the Vulgate's "sweetness" (*dulcedinem*).

scribes the kingdom of Christ in Gen. 49:12: "His eyes are more beautiful than wine, and His teeth whiter than milk." This is a strange King—one who is soft and effeminate in the eyes of the flesh. Psalm 45 also commends Him because of His beauty. That psalm describes the kingdom of Christ most beautifully, too. He is saying: "Extend Your kingdom with Your beautiful appearance instead of with bloodshed." This is the way the prophets describe the kingdom of Christ. What that beauty of Christ is the Spirit adds in the psalm (Ps. 45:2): "Grace is poured upon Your lips, etc." This means the sweetness of the Word of the Gospel.

20. *And Judah will be inhabited forever.* That is, "those whom I have not cleansed up to the time before the Gospel was revealed now will all be cleansed," because the Law leads no man to perfection, as Paul says (cf. Heb. 7:19). Moreover, that new preaching, the Gospel, will cleanse all men and lead them to perfection, if they believe. After all, he is declaring that Christ is our Righteousness, Wisdom, Redemption, and Satisfaction, who is blessed forever and ever. Amen.[8]

[8] The Altenburg manuscript adds the date: "Wittenberg, the Eve of the Festival of St. Lawrence [August 9], 1524."

LECTURES ON AMOS

The Altenburg Text

Translated by
RICHARD J. DINDA

BECAUSE we are flesh and blood, because we have very harmful foes against whom we battle zealously, and because Satan in the meantime does not cease his work, we need extensive instruction and a wealth of the Word of God, lest, misled by the flesh and surrounded by Satan, we extinguish the Spirit—which can happen very easily. The apostle therefore gives us careful admonition that the Word of God dwell in us πλουσίως, in all wisdom, etc., in Col. 3:16. You see, just as the body must die unless one gives it bread and nourishment to sustain it, so also is it all over for the soul when its true food, the Word of God, is taken away. After all, "man does not live by bread alone, but by the Word of God," Deut. 8:3.

THE PLAN OF THE PROPHET

The prophet Amos was a contemporary of Hosea—as the initial verse indicates. Both prophesied against the kingdom of Ephraim, and both predicted that the same calamity would occur. You see, we have here the customary activity of the Lord God. Whenever some great upheaval threatens, whenever some great evil threatens, He sends His prophets or ministers of the Word to announce His Word, to foretell the ills which are coming and, after preaching the Word, to turn at least a few hearts and call them to repentance. No doubt, since we have the Word of God so very clearly, we ought to be waiting for a great upheaval. But only the Lord knows what will happen in the future and when it will happen. Therefore at that time when the deplorable devastation of Israel threatened, He sent His prophet Amos and other great prophets to preach the Word and to warn Israel of the impending destruction and misery. Thus they would not all be completely destroyed but would abound in the Word of God and be called back to repentance. But as the Word has always been held in contempt—just as people despise it today—at that time the Word had no place in their midst. There was no respect for the Word or for preachers of the Word. But a few were concerned with the Word, and among them, few though they were, the Lord worked salvation through the Word. Because the rest of the multitude despised the Word, laughed at it, and blasphemed it; because they dealt badly with the prophets whom He had sent to announce their salvation; because they hissed at them, mistreated them, and finally even killed them; God deservedly rejected them. This is the appearance, shape, and form of God's Word. It is not for us to hope for better things.

The sum and scope of the prophet Amos, then, is this: He rebukes and admonishes Israel to come to its senses and repent of its wickedness. It thus will come to pass that Israel will be able to watch out for the destruction that threatens because of the judgment of God. Israel, however, held his prophecy in great contempt. You see, not only were the Word and preachers of that Word very displeasing to the world and to the wisdom of the flesh; but Amos also prophesied at that very time when the kingdom of Israel was in full flower, when Israel was successful in all its endeavors (when Hosea also prophesied). Amos prophesied under the great and bold, although wicked, King Jeroboam, who with his various outstanding victories restored the boundaries of Israel "from the entrance of Hamath to the sea of the Arabah," as it is written in 2 Kings 14:25. Amos, therefore, became infatuated with that prosperity of the realm, as the wicked generally are infatuated with success and are destroyed thereby, Prov. 1:32. You see, they believe that they have no need for God. They go on in their blindness to act wickedly, until they are caught by the judgment of God and perish. The Word is declared to them in vain, as we see in this prophet. Amos, therefore, prophesied at a very ill-starred but yet very opportune time. From all this let us learn well that in adverse times we must have good hopes for the goodness and mercy of God, but that in good times we must live in fear.

CHAPTER ONE

1. *The words of Amos . . . which he saw.* This is according to the Hebrew text. In Latin we must render it as follows: "These are the things Amos saw" *(Haec sunt quae vidit Amos).*

Who was among the shepherds of Tekoa. So also later,[1] the text says that Amos was not a prophet, but a shepherd, that is, that he did not belong to the class, or order, of prophets. There were various orders among the people of Israel: some were prophets, some were priests, some were wise men. It was according to the will of these men that the people were ruled. They were in charge of the ministry of the Word. Whatever they would establish or teach the people would accept as most sacred. Confident of their own authority, then, they became puffed up. To resist them was looked upon as blasphemy. For, as we read in Jer. 18:18, they said, "The Law shall not perish from the priest, nor counsel from the wise, nor the Word from the prophet." In contempt of those who became so proud, the Lord, however, often aroused humble, common men who belonged to neither the prophetic nor priestly order. These lowly people thus would resist all those others; they would rebuke them for their wickedness, as we can see here and there in the prophets. This, however, is the "folly" of God, by which He makes foolish the world and the wisdom of the flesh (cf. 1 Cor. 1:20 f.). These men were very lowly, very humble people. It seemed insane for them to want to resist kings and so many prophets and priests, who were in charge of the ministry of the Word, as well as a prudent people taught in the Law of the Lord. It seemed insane for such men to want to teach something new and outside of the normal custom. These humble men, therefore, were considered fools. Their word was despised and blasphemed. So also today, to the wise men of the world those things appear

[1] Cf. Amos 7:14.

to be strange (παράδοξα) which are said and written through the Gospel of Christ against so powerful a kingdom as that of the pope, extolled for so long by saintly men. After all, it is by the pope that kings and princes and all the learned, finally, the whole world, stand. This is what the prophet intends when he calls himself a shepherd of Tekoa. He indicates that both the place and the person are insignificant. This, however, is what the apostle Paul says in 1 Cor. 1:27, that God selected the foolish and weak things of the world to shame the wise and powerful people of the world, etc. The Hebrew word[2] which we render here as "shepherds" does not really mean a shepherd but a man who has many cattle. It means an owner of cattle, a herdsman.

Which he saw . . . two years before the earthquake. Here he is indicating the time when he prophesied, namely, under Uzziah, king of Judah, and Jeroboam, king of Israel. There is nothing in Scripture about when that earthquake occurred. This, however, was undoubtedly mentioned in the book of the acts of the kings of Israel, which is so often mentioned in the Books of Kings (cf. 1 Kings 11:41), but which we do not have. Zechariah also remembered this earthquake in chapter 14:5. Undoubtedly, that earthquake, whenever it happened, was a sign of a coming evil. This is something that always happened among the heathen too, as the histories of the heathen bear witness. In this way, as if with a sign already past, the prophet elicits faith for his prophecy.

2. *The Lord will roar from Zion.* This topic is the goal, or main point, of the entire first chapter—in fact, of the entire book. Because it is a custom of the prophets to use poetic figures and expressions, this prophet is completely of this kind. He is completely poetic. It is metaphor then—or allegory, rather—when he says, "The Lord will roar." By this he signifies the great wrath and threat of God. It is as if he were saying: "The Lord, who is from Zion, who lives in Zion, or resides in Jerusalem—that Lord will roar. He is angry. He will stiffen His mane like an angry lion. Watch out! He is threatening you with destruction. For no matter how much you may hold Him in contempt, yet He is warning that He will devour you all. Moreover, for this devouring of you, He

[2] נֹקְדִים.

will use the teeth and throat of the Assyrians. This will happen to all of you unless you repent, etc."

The pastures of the shepherds will mourn, as if to say: "The Lord is threatening you with this: He will devour you. He will reduce your land to a wilderness. Your habitations will become deserted wasteland. There will be grief in your tents, and the areas where your shepherds now are will be forsaken."

And the top of Carmel will wither. Again he is speaking figuratively. There are two Carmels: the first, the place where Nabal lived. Scripture calls him "churlish," 1 Sam. 25:3. It was located toward the south. Here, however, the prophet is speaking about that great and famous mountain, renowned for its varied crops of fruit. The sense, then, is this: Carmel will be reduced to a wasteland and will not be cultivated. What now lies broad and expansive, very rich and fertile, will lie untilled. At the same time, the prophet has included with this prophetic manner of speaking that the entire people would be destroyed. By the habitations of the shepherds he means the common people—people of the lowliest lot. With Carmel he indicates all the best people—the princes and priests. All of these, he says, will perish at the same time. This is how, in accord with their custom, those whom we call the "minor" prophets generally use more figures of language than the major prophets.

3. *For three transgressions of Damascus.* He now goes on to explain in detail what he meant by the habitations of the shepherds and by Carmel. Furthermore, you will read this more accurately according to the Hebrew in this way: "Because of three lies of Damascus, and because of four, etc."

In iron wagons. What our words say here refers to something else in Hebrew. It is not a wagon but some toothed tool for breaking down straw into fodder for cattle. We do not use this tool. I call it a threshing sledge. We have the same words in 1 Chron. 20:3: "iron wagons."

5. *Syria . . . Cyrene.* This reads badly and is also translated badly. After all, Cyrene is located between Egypt and Africa Minor. The king of Assyria, however, never held Africa in subjection. Therefore, instead of Cyrene, we must read Kir. So much about the grammar.

Our translators have treated this passage (v. 3) in different ways. Lyra, perhaps in accord with the sense of the Hebrew interpreters, thinks that we should take the three transgressions as sins which the Holy Spirit does not forgive. Jerome is far more inept. He interprets the transgressions as follows: the first is the thought of sin, the second is the decision to sin, the third is the act itself, and the fourth is impenitence. But when the text is quite clear in itself, what is the need to imagine ἀπροσδιόνυσα ?[3] After all, it is nothing that they think this means four sins, because he lists seven sins. So it is my idea that this is the figurative speech of Scripture, a likeness of which we read in Lev. 26:18, 21, 24, where we find the repetition several times: "I will chastise you sevenfold. . . . I will smite you sevenfold. . . . I will chastise you with seven plagues." That number seven indicates a perseverance in punishing and chastising them. It is as if He were saying: "I shall destroy you completely. I shall not cease smiting you. I shall not lessen My plagues against you." Thus we must take this passage of the prophet Amos to mean that the Lord is saying, as it were: "Because they have obstinately continued to sin against Me, because they have not ceased sinning, because they are not sorry for their wickedness but have continued in their great obstinacy to act wickedly, I will completely destroy them and wipe them out." Indeed, this is the meaning I take from this passage. I see no better one.

3. *Because it has threshed . . . with threshing sledges.* He lists the crimes or transgressions of Damascus, as if to say: "He has threshed and broken and reduced as it were to dust that land of Gilead. He has threshed it as chaff is generally threshed on the threshing floor." But Gilead is in the divided tribe of Manasseh.

I will not cause . . . to return. People have applied this to the returning of repentance. I do not approve of this. Rather, the sense seems to be: "I will not free you from the hand of the Assyrian. I will neither diminish nor turn away the punishment. I will have no compassion on you. I will allow the Assyrian to rage against you, just as you proceeded to destroy Gilead, etc." This expression is used frequently here and there in the Psalms. In Ps. 6:4 we

[3] "Things irrelevant." Cf *Luther's Works,* 19, p. 120, n. 1.

read, "Turn, O Lord, save my life"; and in Ps. 90:13: "Return, O Lord! How long?"

4. *So I will send a fire.* He means that destruction is going to come by fire at the hands of the Assyrians, as if to say: "Watch out! At some time I will send fire. I will cause many evils to come upon you which you will clearly be incapable of bearing."

5. *I will break the bar of Damascus.* He figuratively calls the fortifications "the bar." He is also referring to the aristocracy, those who are brave and strong enough to take up arms against the Assyrian who will come. He says that He is going to send a fear over them like fire when the king of the Assyrians comes, so that they will not defend themselves.

I will destroy the inhabitants, that is, "I will cut them off; I will exterminate them."

From the plain of Aven.[4] Damascus was located on a very beautiful plain, not in a mountainous area. Pleasant fields all around surrounded it. Here the prophet is alluding to this pleasantness of the site. He is saying, as it were: "You live in a very beautiful, very fertile place. The location of your city is very lovely, but I will wipe you out. I will carry you away to the Assyrians."

Of Aven. This is what the Hebrew language calls whatever is not the true religion established by the Word of God. The word is taken from vexation of hearts, for it properly means "toil." The prophet is alluding to those pursuits of wickedness with which the wicked weary their consciences and afflict themselves with a religion they themselves invented.

And him that holds the scepter from Beth-eden. This is again a circumlocution, that is: "I will remove the king and cause him to be taken away. He intends to build for himself a splendid and magnificent palace in a very lovely place, but he will accomplish nothing. He will not enjoy the use of them, for he will be taken away and cast out."

6. *For three transgressions of Gaza.* The prophet goes on to frighten and terrify with the judgment of God all the nations which

[4] For the Hebrew אָוֶן the Vulgate here has *idoli* ("idol").

were living round about Jerusalem. Indeed, the king of Assyria sent against them by the judgment of God was going to sweep over not just the people of Israel but the wicked nations, too, such as the Moabites, the Edomites, etc. All of these the Lord threatens with His roaring as He indicates that they would perish along with Israel. Nevertheless, the prophet is developing this powerful threat against Israel especially. We cannot determine from sacred history what that captivity and transmigration he mentions here are. But from the prophet's context we may gather that this city of Gaza had taken, perhaps in a clash, some Jews and had handed them over to the Edomites as captives. After all, those nations which surrounded Israel always raged against it with a perpetual hatred in whatever ways they were able. They worked with a never ending jealousy and let no opportunity, no time, no energy pass without harming Israel if they could. So exasperated in heart were the wicked nations against God's people Israel. You see, Jerusalem was located in the midst of heathen and had round about it very harmful foes. The Lord says that He will punish this sin sevenfold.

Because they carried into exile a whole people. It is as if he were saying: "They are of such a hostile and aggrieved disposition toward Israel that they are unable to satisfy that eagerness for avenging themselves. It is not enough for them to avenge themselves against the people of God who have the Word of God." So Satan cannot bear the Word of God and strives against it with all his might. In this striving, he stirs up the wicked against the devout who have the Word of God. So also today, our most bitter foes are those who assail the Word at the instigation of Satan. Wherever he takes away the Word, he easily draws all men to himself. This is how exasperated the minds of all those nations were against the people of God.

9. *For three transgressions of Tyre.* The people of Tyre had undoubtedly conspired with the Palestinians in that captivity of the children of Israel which he just mentioned. The people of Tyre handed the Israelites over to be taken away, and the Palestinians took them away or carried them off.

They did not remember the covenant of brotherhood. He says, as it were: "Even though the Tyrians have suffered no harm, they have unilaterally raged against My people and have broken the covenant of brotherhood." No doubt he is speaking about the covenant established between Solomon and Hiram, king of Tyre. See 1 Kings 5.

11. *For three transgressions of Edom.* Dr. Jerome again is snoring as he translates this passage—and no wonder. After all, he was the only fellow who was not equal to the great arduous task of translating, for what he translates here as ". . . he violated his mercy" has been translated with patent absurdity. It ought to be translated this way: "He destroyed his own compassion." It is as if he were saying: "They should have embraced each other eagerly and very warmly, as brothers. They ought to have had a great and necessary union between them. However, they destroyed each other." In German we cannot translate the word *viscera* [5] ("compassion") suitably. It has a very specific meaning in Hebrew. This specific meaning we express approximately in the Latin word *viscera.* The apostles and evangelists in the New Testament also used this word [6] frequently, as we read in Luke 1:78: "Through the compassionate mercy of our God." Paul used it here and there in his epistles, for instance, Phil. 1:8: "God is my witness how I yearn for you all with the affection of Christ Jesus." Also, Phil. 2:1: "If there is any affection and sympathy."

And his anger tore perpetually. You will translate this more accurately this way: "His anger rages endlessly." That is, it knows no limit in revenge against his brother. You see, the Edomites came from Esau, who was the brother of Jacob, who is otherwise called Israel. From him came the Israelites. So both were born of one father, Isaac. See Genesis.[7] This is the same as what follows:

He kept his wrath, etc. The anger of this people against Israel is implacable. Just as this hatred began in Esau, so it has never ceased among his descendants.

12. *I will send a fire upon Teman.* Teman was the grandson of Esau. Later, the entire region of the Edomites was named Teman

[5] Luther means to say that the Hebrew word רַחֲם, translated literally to German, would not yield the meaning of the original, as the Latin *viscera* does.

[6] In Greek, σπλάγχνα.

[7] Gen. 25:21 f.

after him. You see, Scripture in this way generally gives various names to the same region, as we see in the Psalms, where Egypt is named with different names. This land [Teman] received its name from *Auster* ("the South").[8] It was famous because it had many outstanding wise men. It is also mentioned in Job 6:19.

Of Bozrah. This is a well-known and important city of the Edomites.

13. *For three transgressions of the Ammonites.* As they explain this passage, the interpreters vary strangely where it speaks of ripping up the pregnant women. We are sure that the word "rip up" has been correctly translated from the Hebrew. Some, however, want "pregnant women" to be understood as "mountains." They prove this from what follows in this context; "that they might enlarge their border." In this way the sense is this: The Ammonites have been so captivated by the desire to rule and to enlarge their borders that they even ripped up the mountains and took them away in order to enlarge their borders. This, surely, was a useless task. I think these are Judaic and purely arbitrary ideas. I take it very simply—just as the text reads by itself—about ripping up the pregnant women; or I take it as a metaphor, as this is a prophet of the countryside who is full of figurative language. In that case, the meaning may be that the Ammonites have overthrown and destroyed the rich and outstanding cities of Gilead. This metaphor also more correctly agrees with what follows about enlarging the borders. You see, these people were working with a unique crime to make an assault on the borders of the Israelites. But I am not disturbed if anyone wants this to refer really to pregnant women. Yet it is absurd to attribute such savagery to this people.

14. *So I will kindle a fire in the wall of Rabbah.* Every region had some special and famous city from which the entire region would receive its name. This we see in all the sacred accounts.

With wailing, more accurately, "with shouting." After all, he is speaking about the cry or triumphal shout of victors, not of those who have been vanquished, so that, obviously, the enemy are going to rejoice in overthrowing, etc.

[8] The Hebrew תֵּימָן (Teman) means south.

15. *And Milcom will go into exile.* This is not a proper noun but a common noun. Therefore we should translate it as follows: "And their king will go into exile." Furthermore, Milcom was a god of the Ammonites (1 Kings 11:5). You see, just as individual regions had individual cities from which they received their name, so also each people had a special god. The Palestinians had Dagon, the Ammonites Milcom, the Moabites Baal-peor, as the accounts tell us.

CHAPTER TWO

HERE again we are uncertain about the episode of history which he mentions at the beginning of this chapter. The tales of the Jews do not please me, because they do not inform us on the basis of Scriptures and because there is no sacred account which can make us certain. Therefore I think that we must give this a metaphorical meaning, namely, that "bones" does not mean the bones of a body but the strong—the powerful princes—who can do much with weapons and in waging war, for in Holy Scripture the strong and powerful are generally called "bones." The prophet, then, is rebuking the insatiable eagerness of the Moabites for violence when he mentions the burning of the bones of the king of the Edomites (for we should not read "set fire to" but "burned").

In these passages we see the marvelous judgments of God, which we think are accident or luck, especially when some nations become superior to others in battle, when the armies of some nations are cut down. All these things take place by the judgment of God. Furthermore, God Almighty also avenges harm done to the heathen, so that we may learn that God is Lord of all the world and that all things are done in accordance with His will. The apostle Paul also says this—that He is God, not only of the Jews, but also of the Gentiles (Rom. 9:24).

2. *Kerioth.* I think we must read this as a common noun, that is, this is simply "city."

Amid din. More accurately: "amid uproar."

And the sound of the trumpet. In jubilation. He has now finished his prophecies against the heathen. He is returning to what he had begun and is beginning to prophesy against Judah.

4. *For three transgressions of Judah.* He rebukes Judah, beginning with the source of all sins, namely, idolatry, which aban-

dons the true worship and Word of God. After all, he struggled with this wickedness perpetually. You see, abominable idolatry necessarily follows when we depart from the true Word of God—something we see not only here but in all Scripture.

And . . . His commandments. We read this more accurately as "statutes." We shall tell elsewhere what the difference is between commands and statutes. Now it is sufficient to make the following distinction: statutes are ceremonies having to do with God, but which nevertheless can be changed according to circumstances. In Psalm 2 there is a prophecy concerning Christ: that He was going to declare a statute or decree of God or an ordinance of God; He was going to declare a decree of God far different from those which were of the old covenant: namely, that He was the eternal Son of the Father; that He would rule; that He would be King of the entire world; that He would condemn whatever was born of human righteousness, even through the Law of God; that people would have to believe in Him; that they would have to worship Him, etc. The entire psalm has this tone, and says that otherwise we are going to lose the way of righteousness, etc.

Their idols have deceived them. More accurately: "Their lies [1] caused them to sin." He is giving the reason why they are going to be rejected: because they have followed the wicked ways of their wicked fathers; they have followed the lies with which their fathers had acted wickedly against God and which they themselves have kept on perpetuating in their wickedness. So does God in a very simple way want us to have respect only for His Word that we may not follow or approve those things which our fathers followed and approved; that those may become ashamed who today are setting up against the clear Word of God a host of ancestors and a length of time, when they see here that their sons are being charged with following the wickedness of their fathers. This is something the Lord also forbade in Lev. 18:30: "Keep My commandments. Don't do what those who came before you did, etc."

6. *For three transgressions of Israel.* Up to now the prophet has been digressing. He has been giving as it were a prelude to his

1 With the Zwickau and the Halle texts we have read *mendacia* for *idola.*

prophecy. Now he begins the real prophecy he has taken up against Israel. A summary of this entire passage is this: The prophet rebukes the wickedness of Israel and condemns the tyranny and incredible greed in it. He says that Israel sold a righteous man for silver and a poor man for a pair of shoes, that is, they have perverted their sense of justice. In passing judgment they have followed neither fairness nor legality. Rather, they have considered their own avarice. Thus they have not had consideration for the righteous. As a consequence, he must pass judgment on all who have abandoned their fear of God so that they have no respect for the ordinance of God or for human rights but are dedicated to satisfying their own personal cupidity and have completely surrendered themselves to greed, etc.

7. *They who trample . . . into the dust.* You read this more accurately as: "They devour . . . into dust." He is using the word "devour" to emphasize their wickedness and their penchant for perverting justice. It is as if he were saying: "They are reducing the poor to absolute nothingness as into dust. They make no favorable judgments for the orphan, the widow, and the poor, who already are quite miserable enough and the respect for whom I wanted to be considered. Instead, they have perverted their judgments in favor of the powerful aristocrats." This we read also in Hosea, and what follows is more of the same.

And turn aside the way of the humble. According to the Hebrew, it reads thus: "They twist or pervert the way of the afflicted." "Way" means business, personal affairs. The meaning is this: Up to now they have given no consideration to the poor as people whose "ways" they should have protected, whom they ought to support, who ought to be among the first to receive their concern. Not only have they neglected the poor; they have even oppressed them.

A son and his father, etc. Up to now he has been noting the tyranny and great greed of Israel. Now he also condemns their promiscuous lust, which he says was so great that both father and son had no fear of violating the same girl. Therefore they had no consideration for honor and chastity. This could have happened easily in that Judaic people who had girls as their own maids. They were like slaves whom they would abuse as they pleased.

So that My holy name is profaned. The sum of all their wickedness reaches this point, and all things fall back to this point: they are blaspheming and profaning the holy name of God. The name of God has been invoked upon us, that is, by grace we have become the sons of God, coheirs with Christ. In short, we are called by the same names with which God is called. So long as we believe, we are called righteous, holy, wise—even gods! The name of God, however, is blasphemed and corrupted because of us and through us when we walk unworthily, when we live and behave otherwise than befits Christians, when we are given over to wickedness and uncleanness.

8. *And upon garments taken in pledge.* Now he is again rebuking them for their greed. He is talking about goods unfairly acquired and about spoils extorted from the poor, and he says that, contrary to the Law, they have kept garments taken in pledge. You see, there was a provision in the Law that no one who had received a garment from a neighbor in debt to him should keep that pledge through the night if the man from whom he had received the pledge was poor.[2] But they had as much contempt for this law as they had for all the rest.

And in the house of their God they drink the wine of those who have been fined. They used to extort fines from the guilty, and these were unfair fines. Note the terrible wickedness of the priests. Priests who intended to enter the tabernacles had been absolutely forbidden to drink wine. This the Law demands.[3] But here he says that they were not content with the law of God but despised it. Instead, they drank wine which they had taken very unjustly, wine which they had illegally extorted. To such an extent was there utter lack of respect for what is good and godly. The sense is as if he were saying: "They have taken unjust fines with which to buy wine for themselves in order to live well. Of the garments of the poor given in pledge—garments which God had forbidden them to keep overnight—they have made fine beds for themselves to live in luxury and to indulge in their appetite very freely." These are strangely fiery and vehement words of the prophet. You see, he is not charging them with simple luxury and pomp. Rather, he is

[2] Cf. Deut. 24:12.

[3] Lev. 10:9.

saying that they are living well off the spoil taken unfairly from the poor and have forgotten all divine laws.

Here the question is why the prophet rebukes this profanation of the temple that Israel had, when he should rather have praised the profanation of the temples and practices of the wicked which were outside of the Word of God. You see, Israel did not have a temple established by the Word of God except Bethel. Furthermore, the only such temple built by the Word of God and at the ordinance of God was the one in Jerusalem. I answer: They sinned no less wickedly because they acted against conscience. After all, they thought that they had established this worship for the true God, not for idols. Therefore the prophet passes judgment on them in accord with their conscience. You see, much as that was not the true worship of God, much as that worship was established without the Word of God—and, in fact, contrary to the Word of God—and although they did not serve the true God; yet because their own conscience rebukes them, they are charged with ungodliness. Therefore, the prophet says:

In the house of their God. It is as if he were saying: "It was not the true God nor the true house of God." Yet because they thought that they were serving the true God but did not, they acted wickedly. Their neglect of that worship is as wicked as if they had done it to the true God. It is just the same as if one were to say about our sacrificing priests and monks: "They have taken vows of chastity and poverty and who knows what else, and yet no one is more given over to lust than they, they are very rich, and they live very luxuriously; therefore we can charge them with ungodliness as men who have not satisfied their own vows, which are wicked vows and against God because they cannot keep them. But because these men want to appear to keep them and do not keep them, they are wicked."

9. *Yet I destroyed the Amorite.* The Lord reproaches them for an excellent blessing and thus accuses them of ingratitude. They are like people who are not at all moved by His great and innumerable blessings to love God, to follow His Word. They have always experienced Him as their Protector and Father. With outstanding victories He had made them superior to all their enemies. He is saying, as it were: "So this is the thanks you give Me."

I destroyed . . . his root beneath, that is, "I have wiped him out completely—the old together with the young." Therefore He has wiped out and torn out by the roots the Amorites so that not even a single one of them lived and survived.

12. *But you made the Nazarites drink wine.* "It was not enough that you acted wickedly against My law and drank wine in My temple, but you also gave others the opportunity to sin against the Law, namely, when you gave the Nazarites wine to drink." This the Law forbids in Num. 6:3.

13. *Behold, I will creak beneath you.* This is a Hebrew figure of speech. It is as if He were saying: "Just as a cart groans beneath its load of straw, so I shall cause you to groan beneath the Assyrian chariots. That is, you will groan as you are crushed by the great burden and hardship. You who are so proud and haughty now will again be oppressed." This is what He means by saying "beneath you." It is an expression we cannot translate suitably in Latin.

14. *Flight shall perish from the swift.* He removes every protection. He threatens that He will take away everything in which they promise themselves safety and flight, every boldness and eagerness to escape. It is a Hebraism when He says, "Flight shall perish." David also used it in Ps. 142:4: "Flight perishes from me," that is, "I see no way to escape. I have lost every hope of escape. I will have to die, etc." So also here the Lord is threatening the same thing, as if to say: "I will surround you with such a force of enemies, with the might of others; I will send such a terror upon you that you cannot escape. The powerful leaders of your armies will lose hope. Their confidence in your future will disappear, and they will run away. Therefore, there will be no help for you. Your warriors, generals, bowmen, all your cavalry—they will lose every hope of victory." This is the end of the first discourse in this prophet. You see the prophets do not immediately give the whole prophecy. Another sermon follows.

CHAPTER THREE

THE occasion for and summary of this chapter, or the following address, is this: Very many people had been offended because of the prophet's preceding sermon. They were accusing the prophet of foolishness, of being a man who up to now had been not at all afraid of condemning everyone in the same breath and of accusing them of wickedness. Yet the king was good, and a majority of the people devout. Thus the good fortune of the king provided them with the opportunity to resist the prophet. Under this compulsion, then, the prophet returns and goes on energetically to condemn them, saying that the hypocrisy with which they had covered their wickedness would accomplish nothing. And so he begins:

1. *Hear this word that the Lord has spoken against you, etc.* The prophet himself gives the reason for this sermon, as if to say: "Let it be that the Lord has chosen you to be His people. Let it be that you are famous throughout the world—ennobled because of God's many works and blessings on your behalf. Let it be that He has not done the same for every nation. But you are not righteous just for that reason, because you are transgressors of the divine Law. Yet you go on pleasing yourselves with your own innocence. But I take it away and condemn it." The Divine Majesty always treats also us this way, as when we want to be good and holy. Before God we are wicked. He does not want sinners, because they are unwilling to acknowledge their sin. Rather, they swell with pride and convince themselves of their own saintliness. For this reason God rejects them. On the other hand, those who acknowledge their sin, although they may be great sinners, those who do not support their wickedness with some hypocrisy, they ask for and receive pardon. The Lord receives them. In fact, Christ came not to call the righteous, but sinners.[1] This we see here.

[1] Cf. Matt. 9:13.

2. *Therefore, I will punish you.* It is as if He were saying: "You think that I ought to spare you because you are My people. I will, however, punish you the more, that you may learn to know Me and to have faith in Me." Thus He also disciplines His saints whom He loves.[2] This is what Ezek. 9:6 says: "Begin at My sanctuary"; and 1 Peter 4:17: "For the time has come for judgment to begin with the household of God; and if it begins with us, what will be the end of those who do not believe the Gospel of God?" This is the way the puppy gets flogged so the wolfhound may live in fear.[3] God chastises His own children so that He may afflict even more severely the wicked who do not come to their senses, so that He may rage against them even more harshly.

3. *Will two walk together?* Jerome boldly passes by this passage. He can come to no decision as to its meaning. You see, the Hebrew word which we have here נוֹעָדוּ has various meanings: "they know," "they agree," also "they have come together." Some take it to apply to the king of the Assyrians and God, for God was going to send the king of the Assyrians against Israel. To me the text seems completely proverbial. The meaning may be this: Two people cannot walk together unless they are in harmony, unless they agree with each other. We apply the proverb this way: These two are God and His people. The Lord is saying, as it were: "You know from this that I am your adversary, that I am not standing at your side. In fact, we are not walking on the same road as we ought. I am not in agreement with you. Nevertheless, you want to escape unpunished. You are wicked and have transgressed the Law; yet you argue over your innocence. Therefore, because I am just, I will not spare your unrighteousness. I will not stop striking you until you agree with Me, which you now do not, for you are following a road that goes away from Me."

4. *Will the lion roar in the forest?* This has to do with the same point as the preceding verse. This, too, has the force of a proverb. It is as if the Lord were saying: "If a lion is hungry, he will roar in the presence of the prey that he will tear to pieces and with which he will satisfy his hunger. So I would cease roaring against you, I would not be your adversary if you were not wicked and evil,

[2] Cf. Heb. 12:6; Rev. 3:19.

[3] Cf. Juvenal, *Satires,* VI, 122.

if you were not giving Me an occasion for raging against you." We have a similar manner of speaking in Job 6:5: "Will the wild ass bray when he has grass?" Everything which follows is related to this point.

5. *Will a bird fall into a snare?* It is as if He were saying: "Because I am a Fowler, I have spread My nets. I am threatening you with harm. Because you are not fleeing the snares, because you go on acting wickedly, you will be caught. You will not be able to escape My judgment." What follows is the same.

Will a snare be taken away? This looks at the intent of a fowler rather than at his actual task. You see, a fowler can be tricked so that he catches nothing. Yet he stretches his net with this intent or purpose, that he catch something. "In this way," says the Lord, "I am not threatening you with harm in vain. I will capture you through the king of the Assyrians."

6. *If a trumpet sounds in a city.* It becomes more clear if you translate it this way: "Will a trumpet sound?" You see, the Latin translator obscured the meaning when he translated this as a condition. We must apply everything to the prophet's preachment, with which he warns them of a coming captivity unless they repent. He is saying, as it were: "When the trumpet blows, either an enemy is near or the city is on fire. Do not doubt also that harm against you will follow. After all, I do not accuse you rashly."

Does evil befall? He is arguing on the basis of the righteousness of God, just as Paul did in Rom. 9:14: "Is there unrighteousness [4] with God?" He is saying, as it were: "You ought to tremble and fear, but you keep on sinning against Me."

7. *Surely the Lord God does nothing.* That is, if something is going to happen, if harm threatens you, the Lord always makes this known through His prophets, whom He sends to predict a coming harm. So do not doubt that a great persecution remains for you, now that He has sent me." This is what I said at the beginning of this prophet [5]—that the prophets were sent to warn the people of God's plan before a great upheaval should follow.

[4] The Weimar text has *iustitia,* but we have read *iniustitia* on the basis of the Vulgate text, which has *iniquitas* in Rom. 9:14.

[5] Cf. p. 127 above.

8. *The lion will roar; who will not fear?* He goes on to strengthen his earlier sermon against the wicked, self-righteous hypocrites, who have convinced themselves of their own holiness, as we said at the beginning of this chapter. Confident, therefore, of their own privilege, they thought that the prophet was either lying or crazy. So he is again warning them of the wrath and anger of the Lord. He says that it will come to pass that they will perish by the judgment of God unless they repent; that the Lord is roaring and directing harm against them; that He is threatening them with captivity, etc.

9. *Proclaim to the strongholds in Ashdod.* He is comparing the surrounding nations with the people of God so that the latter may become confounded and ashamed of their own wickedness when they see that they surpass even the heathen. It is as if the prophet were saying: "Look, you heathen who live around us! Gather to us. Make a test whether we can be compared with you. The people who want to be called God's people surpass in wickedness you who do not worship the true God." This is how nearly all the prophets almost justify the heathen in a comparison with wicked Israel. Ezekiel writes this way in chapter 16:48: "Your sister Sodom and her daughters have not done as you and your daughters have done." We have the same thing also in Jeremiah (cf. Jer. 23:14).

Assemble yourselves upon the mountain of Samaria. Here he is declaring the wickedness of Israel, of which he has also spoken earlier. He is saying: "In this realm, there is no administration of justice, no civil government; nor is there any limit to greed and ostentation." Isaiah rebukes the same sin in chapter 2:7: "The land is filled with silver and gold, and there is no end to their treasures." This sin—the wicked tyranny of the princes—almost all the prophets condemn in this people.

10. *They do not know how to do right*, that is, "They are so far from being good and devout that they even lack common sense. They became as stupid as unthinking cattle."

11. *An adversary shall surround the land.* The meaning is: "You steal the substance of the poor. Your greed knows no limit; but on the other hand, the judgment of God awaits you. You will be taken captive. All your goods and marks of distinction, your kingdom and your priesthood, will be taken away from you."

And bring down your defenses from you. This word "defenses" in Scripture is often taken to mean "kingdom," just as we must take it here and in many psalms.

12. *As the shepherd rescues.* God does not become angry the way people become angry. Indeed, people hold such bitterness against those whom they hate that they would prefer them to be destroyed completely rather than have them survive for one hour. This anger is worst in those who persecute the Word. Isaiah describes this anger.[6] But no matter how much God may rage, He is angry and strikes out in such a way that a remnant remains safe nevertheless. Here we see the same thing. He is threatening them with terrible captivity, destruction, and plundering of all their property. He says that the Lord will sweep over them by the hand of the king of Assyrians, so that clearly all of them will seem to be swept away. Yet a handful will survive, lest absolutely all of them perish. The prophet certainly is using a harsh and terrible simile, with which he wants to reveal the wretchedness of their captivity. Because this prophet is a shepherd familiar with the countryside, he takes his similes from those situations with which he is most familiar—from flocks, cows, etc. The meaning of this simile, then, is this: Just as a bone or a piece of a sheep's ear snatched from the mouth of a lion is not to be compared—in fact, is nothing—over against all the rest of the body that has been devoured, so also the king of Assyria will devour you. Yet I will keep a very few unharmed, lest the Israelites perish completely. The prophet Isaiah, who is more elegant than this rustic from Tekoa, uses a more pleasant simile also in this sense in chapter 65:8: "As the wine is found in the cluster, and they say, 'Do not destroy it, for there is a blessing in it,' so I will do for My servants' sake and not destroy them all." The prophets are full of passages of this kind.

In a bed curtain. Here even the Jews themselves do not agree about this expression. I translate it "on a corner of a bed and on a couch of Damascus." We must take a guess, however, as to its meaning. I am quite sure that we must apply this to the tribe of Judah. He is calling the kingdom of Israel a "bed." He says that they are indulging their appetite on this bed—that is, in this peace-

[6] The Zwickau text here refers to Isaiah's chapter on the vineyard, Is. 5.

ful and wonderful kingdom. I also take the couch of Damascus to refer to the kingdom. The sense of the prophet, then, is this: Only one corner of the bed will be saved. All the rest of it will be destroyed. Some portion of the people—and this a very small one—must be saved, and all the rest will be destroyed. A few remnants of both Damascus and Samaria will survive. That it did happen this way we know from the sacred accounts. After the Assyrian army had destroyed the Israelites, a very few remained who had joined themselves to Judah and had a devout heart. Just as not all who were of Israel were frequent sinners, so also not all were taken away and destroyed. Because this meaning of mine agrees with history, I like it.

13. *Hear and testify, etc.* He is explaining the statement above. He says, as it were: "They have established in their own judgment a distinguished worship of God. In Bethel they have a rich and fat priesthood. They indulge their appetite extravagantly. They live in great luxury. They have homes in which to spend the winter. The ones in which they live in summer they build at very great expense. They rest securely. The time, however, will come when I shall punish their priesthood, temple and sacred objects. That's when the priests and monasteries will go to pieces." This is the way the prophets everywhere describe the opulence of the false prophets and the wicked priests. Such people must abound in every good thing. Meanwhile, the genuine prophets have no honor. They hunger and thirst; the others lack nothing.

CHAPTER FOUR

HE is addressing those wicked women of the impious. He calls them "fat cows." After all, this sex is much too weak to be able rightly to use prosperous situations which even otherwise generally weary the minds of even the wise. Isaiah in chapter 3:16 also speaks in this sense: "Because the daughters of Zion are haughty and walk with outstretched necks, glancing wantonly with their eyes, etc." This is the way he is speaking here, too, about the wives of bishops, priests, and princes, to whom the goods of the poor are prey.

1. *You fat cows,* that is, "you rich and powerful women among the people. You become a cause for wickedness to your own husbands. Your greed is insatiable. Your luxurious ostentation knows no limit." (You see, this class by nature has a tendency to be given over to such things unless fear is added.) Here is what he adds:

Who say to your lords, that is, "to your husbands."

Bring, that we may drink. More accurately, this reads "that we may feast, that we may live in splendid luxury." Therefore, "Because you seek this one thing, the Lord has sworn by His Holy One,[1] or by His holiness, that He is going to lead the king of Assyria over you. You will become his prey. He will sacrifice you like fat cows."

2. *And who will carry you away with hooks.* Again he is using similes from the countryside. It is as if he were saying: "Just as we generally carry the meat we have slaughtered attached to a spit or a pole, so he will carry you away with a wretched captivity."

And your remnants. This reads more accurately "your remnant,

[1] According to the Zwickau manuscript, this means "by Himself." Cf. W, XIII, 135, 16.

the last of you," that is, your home, your sons and daughters, with whom you are now living luxuriously—even those the king of the Assyrians will carry off.

In boiling pots, or in a fisherman's boiling kettle. They will perish wretchedly along with you in captivity.

3. *And you will go out through the breaches, one before the other . . . into Harmon.* "You will not go out by a direct road, but through the broken walls wherever you can. For so it will come to pass that those of you who now sit securely within well-fortified walls will flee when the Assyrian comes. He will tear down the walls and ramparts and throw you out of the city through those breaches. He will have no consideration for your dignity. Rather, as you fall into his hand, he will make you get out of the city. He will drive you forth. He will drive you out before him as the cowherd drives cattle."

Harmon. The interpreters believe that this means some high mountain or Armenia or who knows what. That, however, is nothing. It doesn't stir me. I am content with the simplicity of the account. Therefore, as he named the city Kir earlier in chapter 1:5, so here we must take this to mean a place or region in Assyria to which the Israelites were taken as captives. For as I mentioned earlier how the Israelites were not carried off into Syria, so here they were not carried off into Armenia, but to the Medes and Persians.

4. *Come to Bethel and transgress; to Gilgal.* Those two places, Gilgal and Bethel, are famous and well known, for in these places the people kept trying to emulate the priesthood of Judah. They established a most elaborate worship of God there, although it was contrary to the Word of God. This passage, then, is a sort of sharp and bitter concession by irony. He is saying, as it were: "I condemn that wicked worship. I always forbid you to depart from the worship established through My Word. But you hold Me in utter contempt and go on behaving wickedly. But go ahead! Continue!—as if you were not already wicked enough before. Yes, yes, just continue." So it happens in the case of all the wicked that when they want to be righteous, when they think that they are behaving well, they sin the more seriously in the judgment of God.

Bring your sacrifices, etc. This also runs out to sarcasm. This prophet was a very brave man. He was not afraid to condemn and reject even those works done for the true God which appeared to be very great and very good.

Every three days. Here I follow the meaning which Lyra gives. It is as if the prophet were saying: "You have established a worship of God, you strive to rival Judah which has the law of God to appear before the Lord three times each year, as the Law says. You also follow the same rule. You come together and preach and thus multiply your wickedness, for you are doing this without the Word of God and without faith. These things are your own inventions. Therefore you are laughing at God, and God is laughing at you. Nothing has any value before God except what He Himself institutes."

5. *Offer a sacrifice of praise of that which is leavened.* According to the Hebrew this reads, "Burn." There were different kinds of sacrifices: burnt offerings, peace offerings, offerings made in connection with vows, and voluntary offerings which would be made in thanksgiving. Therefore a more accurate translation here would be "a sacrifice of praise." [2] You see, they used to make such sacrifices for certain blessings as an act of thanksgiving, as we have it in Moses (cf. Lev. 7:12). So he has taken this passage from Moses and says, as it were: "Go ahead, kindle your sacrifice, you great priests who use leavened material in your sacrifice, about which the Law wants us to be very careful." Or (to treat this as irony) he is here again taking note of their wicked imitation of the Law, although they were doing everything contrary to the Law. There was one place that God had prescribed where He wanted to be worshiped. Also, they used leavened bread in their peace offerings, according to Lev. 7:13.

And proclaim freewill offerings. Wherever the word "proclaim" appears, Paul has translated it with the word "preach." This is the way we should render it in this passage. It is as if the prophet were saying: "With this preaching of yours, you are inviting your people to your own wickedness which you have established." "Freewill" means voluntary. This is legal terminology taken from Moses, for in the Law certain sacrifices would come under this name. We have

[2] That is, "sacrifice of praise" would be better than "praise" alone, as in the Vulgate.

the following in Ps. 119:108: "Accept the freewill offerings of my mouth, O Lord."

6. *Consequently I gave you cleanness of teeth.* He is saying, as it were: "I cannot draw you away from that wickedness. I am accomplishing nothing with the tribulations I give you, no matter how many and great they may be. Therefore I am forced finally to reject you completely. I accomplished nothing with famine, nothing with pestilence, nothing with thirst, nothing with failure of crops. For whenever you should have returned to Me—for that is why I chastised you—you always returned to that worship of yours, although it is an abomination to Me." Furthermore, we have here a metaphor of the Hebrew language which is rather farfetched. We cannot render it in our own words. The literal Hebrew reads as follows: "I have given you cleanness, or inactivity, of teeth," that is, "You had eaten nothing for a long time. I had sent you a famine, but you continued to sin." You see, whenever the Lord chastised the Jews, they thought that the reason was that they had neglected worship at Bethel. Actually, the Lord's plan was to chastise them so that they would recognize their error and would flee to Him to obtain forgiveness. So we, too, struggle with equal wickedness. When the Lord becomes angry and sends us some evil, we establish processions around our fields to pray for a good harvest, we celebrate many Masses, although in doing so we provoke the Lord more seriously. The same thing also happens annually when we have to do battle with the Turk. As a consequence, it happens that the Turk is always superior to us.[3] This is the same thing I have said before: Whenever the wicked think that they are behaving well, they fall into worse sins.

7. *One part would be rained upon.* This means a field, for in the Hebrew a field is called a portion, because the fields were allotted to each city.

8. *And two or three cities came.* The Hebrew reads "would totter." He means the movement and going to and fro of a thirsting people.

9. *I laid waste a multitude.* This means the supply of all fruits. You see the same thing in Hosea (cf. Hos. 2:12).

[3] Cf. p. 88, n. 1, above.

10. *I sent among you death.* More accurately this reads "I sent among you a pestilence." I do not know where or when this episode occurred.

I carried away your horses to captivity. According to the Hebrew, this reads "in captivity."

11. *I overthrew you, as when God overthrew, etc.* One can read this either as a subjunctive or as an indicative. The meaning is the same, as I said earlier in chapter 3:12 about the remnant that was saved. "I have caused you to be overthrown and afflicted with misery, to be led away and treated with contempt. Yet, some tiny remnant has been rescued. A very small part has been saved, lest Israel perish completely. Although I afflicted you very much with great wretchedness, yet you have not reversed yourselves in striking out at Me, namely, the Lord your God." But he uses a simile according to his custom: "Just as one single brand, kindled and taken from the fire must not be compared with the burning of the entire house; so also that remnant of you is not compared with the entire people." In this way, too, as the Lord is about to justify us, He deals with us, terrifies and so shames our consciences that we believe that it is all over with us, as if He intended to condemn us eternally. Yet, He always leaves us some hope, lest we utterly lose hope. He snatches us away like a brand from the fire. This passage and similar ones, then, have been written both to terrify and to comfort. They terrify those who have a stiff neck and persevere obstinately in their own righteousness. They comfort the humble and afflicted who recognize their sin. Blessed is the man who understands this.

12. *Therefore thus I will do to you, O Israel.* Some people want to assume that something has been left out here, so that the meaning is this: "Up to now I have done this to you. I go on to do still more." I do not approve of this meaning. After all, why should the Lord add this to those whom He had already overthrown like Sodom before and whom He had overthrown in such a way that a very tiny remnant was barely saved like a bone of a lamb snatched from the lion's mouth or a brand from a fire? The meaning I take is this: The Lord is saying, as it were: "O Israel, you think that you have a God who is kindly disposed to you. You seek and invoke Him in Bethel contrary to the Law. But take a look at Me. I am the

One who is persecuting you, and I am doing that so that you should return to Me and prepare yourselves to meet Me. But you are not doing this."

To meet Me. Here again the translators differ. The sense of the Septuagint is beautiful, but the grammar of the text militates against it. This passage applies to the same point as many others in the prophets, as that in Ezek. 13:5: "You have not gone up into the breaches or built up a wall for the house of Israel that it might stand in battle in the day of the Lord"; also, Ezek. 22:30: "And I sought for a man among them who should . . . stand in the breach before Me for the land that I should not destroy it; but I found none"; also Is. 64:7: "There is no one who bestirs himself to take hold of Thee, there is no one that calls upon Thy name." So also here the sense is the same. He is saying, as it were: "With those blows with which I struck you I wanted you to return to Me, to meet Me, to come ahead of My wrath and set yourselves before Me, lest I continue to wreak vengeance. But you are clearly doing the opposite." Everything agrees with what has gone before when He constantly repeats, "And you did not return to Me."

13. *For, lo, He who forms the mountains.* He is declaring the greatness of His power. "Why is it," He says, "that you flee for refuge to idols or to human protection, when you ought to be fearing Me, for you know I create all things and can cause them to perish? I am the Creator of all the finest things; night, day, life-giving air—these all come from Me. You are fools—you who think that you are going to escape My hand. I am so powerful that I hold all things in My hands. Once I have taken hold of someone, there is no one who can take him away." In this way He sets His omnipotence against their wicked obstinacy. He also speaks in a similar vein in Is. 51:15: "I am the Lord . . . who stirs up the sea, etc."

And creates the wind. I take this to mean spirit or breath. It is as if He were saying: "To this extent you are not able to slip out of My hands when I plan to take vengeance on you, that you even have your life-giving spirit from Me. When I take that away, you cannot live even for a moment."

Who gives to man His own eloquence. I explain this as follows: He gives man the power to speak. His Divine Majesty belongs so properly to us that He even gives us the words which we are going to utter. You see, the Hebrew word properly means this. When Scripture speaks about the eloquence of God or the Word of God, it uses the word אֵמֶר or דָּבָר.

Who makes the morning darkness, that is, "You still do not fear the Lord, who can take from you the day, without which you cannot get along."

And treads on the heights of the earth. Whatever on earth is great and lofty is subject to Him. Because of the literal meaning, one may play around with allegories here with little trouble. The Lord forms the mountains; that is, every power, every dominion, comes from Him. As He wishes, it yields and is subject to Him, just as He says, "And treads on the heights of the earth." He also makes the dawn and the day and the clouds—that is, the good weather. According to His will, our affairs prosper. Again according to His will, all things become unsuccessful and upset.

CHAPTER FIVE

EARLIER, at the beginning of the third chapter, I said that the prophets did not complete these books of prophecies or sermons in a single year. Also, they did not make all their prophecies in one year. Here, too, we have another sermon that the prophet held in another year. Its meaning is the same as that of his earlier ones. Everything comes back to the same point, except that in each sermon he uses different words and different ways of speaking. You see, these books of the prophets are nothing else than sermons.

1-2. *Hear this word, O house of Israel, for I take up over you a lamentation: Fallen, no more to rise, is the virgin Israel.* "I take up over you" is a common Hebraism in all the prophets. When they call the Word of the Lord "the burden," the prophets are announcing an evil which is going to come to oppress the people. So they give the Word the title "burden." After all, the prophets were troublesome, hateful, burdensome people, announcing as they did nothing but a burden—destruction of regions, the threatening wrath of God. Paul (along with all preachers of the Word) says, "The wrath of God is revealed from heaven against all ungodliness, etc." (Rom. 1:18). The flesh is unwilling to bear this preaching which is harsh and oppressive in appearance, for it relies on its own righteousness and thinks that it does not deserve punishment. But the prophets threaten temporal ill, lest we be forced to endure an eternal one if we do not repent. We also have the same expression in this passage, when he says, "I take up over you." We cannot accurately reproduce this Hebrew phrase in Latin.

Fallen . . . is the virgin Israel. Israel had been betrothed to the one God because of the Word of God and because of faith in the Word, which kept their souls chaste. He is saying, however, that Israel has fallen or will fall, that she would be destroyed and devastated by the king of the Assyrians. Thus the prophet is placing before their eyes the evil which was going to befall them as if it were happening now or had already happened. This is the custom of the prophets. He is not speaking about virginity, as translators—and with them Jerome—mistakenly think.

No more to rise. This is what Hosea prophesies in chapter 1:6: "I will no more have pity on the house of Israel, but I will utterly forget them." [1] You see, they were so ruined and scattered that they were never brought back to their own kingdom. This we have in the sacred accounts.

On her land. She will lie desolate and deserted, and only a very small remnant will survive. This handful, however, is not to be compared with those who will be rejected and who will perish. Scarcely ten percent will survive, as we see from what follows.

3. *The city from which a thousand used to go forth, etc.* This is the same as what he said earlier about the remnant who were going to be saved like a legbone snatched from the lion's mouth and a brand snatched from the fire.[2] Here he is speaking clearly and without figurative language. It is as if He were saying: "They will be devastated in most wretched fashion. Yet a very small handful will survive."

4. *Seek Me.* Now the Lord begins a very gentle admonition and warning. He is saying, as it were: "Seek Me! Me! I am the One who is striking out at you," as He said earlier.[3] "I, too, will be able to heal. Why do you run to your wicked worship at Bethel? Run back to Me!" The Lord always keeps one eye on Bethel, as He immediately adds. We seek the Lord, not with outward works or an external hypocrisy, but as we have it in the psalm (cf. Ps. 119: 2, 10), we must seek Him with a whole heart. The heart does not require an external rending of clothes, as Joel 2:13 says: "Rend your hearts, etc." We also read in Is. 21:12: "If you seek the Lord, seek; turn and come back."

And you will live. This is a Hebraism which we translate in

[1] According to the Vulgate.

[2] Amos 3:12.

[3] Amos 4:9.

Latin[4] as well as we can in this way: "Things will go well with you." This Hebraism is a common one in Scripture. We have it in Ps. 142:5: "My Portion in the land of the living." It is also in Hezekiah's song in Is. 38:11: "I said, I shall not see the Lord in the land of the living,"—that is, in a land where everything prospers and turns out well.

5. *To Beersheba.* This people had the same foolish wickedness which our people have, who have built a temple or an altar in honor of the saints wherever the saints lived or did something. The people of Judah reflected exactly the same madness. Jacob had been at Bethel, they had been circumcised at Gilgal,[5] and Abraham had lived at Beersheba. Therefore they picked out these locations as places holier than others and there established some sort of worship of God. The Lord, however, did not want us to imitate the deeds of the saints, but their faith. This is something which He always teaches in the Law: "Observe what I command you" (Ex. 34:11), as if to say: "Not what I did with the saints." Because the holy prophets taught such things, they were considered heretics—wicked men who were forbidding the worship of God. The prophets, however, were doing this completely and simply to call Israel back from works to the Word alone. This is something we, too, must do; but as the prophets then were despised and killed as evil-speakers, so also the same thing happens to us, etc.

Bethel shall come to nought. She will be in אָוֶן. Here we have the word אָוֶן, which I mentioned earlier.[6] The prophet has used it here in its germane and native sense, as it is also used in Ps. 90:10: "Their span is but toil and trouble." So also here: "Bethel will be in אָוֶן," that is, "As you have performed your wicked righteousness at Bethel and as a result were unhappy and disturbed, so the Lord will bring the same thing to pass for you: [He will turn] Bethel into Bethaven,[7] that is, you will have trouble and misery on account of it. This Bethel will become for you an occasion for a very great evil."

[4] *Bene habebitis* for the *vivetis* of the Vulgate text.

[5] The Weimar text has Gilead, but we have read Gilgal in view of Joshua 5:9.

[6] Cf. pp. 67 and 69 above.

[7] "House of God" into "House of Trouble."

6. *The house of Joseph.* The kingdom of Israel is at times called the house of Joseph or of Samaria or of Israel. The prophets also call it Mount Ephraim, the house of Ephraim, etc.

7. *O you who turn justice to wormwood.* These two words [justice and wormwood] Scripture always joins together. But this passage is taken from Moses in Deut. 29:18: "Lest there be among you a root bearing poisonous and bitter fruit." The author of the Epistle to the Hebrews has also quoted this passage (Heb. 12:15), and so has Acts 8:23. The idea is this: "Secure in your own righteousness, you despise God, whom you ought to fear. Therefore, what otherwise is very sweet you turn into bitter poison for yourselves and others."

8. *The Pleiades.* Here the Jews contrive various things, but they are not certain. Let us make a stab at it, too. The prophet surely aims at this point that, just as before, he again places the power of God in opposition to the wicked despisers. What follows also indicates this.

And darkens the day into night. It is as if He were saying: "The gods whom you are seeking in Bethel and Gilgal and Beersheba will not help you. In vain do you run back to them, as you take them your substance and call upon them. I am Lord and Creator of all things. Come to Me, and you will live."

Who calls for the waters of the sea. This is what the psalmist says (Ps. 147:8): "He covers the heavens with clouds, He prepares rain for the earth." When He intends to give rain, He causes the clouds to ascend [8] from the sea, as we see from the account of Elijah, etc.[9]

9. *Who smiles at destruction.* This has been translated very poorly.[10] In the Hebrew it goes this way: "who confirms destruction." It is the same word [11] which we have in Ps. 39:13: "That I may be refreshed before I depart and be no more." The translators differ strangely. The prophet seems to me to be speaking completely figuratively, so that "to confirm destruction" is the same

[8] For *descendere* we have read *ascendere,* as in the Halle manuscript.

[9] Cf. 1 Kings 18:44.

[10] That is, in the Vulgate's *qui subridet vastitatem.*

[11] בָּלַג.

thing as to bring on with powerful violence a destruction that nothing can resist.

Against the strong. More accurately: "against power or the kingdom and authority *(Gewalt)*," as in Ps. 62:11: "Power belongs to God." All things are subject to Him. All things are in His hand. There is no force or power so great that it can resist Him, in fact, that does not come from Him, just as the prophet said earlier.

10. *They hate him who reproves in the gate.* Where the court is, where the judges sit and senates pass judgments—this the Jews call "the gate." The meaning here is this: "Those wicked people do not wish to be censured in a gathering of people, in public, in the assembly." So too, our own princes and bewitched bishops turn away from the Word of God with a sin that causes their wickedness to become obvious to the common people, etc.

Who speaks the truth. We have the same expression [12] in Ps. 119:1: "Blessed are they whose way is blameless," that is, blessed are those who are sound in their way. Paul interpreted it in this way (cf. 2 Tim. 1:13). They were unwilling to endure those whose doctrine was sound, whose love and faith were sound. We daily have the same experiences; wickedness cannot bear sound doctrine.

11. *Therefore, because you trampled.* After a very friendly exhortation, he adds a warning by means of another parable. He laments that which he has always lamented before, namely, that the sum of all wickedness is lack of faith toward God and violence against one's neighbor.

You trampled. More accurately: "You burden, you oppress the poor and impose burdens on them. They are not up to bearing those burdens. You husk the wretched masses, you demand intolerable taxes. You erode their goods legally and illegally."

Exactions of precious goods. That is, "Whatever good things the poor have you take for yourselves. Their good fields, farms, gardens you make your own through plundering and tyrannical greed." Let the pope and his men, and let our princes—those takers and devourers of the poor—give thought to this, if they have ever forced

[12] תָּמִים.

some poor man to pay as tribute his good field or anything that he has.

Pleasant vineyards. These are desirable vineyards. This is a very common word both with the prophets and in the Psalms: Beautiful, inviting, pretty vineyards.

12. *For I know how many are your transgressions.* When He uses this word "I know," He is indicating both their and His state of mind. It is as if He were saying: "You are very savage to the poor. You oppress as if I would neither see nor know it. But I see it well. I fix My eyes on the poor. Nothing of all the things you do is hidden from Me, much as I may temporarily make believe [I don't see]. This is what blinds you." We have this also in Ps. 10:11: "The wicked say, 'God has forgotten. He has hidden His face lest He see at the end.'" We read in Ezek. 8:12: "The Lord does not see us. The Lord has forsaken the land." The same thing is found in Ezek. 9:9. In Is. 29:15 we have: "Who sees us? Who knows us?"

13. *Therefore he who is prudent will keep silent in such a time.* To this, all of Ps. 11 pertains: "For lo, the wicked bend the bow, they have fitted their arrow to the string, to shoot in the dark at the upright in heart; if the foundations are destroyed, what can the righteous do?" Let him perish who does not want to be saved. Let him who is filthy continue to be filthy.

It is an evil time. He calls it an evil time because evil people are in the majority.

14. *And the Lord of hosts will be with you, as you have said.* This is an anticipation. The wicked Jews did not recognize their own ungodliness. They kept protecting themselves with the promises of God: that they were the people of God; that the Lord had promised that He would be in the midst of them; and that the Lord had not done the same for every nation. Therefore they were accusing as liars the holy prophets who were announcing that the wrath of God was going to come. They charged them as men who were speaking against the law of God and against the promises of God. Micah described the voices of this kind of wickedness beautifully in chapter 2:6-7: "'Do not preach'—thus they preach—'one should not preach of such things; disgrace will not overtake us.'

Should this be said, O house of Jacob? Is the Spirit of the Lord impatient? Are these His doings, etc.?" Here the prophet Amos washes away all these wicked voices when he says, "Seek good and not evil, etc." It is as if he were saying: "The Lord has promised that He would be with you, but only with you who are devout, who will have kept what He has commanded you." Micah also adds (Micah 2:7): "Do not My words do good to him who walks uprightly?"

16. *In all the squares there shall be wailing.* With a quite harsh transition, he passes over to a threat and says, as it were: "Because you do not pass right judgment, you will fall into a fearsome judgment. All places will be filled with wailing—all your streets and squares. Not only will the city dwellers weep, but the farmers, too," as it now follows:

And to wailing those who are skilled in lamentation. It is as if He were saying: "I will cause a general grief throughout the entire kingdom so that whoever can wail will wail. So great will the wretchedness be that there will be no one who is not sorry to be alive. Both old and young will wail, all that can."

17. *In the vineyards,* that is, among the vinedressers. "In the ways" is a bad reading.[13]

For I will pass through the midst of you, that is, "when I shall have trod you under and struck you down in My anger, as I struck down Egypt."

18. *Woe to you who desire the day of the Lord!* He is speaking this against the stubborn who despise his preaching, who kept accusing the prophet of lies and foolishness, who kept scorning him and saying that all such things which he was preaching would not come to pass. About such people we read in 2 Peter 3:4: "Saying, 'Where is the promise of His coming? For ever since the fathers fell asleep, all things have continued as they were from the beginning of creation.'" Just as the wicked since the beginning of the world did not believe the promises of God, so they also despised His threats until they utterly perished without thinking about such things. Our wicked priests do exactly the same thing today, too. In their complete smugness they blithely despise the

[13] *In viis* for *in vineis* in the Vulgate.

Word of God now again revealed to the world in His great goodness. They laugh at those who threaten them with evil and destruction. They talk like this: "This thing about the clergy is temporary. The situation will change. The time will come when all such things will cease and the priests will have the very best reputation." They are in the same condemnation in which the wicked Jews were whom Amos mentions here and to whom Peter referred.

The day of the Lord is darkness and not light. "Day of the Lord" he calls the whole time of that affliction which he is prophesying. As I have said before,[14] day [15] means good fortune to the Jews—a time when everything is successful and happy. This is a common figure everywhere in the Psalms. He is saying, then, that all successful things will be unsuccessful and filled with sorrow.

19. *As if a man fled from the face of a lion.* Now He is threatening a terrible death to those despisers. It is as if He were saying: "Go ahead! Completely despise the Word of the Lord! You are secure. You think that it will not come to pass that you will fall into the coming evil. But that is why it will be impossible for you not to be destroyed, as it is impossible for a man to escape who flees from a lion and meets a bear. Therefore you will be unable to escape. When you become confident that you are going to get away, you run into the midst of evil. I will remove all of your protection." Today our clergy are going to consider as enemies the very princes to whom they are fleeing for refuge. Obviously they are looking for genuine protection against the God whom they are fleeing.

21. *I hate, I despise your feasts.* Here again, as if by anticipation, He responds to them because they undoubtedly thought that worship of God Almighty which they had established and considered of the highest value was very pleasing to God, inasmuch as they sang many hymns, did much sacrificing, and built great temples. They set up all these as objections to the prophets, just as our wicked people today set up as their objections to us their expensive cathedrals and their hymns of praise. The prophet responds: "I hate and despise all these things. Even your most hallowed activities displease Me, because you are wicked and do everything

[14] Cf. p. 156 above.

[15] The Zwickau manuscript has "light" instead of "day."

with a wicked heart." We see the same thing in great detail in Is. 1. So Scripture and the Spirit in Scripture totally condemn everything the wicked do, everything they establish, with which they believe they are pleasing God and with which they think they have followed the works of the Law. But their heart is wicked and faithless. This is what is said in Prov. 21:27: "The sacrifice of the wicked is an abomination"; and in 1 Sam. 15:22: "To obey is better than sacrifice." If such works, so holy in the sight of the Jews, who were the people of God and had the Word of God, are condemned as works done outside of faith, what about the insolence with which our wicked papists strut around in their foolish, frigid works?

I take no delight in your solemn assemblies. Moses adds this expression to all sacrifices, saying that the sacrifices of the righteous would be a sweet fragrance to the Lord, as we can see everywhere. But here He is clearly condemning the sacrifices of the wicked, saying that He will not receive their fragrance, that is: "When you come together to sacrifice, I will not receive the fragrance, I will not accept your sacrifices. They will be a stench to Me."

22. מִנְחָה. These are cereal offerings, *Speiseopfer,* which they would always add to the burnt offerings.

And the peace offerings of your fatted beasts. That is, "Nothing will please Me, regardless of what you may have offered. I will not accept the peace offerings you sacrifice, regardless of their fatness, even if you may have offered your fattest."

23. [*Take away from Me the noise*] *of your songs.* Here we also see that they used to sing, but just as he thinks that everything else is wicked, so he also condemns their songs or chants. This surely is great boldness on the part of the prophet, who dared to condemn works that appeared to be so very holy. Yet, those prophets who kept condemning such practices were killed as wicked men, perverters of the Law, who forbade the worship of God. So, too, today we are forced to have the same objections thrown up against us. The Lord, however, wants people to worship Him in faith. The wicked do not please the Lord, regardless of how great and splendid their works may be.

24. *But let justice roll down like water.* Here, after the threat, he has blended in the kingdom of Christ. This is a transition. It is as if he were saying: "Why is it that you boast of your sacrifices, peace offerings, and all such? There will come a time when all those external ceremonies will cease and righteousness will roll down in a great supply." It seems to me, then, that he is speaking about the Gospel which is going to be revealed through Christ. After all, "to be revealed" means to be preached and manifested—and that had not yet occurred. So here he is passing over from the worship he has censured to the true worship which pleases God. This, you see, is the custom of all the prophets; when they intend to set forth genuine righteousness through Christ, they condemn all the works of the faithless, even those which appear to be very holy. We have the same thing in Ps. 40:6: "Sacrifice and offering Thou dost not desire, but ears Thou hast finished for me." So when he says "like water," he is indicating an abundance of grace that is to be declared through the Gospel. We also have similar passages in Isaiah.[16]

Like an everflowing stream. He is signifying the power and efficacy of the Word. You see, the Word bursts forth and runs even when the madness of Satan and its foes stand in its way. Whether the princes are willing or not, it breaks through like a stream. They are unable to hold it back.

25. *Did you bring to Me sacrifices and offerings?* Stephen cites this passage in Acts 7:42 but in different words. Yet he hit the sense beautifully, as all the apostles have a way of doing when they cite the statements of the prophets. But what shall we say to this passage which militates against many other passages of Scripture? After all, it is very clear that not everyone in that people was wicked. Scripture here and there bears witness of this, as does Balaam in Num. 23:21-23: "For there is no enchantment against Jacob, no divination is seen against Israel: the Lord their God is with them." There he praises the people wonderfully for their great devotion, so that some interpreters are offended and disturbed here in various ways. But here is the harmony: In Holy Writ we must especially watch for and take note of the figure of speech which grammarians call synecdoche, so that both things

[16] Cf. Is. 48:18.

are being said about the same people. So this passage, too, must be understood. Thus in Ps. 78:18 [17] the psalmist rebukes them for their wickedness and accuses them of unbelief because they asked for food. He says, "They tested God in their heart, by demanding the food, etc." In another psalm [18] he commends the same sin, saying that their demand for food was made in devotion. Thus from a single episode of history we get differing and contrary meanings. But as I have said, this is a case where the Word of God takes a look at an entire people and yet also divides it into two parts. After all, there undoubtedly were among them some devout people whom it does not rebuke when it mentions idols. Also, on the other hand, it makes an exception of the wicked when it mentions godliness and the true worship of God which the devout followed with Moses. Those people were wicked who kept muttering for their food. Yet food was given because of the faithful. Therefore both ideas are true. Because of that testing those were condemned who did not believe, but the godly were saved—because of whom the food was given. This is how we must understand this passage in Amos: There were many godly people in Jacob who did not worship idols. He is not speaking about these, although he makes mention of Jacob. But the greater part was wicked. It is their idolatry which he rebukes. They committed many wicked acts which the Lord meanwhile endured, as we read in Ps. 95:10: "For forty years, etc." See also Heb. 3:8-12. Here he is accusing them of idolatry and says, as it were; "You are like your fathers. Your fathers sinned against God with their abominable idolatry, and you are pursuing the same wickedness. Therefore He will overthrow and take away from you everything in which you trust—all your righteousness—and you will be carried away."

The star of your god. What this star was we are unable to determine from Scripture.[19]

[17] The Weimar and Erlangen Texts have "Ps. 11," but the Zwickau manuscript has the reference obviously intended, "Ps. 77," which in our reckoning becomes Ps. 78.

[18] Cf. Ps. 105:40.

[19] Cf. Acts. 7:43: "The star of the god Rephan."

CHAPTER SIX

THE prophet continues to declare the captivity to come, which he has continually threatened earlier. Here he again begins another discourse, in which he includes at the same time the two tribes—those which were in Samaria as well as those in Israel. He prophesies that they are all going to be laid waste and carried off by the Assyrian. We shall remain with this simple meaning, that we understand this as the Babylonian captivity, not that last captivity, as some would have it, because necessity does not force us to depart from this simple meaning of the text. Furthermore, he is prophesying against the princes and aristocrats of the people, who abounded in luxury and all riches. But he does not accuse them of wickedness in this, that they are wealthy, but that they acquired that wealth by deceitfully plundering and oppressing the poor, as we have seen earlier. Otherwise the possession of wealth is not bad. Acquiring wealth unjustly and misusing it—this is bad.

1. *You who feel secure on the mountain of Samaria.* The expression "you who feel secure" we must not construe with what follows. Rather, the meaning is this: "You are insolent and stubborn; you have an odd kind of pride, you who are on the mountain of Samaria, that is, you who are sitting securely in your kingdom."

You who pompously enter the house of Israel. This statement is not altogether bad: "You are proud. You stride about arrogantly in the house of Israel." However, we cannot read this from the Hebrew in this way: "You enter into the house of Israel" that is, "You seek your own advantages in the kingdom of Israel, you turn everything into your own profit." In fact, "to go in and out" in Hebrew terminology means "to be involved with," as Luke spoke in Acts (cf. Acts 9:28) and as we read in Deut. 28:6: "Blessed shall you be when you come in, and blessed shall you be when you go out." So also here. It is as if he were saying: "You are doing everything for your own tyranny and are seeking only your own gain. Everything you do you do for yourselves in order to profit yourselves."

2. *Pass over to Calneh and see.* Here you see his intent when he says, "You who enter the house of Israel." The meaning of this passage is this: "Yours is a small kingdom, and yet it feeds so many plundering powerful princes that far more powerful realms would barely suffice to feed them." This is exactly as if we were to say in regard to Germany that Germany feeds so many bishops who are robbing the people that the riches of the Assyrian kingdom would hardly have sufficed to feed them. The interpreters have strangely different meanings for Calneh. Take a look at them.

Hamath. This is the region which today is called Antioch in Syria.

To all their finest kingdoms. That is: "See these kingdoms! Look at their princes! Compare with your realm whatever is very fine in those kingdoms! You will see that you far outstrip them both in princes and in luxury. We can also read this in the masculine gender: "all their finest men."

Is their territory greater than your territory? This is exactly what Is. 5:8 says: "Woe to you who join house to house, who add field to field up to the boundary of the place." That is, "You grab everything for your own use so that there is no longer a place for the poor. So also here, "your territory, that is, the limits of your possession, are very broad, etc."

3. *O you who are kept away.* That is, "You will be reserved until the day of the captivity, when you will all be led away."

And you who approach the seat of violence. The Hebrew reads as follows: "You who approach to sit in injustice," that is, "everything you do, all your interests—all this is destined for one purpose: that you come out wealthy, that you abound in all things, whether this be done justly or unjustly. You think that it does not matter how you accomplish your purpose."

4. *Woe to you who lie on beds of ivory.* Now he is describing their wicked pomp and luxury.

And stretch yourselves. More accurately: "You who luxuriate, or enjoy abundance." He condemns the luxury and richness of their courtly couches and regal bedrooms, with which our princes today also abound.

You who eat the choice lambs from the flock. This refers to all the best things.

And calves from the stall. The best is reserved for the big shots.

5. *And, like David, have invented.* That is, as if in imitation of David, they, too, play the psaltery, although they are actually the poorest sort of imitators. David used the psaltery to praise God, to encourage his love toward God, and to stir up the spirit through the Word of God. They, on the other hand, use it for their own luxury, to satisfy their own ears, etc.

6. *But are not grieved over the ruin of Joseph.* This refers to what I said at the beginning of this chapter: the Lord is not condemning the possession of wealth but the misuse thereof, that is, solely for one's own pleasure rather than to support the poor, not as a faithful dispenser of those things which God has given. Here He is condemning this wickedness, that they are not grieved over the ruin of Joseph, that is, over the poor and afflicted in the kingdom of Israel. They did not pass just judgment but oppressed and afflicted the poor in the gate, as I mentioned earlier. So, too, today our princes in all things operate with the same wickedness. There certainly is no limit to their luxury. They want to abound in all things. Meanwhile the poor freeze and go hungry. Everywhere there is pure deceit. They do not listen to their own subjects, in fact, they oppress them with unbearable taxes and then drain off whatever they still have. This is a situation which does not require many words, for the situation speaks for itself.

7. *At the head of those who go into exile.* That is, those who are most to blame shall be first in the punishment.

[*And the revelry of those who stretch themselves*] *shall be taken away.* That is, "the revelry of the proud shall cease." That is how it reads accurately.[1]

8. *The Lord God has sworn in His own soul.* Hilary used to note

[1] Luther suggests *convivium pomposorum* for the Vulgate reading *factio lascivientium.*

passages of Scripture of this kind in his little books. This is similar to a passage in Genesis (Gen. 19:24): "The Lord rained . . . from the Lord." See Hilary.[2]

[*I hate his*] *houses*, more accurately, his palaces; that is, the buildings magnificently constructed at great expense, buildings in which they strutted proudly.

Along with its inhabitants. In Hebrew this reads, "With its entire fullness." That is, whatever is in the land will perish. This is a Hebrew phrase which also occurs in the psalm (Ps. 24:1): "The earth is the Lord's and the fullness thereof."

10. *And he will take him up.* He is describing the misery of the captivity. It is as if he were saying: "The misery, the disaster, will be so great that, because of the great number of the dead, there will be no opportunity to bury the bodies of the dead. Rather, they will be forced to burn them in the houses." This is a harsh threat with which he is frightening them.

He will say: Hush! You must not mention the name of the Lord. In this passage the interpreters trouble themselves in various ways. In my judgment, however, this is Hebrew phraseology which occurs frequently in Scripture. We read the following in Ps. 45:17: "They will remember Thy name, O Lord"; and we find it in various places in the Psalms. Therefore, to mention the name of the Lord is to preach and utter the name of the Lord, to spread it by preaching. Christ also spoke with this phraseology: "Do this in remembrance of Me,"[3] that is, "Remember Me. Use the Word when you do this." We have it also in Is. 64:5: "Those that remember Thee in Thy ways." Therefore the meaning in this passage is as follows. It is as if the Lord were saying: "Everything will be filled with wretchedness. There will be no source from which they will be able to receive consolation. Everything will be so full of weeping that they clearly will no longer recall the preaching of the name of the Lord. They will be able to do nothing but complain. Filled with grief, they will not preach the name of the Lord. Every worship and praise and preaching of the name of the Lord will cease."

11. *And the great house shall be smitten into fragments, and the*

[2] Cf. *Luther's Works,* 3, pp. 296 f. and n. 66.

[3] Cf. Luke 22:19; 1 Cor. 11:24.

little house into bits, that is, "He will overturn all your houses, the great ones as well as the little ones, in which you now glory and are secure in your own wickedness.

12. *Can horses run* [*on rocks, or can one plow with wild oxen?*] Again we have a rustic metaphor of the Tekoan rustic. This shepherd is always consistent. He remembers the farm animals, the horses and the cows. Perhaps the prophet wants this to mean cows that will be kept for threshing rather than for plowing; or that pregnant or calving cows are not suitable for plowing. Otherwise we are certain that they plowed with oxen or cows. The sense of the metaphor is as if he were saying: "Those people are useless. They are not at all fit for that for which the Lord uses them. They are absolutely useless for every ministry of God. God has no use for them. Since He is so weary of them, He despises and rejects them. They no longer please Him. They do nothing more to please God." This is the same as what now follows:

[*But you have turned justice*] *into bitterness*, more accurately: into poison. This is what I mentioned earlier, that is, "You afflict and strike down the wretched and afflicted. You do not pass fair judgment upon the poor."

Horns. This, too, is a metaphor which the Latins use generally. It is as if He were saying: "You boast about your tyranny. With a stiff neck you proceed against the Law and the Lord as if you were behaving justly. Thus you please your own selves with that wickedness of yours. Therefore you will be carried away. I will send upon you the Assyrian army to grind into dust everything from the entryway of the kingdom of Israel all the way to the exit thereof. There will be nothing left over."

CHAPTER SEVEN

WHAT up to this time he has prophesied and threatened with clear language he here prophesies through enigmas and visions. God's mercy and patience are commended to us. God does not want the death of the sinner, but rather that he be converted and live.[1] For this purpose, He defers the punishment as He invites to repentance. But finally, when He sees that He is moving things forward neither with threats nor with blandishments, He becomes very angry and takes to blows. This is the way He always acted with the Jews, with Pharaoh, with Judas, the betrayer. In these instances He revealed His terrible judgments that they might be examples of His wrath. We see the same thing here. He sent out His Word in such detail, He gave various exhortations through His prophets both openly and in visions, to invite them to repent. However, because all of this accomplished nothing, He rejected this entire people terribly.

1. *Behold, He was there as a Creator of locusts.* That is, He was forming locusts when the late rain began to increase or develop. This is a chronology with which he is indicating that locusts developed at the least opportune time, namely, when the crops first shoot up, when the grains and all the fruits can scarcely tolerate any adversity, least of all locusts that devour them.

After the king's mowings. [These words] are to signify the cutting off of shoots in the field, as our farmers do at the beginning of the sprouting crops. The kings would keep and use that cutting or mowing of the crops for themselves, just as our princes keep for themselves the fish and beasts of the forest.

2. *When they had finished eating.* More accurately: "When they had devoured all the grass of the land." This is God's threat with which He indicates that the army of the Assyrians—which He calls

[1] Cf. Ezek. 18:23.

locusts—will come to destroy everything so that there will be nothing left to remain.

O Lord God, forgive, I beseech Thee. Here the prophet is setting himself up as a wall in front of the people to turn away the wrath of God that they may not perish. Yet he does not completely turn aside the wrath of God, for the Lord has postponed the blow, lest He punish at the beginning, as He had threatened. This, then, is the prophet's state of mind when he says:

Who will lift up, etc. It is as if he were saying: "O Lord, spare him, lest You destroy him. Don't send the king of Assyria against Jacob, for Jacob is nothing when compared with the Assyrian. Who, then, will lift him up?" That is, "Who will cause Jacob to stand up against the Assyrian?"

6. *The Lord repented concerning this; This also shall not be,* namely, "This is not to happen in this time while the kingdom is still flourishing." You see, the kingdom of Israel was enjoying its greatest flowering during the reign of Jeroboam, a good and outstanding king in appearance, as we mentioned at the beginning.

4. *Behold [the Lord God] was calling for a judgment by fire.* That is, "I saw a case being tried. In it they demanded that the case being investigated be judged by fire." He does not describe the lawyers and judges before whom the case was tried. But the fire was so great that it consumed not only wood but even—and this is against nature—"the great deep," that is, the standing waters and other seas. He is pointing out the vehemence of a fire in that it dried up not only that water which the burning sun generally dried up otherwise too but even the deep waters.

The land. More accurately, "the fields." Let me summarize all this. He is comparing the kingdom to the great deep and to a fertile field. At that time, as I have said, the kingdom of Israel was flourishing under the rule of Jeroboam. That this kingdom would be destroyed appeared impossible and even incredible. Yet, he is here threatening that everything will be destroyed and consumed by fire. After all, just as the great deep or an ordinary field is nothing compared to the devouring fire, so also the kingdom of Israel is considered as nothing in comparison with the power of the Assyrians, who were going to come because of the judgment of God.

7. *And in His hand was a trowel of mortar.* The Hebrew word does not mean a trowel but a level, or a plumb line—what we commonly call *Richtscheit.* Masons use it to keep their walls straight. When he says here, "The Lord standing beside a wall of a plumb line," it is a Hebraism. That is, the Lord was standing beside a wall which He was keeping straight with a plumb line.

8. *I will never again pass by them.* That is, "Even if I postpone for a time that captivity with which I have threatened Israel, yet I will no longer pass over its sins. In some respect I will punish. I will straighten and fit in with My plumb line the stones which project. That is, I will punish the sins or the house of the king." In this third vision, the Lord is threatening evil to the royal household of Jeroboam and excludes the other people, whom He says He is willing to spare temporarily. The meaning, then, is as if He were saying: "The mason uses his plumb line to set in order the stones which stick out and do not square well with the others. He does this to make a good fit. In the same way, I with My judgment will straighten the household of King Jeroboam in the midst of the people before that great captivity of the entire kingdom," as He adds immediately.

9. [*The high places of the idol*] *will be made desolate.* He is mixing those three visions simultaneously here. It is as if He were saying: "Those things which I have prophesied will come to pass. Yet those two with which I have already threatened the entire kingdom I will put off for a little while. That third one, however, I will not postpone."

The high places of the idol. What we read here you will read more accurately as "the altars of illusion." He aptly calls that wicked worship of ungodliness "altars," or "houses of illusion." You see, the ungodly laugh aloud at God with the worship they themselves have invented. Thus Ishmael mocked good Isaac, as Paul says in Gal. 4:29: "But as at that time he who was born according to the flesh persecuted him who was born according to the Spirit, so it is now." Thus the ungodly with their own traditions always mock the preaching of the godly. This battle between Isaac and Ishmael will never cease.

And the sanctuaries. A sanctuary is an endowed institution

(Stift). We read in the psalm (Ps. 114:2): "Judah became His sanctuary, Israel His dominion." That is, Judah is His bishopric *(Bistum).* In Judah he wanted to have His priesthood, and in Israel His dominion, His kingdom. He is saying that all this would be laid waste.

And I shall rise up against the house of Jeroboam. This properly refers to the king. He is threatening the king's house; that is, death to the descendants of the king. This happened after Jeroboam died when Zechariah, the wicked son of Jeroboam, was killed, according to 2 Kings 15:8-10.

10. *Then Amaziah . . . sent.* Here we have an example of that struggle and mockery about which I spoke a little earlier. This account is well worth noting. In it one can see what that ungodliness is and what it thinks of the Word of God, how it despises everything that is of God in order to keep its own things safe. Here the wicked priest Amaziah mocks and despises the pious prophet Amos, a contemptible, lowly shepherd. So he urges the king not to believe the prophecy of Amos. He says that it is a lie since Amos indeed speaks against the king and against the kingdom which they were very sure God had instituted. This is how the wicked blind and mislead each other with their wickedness, as the apostle says in 2 Tim. 3:13: "Evil men and impostors will go on from bad to worse, deceivers and deceived." He now adds the wicked doctrine of the wicked priest.

Amos has conspired against you in the midst of the house of Israel. This is an argument from the royal dignity, from multitude and magnitude. So also today, the enemies of the Gospel wickedly set against us the dignity and majesty of the emperor as well as the authority of the church. So here, the wicked priest is setting against the prophet the kingdom of Israel and its king, both of which they were very certain God had established. This the prophets could not deny. And because the wicked knew that God had instituted both king and kingdom, they would not listen as the prophets condemned both king and kingdom. Instead they would argue this way: "If the king has been divinely established, it follows that God is with the king and confirms the kingdom. Therefore the king does not err." When therefore the prophets would condemn king and kingdom, they would be killed. They would be accused of inciting rebellion, as Amaziah says here: "The land is not able to bear all his words." Christ heard the same thing: "He stirs up the people, teaching throughout Judea, etc." (Luke 23:5). This, however, is the form of the Word of God; this is the appearance of the preachers of the Word.

11. *Jeroboam will die by the sword.* Here Amaziah is wickedly misrepresenting the words of the prophet to make him a greater object of hatred. You see, he is telling a lie. He adds a sinister touch as he sets the prophet's words before the king. The prophet had threatened death to the house of Jeroboam, that is, to his sons. This prophecy he twists perversely for Jeroboam. We see the same thing happening to us today in every detail. This wickedness all the prophets condemn. They condemned the ungodliness of the people, but the wicked people opposed them, defending their own wickedness by saying that they were the people of God, that they had the Word of God, etc. But the prophets would say that these promises pertained not to the wicked but only to the faithful, of whom there always were very few. They kept saying that only those would be saved because of the promises made to their fathers, but all the rest would perish. This is the same thing as Isaiah says (Is. 10:22): "Though the number of the children of Israel be as the sand of the sea, only a remnant will be saved"; and as Paul says in Rom. 11:1: "I ask then, has God rejected His people? By no means! I myself am an Israelite, etc." Clearly [he is referring to] the best part of the people.

It is the king's sanctuary. It is as if he were saying: "Go away. You will make no prophecy here. This is the king's sanctuary. Take care that you don't oppose the kingdom of Israel, which God Himself established. Flee, lest you be caught and killed. Here there will be nothing for you to eat. Go to Judah." This is what ministers of the Word hear. This is how they have to be chased away.

14. *I am no prophet.* The interpreters upset themselves in various ways with this passage, but in vain. After all, what I said earlier about the orders of prophets also applies to this.[2] The sense then is this: "I do not belong to the rank, or order, of prophets." You see, there were orders of prophets. Hence the sons of the

[2] Cf. p. 129 above.

prophets are called hearers or followers of the prophets in the sacred accounts.

I am a herdsman, etc. It is as if he were saying: "I do not prophesy for the purpose of getting my food from it. I am not in pursuit of my own profit or wealth. Rather, I seek food with my own hands. I am content to dress the sycamore figs (mulberry figs)."

16. *You shall not drop your words against the house of Israel.*[3] The prophets frequently use this word "drop words" *(stillare)* for the verb "to preach." Indeed, whoever preaches drops his words, namely, when he declares the wrath of God and the coming punishment, that is, when he warns and admonishes before the calamity comes; for when it comes, there is a heavy shower of it.

17. *Will be a harlot.* That is, she will be raped.

By line. That is, your farmland will be parceled out.

In an unclean land, That is, in captivity.

[3] The Vulgate Text has *non stillabis super domum idoli,* but in the parallel line before it reads *non prophetabis super Israel.*

CHAPTER EIGHT

The final two chapters in this prophet are his last two discourses. With them he acts as if he were tired of preaching and prophesies that the entire people will be utterly destroyed both for the kingdom and for the priesthood. The way he speaks about the destruction and captivity at the hand of Babylon is really very similar to the very last destruction and captivity which took place at the time of Christ, when the priesthood, too, perished along with the kingdom.

1. *A basket of summer fruit.* Puns in one language cannot be translated into another tongue. Here there is a pun in Hebrew that we must circumscribe. The Hebrew word means a basket, a kind of cage, or a woven canister, in which birds are kept and fattened. The interpretation is twofold. Some translate it as a basket of fruit, others as a cage of birds. I like the latter translation, a place where birds are fattened for slaughter. The meaning, then, is this: The prophet seems to be saying: "Because I say everything to this people in vain, destruction and death threaten it. Nothing else remains for it but a wretched death, because I see a cage filled with animals for slaughter. Whatever belongs to this people will be totally finished and devoured." This we see clearly from what follows, where he explains that pun.

2. *The end has come upon My people Israel.* We have the same figure of speech in the Hebrew as if one were to say in German *Ich sehe ein Reis* and someone were to answer *Ich will dich recht reissen.*[1] There is a big difference between *Reis* and *reissen*, yet there is a relation by paronomasia between the words. We have

[1] This German pun depends on the similarity of sound between words unrelated in meaning. It might be approximated by an English pair of words as follows: "I see a shoot." "I'll shoot you properly." The two Hebrew words involved in the text are קַיִץ ("summer fruit") and קֵץ ("end").

the same allusion here, too, in the Hebrew, which we cannot render in the Latin language.

I will never again pass by them. He used the same phrase in the preceding chapter (v. 8): "I shall never again pass by them," that is, "I will no longer shut My eyes to their wickedness. I will no longer spare them."

3. *The hinges of the temple will shriek.* When that last captivity and that end about which I have spoken will come, all the palaces [2] will be knocked down and destroyed. The entire kingdom will fall and the royal house will fall into ruin. It will be completely destroyed by an attack.

Many will die; in every place. This is translated poorly. We read it in the Hebrew as follows: "The multitude of dead bodies will throw forth silence everywhere." He is describing the wretchedness of the captivity. He means two things: first, that the kingdom would cease and whatever belongs to the kingdom would perish utterly. Next, he also foretells that people everywhere would be crushed and destroyed. He is prophesying that there would be so many dead bodies that there would be a great silence, great misery, great loneliness everywhere. This is what the Hebrew word "silence" means, namely, the destruction, devastation, and death of everything. Silence follows this; that is, it is like a lonely desert, as when a plague rages in some city and few people are seen. Vergil calls this the "voiceless shades." [3] But when the prophet says, "In every place," he means the destruction and death of the entire people, as I mentioned at the beginning of the chapter.

4. *Hear this, you who trample upon the needy.* He now warns them of their own wickedness, namely, that they themselves are the reason for this disaster because of their sins, which he also censured above.

Who trample upon. More accurately: "You who swallow up the poor and cause their demise." You are still oppressing the poor so that nothing of what was theirs is left over. All their goods go to you because of your wicked greed and tyranny.

2 Luther here uses *palatium* as a synonym for *templum* in the Vulgate text. In the next sentence *domus regia* provides the same interpretation.

3 Vergil, *Aeneid,* VI, 264.

5. *When will the month be over?* Month, not harvest.[4]

That we may sell grain . . . that we may make the ephah small, etc. He touches on the main points of their wicked greed. He finds in them four things that are reprehensible, as you see. It is as if he were saying: "You have no equals in greed. So do you swallow up the poor and with your greed cause whatever the poor have to come to you. You do this with your wicked cheating, when you corrupt the measures and the merchandise."

6. *For a pair of sandals.* That is, you consider them to be very cheap.

The refuse. This is the fourth sin with which he finds fault—that they sell the refuse and sweepings, or chaff and dust, of the grain for good grain; that they do not sell the pure grain to the poor but mix it with dust and sweepings that they may have a greater profit. This is something which our own merchants do as well as all those who have things to sell. But he is reproving the excessive greed of the priests when he says that they are impatient with the month, that is, with the new moon. You see, this was a holy day on which they would relax. He says that the priests did not like the new moon, because they were not allowed to do business on that day and lie in wait for the money of the poor. Therefore, because something would thwart their wicked greed, the celebration of feast days or of sabbaths used to irritate them.

7. *By the pride,* that is, against it.

8. *And all of it rise like a river.* Again this has been poorly translated in our Latin Bibles. The Hebrew has this meaning: "And its consummation will rise like a river. It will be cast out and drunk up like the river of Egypt." The Hebrew word (יְאֹר) has two meanings, for it signifies both river and light. It is uncertain, then, which of the two He intends to use. The sense is as if He were saying: "Just as some sudden storm cloud appears, so the end and destruction will come upon My people. They will flow away like the river of Egypt; that is, the Assyrian will swallow them up. They will move to Assyria and will be sucked up and swallowed like the river of Egypt which flows into the sea and is swallowed up."

[4] Luther means to say that the correct reading in the Vulgate is *mensis,* not *messis.*

9. *The sun will go down at noon, etc.* These are Hebraisms, as I have said earlier. After all, we never read that it happened that the sun set at midday. Darkness signifies adversity and misfortunes; light means success and good times. Consequently, serenity of face indicates gladness, as we have it in Ps. 38:10: "And the light of my eyes—it has also gone from me." Therefore, just as he says earlier in chapter 5:8: "Who darkens the day into night," so, too, he says here that the sun will set at noon (which is what he calls daylight) when the sun is most visible and clear. That is: "When the kingdom is flourishing at its height, when it will feel the most secure, then all of you will perish, suspecting nothing like that. You will be taken off into the deep, so that you topple the more ruinously." This is what God does in the case of all the wicked. And when they believe that nothing is farther from happening than that they are going to perish, then the Lord punishes them and causes them to perish. This is what Paul says in 1 Thess. 5:3: "When people say, 'There is peace and security,' then sudden destruction will come upon them." Jerome transfers this to the time of Christ's Passion, but both the context and what follows do not allow him to do this, if you were to take a very close look.

10. *I will bring sackcloth upon all loins.* It was the custom for the Jews to put on sackcloth when they wept and were filled with grief. With this external garb they indicated an internal sadness and grief of heart. There was no need to do this, but this was their custom. Therefore Christ says in Ps. 69:11 that He made sackcloth His clothing, that is, that He was filled with grief. Also the "baldness of every head" means this. When we are grieved, we are accustomed to tear at our hair.

Like the mourning for an only son. He means that the captivity will last forever; that they will never be brought back. He is drawing a simile from the grief of a mother over her only son. A mother's grief is deepest when her only son has died and there is no further hope for having other children.

The end of it. More accurately: "its descendants." [5]

11. *I shall send a famine on the land.* This is the last blow. It is the worst, the most wretched, of all. All the rest of the blows

[5] Luther suggests interpreting *novissima* to mean *posteros.*

would be bearable, but this is absolutely horrible. He is threatening to take away the genuine prophets and the true Word of God, so that there is no one to preach, even if men were most eager to wish to hear the Word and would run here and there to hear it. This happened to the Jews in the Assyrian captivity and in that last one. We must watch and pray lest that same famine be sent on us, too. Now we are by the grace of God overwhelmed with a manifold abundance of God's Word. But we must watch and pray that it may not be taken away again and that palpable darkness and the foulest errors may not be sent upon us, so that even if we wanted to hear the Word, there would be no one to preach it, as happened to the Jews, Greeks, and Romans, who once abounded in the Word of God. For when the Word has been taken away, what else remains but the most terrible darkness of human reason which wants to be our mistress and which can teach nothing else than the doctrines of the demons? After all, what else would darkness teach except darkness and errors? There is no light except through faith in the Word. What happens next the prophet here adds:

12. *They will wander from sea to sea.* That is, they will look for the Word. They will run here and there, and they will not find it. This we experienced well enough before the Word was published through the grace of God. This is why we have the countless sects of monks. One becomes a Carthusian, another a Franciscan. One establishes one kind of life, another another kind by which he believes he is pleasing God, but there is no peace of conscience. One runs to Rome, another to St. James.[6] So we ought to be thankful now to almighty God and we should use that invaluable gift correctly lest it again be taken away from an ungrateful people and we fall into greater errors than ever before; lest we who are now fed with dainties again lie in the gutters, as Jeremiah says in Lam. 4:5. After all, before the Gospel again was spread, what else did we eat but the filth of the pope—and this at the expense of both money and soul? But we are ungrateful. The princes go on to play the role of Midas. Their responsibility ought to be to stir up and nourish the studies of learned men. Here they ought to be using their great resources that the Word and correct studies thereof be

[6] The shrine at Santiago de Compostela in Spain, supposed to contain the bones of St. James. Cf. *Luther's Works,* 22, p. 250; 29, p. 63.

widely taught. Before, these princes had spent large amounts of money for the ministry of Satan, but no one listens. We are telling a tale of a deaf man. But if we go on to be such people, the same judgment will come upon us which the prophet is threatening here. This is at the point of starting now through the wicked prophets.

13. *In that day the fair virgins . . . will faint.* This is the fruit of that very bleak famine. It is as if he were saying: "There will be many beautiful and lovely maidens; there will be many fine young men. But they will all waste away and perish, so that none of them can be useful." That is, that fine young manhood will perish. Had it been taught and brought up in the Word of God, it could have been placed in leadership roles for the state, it could have taught others, it could have administered the state correctly through God. But because the Word of God has been taken away, the young people are misled by errors, they perish, they are useful to no one. Up to now what have our universities throughout the world been except devourers of our finest youngsters? When they were sent away by their parents to learn godliness, to learn good skills in order to be able to serve in positions of leadership in the state, they learned nothing else but to excel in drinking and fornication. Thus imbued with every barbarous wickedness, they perished, and all their finest talents also were destroyed on account of that wickedness. The monasteries have produced the same fruit too. It becomes necessary, then, at the height of midday to feel our way like a blind man in that darkness of not having the Word of God, which might rule us and provide us with light.

14. *Those who swear by the sin of Samaria,* that is, by the idol of Samaria. He aptly calls that worship of human reason established outside the Word of God "sin." Thus he shows that he wanted them to worship and adore not Satan but the true God. You see, they kept thinking—as we have said before in great detail—that they were pleasing God with that worship, inasmuch as they had instituted it in honor of the true God and not for idols. But because they were thus binding God to a worship they had invented themselves and about which they had no Word of God and yet thought that they would please God in it, therefore this was an abomination to God. So also have been all the works of our monks and priests. See above.

CHAPTER NINE

As I have said, the last two chapters are devoted completely to the final destruction of the entire kingdom and priesthood. The preceding chapter deals strictly with the ruin of the kingdom. This final one takes a look at the destruction of the priesthood, as we shall see in the vision.

1. *Smite the hinges and let the thresholds shake, and he tore (or rent) them all onto their heads (or onto the heads of all); and what is left of them, etc.* This vision has it that the door hinges are going to be struck. When they will be struck, the thresholds will rattle. In summary it means this: "I will break the priesthood and carry it away totally along with the kingdom and whatever is left of the people. Thus when both the kingdom and the priesthood will have been destroyed, they will wander here and there throughout the earth. They are going to have no established home where they may be able to stay. They are always going to have an unstable dwelling." This is what he means with the shaking of the thresholds. The smiting of the hinges—that is, the removal of the capital, as he says here—means the complete removal of both kingdom and priesthood. We find this figure of speech here and there in the prophets, as in Ps. 68:21: "God will shatter the heads of His enemies, the hairy crown of those who walk about in their guilty ways." We have the same thing in Hab. 3:13: "Thou didst crush the head from the house of the wicked, laying him bare from thigh to neck." In summary, all this indicates that both kingdom and priesthood are going to be taken away from them, as Christ says in Matt. 21:43. After all, what else are the Jews today who are still alive but a wretched trunk without a head? They have been scattered wretchedly throughout the world. They have no stable dwelling place, no kingdom, no priesthood. This smiting of the hinges he himself explains when he immediately adds:

And rend them on the heads. That is, He will take away the kingdom and the priesthood. The shaking or movement of the thresholds he explains in very great detail in the verses which follow: And what is left of them I will kill with the sword. There will be no way of escape for them, and no one shall be able to escape."

2. *Though they go all the way down to hell, etc.* We must take this in a potential sense, just as we have the custom of speaking in the same way. He means that they will never be safe, regardless of where they may have fled. Moses also gave them this very terrible warning in Deut. 28:66: "Your life shall hang in doubt before you. Night and day you will be in dread and have no assurance of your life. In the morning you shall say, 'Would it were evening,' etc." We see the same thing here in every detail.

4. *I will set My eyes upon them.* That is, "I will watch them carefully that I may harm them, that I may destroy them, not that I may do good to them." He gives the reason for this, namely, why they will be unable to escape. He says that they have against them the Lord God omnipotent, the Creator of all things, whom no man can deceive, no man can escape, and before whose magnificence all creatures must tremble. They will be unable, then, to escape His wrath. Therefore, he is setting against them divine power and majesty when he says:

5. *The Lord . . . who touches the earth, etc.* It is as if he were saying: "You are entertaining vain hopes that you will escape."

6. *And founds His vault upon the earth.* This is the same word [1] that is used in the translation of 1 Sam. 10:5: "Lo, you will meet a *band* of prophets." [2] The word appears in Moses, too, where it is translated in Ex. 12:22: "Dip a *bunch* of hyssop." Some want this to mean the gathering of the elements. The statement of Jerome, however, pleases me more, as if to say: "The Lord sits and dwells in the heavens, and yet He keeps His band, His people, that is, His church, on earth, and protects it." You see, He has founded it very

[1] The word *fasciculum* is used in Amos 9:6 in the Vulgate to translate the Hebrew word אֲגֻדָּה.

[2] In 1 Sam. 10:5 and 10 the Hebrew word is חֶבֶל, and the Vulgate translates *grex* and *cuneus* respectively.

firmly, lest Satan be able to do anything against it. But if anyone proves another meaning, it will be fine with me.

7. *Are you not like the Ethiopians?* The prophet is anticipating an objection and responds to their question with silence, as he also did earlier in chapter 5. There we spoke in detail about this matter when he said (v. 14): "The Lord God of hosts will be with you, as you have said." Let me summarize this entire passage. There is no acceptance of persons before God. It is as if he were saying: "It is not that you are boasting that you are the people of God, that the Lord has called you His own ahead of all peoples of the earth, as Moses said.[3] It is because you do not observe the covenant of the Lord that you will be taken from the earth. Whoever has sinned will be guilty before the Lord, whether he be Israelite or Egyptian. Nothing will profit you, because you defend your own wickedness with the promises God has shown to you. But they have nothing to do with you, so long as you do not believe the Word of God but are wicked, as Peter says in Acts 10:34-35: 'Truly I perceive that God shows no partiality, but in every nation anyone who fears Him and does what is right is acceptable to Him.'" It is as if he were saying: "He has respect for those who fear [Him] and keep His Word. Those who despise He destroys, whether they be Jew or Egyptian or Ethiopian."

8. *Behold, the eyes of the Lord are upon the sinful kingdom.* Here we see very clearly that the Lord transfers kingdoms and stirs up one people against another to make it its tributary, to overturn a kingdom and to use it for itself. This is how He caused the very powerful Roman empire to perish. Barbarians, whom the Romans held in utter contempt, gained superiority through victory. He does the same thing with every kingdom which He wants to destroy, just as He says here: "The eyes of the Lord are upon the sinning kingdom," as if to say: "No matter what kind it may be." He Himself lists here examples of kingdoms He transferred—the Egyptians, the Palestinians, and the Syrians from Kir. This last one is mistakenly read as Cyrene, as we mentioned in detail in the first chapter of this prophet.

Except that I will not destroy . . . Jacob, says the Lord. This is

[3] Cf. Ex. 19:5.

what we spoke about in detail earlier in chapters 3 and 4 about the remnant saved. You see, the prophets have this custom: after a threat they also add a consolation because of the devout. The meaning, then, is this: "Even if the entire kingdom and the entire priesthood perish, yet I will save a remnant for Myself, lest they all perish." Isaiah says this, too (Is. 10:22): "For though your people Israel be as the sand of the sea, a remnant will be saved."

9. *For lo, I will command and shake, etc.* This is a clear exposition of all the previous statements. He is saying: "I will give the command, for when I will it, then it cannot fail to happen. I will overthrow the whole house of Israel."

And shake . . . among all the nations. He means the kind of emotion Scripture says was in Cain [4] and the kind people have at times when they shake their heads. This is the same thing that Hos. 9:17 says: "They shall be wanderers among the nations." With quite a harsh simile He declares how He is going to strike Israel, and, in such a way:

That no pebble will fall upon the earth. Lyra says that this is a Hebrew idiom, so that the idea is this: Not a single word from the prophets will fall rashly so that it goes unfulfilled. He follows the passage in 1 Sam. 3:19: "And none of his [Samuel's] words fell to the ground." However, I do not like this. Rather, in my judgment the meaning seems to be as if he were saying: "I will sift and shake the house of Israel so that not even a pebble will fall on the earth; that is, so that no one can escape that shaking. No one will fall out of that sieve. No one who comes into this sieve of Mine will be freed forthwith." We also see this today in the case of the Jews. I simply have no better idea than this. Up to this point that anticipation of the prophet over the coming destruction of all Israel has endured. Now follows a beautiful passage about the kingdom of Christ, who is going to restore the despised kingdom of David and lead Israel back into an eternal security, namely, in a spiritual way by the preaching of the Gospel of faith.

11. *In that day I will raise up the tent of David.* This passage is quoted in Acts 15:16-18. Let me summarize it. "When I have thus destroyed the kingdom and the priesthood, I will gather together

[4] Cf. Gen. 4:14.

the pieces of the tent of David which has fallen and rebuild it. Into it will come even people from every nation who are going to believe, although they are not of the house of David." As I have said, we must properly take this to mean the kingdom of Christ.

The tent of David. Understand this as the people of David, the descendants of David *(den Stamm Davids),* as we also have it in Is. 11:1, where he says to the same effect: "There shall come forth a root from the stump of Jesse." This is the kingdom of David, from which the Messiah was to rule. It clearly had been an object of contempt; it had almost died out and ceased to exist when Christ came. Only insignificant dregs survived. It was like a dead torso. It was not in flower. It had fallen, it had been broken. But when Christ came, it was revived. The dead stump flowered and brought forth an outstanding Flower and Fruit. Everything was renewed and restored. All that had been broken down was rebuilt, and everything was made most beautiful. In a wonderful way this is an elegant and beautiful prophecy, because He has said that out of that very despicable tribe of Judah, which had nearly ceased to exist, He would build for Himself an outstanding church of the elect—a church filled with grace and the Holy Spirit and made noble by the Spirit. He is of course speaking of the retinue of the Spirit, in which the entire kingdom of David was administered, for it had rulers filled with the Holy Spirit.

12. *The remnant of Edom.* That is, Jews will not be the only ones inside this tent. There will also be the remnants of Edom and of all nations who are going to believe the Gospel. This is a wonderful and delightful prophecy. In the Hebrew this is all said with far greater charm.

13. *And the plowman shall overtake the reaper.* A miraculous metamorphosis of this kingdom will occur, so that the reaping will immediately follow the plowing. He is saying that He will establish and rebuild this kingdom with such speed and so quickly that everyone will be amazed, that they will plow and harvest at the same time. He signifies the very swift course of the Word of the Gospel among the Gentiles. It is as if he were saying: "The Word of God will move forth among the Gentiles so quickly that they will be converted from their sins and bear fruit at the same time. They will believe simultaneously with the Jews who have been trained

and taught already for a long time." You see the same thing in Joel 2:32.

The mountains. These are the apostles and the preachers of the Word.

14. *And I will turn back the captivity of My people.* He is speaking about a spiritual leading and turning back. After all, He made the corporal threat earlier that He would hand them all over into captivity. All were brought back with this leading back—as many as believed the Gospel when Christ came and were brought into that tent of David by faith. There there is the greatest security, peace, and joy of conscience. Those who dwell there produce rich fruit. Strengthened in faith by the Holy Spirit given from heaven, they will not be moved out of it forever. Moses always ordered them to act, and they never did. Therefore the promises which were also made to them were promised in vain. Here, however, the Lord Himself is promising that He will act, that He will bring back, that He will set in place. Therefore it will be fulfilled that they will not "be plucked up, etc."

The end. Praise be to Christ. 1525

LECTURES ON OBADIAH

The Altenburg Text

Translated by
RICHARD J. DINDA

THE interpreters are not agreed as to when Obadiah prophesied. They make various judgments about him, since he mentions at the beginning of his prophecy neither the time nor the king under whom he prophesied. This, however, is something one may notice in the books of several of the prophets. Jerome says that this was the Obadiah who, under wicked Ahab and Jezebel, feared for the hundred prophets in the caves, as it is recorded in 1 Kings 18:3-4. As a result of this [according to Jerome] Obadiah received the gift of prophecy.[1] But this is much like the dreams of old women—like many other points of Jerome whenever he makes rash judgments about sacred matters. In their own commentaries, the Jews draw a different conclusion. To me it seems certain that he prophesied after the Babylonian captivity and that he took his prophecy from Jeremiah, which certain points in this prophet indicate. Also there are clear-cut details that convince me that he was a contemporary of Jeremiah. He sets up his prophecy against the Edomites who were boasting about and taking great pleasure in the destruction and abduction of Jews at the time of the Babylonian captivity. This we can see in Ps. 137:7: "Remember, O Lord, against the Edomites the day of Jerusalem, how they said, 'Raze it, raze it! Down to its foundations!'" This means: "Remember, O Lord, and avenge that reviling of the Edomites with which they insult in the time of adversity Your people as they were being led captive. Remember what kind of people they were when Jerusalem was being destroyed." As I have said, this is the consideration that

[1] Jerome, *Commentaria in Abdiam prophetam, Patrologia, Series Latina, XXV,* 1099: "Obadiah is the man of whom the Hebrews say that under Ahab, the king of Samaria, and under that most wicked Jezebel he fed a hundred prophets in caves, prophets who did not bow the knee to Baal and who were among the 7,000 of whom Elijah knew nothing, as he is charged. . . . Because Obadiah had fed a hundred prophets, he received the gift of prophecy himself and from a leader of the army turned into a leader of the church."

moves me to think that Obadiah was a contemporary of Jeremiah. Here is a summary of the prophet: Against the Edomites he prophecies that the vengeance of God would occur because the Edomites were quite delighted at the time of the Babylonian captivity that the Jews were being grievously afflicted and led into captivity. Yet, because the Edomites were brothers of the Jews,[2] they should have showed compassion. Then, from the destruction of those nations which by the judgment of God had destroyed the kingdom of Judah, he goes over to the kingdom of Christ, which is going to come through the Gospel and in which the remnants of Ephraim, Israel, and others were to flourish. Thus the transition will not appear abrupt, and everything fits together well—which somehow coheres only with great difficulty in the other interpreters.

1. *Thus says the Lord God concerning Edom: we have heard tidings (a report).* He is using metaphors drawn from the military to terrify the Edomites and to exaggerate the calamity which would come to them. The metaphor is drawn from the military custom in which envoys, who have a way of reconciling estranged friends, are usually sent to the foe in regard to important matters. It is as if He were saying: "Other kings and princes accomplish their business through their envoys. I take care of things by Myself through My Spirit."

Rise up, and let us rise against her for battle! These words are those of the envoy. With them He stirs up to battle those nations whose effort and aid He wanted to use against the Edomites He planned to destroy.

2. *Behold, I have made you small among the nations.* He crushes their confidence and uplifts the might and arrogance of Edom with which they were accustomed to be haughty against the Jews. You see, between the Jews and Edomites there were very bitter mutual hatreds—the kind of hatreds and animosities which generally exist between brothers. So the Edomites had ἄσπονδος πόλεμος ("an implacable strife") with the Jews, not so much because Jacob had taken the blessing away from his brother Esau as over the fact that they were forced to wear the yoke of Israel, a yoke they certainly could not strike from their necks because they were weaker than

[2] As descendants of Esau, the brother of Jacob.

Israel. Here, then, the meaning is as if the Lord were saying: "So great a force and so powerful an army of nations will I raise up against you that, when your strength is compared with theirs, you will appear like a mosquito, and they will hold you in contempt in comparison with themselves. They will consider you worth nothing. They will gulp you down in a single mouthful so that you will no longer exist."

3. *The pride of your heart has deceived you.* He adds the reason why He is going to expose the Edomites to scornful plundering at the hands of an opposing army. He says: "It is because you take great pleasure in yourself and your own self-esteem and strength. You grow haughty. You lack no confidence in your own future." And so he also adds:

Because you live in the clefts of the rocks. He indicates the reason for this insolence: that their well-fortified region, cities, and fortresses [3] are giving them the courage to be so proud. You see, it is also clear from Moses that this land of the Edomites is rocky. We read in Deut. 2:2-4: "For many days we went about Mount Seir . . . . 'You are about to pass through the territory of your brethren, the sons of Esau, who live in Seir, etc.'" The Latins call it Arabia Petraea, which received its name from Sela, the great and well-known city of Arabia Petraea. To the Jews, Sela means "rock" *(petra).* A good part of this Arabia is the land of the Edomites. The sense of the verse, then, is: "You trust in your own strength because your land is hilly, so that there is no open approach for an army, and because your land will be hard to attack. This hope, however, I will take away from you." He alludes to that outstanding city Petra in the Hebrew fashion, as if to say: "You have a royal city, carefully fortified—a "rock" in whose clefts you believe you will be safe. But your hope will deceive you. You see, you are so far from being safe in those clefts of the rocks or in the most hidden places or, in fact, anywhere in your entire land that you will be unable to hide from the army that is about to come against you."

Whose dwelling is high. That is, you have fortified citadels in the mountains.

Who will bring me down to the ground? He describes their in-

[3] With the Halle manuscript we have read *arces* for *agros.*

solent pride and their confidence in their might and says that their confidence certainly lies not in the help and protection of the Lord but in their own rocky fortifications. "But listen!" He says, "However much you may be fortified with your mighty fortresses, I will nevertheless take every hope away from you. I will reduce you to absolutely nothing, and I will do this even

4. *Though you soar aloft like the eagle and though your nest is set among the stars, etc.* So little can God Almighty endure our self-confidence, so much does He hate the trust of the flesh and the prideful insolence of impious hearts, that we see scattered throughout all Scripture that He calls us back from the arm of the flesh, from confidence in ourselves, to place our hope in Him. Only then, He says, will we be safe, etc.

5. *If thieves came to you.* To summarize this passage: "You ought to prefer to wish that thieves and robbers might attack your land and take booty from it (for, since they would not take everything, something would be left for you) rather than that I come against you, for I will seek out all things and search out all the most secret places in all the hollows of the hills so carefully that nothing will remain for you, that everything will be destroyed, and that all of you will perish with it."

How you would have been destroyed! This verb[4] is used in various ways in Scripture. Interpreters render it in different ways also. It occurs in Hos. 4:5: "I had your mother destroyed." It also appears in Ps. 49:20, where we read: "Man cannot abide in his pomp, he is like the beasts [that perish]." We also read in Ps. 4:4: "Commune with your own hearts on your beds [and be silent]." This properly means to reduce something to silence and to nothing, to demolish some kingdom or people to such an extent that scarcely traces remain to be seen, that they keep their silence and dare not utter a sound, etc. This is just the way the Germans say about someone who has learned from his own evildoing *Er ist so fein still worden.*[5] Here the meaning is the same in every detail, as if he were saying: "I want to make you so small that you will be forced to

[4] The verb דָּמָה ("cause to cease; destroy"), which the Vulgate translates with *conticesco* ("fall silent").

[5] "He has really learned to keep silent."

be very quiet, for that calamity which is going to happen to you when I come against you with My army will be such that the attacks of thieves and robbers, no matter how great they might be, compared with this calamity are not to be considered attacks or depredation. You should have preferred to be oppressed and to be reduced to silence under the oppression of thieves. This, however, is not to be compared with the ruin that will occur when I come, etc. For I will leave you not a single bunch of grapes. I will take away everything you will have hidden, whether this be money or men whom you hoped you would save. So nothing will escape when I destroy."

7. *They have driven you all the way to the border.* This is the same phrase we find in Is. 5:8: "You have added field to field all the way to the border of the place." The meaning, then, is: "They will force and drive you out all the way to the borders or limits of your land. They will throw you completely out of your land, so that you will not have a territory."

All your allies have deceived you. He takes away all their confidence—so completely that there will be nothing in which they can place their confidence as the destruction breaks upon them. Not only will their most strongly fortified cities and fortresses avail them nothing, but even their neighbors, allied peoples, will betray them and disregard their treaty with them.

There is no understanding. In German we express this with *Du Narr, du merkst nicht.*[6] "You do not notice that you are vainly trusting in the arm of the flesh. You will have crutches of reeds, and if you will want to support yourself with them, you will fall. No understanding, no planning, no might will avail you. I will even make fools of your wise men so that the very men you are confident will stand by you will change their minds and oppose you. This is the same thing that Ezek. 23:22 says: "Behold, I will rouse up against you your lovers from whom you turned in disgust, and I will bring them against you from every side, etc." And we read in Jer. 30:14: "All your lovers have forgotten you." Exactly the same thing happened to the people of Constantinople when they took the Turk into an alliance with them. Shortly after that they became

6 "You fool, you do not understand."

a tributary of the Turk. The same thing occurs often in our day in the case of the emperor and pope. While the emperor believes that the pope is standing by him because they have struck a treaty, when the situation becomes serious, the pope changes his mind and turns against the emperor, etc. The Jews, too, have experienced the same thing. When they solicited the friendship of the Romans with the thought that they would come out victorious against all nations, those Romans whom they had wanted as their auxiliaries immediately became their masters. This is also what Latin writers say with such elegance, that we must seek out our peers as friends and watch out for those who are stronger.

8. *Will I not destroy the wise men out of Edom?* He threatens to remove not only their external protection—arms, might, fortifications—lest they be able to feel safe, but also their wise men, who with their advice might provide help in those periods of tumult. After all, this land did have wise and far-sighted men—Esau was one—but all these, He says, He will make fools of and destroy. Many scattered passages of Scripture point to this idea of the confounding of human wisdom and the plans of the flesh. Ps. 107:27 reads: "They reeled and staggered like drunken men and were at their wits' end"; and Ps. 33:10: "The Lord brings the counsel of the nations to nought." The flesh, therefore, cannot in time of temptation cure itself with its own counsel and wisdom.

9. *And your mighty men shall be dismayed, O Teman.* More accurately this reads: "Your mighty men will become fearful," *flüchtig und schüchtern.* You see, this properly means that fear which generally pervades an army that is about to be cut to pieces and sees no way of escape. Also, what we have rendered in our translation as a common noun [7] ought to be translated with a proper noun, namely, "in Teman." For that is what He calls the land which Teman, a grandson of Esau, mentioned in Genesis (36:11, 15, 42), named after himself, as princes and kings sometimes do.

So that every man from Mount Esau will perish. The Hebrew adds "by slaughter, etc." "Thus I will take care that everyone from Mount Esau will be wiped out, that not a single person will survive." Yet the Hebrew has far greater significance than can be rendered conveniently in another language. It is as if He were say-

[7] The Vulgate text has *a meridie* ("to the south").

ing: "There will be a heap [of bodies] lying here and another heap there. They will be killed everywhere in the cities if any care to resist. Also in that terrible slaughter your wise men will be so greatly terrified that they will become completely stupid, etc."

11. *On the day that you stood aloof.* This is the reason why He is so angry with them. Also, this clearly reveals the fact that the prophet prophesied around the time of the Babylonian captivity—as I said concerning the time of this prophet at the beginning of this chapter.

His army. More accurately this is "his wealth." This is the passage that moves me to believe that this prophet worked at the time of the Babylonian captivity, for Jerusalem was never captured before that captivity of the Chaldeans.

12. *And you will not look down upon.* The Hebrew reads, "Therefore you will not see." And yet, that Hebrew word does not simply mean "to see." Instead, it is what we mean when we say in German *Du wirst nicht mehr deine Lust sehen,* "No longer will you amuse yourself" over the unfortunate circumstances of your brother.

You will not boast. "You will no longer taunt him in the day of his affliction. Indeed, also upon you will fall a hailstorm of disasters."

In the day of their ruin. For this there are only two words in Hebrew.[8] The Latin translator, however, delighted as he was with an unfortunate supply of Latin verbiage, renders it sometimes with *perditio,* sometimes with *angustia,* sometimes with *ruina,* etc.

14. *And you will not stand at the parting of the ways.* The Hebrew word פֶּרֶק means two things: both "a forcible taking away" and "destruction," as one may see in Ps. 50:22: ". . . lest at any time He carry you off and there be no one to snatch you away."[9] So also here we can understand both meanings. The sense is this:

[8] It is not clear which Hebrew words Luther has in mind, for there are three synonyms of "calamity" in v. 12, another in v. 13, and two in v. 14. Their Vulgate equivalents are *peregrinatio, perditio,* and *angustia* in v. 12; *ruina* and *vastitas* in v. 13; *exitus* and *tribulatio* in v. 14.

[9] The passage cited does not contain the verb פָּרַק, but its synonym הִצִּיל.

"You, O Edom, were not content with plundering your brother, with taking away his wealth from him when at My urging you were sent out with the other nations against him, but you also held back and delayed those who wished to take refuge in flight, and you delighted in killing those who were thus held back."

Nor cut off. That is, "Those who were unable to flee you kept under pressure and crushed to insure that all would be killed."

16. *For as you have drunk upon My holy mountain.* He threatens all nations with destruction, as if to say: "I will put you and the other nations into the same pot. You will be destroyed together, just as you destroyed My people and ate and drank My blessings in My sanctuary. But I will see to it that other peoples may in turn eat up and swallow all your possessions." Thus with His marvelous sense of judgment God Almighty always punishes the old sins of a kingdom by means of new sins of other peoples whom He rouses to act, as we see here. The nations that have sorely tried the people of God have sinned. Here the Lord threatens vengeance for this sin—that other nations will rise up against those destroyers. In this way some new sin would punish that old one. Thus the Tartars and the Goths with their new sins rose up against the old sins of the Romans, who had oppressed the Jews in so many ways. Today the Turk is powerful. However, if the earth will not immediately pass away, another stronger country will rise up that will be stirred by the judgment of God to subdue the Turk, etc. Up to this point we have considered the first part of this prophecy concerning the threatened destruction of the Edomites at the hands of other nations, who I believe are the Romans.

17. *And in Mount Zion there shall be salvation.* Here begins the latter section of this prophecy. Now that the Jews have been carried off into captivity and the Edomites who mocked the Jews have in turn been destroyed, he promises another kingdom, which we can understand in no other way than as the spiritual kingdom of Christ spread among all nations through the Gospel. The Jews had been divided into two kingdoms: the kingdom of Israel, which was never again established after its destruction; and the kingdom of Judah, which was changed into the kingdom of Christ. This is an absolute essential to the understanding of those who read the prophets, whose books frequently mention these two kingdoms.

It is important, then, to know that the prophet here is speaking about Christ's spiritual kingdom. The very words force us to accept this, for when he says:

The house of Jacob shall possess those who had possessed it, he is indicating that the house of Jacob would recover and extend its kingdom for itself and would reduce to subjects those under whose dominion it had suffered before. This is the meaning of the Hebrew word (יָרַשׁ), which our translator rendered "possess" but which he did not render with the force of the Hebrew word. For it more properly signifies what the Germans call *einnehmen.* So this magnificent word can fit neither the external kingdom of Judah nor the Israelites, for the kingdom of Israel was never destined for restoration—as is quite clear from the sacred accounts. That contradiction, therefore, forces us to understand that this is Christ's spiritual kingdom, that from the people of Israel the apostles and other disciples of Christ would come who were going to make subject to themselves the whole world by a new preaching of the Gospel and thus were going to establish a new and eternal kingdom. This is why he says that in Mount Zion there would be an escape, or a new salvation, that is, that from Zion there would come forth the sort of preaching which, if believed, would free one from death, sin, and hell. This preaching would come first from Zion, as Is. 2:3 says: "For out of Zion shall go forth the Law, and the Word of the Lord from Jerusalem"; and Joel 2:32: "In Jerusalem there will be salvation."

And it shall be holy. That is, the nations will no longer be able to corrupt it, as had happened before.

18. *The house of Jacob shall be a fire, etc.* He says that in the universal subjection of all nations even the Edomites are going to be subjects of this kingdom. If we take this to mean corporal subjection, this all becomes absurd and conflicts with history. After all, what is less fitting than that the house of Jacob will be a fire and the house of Joseph a flame and the house of Esau—that is, the Edomites—straw destined to be devoured by the flame? In response to this, the house of Joseph never returned after the Babylonian captivity.[10] Furthermore, the house of Judah never

[10] The Assyrian captivity is meant.

took possession of the Edomites. Finally, what is most absurd of all is that he here finally says that the Edomites would also be consumed by fire after he has already prophesied that the Edomites will all perish and be reduced to nothing. All this, then, completely compels us to understand this to refer to the preaching of the Gospel among all nations by the apostles and other disciples. By this preaching all nations have devoured—that is, have become incorporated with—the kingdom of Christ spiritually, so that they can no longer be snatched from Christ's hand, as Christ says in the gospel.[11] After all, it is true that, once one has grasped the Gospel, Satan does not easily prevail. This is something which history reveals, for that Arabia Petraea, in which the Edomites lived, has been a place for holy men since the Gospel was revealed. St. Anthony [12] and many other holy fathers have lived there.

There shall be no survivors. He will subjugate the house of Esau in such a way that not even remnants will survive. Nothing will survive that can prevail against this kingdom of Christ. For through the Gospel Christians become the lords of all creatures. So much for the power and efficacy of the preaching of the Gospel among the Gentiles.

19. *And those who live toward the south shall possess, etc.* Here we have a strange contradiction if you take this literally, to mean some external kingdom. First he says they will take possession of; then, they will be possessed. The kingdom of Israel had been divided into twelve tribes and had been carefully cautioned by the law of Moses not to mix the tribes, as one can see in Moses.[13] But since he here plainly says that those of the Negeb—that is, those who live to the south—will take possession of Mount Esau, etc., we must take this to mean something completely different from the literal sense. The sense, then, is this: The Christian apostles and other disciples who are going to live toward the south on Mount Zion, where the Gospel is preached first—these men, I say, will with their preaching produce fruit among the Edomites.

And those of the plains (more accurately, the low places, the

[11] John 10:28.

[12] Cf. *Luther's Works,* 24, p. 65; 28, p. 322.

[13] Num. 36:9.

pleasant valleys amid the mountains, *die Gründe) will possess the Philistines.* This is something that never actually occurred after the Babylonian captivity, for even the entire kingdom was unable to overpower and subject the Philistines. We must, then, take this as a reference to that spiritual subjection through the Gospel.

Ephraim. This, too, is contrary to the Law. This happened, therefore, through the apostles when they went into Samaria to preach the Gospel. What follows this is also quite similar.

Benjamin shall possess Gilead. Benjamin is on the west side of the Jordan, but Gilead is on the other side, in the tribe of Gad. Necessity compels us, then, to relate all of these references to the preaching of the Gospel.

20. *And the exiles of this army, etc.* This is far more absurd than the previous references. What can we call more absurd if you look merely at the words than that they who were taken away into captivity and were never led back would oppress all the land of the Canaanites? This is the same as what follows about the exiles of Jerusalem: that is, that the captives from Israel would take possession of the cities of the Negeb, those cities which were located around Jerusalem and in Edom.

As far as Zarephath. This is the same word as that which we see in 1 Kings 17:9 concerning a city near Sidon where there lived the widow who fed Elijah. Lyra here suggests some trifling observation or other and wants this to refer to France. This seems very inappropriate to me. This is a violent and twisted gloss that bears no resemblance at all to the truth. The translators make a similar error in our translation in the words.

In Bosphorus.[14] Jerome produces the testimony of his own Jew from whom he learned his Hebrew that the emperor Constantine transferred the Jews to Bosphorus in Thrace and that there they would wait to again establish their kingdom, as well as all sorts of other lies. But that good man [Jerome] has been deceived by a figment of Judaic imagination. We clearly see that the prophet is speaking about those places which are in the land of Canaan, where the kingdom of Christ first began through the Gospel. Furthermore, the Hebrew is *Bisphorod,* that is, "near Phorod." This word is

[14] In Sepharad.

found nowhere else in the Bible. So the Jews, too, devise a story—namely, that this is Spain. But this simply doesn't fit. In fact, I don't think any Jew knows what it is. Our translators,[15] fooled by the similar sound of the name, have also interpreted Bosphorus for בִּסְפָרַד. This is ridiculous. Therefore we must take this to refer to some inconsequential town in the land of Canaan which has been obliterated by the ravages of time so that today it is impossible for us to know what was there. You see, the fictions of the Jews are worthless—similar to old wives' tales.

21. *Savior shall go up.* He calls leaders "saviors," as we find in the Book of Judges (Judg. 3:9), where He sent them many saviors, that is, leaders to lead them and take charge of them, to be in the lead if they ever had to fight with enemies. So here the apostles and other disciples are called "saviors," men who by preaching that joyful Gospel message have certainly freed them from all the assaults of Satan and from the gates of hell; men who have judged them in faith, who have ruled them with just judgment, and thus have prepared the eternal kingdom for the Lord.

Praise be to Christ!
Wittenberg, February 1, 1525

[15] The Vulgate.

LECTURES ON MICAH

The Altenburg Text

Translated by
RICHARD J. DINDA

PREFACE TO MICAH

WHEN the destruction of the Jewish people was imminent, when the new age and kingdom—namely, Christ—were coming, God sent many great prophets to cry out and lament about the coming destruction of the entire people so that at least some who heard the preaching of a threatening evil might believe, be converted, and, thus converted, be saved. In this way they might delay that terrible and wretched destruction. Thus at the same time prophesied Amos, whom I regard as the first, Hosea, who must be counted after Amos, and Micah. Isaiah also prophesied at the same time, although he would have been the last of these. Now all of them prophesied about the destruction of the old people and the bringing in of a new people, about the abolition of the external kingdom and the establishment of a new spiritual kingdom which would happen through Christ. You see, when the physical kingdom ended, the spiritual kingdom of Christ succeeded it. It was impossible for the external kingdom of the flesh to stand along with the spiritual kingdom. Therefore the external kingdom had to be abolished, and that was accomplished by the miraculous counsel of God when He caused His people to be carried off into captivity, a people who were boasting smugly about their external kingdom and external righteousness. And yet, after the dispersion—massive though it was—God Almighty preserved for Himself a remnant of the people which He caused to be brought back from both sides—from Israel and from Judah. Of these remnants saved, nevertheless, the greater part was numbered from Judah rather than from Israel, in order that there might be some in whom this new kingdom might begin. After all, there had been a promise that Christ would be born of these people and that from them would come forth the Savior and that new Word of the new kingdom. Therefore, in order that God might stand on His promises, He saved some—although very few—among whom He might present what He had promised and might be found truthful. The prophet Micah thus was sent to declare that the destruction of the entire people was imminent. But all the prophets cried out in vain.

Today through God we have received the sound Gospel in rich measure. We, too, must have no doubt that some great calamity and change of all things threaten. Because of His goodness, God Almighty warns us, just as He warned the Jews with many prophets and an abundance of words. He calls us to repent, but just as they held all things in great contempt, so also do we. After all, our princes rage against the Gospel and its preachers. They persecute its preachers, arrest them, throw them into prison, and kill them. Even the bishops, whose responsibility it is to promote the Gospel, persecute them very much and confirm wickedness against the Word of God. So what happened to the Jews when they despised the Word is undoubtedly going to happen also to us when we despise it.

In general, the prophet Micah discusses the same thing in his prophecy as Hosea does in his. They both saw so many prophets and such a complete expression of the Word sent in vain, they saw so many prophets despised and, in fact, killed that they foretold that both kingdoms would be destroyed. Yet there was the clear promise of God that the kingdom of David would be an external kingdom, that no leader would be taken away from the throne of David until the Messiah would come. The promise says this openly. In appearance this certainly was contrary to the prophets, who kept threatening and prophesying that both kingdoms would be ruined. Even the wicked people of Judah kept pressing the prophets with these prophecies about the kingdom of Judah. (Our people do not have a clear word of this sort with which they could oppose the Gospel, like the Jews.) And yet God miraculously kept His promise, so that He provided both kingdoms with a very wretched destruction. But He was not unaware of His promise, for the kingdom did not disappear completely. King Jehoiachin, who was carried off to Babylon [1] and put into prison, nevertheless was saved. He was finally honored and elevated above all the kings in Babylon,[2] as the sacred histories have it. This flesh, however, does not notice that God thus reveals in one man what He has promised. This is God's

[1] The Weimar text has *in Assyriam,* but see 2 Kings 24:15.

[2] The Weimar text has *Assyriorum,* but see 2 Kings 25:27-30.

way. Thus also in Rom. 11:1, Paul proves that God did not reject His people and says: "I ask then, has God rejected His people? By no means! I myself am an Israelite, a descendant of Abraham, etc." A special part of that otherwise numberless people was saved. Isaiah, too, says (Is. 10:22): "For though your people Israel be as the sand of the sea, only a remnant will be saved." The Jews, however, understood the promises in a different way. Therefore they did not at all accept the prophecy of Hosea, Micah, and the other prophets that both kingdoms would be destroyed. Our people have no such word, although they boast that they are the church which God is not going to forsake. But let them look at the example of the Jews. Let them be frightened and cease being confident. God will be able to save His church here and there throughout the world—one in one city, another in another. In the meantime, all the princes, the pope, and all the bishops will perish. This is just the way He miraculously saved the kingdom of Judah, although almost the entire kingdom was wiped out. Thus God acts in miraculous fashion so that the wicked are ashamed and blinded and die. In this way He sometimes acts so that the prophets appear completely contrary to Him. This appears very clearly in Jeremiah and Ezekiel. Jeremiah prophesies about Zedekiah, king of Judah, and says that it will come to pass that Zedekiah will be captured and surrendered into the hands of the king of the Chaldeans. Then the prophet adds (Jer. 32:4-5): "And he shall speak with him face to face and see him eye to eye; and they shall take Zedekiah to Babylon, etc." Ezekiel prophesies about this same king (Ezek. 12:12-13): "He shall cover His face that he may not see the land with his eyes . . . and I will bring him to Babylon in the land of the Chaldeans, yet he shall not see it, etc." This is the way Micah prophesies. Ezekiel had foretold that the king would not see the land, and indeed he was correct, because they tore out his eyes before he was taken into Babylon. Jeremiah had foretold that Zedekiah would see the eyes of the king of Babylon, and he, too, was correct, for he was brought before the king first before his eyes were put out. The wicked Jews were offended by this contradiction —for such it seemed to be—so that they charged the prophets with insanity, as people who contradicted themselves. But this is God's way if He wants to blind us, and so He acts against the presumptuous who are too smug, etc.

CHAPTER ONE

1. *In the days of . . . the kings of Judah.* He does not mention the kings of Israel, although he nevertheless is prophesying the destruction of both. Both Amos and Hosea implicate the kings of Israel and Judah simultaneously. But because Micah prophesied in the kingdom of Judah, he mentions only the kings of Judah.

Of Moresheth. This is a city in the kingdom of Judah, as we see from Joshua (15:44). Consequently he is called a Morashite. In addition, Micah was a minister of the Word for a long time. We can draw this conclusion from the time when the individual kings under whom he prophesied ruled. Therefore he did not make his prophecy all at once in one sermon or during a single year. Instead, he said some things in sermons in one year, others in other discourses in other years. Therefore, just as we earlier divided the prophet Amos into many discourses, we must also do the same thing in the case of Micah. In the same way, Luke calls the prophecy of Isaiah the "book of the words of Isaiah." [1]

Against Samaria and Jerusalem. Surely it is great audacity on the part of the prophet to mention Jerusalem immediately at the beginning of his prophecy. You see, he has quickly touched, as it were, the pupil of the eye of the Jews. It is a wonder that the prophet was not killed immediately. However, he did not have altogether bad kings, and he even prophesied under pious Hezekiah. Otherwise this prophecy appeared to be completely contrary to the promise regarding the kingdom of Judah, as we said earlier. The elders of the people, who intended to free the prophet Jeremiah from an unjust death, used this example against the furious priests who wanted Jeremiah killed. This we read in Jer. 26:18: "Micah of Moresheth prophesied in the days of Hezekiah, king of Judah, and said to all the people of Judah, etc."

[1] Cf. Luke 3:4.

2. *Hear, you peoples, all of you; hearken, O earth.* He speaks with great vigor and vehemence at the beginning of his prophecy. He visualizes the coming destruction with such certainty that he does not see how anyone can resist it. He would willingly give advice to the people as he sees the wretched destruction as if it were already present. He urges them with spirited vehemence. He is even more urgent when he adds:

And let the Lord God be a witness against you. That is, "What I am saying certainly comes from the Lord. When you hear me speaking to you, imagine that it is in fact the Lord speaking to you. Listen! Listen! All of you, pay attention to me. Come together and have no doubt that you are listening to the Lord when you hear me. Therefore, believe me!" This is the way I understand simply the fact that he says, "Let the Lord God be a witness against you." That is, "Don't take my preaching in any other way than as if God Himself were speaking to you."

The Lord, from His holy temple. It is as if he were saying: "I am speaking of this Witness and this Lord who is in the temple at Jerusalem." With this preface he rejects and throws out completely whatever there is of their worship about which they were boasting: namely, the temple, their sacrifices—briefly, whatever they thought was the only thing that pleased God.

3. *For behold, the Lord will come forth out of His place.* Now he is setting forth what he intends to teach. He says, as it were: "Don't please yourselves! You deceive yourselves when you imagine that you have a God who is kindly disposed to you. Don't be so smug! By no means can He endure the smug and presumptuous. He who you think is hiding and silent will come forth. He will surely come."

He will come down. That is, "He will reveal Himself as present in effect, namely, through the kings of the Assyrians and the Babylonians."

He will tread upon the high places of the earth. The Hebrew word בָּמָה which the Latin translator renders here as "high places" *(excelsa)* is frequently taken as "altars," but it also means in general whatever is high or lofty, for I believe that the Latins call altars *(altaria)* by that name because of their height *(altitudo)* or loftiness. The meaning, then, is this: "The Lord will tread upon the high places of the earth," that is, upon the heights of the earth and upon those places which stand out above others. That is, the Lord will tread upon and is going to reduce to absolutely nothing princes, kings, priests, temple, sanctuary—all the things you believe are going to endure and stand firm. This is the proposition, the theme, the sum, or the scope of this entire prophecy, for everything which follows relates to this.

4. *And the mountains will melt under Him.* This is a synecdoche: the container for the thing contained. With these two words (mountains and valleys) he includes, in my judgment, the whole people. It is as if he were saying: "All things will be dissolved, all things—both in the mountains and in the valleys—will be consumed. No cities will be safe, whether they are built on the heights or in the valleys." So he is alluding to the makeup or terrain of the land, because it is filled with small mountains.

Like wax before the fire, like waters poured down a steep place. He is still bearing down on the destruction and says, as it were: "The Lord will overthrow you very easily and with no difficulty. For as wax cannot but melt before the heat of fire, and as water rushing down a steep course cannot be kept from flowing downward, so that great destruction of yours comes with such force and headlong rush and so threatens you that, as wax cannot resist the heat of fire to keep from melting, you will by no means be able to counteract this evil." That is how great the wrath of God is when He becomes angry against the wicked who despise His Word.

5. *All this is for the wickedness of Jacob.* These matters the prophet certainly taught with great courage and audacity (παρρησία). He dared to accuse of wickedness men who appeared to be very holy, who were very careful about doing the works of the Law, lest they transgress it in any part, who kept promising themselves a complete and perfect holiness. If you were to compare with them our self-righteous monks and whatever there is of this ilk, the latter would be nothing. After all, the former were well versed in the works which God had commanded, and they performed them with great care and enthusiasm, while our people are engaged in foolish and ridiculous works which they themselves have made up. But this ought to have been translated more accurately: "This

whole thing is on account of *(propter)* the transgression of Jacob." It ought to be translated as in the case of Hos. 12:12: "And Israel did service for the sake of a wife *(propter uxorem),*" where our books [2] read "in regard to a wife *(in uxorem).*" But with this preaching the prophets stirred up against themselves the wrath and bitterness of all men. After all, the work-righteous Jews took nothing harder than that their own righteousnesses were condemned. This is just like our people today who cannot stand this, although they are already convicted by the Word of God.

What is the transgression of Jacob? etc. The prophet himself is indicating that the wicked work-righteous had guarded their own acts fiercely. Therefore he raises an objection to his own statement in roleplay style *(per* μίμησιν*),* saying in the role of the people: "What is the transgression of Jacob?" [And he answers:] "Is it not Samaria?"

And what are the high places of Judah? This expression "high places" means altars. The sense, then, is this: "I will uncover for you the sin of both Israel and Judah." Israel sins in Samaria, Judah in Jerusalem. This is the source of every wickedness—namely, worship and sacrifices which God has not instituted and which the Word of God has not commanded. And here we see again—as we do in all Scripture—how it does not please God, and in fact, how He hates it, if we establish anything outside the Word of God, however good and holy it may appear. Those rites and sacrifices of the Jews which they were performing for the true God were like this. Thus finally our people should be ashamed and repent of their error and know that none of these things which they have instituted themselves are pleasing to God.

6. *Therefore I will make Samaria a heap of stones.* He responds to their objections, with which they were supporting their wickedness against the Word of God. What we read here as "a heap of stones" is the same expression [3] that we also have in Ps. 79:1: "They have laid Jerusalem in ruins." This is the sort of wall of stones around vineyards. In this wall the stones are not put in and fitted together with cement.

[2] The Vulgate text.

[3] The Hebrew word עִי ("heap of ruins").

And I will pour down her stones into the valley. That is, "I shall forcefully tumble them down and hurl them into the valley in a heap so that neither tower nor wall remains."

And uncover her foundations. That is, "I shall mow her down in such a way that no stone remains upon another, so that her very foundations are visible to anyone."

7. *And all her images.* That is, "The king of Assyria will topple everything in which alone you take pride—your idols, calves, and other images."

All her hires. These are the unredeemed offerings (ἀναθήματα), presents, and gifts which they give to the priests or to the temples to encourage the worship of God. We had this earlier in Hosea (cf. 2:5).

For from the hire of a harlot she gathered them. This is a proverbial figure of speech. He calls the entire population a harlot. The idea, then, is as follows: "With your fornication you have gathered these statues, images, and hires, or unredeemed offerings (ἀναθήματα). They are the hires of a harlot. That is, you have obtained them all out of wickedness. Therefore I will again hand them over to a wicked king who also delights in idolatry. Just as they were obtained, so will they also perish." This is exactly the same expression as the Latin *Male parta male dilabuntur* ("Goods ill got must ill be lost").[4] Doubtless so also by the judgment of God the goods and treasures of the monasteries will become the prey and plunder of some wicked soldiers. After all, these were obtained from the hire of a harlot no less than was the hire of the Jews, as he calls it here. The Word of God will not tell a lie, etc.

8. *For this I will lament and wail.* The remaining part of this chapter is very difficult. So great is the difficulty of this passage that in nearly every word the prophet has used Hebrew tropes or figures of speech. It makes me think that almost every figure of speech of the Hebrew language has been gathered together here. We are absolutely insane, then, when we undertake the interpretation of the prophets without a very great skill in and understanding of the Hebrew language. But in explaining this, I shall merely

[4] Cf. *Luther's Works,* 19, p. 126, n. 10.

present as much as I can with the help of God. I can do nothing else; also, I should promise nothing else.

Up to this point he has been prophesying the destruction of the kingdoms of Israel and Judah: that all the idols and "unredeemed offerings" were going to be reduced to nothing by the king of the Assyrians, who would come as a destroyer against them because of the judgment of God. Here he has placed before their eyes the devastation as if it had already occurred. He is acting like a spectator of that destruction. With great affection he begins to speak about their destruction as if it were already present: "For this I will lament, etc." If we should want to translate this into Latin, we would have to read and understand it all in a potential sense. You see, the Hebrew lacks an optative mood; therefore the Jews cannot speak the way we do. The Latin would say it this way: *Posset aliquis, vel deberet quilibet, lugere et plangere* ("Someone could—or, anyone should—lament and wail").

I will go stripped and naked. We must apply this being naked to beautiful adornment, that is: "I will put on poor and cheap clothing after taking off all the more decent clothing. With this action I will signify the wretchedness of the destruction." In the same way also, Isaiah went about naked at the bidding of the Lord. With this nakedness he meant to show, as the text of Isaiah has it (Is. 20:3), the captivity of Egypt. It is not that we believe that Isaiah walked about completely naked but that he wore only modest and very poor clothing and abandoned his long and decent garb. This is the way we must also take the passage in the gospel account about the disciple who "left the linen cloth and ran away naked" (Mark 14:52).

I will make lamentation like the dragons. The Hebrew word means both sea monster and dragon. I don't know what sort of lamentations dragons make. The prophet is mentioning huge beasts that make their noises in accordance with the size of their bodies. With this he exaggerates the impending wretchedness.

And mourning like the young of ostriches. The nature of the ostrich is described in Job 39:13-18. She abandons on the ground the eggs she has laid and completely neglects her chicks. Therefore he calls them "the young of ostriches"—chicks which their mothers have completely deserted and abandoned.

9. *For her wound is incurable.* That is, it is a very wretched and lamentable wound. You see, this is what the Hebrew word means: a wretched, poor, depressed creature.

And it has come to Judah, it has reached the gate of My people, to Jerusalem. I think that the prophet is speaking not about the Babylonian [5] captivity but about the terror of a captivity at the hand of someone close by. In the same sense, if the Turk were to destroy some nearby city, this closeness would terrify us all so that we would be afraid that the Turk would come to us too. In this passage, then, I think the sense is as if he were saying: "The wound of the kingdom of Israel is huge and pitiable. The damage is irreparable. This wound frightens Judah and causes it to be terrified also so that it, too, believes that it is going to be ruined and destroyed."

10. *Tell it not in Gath, weep not at all.* The word *lachrimis* ("with tears") was added in the Latin translation. It could have been omitted. This passage has been taken from the song of David in 2 Sam. 1:20. The prophets have the custom of repeating many things from the historical books. You see, here we have the same words as there: "Tell it not in Gath, publish it not in the streets of Ashkelon, lest the daughters of the Philistines rejoice, lest the daughters of the uncircumcised exult." You see, it was a great disaster for Israel that King Saul was killed. If the enemies of Israel had discovered this, they would have rejoiced at the death of the king. Micah here is imitating the same idea. It is as if he were saying: "Conceal this if there is some way you can, lest your enemies rejoice when they learn about the calamity you have sustained." You see, not merely destruction but also great fear of impending disgrace was involved. They were afraid that their enemies would revile them and mock God, of whom they had always boasted as their Protector and Defender.

In Bethleaphrah. The Hebrew word properly means ground which has been dug up, ground which has not been packed down —the sort of dirt that is thrown up from graves. In other places it is generally translated with the word "earth." "Bethleaphrah" is a Hebraism: "in a house of dust," as if to say: "In a house where dust is sprinkled, where dirt is generally scattered." The idea,

[5] The Weimar text has "Assyrian," but the Halle manuscript reading "Babylonian" is probably the correct one.

then, is this: "Don't mourn openly. It is best for you to hide in some corner where mourners generally mourn. Hide in corners, lest your foes hear about your very wretched disaster and revile you."

Sprinkle yourselves with dust. In the Hebrew this is: "Roll in the dust there," obviously, "lest your enemies find out about your destruction." Thus in all these expressions he is setting forth a coming situation as if it were already present in order to move them to repent by declaring the misery of the impending destruction.

11. *Pass on your way, inhabitants of Shaphir* [i. e., *of Beauty*]. Here we have a strange difficulty. I read it according to the Hebrew as follows: "Pass on your way, O Habitation of Beauty, in nakedness and shame. The habitation of Zaanan (or Zenan) does not come forth. The House of the Neighbor (Bethezel) will take its mourning from you while it continues to stand." It is Jerome's custom in his translation of the Bible always to render proper nouns with common nouns; in his commentaries, on the other hand, he always translates the common nouns with proper nouns. So here, what he translates "which dwells in the way out" *(quae habitat in exitu)*, should absolutely have been translated with a proper noun. There is a Hebraism in the word "habitation." You see, the Hebrew word means citizen. We would translate it accurately if we were allowed to make up a word like "citizenplace" *(cividitas)*. In addition, the prophet is speaking with a sharp and bitter concession: "Pass on your way!" as if to say: "Go, Beautiful City; go, you great realm of Samaria! Go on your way. On your way, Precious City! There is no salvation for you. It's all over as far as you are concerned. There is no one to hold back the Lord. The wrath of God is running against you like a waterfall," as he has said before (v. 4). "Beside this, 'your shame has been uncovered,' that is, it has clearly happened that you are passing on your way and are being destroyed. No one is in the dark about that." You see, our reading,[6] "your shame has been brought into disorder" *(confusa ignominia)*, is unsuitable.

Do not come forth. This the prophet seems to me to be saying in imitation style (μιμητικῶς). Zaanan is a city of the tribe of Judah.

[6] In the Vulgate.

This is clear from Joshua 15:37. The prophet has added an extra "a." This city along with the others named here was close to the prophet while he was making this prophecy, for he prophesied in the kingdom of Judah, as we have said earlier.[7] So he is addressing himself to neighboring and adjoining cities. And there is a double meaning to this passage: (1) "Go on your way, O Kingdom of Israel; begone; our city in which we live is not yet on the way out with you; it is safe, etc."; (2) (and this second meaning I like better) as if the prophet were saying: "My Zaananites are still safe and are saying, 'The Assyrian will not come to us. This evil will not come close to us. We shall be safe, etc.' " Thus everything here is in very figurative language, as if he were saying: "Oh, no, Zenan will not depart." This seems to me to be the most suitable interpretation. If this does not please someone, let him show me better ones. But, as I have said, we should certainly read this as a proper noun.

The House of a Neighbor will take its mourning, etc. That is: "You are now on your way out. The Assyrian is carrying you off into captivity. Therefore the House of the Neighbor—that is, the kingdom of Judah—will take its mourning from you, for it is still standing, that is, it is still safe and standing." Although it still stands, nevertheless it mourns because of its fear on account of a neighbor's captivity, as I have said earlier.

12. *For the inhabitants of Maroth have been weakened in a good thing.* He gives the reason for the wailing. We can take also this passage to have two meanings. First, he is saying: "They have been weakened for a good thing," so that the sense is: they are weak for doing good. The inhabitants of Maroth,[8] that is, of disobedience, are not training themselves for good. We thus apply this to their sin. It is as if he were saying: "They have deserved to be frightened and to weep because of their own bitterness." The other meaning is this: They stand, they are safe, but they grieve, mourn, and are sad over you. In fact, they are afraid of evil for themselves. This meaning applies to the punishment. I prefer the latter idea.

Because evil has come down from the Lord to the gate of Jerusalem. That is, it even comes close to Jerusalem.

[7] Cf. p. 210 above.

[8] The Hebrew name Maroth means "bitterness."

13. *The rumble of the chariot, etc.* As everything of this passage at the end of this chapter is very difficult, so also this verse corresponds to the rest. I translate it from the Hebrew as follows: "Hitch up (or harness) the chariot for driving, O inhabitants of Lachish." There is nothing to what Lyra brings out about this city. In fact, this city on the plains of Judah close to the Palestinians is quite well known. It is in the immediate neighborhood of the others listed here. Because the prophet is prophesying among these cities, he suits his prophecy to them, as we have mentioned. Moreover, the prophet is saying this with bitter concession, as he did earlier. The meaning is this: "Hitch up your chariots and get ready, O Lachish. You, too, must leave. Captivity is close to you also."

Because you are the beginning of sin for the daughter of Zion, etc. These episodes of history are unknown to us. They are not recorded anywhere else in Scripture. Therefore we must have faith in the prophet that this city instigated and provided the opportunity for the kingdom of Judah to follow the wickedness of the kingdom of Israel. To summarize this passage, then: "Because you, O Lachish, were an accomplice in the sin of Israel, because you provided Judah with the first opportunity to pursue the wickedness of Israel, you will also share the penalty and be the first to go into captivity." This did happen, for this was the first city in the kingdom of Judah to be taken. Therefore when he says, "For in you were found," the prophet does not mean that this city was the first to have discovered these sins, but that it was the first—ahead of all the other cities of Judah—to follow this wickedness, led as she was by the example of Israel.

14. *Therefore give* (or *send*) *parting gifts to Moresheth-gath.* The Hebrew word Siloam appears in John 9:7, where John adds "which means Sent." שִׁלּוּחִים, "sending," means a gift as well as an emissary to the Jews. I translate it as emissaries here, so that the meaning is: "Go, send [people with] gifts, ask for supporting forces because of whose presence you think you will be safe. But, oh, how badly things will turn out for you,[9] for you are trying everything in vain."

The houses of Achzib (falsehood) shall be a deceitful thing. Here again he has translated poorly and ineptly with common

[9] We have read *tibi* for *sibi.*

nouns when he ought to have translated with a proper name, as above. After all, this city [Achzib] is also in the kingdom of Judah, as we see from Joshua 15:44. The translator himself renders it "the houses of falsehood." Such was the blindness of the translator. The meaning, then, is this: "You, O Lachish, and you, O Israel, are in agreement in your wickedness. So go ahead! Gather the Palestinians around you. Send an embassy to the houses of אַכְזִיב regarding a treaty. This is how the kings of Israel will be deceived." This means the kings of Israel will enter into an alliance with the Palestinians. They will rely on that security, but the very thing on which they rely will be the source of their destruction.

15. *I will again bring an heir to you.* We can take this either ironically or simply. Ironically, we understand it in this way: "I will bring you an heir of whom you are deserving, namely, the king of Assyria. You are equals in sin; therefore I will make him an equal heir." Here we have pure allusion, which is impossible for us to translate into Latin. To the Jews Mareshah means inheritance. He is alluding to this word, as if to say: "Just you wait, Inheritance, I'll send you an heir!" The simple meaning of this passage—and I prefer it—is this: "You, O Mareshah, are still standing and safe. You are in safety. The destroying foe has not yet come to you. An heir is being sent to you, namely, I myself, to declare repentance to you with my prophecy. If you believe my preaching, you will be saved and will escape the captivity. This prophecy of mine is 'the glory of Israel which comes even to Adullam.'" This is how we have solved in unusual ways this intricate and difficult passage. We have shown only what we could with the help of God. What follows now is an explanation of the preceding.

16. *Make yourselves bald and cut off your hair.* Baldness was a sign of mourning among that people, as we have said earlier in other prophets.

For the children of your delight, that is, for the offspring in whom you delight and from whom you have received great joy.

Make yourselves as bald. That is, "Weep and mourn seriously. A great and wretched captivity threatens you. Shave yourselves completely bald, just as an eagle regularly sheds its old feathers and grows new ones, so that his youth is renewed, as we have it in the psalm (Ps. 103:5).

CHAPTER TWO

In the first chapter he completed his first discourse. In this chapter he begins a new one. You see, he delivered these sermons on different days or at different times rather than at a single time, as I mentioned at the beginning.[1] In the first chapter he declared that their captivity would come to them because of their holiness,[2] that is, because of their idolatrous worship of God which they themselves had established according to their own will and contrary to the clear Word of God. Here he is announcing the same captivity as a result of the fruits of their wickedness. For as faith cannot but produce good fruits, so wickedness cannot but produce bad fruits like greed, violence, unjust judgments, etc., all of which the prophet lists here and the apostle Paul lists in Gal. 5:19-21. Therefore, as he rebuked their hypocrisy and disguised wickedness, so in this chapter he censures those crass and manifest sins which lack every guise of holiness and which cannot but follow when the heart is wicked.

1. *Woe to those who devise trouble.* The Hebrew word אָוֶן is quite familiar. It properly means trouble. This we see from Ps. 90:10: "If by reason of strength they be fourscore years, yet their span is but toil and trouble." From this, metaphorically, any iniquity came to be called by this name among the prophets.[3] Therefore it is a metaphor also in this passage. It is as if he were saying: "You are doing this in your own bed." When he says "in your own bed," he is periphrastically stating their interests and strivings, so that the idea is this: "You have been doing this one

[1] Cf. p. 210 above.

[2] Cf. p. 212 above.

[3] The Zwickau text states it this way: "From this, in a transferred or metaphorical sense, any wickedness derives its name, because wickedness afflicts both doer and sufferer 'with trouble' (*dolore*)." Cf. W, XIII, 268, 7—9.

thing day and night. This is your interest. You meditate solely on this one thing—how to harm the poor and treat them violently." We have the same expression in Ps. 36:4: "He plots mischief while on his bed," that is, "He did this, he set this as his task, etc." In sum, then, the prophet is saying here: "You never consider doing good. No thought of righteousness ever enters your mind."

When the morning dawns they perform it. He is designating a certain time. In my opinion, the prophet is speaking about the evil which they commit in the areas of justice and doctrine. That is, they have corrupted justice for the poor and the oppressed; they do not promote fair justice, and they teach wicked things instead of the Word. The meaning, then, is this: "You have a concern for only one thing—oppressing the poor. In doing this you make up and redo the laws. You do not render fair judgment. In the morning you teach the people and pass judgments, but at night you meditate on something else entirely, namely, how to make a profit on the Word of God and how to do with your perverse sense of justice nothing else but to swallow up the poor that their fields and possessions might become your booty." These are the fruits of wickedness. After all, what fruits other than evil ones should an evil tree produce? We see an excellent reflection of this sort of thing in the rule of the pope. There they do nothing else and watch for nothing else than that those who belong to that rule live in style. All the pope's laws and rules aim at this point, that his clergy, as he calls them, lack nothing, that they have an abundant supply of all things. Lest they lack anything, they proscribe the poor as debtors and consign them to hell again and again.

Because their hand is against God.[4] The prophet is explaining what he intended to say. It is as if he were saying: "Whatever they do and whatever they teach is against God, much as they strive to give a different impression." This is the way our papists have appropriated to their own use almost every good thing under the pretext of the name of the Lord, of the holy apostles Peter and Paul, and of the holy church. Finally, whatever money there is comes back to them. They have devoured the houses of widows, as Christ says (cf. Matt. 23:14).

[4] The translation as well as the commentary is based on the Vulgate text: *Quoniam contra deum est manus eorum.*

2. *They have oppressed a man and his house.* The Jews use their own little word (גֶּבֶר), which we translate in Latin as *virum.* We speak the same way in German when we say impersonally: *Man sagt also.* The prophets everywhere mention these pursuits of the wicked, as we have seen earlier.

3. *Behold, against this family I am devising evil.* The Lord is placing His own thoughts in opposition to their wicked plans. It is as if He were saying: "You are plotting evil against others; so I am planning evil against you."

From which you cannot remove your necks; and you shall not walk haughtily, for it will be an evil time. "I shall see to it that your pride is restrained, that you do not strut proudly with heads held high as you do violence to others, because the time will be an evil one. The Assyrian will come. He will tame you who now are so wild and haughty."

4. *In that day they shall take up a taunt song against you and lament with lamentation.* That is, "There will come a time when I shall cause you to become a tale for all men. You will become the subject of the song of your enemies who will conquer you." He is setting out the theme, or summary, of the song, as if to say: "They will sing about you in this way":

We are utterly ruined. The land of my people has been completely changed. We discussed this word *(pars)* earlier in Amos.[5] It properly means the inheritance, portion, or fields assigned to individuals.

How he removes it from me! This, too, is part of the song. Furthermore, this passage has a double meaning. The first is that the land was invaded twice, first by Tiglath-pileser, the king of the Assyrians, and then also by his[6] son. But this does not seem right to me. I translate it this way: "How will anyone take it away from me, so that our fields may again be distributed?" Thus I translate the Hebrew verb as an adverb. You see, this is customary for the Jews in expressions of this sort, a fact that becomes very clear from Ps. 71:20-21: "Thou hast turned and revived me"; and "Thou

[5] Cf. p. 153 above.

[6] We have read *eius* for *eis.*

hast turned and comforted me"; that is, "You have comforted me again, and You have received me again." The idea, then, is this: "All our possessions have disappeared. Who will therefore [7] loose us from this yoke, that our fields may again be apportioned to us?" But that will not happen. They have been allotted to another lord and possessor. So, if the enemies are singing this song, it is indeed a song. If the vanquished are singing it, it is a dirge. This is the meaning I take from this passage. I do not think that I am wrong, although I do differ with others.

5. *Therefore, you will have none to cast the line.* He certainly is speaking about the total destruction. Therefore we must not take this to mean only part of the people, as the Latin reading has it. It is as if He were saying: "The entire population will perish completely. No one will remain in the assembly or in the church of the Lord—that is, in that people where the Word of God is—to measure out the boundaries again." In this way the Lord has set the sum and substance of His plans against their wicked plans.

6. *They preach: Do not preach!* Everything in this passage has been translated with great confusion.[8] This is a new passage. The song has now been finished and completed. I translate it: "Do not drip a drop," [9] for that is the way it reads in the Hebrew. The prophets use the verb "to drip" *(stillare)* for "to preach," and "rain" means "preaching." To summarize, then: He is accusing the public officials who were forbidding the prophets to preach and to prophesy the destruction of the people whom God had chosen to be His own possession. He is accusing the public officials who kept charging the prophets with lying, who kept on quoting against the prophets the promises of God made to the people of Israel, as we said in detail at the beginning of this prophet.

They should not preach of such things; disgrace will not overtake us. These words are theirs, and they are saying them to the prophets. But we can understand them as a threat in this way: "We are warning them not to preach; otherwise, disgrace will overtake them." Or we can take them as follows: "Let them not preach of

[7] We have read *ergo* for *ego*.

[8] I. e., in the Vulgate.

[9] *Ne stilletis stillam.*

such things, because disgrace will not overtake us. The prophets are liars. The Lord will not thus confound His own people, whom He has chosen and to whom He has always promised He would be near." Both meanings are good.

7. *It was said in the house of Jacob.*[10] This is a new statement. It is as if he were saying: "This is the confidence of those who have been thus encouraged by a false understanding of the promises and hold our threats in contempt." Either Isaiah has imitated Micah, or Micah Isaiah, for both have this passage. In my judgment it seems that Isaiah has imitated Micah. Isaiah says (cf. Is. 50:2): "Is the hand of the Lord shortened?" The sense of the passage, then, is this: "You prophets are threatening us with evil. You are lying. God is with us. He is the Lord, our God, and we are His people. He has promised to be our Leader and that He would subject our enemies to us. But you are prophesying that our foes will be powerful against us. You are crazy. You are opposing the promises of God." This is how our papists also boast, contrary to the Gospel, that God will be with the church to the end of the world. But the prophets wanted to say that not everyone from Israel belonged to Israel and that the promises pertained not to the wicked but to the devout.

If such are His thoughts. It is as if they wanted to say: "Yes, yes; but the Lord's thoughts are not like that. He will not reject us." They speak this way in the Hebrew fashion.

Do not my words do good [*to him who walks uprightly*]? The prophet responds and in a few words breaks down and silences all their objections. It is as if He were saying: "I do not acknowledge the wicked as My own. I do not want you unless you are devout." This is a very clear and manifest passage against our papists, who still do not believe the Gospel and who bring up an argument drawn from the many: So many holy men could not have been wrong in the church for so long a time. The Lord says: "My words certainly are good. I am the Keeper of what I have promised. As I have promised, I am present—but for the devout, because they trust in Me and believe My Word. But My people have risen up to

10 The Weimar text has *Numquid dictum est in domo Jacob, etc.* The Vulgate has *Dicit domus Jacob, numquid, etc.* The Zwickau text has *Dicitur in domo Jacob, numquid, etc.*

be My enemy.[11] That is, the devout man is so far from being a 'good' man that He is even My enemy. He rises up against Me and opposes Me."

They take away the garment along with the tunic. "They are robbers who swallow up the wretched poor. Therefore I shall not spare them. I do not acknowledge them among My people."

And you are turning to war those who walk in safety. That is, "You initiate legal action where there is no litigation. You grasp at opportunities to sue." This is something with which we have had much experience under the rule of the pope.

9. *The women of My people you drive out from their pleasant houses.* Some take this statement to refer to the captivity, but it seems to me that he is still speaking about the plundering of the wicked priests, as if to say: "With your demands you have so upset the poor widows and matrons that they are forced to sell their homes. You have reduced them completely to dust." Also:

From their young children you have taken away My praise forever. Our translator [12] has rendered the Hebrew word poorly with the word *laudem*. You see, it properly means glory, or adornment. In Ps. 110:3 we have "in holy array." There we have the same word: *im heiligen Schmuck.*[13] The meaning, then, is this: "So great has been your greed, so consumed have you been with a desire to acquire wealth, that you take away even the glory of little children. The good things with which the little ones should have been adorned you have confiscated and diverted to your own use after driving out their mothers. There was nothing of the reasoning of a just and honorable man in you. You have taken away everything in such a way that the loss would never again be recovered." So I think that this is a description of their violence against women and children.

10. *Arise and go, for this is no place to rest.* "Because you have driven out the wretched women and children, your reward will be this: I will drive you out in turn. I will take away from you your glory, just as you have taken away the glory of the little children."

[11] This is a paraphrase of the beginning of v. 8.

[12] The Vulgate.

[13] This is Luther's German translation for *in splendoribus sanctis* (or *sanctorum*) in Ps. 110:3.

Because of uncleanness they will be destroyed, and the destruction will be harsh, or violent, or fierce. This is what the Hebrew word (מָרֶץ) means, that is, "You who walk handsomely in splendor and elegance, you who please yourselves extraordinarily, you are completely filthy before Me. Therefore, I will destroy you, and this destruction is going to be cruel and savage. You will be done for."

11. *Would that I were a man walking in the wind.* What we read in our [Latin] Bibles as: "Would that I were not" is an error.[14] But the Hebrew idiom "a man of wind," "a windy person," we had earlier in Hosea.[15] So also here: "Would that I were a windy man, would that I were a futile, false liar, so that those terrible things with which I threaten you may not take place."

Then I would preach to you of wine and strong drink. "I would want to lie. I would keep silent about the cross, the vengeance, and the destruction that will come to you. This is what your false prophets are doing. I would even declare to you promises and good times."

And that will be a preacher [for this people]. That is, "The Lord will send him to you as your preacher, and you will listen to him. Because you are not listening to me, a prophet sent by God, you will be compelled to listen to the king of the Assyrians."

12. *I shall surely gather all of you, O Jacob.* Up to this point the Lord has been setting His plans against the wicked devices of the impious pontiffs and priests who were taking over everything. In a sort of transition, He now passes from the kingdom of Israel to the eternal, spiritual kingdom of Christ. You see, it was the custom of all the prophets—something we have seen earlier in those prophets whom we have interpreted—to prophesy first about the destruction of the people and about the external kingdom and then to pass over to the spiritual and eternal kingdom of Christ. This kingdom, they had prophesied, would come after the external kingdom was destroyed. It is very important to notice this in the prophets. After all, we certainly cannot take this passage to mean the restoration of the entire external people, as the words surely sound. This passage, then, will force and most certainly convince one that he must understand it to refer to a spiritual kingdom. For

[14] The Vulgate has *utinam non essem.*

[15] Cf. Hos. 8:7.

it was absolutely certain that the kingdom of Israel never was going to be brought back and restored. We do not read that it ever was restored, as the sacred histories show. Yet, although it was completely ruined and destroyed, the prophet is crying out about bringing back Jacob, a name by which he certainly means the entire populace. We are forced, then, to admit that the prophet is speaking about a spiritual gathering which takes place when the Gospel has spread throughout the world, to which scattered Israel is to be gathered together. The words "all of you, O Jacob" certainly sound as if He would gather the entire people, although not all of them were gathered. Thus throughout everything echoes the promise about Christ: "In you will all the nations of the earth be blessed," although all nations nevertheless were not blessed. It is, then, especially important to notice this in the prophets. Otherwise incautious readers will slip and cannot but stumble over passages like these. It is one thing for all nations to be blessed; and another that all nations take or believe this promise of their blessedness. After all, just as the blessing is promised to all, so also it is offered to all in Christ through the Gospel. God does give what He has promised, but not all accept this blessing. Not all believe it; therefore they do not receive the blessing. Here the Lord is also saying the same thing. He says, as it were: "I have stretched out My net over all the children of Israel by sending out the Gospel Word about Christ. But not all are obedient to this Word. They do not wish to be gathered into this sheepfold of Christ, and so they are not gathered." In this passage, then, he is speaking about the ministry of the Word, just as all the prophets do in similar passages. This it is absolutely necessary for us to note in all the prophets.

I will gather the remnant of Israel. This is the same thing which he had said about gathering Jacob through the ministry of the Gospel.

I will set them like sheep in a fold and like a flock in the middle of its pasture. That is, "I will gather them into a single flock, to one sheepfold, and to the same pasturage. I will nicely bring them together to one flock. I will give them the Gospel and one spirit, etc."

The multitude of people will bustle about. That is, there will be such a crowd and multitude of people who believe the Gospel that there is going to be a great thronging and crowding and coming together of those who will approach. This is a clear passage about the conversion of the heathen.

13. *For he who opens the way will go up before them.* What we have here,[16] "who opens the way," is quite gentle. In the Hebrew the meaning is this: "He who breaks through will go up before them. Therefore, they will break through and pass through the gate." In a marvelous way this is an elegant passage, filled with comfort. There is the sign of the cross in it. It is as if He were saying: "I am leading them to the pasture and to the fold, just as Christ says, 'I give them eternal life.' But one important thing is sure: it is not a well-beaten path. There are many things that keep the elect from breaking out—Satan, sin, the Law, death, and the entire old Adam. However, I will see to it that absolutely nothing holds them back. I will promise them Him who opens a breach,[17] who will break through and take away every hindrance, who will prepare the way for them. Thus they will have an easy passage." But, as I have said, this is not the sweet way of the flesh, for the entire flesh must be mortified. The world, sin, Satan, and our entire old Adam set themselves up against us, lest we break through, lest we follow this "Breachmaker" of ours. Christ, however, says: " 'Be of good cheer. I have overcome the world (John 16:33).' I have broken through. Nothing will now bar the way, and you, too, will break through—namely, through this gate, which was beset by sin, the world, and the Law; you will break through to eternal life." In this way the Lord is our Head, that is, our Leader and Conqueror. As He Himself has broken through, so also we are going to break through through Him. And thus, under the leadership of Christ the Prince, Jacob has been gathered together. From this text—although it appears to be vague—it is very clear that Christ is both God and man, that He died and rose again, that He ascended to the Father and now rules eternally, etc.

[16] The Vulgate text *pandens iter.*

[17] Luther's German Bible translates *diruptor* literally — *Durchbrecher.* This name for Christ appears in the German hymn *O Durchbrecher aller Bande,* which prays characteristically (st. 6):

Herr, zermalme, brich, vernichte
alle Macht der Finsternis.

CHAPTER THREE

I BELIEVE that this chapter is spoken through ἀνακεφαλαίωσις ("recapitulation, summary"). It was not preached immediately after the preceding chapter but much later. But everything in this chapter is easy, for he is censuring only outward sins as he has done before. All are moral matters, and there is nothing that could delay the reader.

1. *Justice*, that is, legal rights.

2. *Who tear the skin from off my people and their flesh from off their bones.* This is figurative and poetic speech with which he reproves the violence of their leaders, as we have seen from the previous chapter. The Germans have the custom of speaking in the same way about those who wickedly swallow their subjects: "He skins them to the bone."[1] So also in this passage he has used a strong figure of speech against the wicked tyranny of the impious princes. "Tearing off the skin" continues the description of violence, as if he were saying: "They take away all the substance of the entire populace with very great violence."

4. *He will hide His face from them.* The prophets generally imitate Moses, and this, too, is taken from the song of Moses (Deut. 31:17-18). Therefore "God hides His face" means that He is angry; "He shows His face" means that He is kindly disposed, that He favors us and wishes us well, as in Ps. 80:3: "Show Thy face, and we shall be saved." The same phrase of Scripture we find at various places in the Psalms.

5. *Thus says the Lord God concerning the prophets.* From this it is clear that this chapter is against the princes, prophets, and priests of the people. To summarize this passage: The prophets and

[1] *Er schindet sie bis auf den Grat.*

priests fawn over the princes and thus mislead the people. They keep the people from repenting from their wickedness. But because they despise the word of the prophets whom the Lord has sent, they confirm the people in their wickedness. This is what he is saying:

When they have something to eat. That is, they are opposed to the good prophets who declare rightly the Word of the Lord. They cry out against and persecute the prophets of the Lord. They confirm the people in their wickedness when they cry:

Peace. We have the same thing in Jer. 6:14: "Peace, peace, when there is no peace." This is also taken from Moses.[2] The meaning is this: "They are commanding the people to rest securely. They say that destruction is not going to come. They accuse us prophets of lying when we threaten with a captivity. They say that God is not going to desert His people, as He promised to be with them." The monks and all who preach confidence in works are false prophets of the sort who say "Peace" where there is no peace.

But declare war against him who puts nothing into their mouths. "Mouth" in Scripture is almost always related to the ministry of the Word. On the other hand, gluttony and devouring are related to the throat, as we have it in Ps. 5:9: "Their throat is an empty sepulcher." Although it seems otherwise to others, the sense here appears to me to be as if he were saying: "So great is their wicked bitterness against the prophets of the Lord that they prepare for war against him and persecute and kill him whose preaching does not agree with them and who does not approve of their wickedness."

6. *Therefore it shall be night to you without vision.* That is, "Your preaching of peace will cause you to become blind, so that when the calamity comes there will be a great need for you to prophesy. But you are going to see nothing, you are going to foresee nothing. The disaster will be so great that you will desert your people. You will find no remedy for the ill and will perish along with the people." This is the way God ultimately confounds the wicked preachers.

7. *And the seers shall be disgraced.* This will happen because

[2] Cf. Deut. 29:19.

their falsehood will become manifest when they preach peace falsely. "The calamity, then, will come, and the entire people will see that a deplorable destruction threatens them, as we have prophesied. Then those preachers will be charged with lying, and we shall be found to have been truthful."

They shall all cover their lips. This, too, has been taken in imitation of Moses. Moses speaks in this way about the leper in Lev. 13:45 that he should keep his mouth covered with a garment. The prophet, then, has spoken figuratively: "They shall cover their lips," that is, "They shall suffer such disgrace that they will not dare to speak with others." They will not be allowed to speak. In fact, they will be in such wretched disgrace that they will not even be able to speak. The Germans also speak this way: *Sie werden müssen das Maul zuhalten* ("They will have to keep their mouths shut").

For there is no answer from God. When it is present, the calamity will teach them what they have taught, because the Lord will give them no answer.

8. *But as for me, I am filled with power.* He is boasting of his own power and boldness in the ministry of the Word which God has entrusted to him. It is as if he were saying: "Although all the princes and priests resist me, yet I go on preaching because I must. I do not forsake the established office of teaching, no matter how much their frenzy rages against me. I pay no attention to any outward appearance on their part. I shall finish what I have started with God's help, even if I am going to be killed, because by the efficacy of the Spirit of the Lord I am filled with both power and a sense of justice. This 'sense of justice' is that I am sure that I am teaching correct things. Therefore, even if the enemies of the Word of God threaten me with death, I pay no attention to it. The Spirit of the Lord is with me. He enlivens and comforts me." Surely, to accuse so freely the princes and all those who are in positions of power and who rage against the truth is not characteristic of human boldness but of the boldness of the Spirit of the Lord.

9. *Hear this, you heads of the house of Jacob.* He goes on to censure the wickedness of the princes, priests, and prophets. These, you see, were the most important ranks among the Jews. In these ranks there were always a very few who were devout, but

all the rest were very wicked. These are the results of wickedness —as I have mentioned several times already—when we have stopped worshiping God in pure faith. Our princes today work with the same wickedness and also regard justice as an abomination; that is, they do not produce fairness in law. As a consequence, nothing else will happen except that they will perish. The Word of the Lord will not lie.

10. *You who build Zion with blood.* The prophet explains himself. "You build with blood" is a Hebraism. It is as if he were saying: "You build great palaces, mightily fortified citadels. But it is your plundering and oppression of the poor that supplies you with the expenses for these. You make yourselves rich, you build beautifully, but in the meantime you are swallowing up the poor."

11. *Its heads give judgment for a bribe.* He is explaining himself still more clearly. Furthermore, his phrase "give judgment for a bribe" is a Hebraism. We translate it in the Latin more accurately: "for the sake of gifts" *(propter munera).* I mentioned this earlier when I commented on the passage from the psalm: [3] "Israel did service for a wife," that is, for the sake of a wife. The meaning, then, is this: "The highest orders of the people, whose job it was to restrain wickedness, themselves act wickedly. The princes do not practice justice as they should. Corrupted and overwhelmed by money as they are, they pass judgment on the basis of the person. The priests, too, say what pleases their people. Their tongues are for sale. They traffic in the Word of God, which ought not to happen at all. The prophets do the same thing. They flatter the people; they preach peace, as Jeremiah says; and, in doing so, they confirm the people in their wickedness." Thus he throws the entire burden of this evil back on the wicked prophets. This was also Jeremiah's chief lament (cf. Jer. 6:14). In short, this greed is everybody's chief concern. Cf. Amos 8:4 f. There can hardly be anything more destructive in a state than this evil: namely, when the princes do not promote equal justice but allow money to overwhelm them so that they corrupt justice.

Yet they were leaning upon the Lord. This is an outstanding passage, well worth noting. It helps us understand many of the

[3] The text here says "psalm" for "prophet." The reference is to the commentary on Hos. 12:12. Cf. p. 68 above.

prophets. It causes us to see what sort of listeners the prophets had: very wicked people who nevertheless wanted to support this wickedness of theirs with a kind of sanctity. The apostle Paul explains this also in Rom. 2:17, 21: "You . . . rely upon the Law . . . and you preach against stealing but steal." This is something God cannot but hate very much, as we also see here. After all, these were the wicked voices of the impious raised against the true prophets: "God has promised to be with His people. Therefore those prophets are insane who threaten us with evil, as if God were not in the midst of us. You must not preach, as we said earlier.[4] Evil will not come upon us. God will not drive away His people whom He has selected above all nations and to whom He even entrusts His own oracles."

12. *Therefore because of you Zion shall be . . . a wall without mortar.* These are prophetic figures of speech. It is as if he were saying: "Because you, being wicked, yet are supporting your wickedness, as if the Lord approved of it, therefore Zion will be reduced to nothing so that it can be plowed.[5] For beside the fact that you are wicked, you are also boasting of that wickedness of yours. Thus you commit two sins."

A wall without mortar. I have already commented on this word earlier.[6]

And the mountain of the house a wooded height. That is, thorns and brambles will grow there. No one will till it, no one will go to see it. Everything will be deserted, just as Jeremiah says in Lam. 1:4: "The roads to Zion mourn." These statements and others like them of the prophet seemed impossible to the Jews, for there were other prophecies that said the opposite, as I also mentioned at the beginning of this prophet.[7] You see, there was a very clear prophecy about Jerusalem in Is. 31:5: "Like birds hovering, so the Lord of hosts will protect Jerusalem." There is

[4] Cf. p. 224 above.

[5] The Hebrew text for this verse has "Zion shall be plowed as a field."

[6] Apparently Luther's text here reads: *Sion quasi ager arabitur et Jerusalem erit quasi maceria.* In his comment on Micah 1:6 Luther defines *maceria* (*maceries*) as a wall in which the stones are not held together by mortar. For *maceria* the Vulgate here has *acervus lapidum*. Cf. p. 213 above.

[7] Cf. p. 208 above.

a clearer one in Is. 37:35: "I will defend this city to save it, for My own sake and for the sake of My servant David." Stirred by these prophecies, the wicked smugly kept on sinning. They kept laughing and hooting at the prophets who were threatening something else. Yet God miraculously did both things: He defended it for a time, but finally He nevertheless had it destroyed.

CHAPTER FOUR

WE find this prophecy, almost to the word, in Is. 2 also. It definitely seems to me that Isaiah took his from Micah, as I also mentioned earlier that Micah was older than Isaiah, although they were contemporaries.[1] But here again, with a sort of transition the prophet moves from the destruction of the Judaic kingdom to the new and eternal kingdom of Christ. We cannot take this passage to mean the rebuilding of the external kingdom, although this is what the Jews do because there is such a wealth of promises. Here we must also note the contrary prophecies which were completely blinding the wicked to keep them from being able to believe the prophets. How were they to believe men who declared contradictory things? Thus divine majesty acts in miraculous fashion. We have exactly the same prophecy in Zech. 7 and 8. First he announces the terrible destruction of Jerusalem and of the entire people, for he speaks as follows: "And I scattered them . . . among all the nations which they did not know, and the land they left was desolate, etc." (Zech. 7:14). Then he immediately adds: "Old men and old women shall again sit in the streets of Jerusalem, each with staff in hand because of their age. And the streets of the city shall be full of boys and girls playing in its streets, etc." (Zech. 8:4-5). In this way, too, Jeremiah was sent to buy a field to cultivate after the Chaldeans had already taken the city (cf. Jer. 32:7). Thus prophecies used to be diametrically opposed to each other. Jeremiah had been sent to proclaim devastation, destruction had already come to the city, the Chaldeans had already taken it, and the citizens were at the point of being led away to captivity. Suddenly Jeremiah is sent to announce their salvation by the fact that he was to buy a field. All of this was done for the sake of the kingdom of Judah, for the eternal promise had been

[1] Cf. 207 above.

attached to it. Therefore it had to be preserved until Christ came. This is how the Lord anticipates[2] us with His words. Although He also intended to punish this kingdom, yet He would comfort the devout. It is as if He were saying: "Even if destruction is imminent, even if you will be taken prisoner and will suffer for a time, yet hang on, you devout people. You will be saved. I will take you back out of captivity. I will restore your city to you again, and you are going to live safely in it. Your captivity will not last long." And so it happened, for the faithful whose hearts God had touched finally were brought back from Babylon, as we see in Ezra 1:5. Such are the wondrous counsels of God. He orders the prophets to declare both destruction and salvation, but the former for the wicked, the latter for the devout. It is very important to note this in all the prophets. In this way those wonderful counsels of divine majesty made fools of the wicked. In fact, even the devout were unable to understand them. We see clearly in Jeremiah how he wondered at the counsel of the Lord. For he says (Jer. 32:24-25): "Behold, the siege mounds have come up to the city to take it, and . . . the city is given into the hands of the Chaldeans . . . and yet Thou . . . hast said to me, 'Buy the field for money and get witnesses,' though the city is given into the hands of the Chaldeans." But God caused both to happen, as we have said. This will be the summary of the two chapters that follow.

1. *And it shall come to pass in the latter days.* The Jews connect this text with the preceding verses of the last chapter and take it to mean the external restoration of the kingdom in this way: " 'Zion shall be plowed like a field, and Jerusalem shall be like a wall without mortar, and the mountain of the house a wooded height,' but finally I will rebuild this mountain. I will restore its glory again. It shall be more sublime and glorious than it ever was before." But I do not like this idea. After all, we know that the latter temple was not as large and magnificent as was the former, so that some people who had seen the earlier one wept. We see this from the account of Esdras, 1 Esdras 5:63.[3]

That the mountain of the house of the Lord shall be established. That is, it will be definite, something one may be confident of.

[2] With the Erlangen text we have read *praevenit* for *provenit.*

[3] See also Ezra 3:13.

It is as if he were saying: "It has now been reduced to a wooded height, deserted and overgrown, with no building on it. But it will again be a definite place, well established on that very place where it is now. I will cause it to become more famous and more glorious in the world than it ever was before. It will be more renowned than every other temple." It is not altogether bad that the Jews apply this to the worship in the temple before Christ, when even the Gentiles who were taking up Judaism went up in great crowds to the temple along with the Jews. It is my idea, however, that this mountain became very famous because of Christ.

2. *For out of Zion.* For nowhere but in Zion is the Law. "They were entrusted with the oracles of God," says Paul in Rom. 3:2. Therefore we should take this not only as a literal mountain or a literal Jerusalem but as spiritual mountain and Jerusalem. We should follow the apostle Paul in Galatians, that is: Through Christ the holy church is exalted and glorified by the preaching of the Gospel among all nations throughout the world, although it was necessary that there be a first, external place for the Gospel to be first published. This happened through Christ and the apostles in the temple at Jerusalem.

3. *He shall judge among many peoples.* Here he seems to have looked forward to Christ in Luke 24:47: "Repentance and forgiveness should be preached in His name to all nations, beginning from Jerusalem." This is the power, or fruit, of the Gospel, that it was sent out from Jerusalem by that new King, who judges in the Word and in the Spirit. He will judge not just the Jews but many people.

And shall decide for strong nations. The Gospel is "the power of God for salvation to everyone who has faith" (Rom. 1:16). Therefore it sweeps over whatever is strong and firm, whatever is lofty and glorious. Thus that humbleness of the Word subjects to itself whatever is very strong and powerful in the world.

Afar off. It will go not only into Jerusalem but throughout the world, as the psalm says.[4] We certainly cannot take this to refer to the external kingdom. Indeed, by comparison with this glory external glory was of no account.

[4] Cf. Ps. 19:4.

And they shall beat their swords into plowshares. This is a periphrasis for peace, as he himself explains: "Nation shall not lift up sword against nation." To summarize, then: "The Gospel will bring peace to all. They will all change war into peace." But he is not speaking about physical peace, as some inappropriately think who say that there was peace throughout the world under Caesar Augustus. This is not true. Indeed, the world is always the same—it has a constant thirst for blood, after the example of Cain, the first murderer. He is speaking about the peace which the Word works in Christians who are ready to "strip off the robe along with the tunic," who have peace with all men, who do not battle in the courtroom, who endure injustice, etc. Here again we see how we cannot take this to refer to the restoration of the kingdom.

4. *And there shall be no one to frighten him.* In the Hebrew it reads: "And he will not be afraid." This expression is taken from Moses.[5] That is, he will live in peace. He will dwell in his own house. He will not live in an armed camp. Everything will be peaceful.

4. *For the mouth of the Lord of hosts has spoken.* This is a confirmation to arouse their faith. After all, as we have said earlier, even the saints could not understand the counsel of God about destroying that very glorious kingdom which God had instituted and which had the eternal promise. Therefore he is confirming all those earlier particulars.

5. *For all the peoples will walk.* With clear words he is explaining what he had said a little earlier with obscure language. Many nations will come to Mount Zion, but yet not all. Many will remain in their wicked idolatry and will not walk with us to the house of the Lord. They will not take up the true faith of this new kingdom through Christ but will persevere in their unbelief. We, however, shall walk in a new way which will never cease. That light of the Gospel will endure forever. There will be no end to this religion. Thus that new and great and eternal kingdom consists of nothing else than walking in the name of the Lord. It will not flower with external pomp and force of arms, as do the king-

[5] Cf. Lev. 26:6.

doms of this world. Its thesis is this—that however we live, we must live in the name of the Lord, the only name in which we must be saved. The entire substance of this kingdom is to believe in the name of Christ.

Forever and ever. These words include the coming resurrection from the dead. You see, the prophets have the custom of embracing the entire kingdom of Christ at one time whenever they mention it. They generally speak about it with other words and more beautifully and in greater detail than we can with our limitations. In this mortal flesh we shall not be able to walk in the name of the Lord forever. That flesh, then, which cannot but die, must be raised again. We must be raised up again and be placed in that eternity with our eternal King. The prophets have almost no regard for that very brief moment of time when we sleep in death with all the faithful and await the glorification of the sons of God, as the apostle says (cf. Rom. 8:30), for it is so short a moment. Therefore they immediately include the resurrection and the glorification of the devout in that eternal kingdom.

6. *In that day I will assemble the lame.* With wonderful words and promises He comforts the people, but they are completely incapable of laying hold on such broad promises. You see, diametrically opposed to each other were the prophecies about the destruction and annihilation of the kingdom and about a most magnificent restoration and a future kingdom more glorious and a future people more handsome than had ever existed before. Obviously this seemed impossible to them. They were unable to understand those prophecies, as we also noted earlier from Jeremiah about buying the field. Here He is saying the same thing in every detail: "I will not allow you to perish, no matter what wretched affliction you will suffer when you have been taken away into captivity." "Yet I will assemble the lame." I take this to mean the punishment. That is, the people are broken to bits. The kingdom has been taken away from them. They flourish no longer. They have lost all their property and have been led into captivity. Divine goodness has always enlivened the devout with wonderful promises, so that even though they were about to go into captivity and about to suffer for a time, yet that would be a short time; they would be brought back and be restored to their original freedom and glory. But He adds, not rashly:

7. *And the lame I will make the remnant, and the weak a strong nation.* Here the flesh is greatly offended. It cannot understand the counsel of God about miraculously fulfilling these promises. The Lord had promised an eternal kingdom, a glorious return from captivity. All the Jews, therefore, kept thinking that they would be saved and brought back, that they would be placed in that new and glorious kingdom. The Lord, however, is saying here that He is not going to save all the lame but some remnant of those lame people. After all, only very few of the devout were after some years brought back from Babylon, namely, those whose spirit God had touched, as the account in Ezra 1:5 says. Therefore He is separating the faithful from the wicked and says that the latter will remain in an eternal captivity, while the former will be brought back and glorified.

A strong nation. Thus the church was built through the Gospel throughout the world against the gates of hell and all the attacks of sin. It has been absolutely invincible to death. It has been built on the firm Rock, Christ, its King, through whose Spirit it has been daily enlivened and confirmed, lest it be afraid or be able to be overcome by any creature.

And the Lord will reign over them on Mount Zion from this time forth. Here is a clear and magnificent passage about the divinity of Christ. For this is the way David used to call Him who was going to sit upon his throne his Seed. Ps. 110.[6] This passage Christ Himself quotes in the Gospel account (cf. Mark 12:36). So also here he calls Him Lord who is going to rule forever over His people on Mount Zion. It is necessary, then, that this be not a physical kingdom but a spiritual and eternal one, as we have said earlier in sufficient detail. Therefore the kingdom will be spiritual and eternal, its King eternal and glorified, its people glorified and eternal in that kingdom. How else could He be the Lord and sit on the throne of His father David forever, except the people also be eternal? But He will not be eternal in a mortal or dead body, but in a body raised again and glorified. Here again the prophet includes the resurrection of the dead.

8. *And you, O tower of the flock, cloudy [hill of the daughter*

[6] Ps. 110:1 contains the thought, but Ps. 132:11 presents it more literally.

of Zion]. I think that what we read as "of the flock," a common noun, ought to be read as a proper noun, as it also is in Gen. 35:21. There Moses mentions this mountain: "He journeyed on and pitched his tent beyond the tower of Eder."[7] This was a sort of citadel or tower or fort. You see, what we read as "cloudy" *(nebulosa)* we read from the Hebrew as "citadel" *(arx)*.[8] The Jews say that the Hebrew word means a battlement or fortification. Therefore we should read it this way: "And you, O tower of Eder, citadel of the daughter of Zion, etc." There are some who take this passage to mean the temple at Jerusalem, but I do not approve of this. After all, nowhere else in Scripture is that building called a tower. I believe that the prophet is speaking metaphorically, that he is calling the entire city of Jerusalem the tower of Eder or that the kingdom of the daughter of Zion extends even outside the city, that it has spread throughout the world to all nations, so that Eder means some obscure part of the world. After all, this mountain was not otherwise famous or renowned. The meaning, then, seems to me to be this: The Gospel is going to be so effective, it will be so broadly spread, it will travel with such speed that it is going to come even to the most obscure places of the earth—in short, to the ends of the earth. This is the meaning I get from this passage. I neither have nor find a better one.

To you shall the former dominion come. He is speaking as it were to those who are in captivity, as if they had already been taken out of their land. It is as if he were saying: "You are done for. Your kingdom has been lost. But be confident! The former dominion shall return. Just as you were not originally a captive people, so also shall you again be completely free after the captivity. You shall not be deserted, nor shall you always be in captivity, but you shall again return to your own place."

9. *Why then are you now afflicted?*[9] The prophet is saying all this to set the situation before their eyes. It is as if he were saying: "It is certain that you are going to be led off into captivity. Indeed, your sins have earned this. You will be terribly afflicted —in such a way that you will think that you are never going to be

[7] Cf. *Luther's Works*, 6, p. 274.

[8] Hebrew עֹ֫פֶל.

[9] The Vulgate text has: *Quare ergo nunc affligeris?*

brought back. But have faith! I promise to be with you to bring you back." Thus everywhere the prophet stresses both threats and promises—threats against the wicked, promises for the sake of the devout. What follows also has to do with the same point.

Is there no king in you? "You are not completely going to want for a king. You will not always lack counselors and princes." With these words he removes the anxious doubts of the flesh with which the flesh is being driven almost to desperation. You see, the flesh absolutely cannot endure the hand of the Lord. It must despair when the Lord afflicts it. In fact, even the devout barely understand that work of the Lord, as we have said earlier. Here the prophet appropriately alludes to the thoughts of the wicked and then also to the thoughts of the faithful with which the latter still have good hopes even in the midst of persecution. While they are still thinking these thoughts and are completely unaware, "the Spirit intercedes with sighs too deep for words" (Rom. 8:26).

That pangs have seized you like a woman in travail. This is the very elegant and very fitting use of the simile that Christ also used in John 16:21. You see, the pangs of the apostles and disciples were of exactly the same kind. They thought that it was all over for them, just as a pregnant woman in peril of her life thinks as she goes into labor to deliver her child. Such was the anxious concern of the church which was being born, as they say in Luke 24:21: "We kept hoping that He was the One who was going to redeem Israel, and now, beside all this, today is the third day that these things happened." We see the same thing in every detail here. A great and eternal kingdom was going to be raised up, but first its birth had to happen. This birth could not happen without the great sadness and travail which generally occurs to those giving birth. So the prophets interpret the Babylonian captivity as birth pains. Divine goodness always acts thus with all the devout in every temptation. It first torments us in strange ways. It first tortures us and throws us into hell to kill the lusts of the flesh so that it may afterwards bring us back and save us. Meanwhile the flesh is unaware that these are labor pains, that a wonderful birth is going to follow. With exactly the same line of reasoning, the prophet here is encouraging his people. It is as if he were saying: "Hold out! Endure it—however great the pain may be. A wonderful child is about to be born. Bear the hand of the Lord. Without doubt He will rescue you, and you will produce abundant fruit. The time is short. This will be merely the pangs of labor, which will be absolutely nothing, once the child is born." This is an elegant and wonderful simile, even as it also delighted Christ (John 16:21 f.): "When a woman is in travail, she has sorrow . . . but when she is delivered of the child, she no longer remembers the anguish for joy that a human being is born into the world. So you have sorrow now, etc."

10. *Writhe and groan, O daughter of Zion.* As we generally help women in childbirth with our cries of encouragement, so also here the prophet is helping the people with his cries of encouragement to endure that very brief period of captivity and to think that this is merely the pain of childbirth. He is saying that the birth will soon take place and that a very great comfort is going to follow. He immediately adds:

For now you shall go forth from the city. That is: "I certainly admit that you will be moved out of the kingdom of Jerusalem, but you don't like this. You will go forth from the city. That is, you will no longer live in your own cities. You will no longer hold cities in subjection to you. Rather, you will be subject to the Assyrian. You will endure a wretched slavery, but it will not last long, for the Lord will free you, ransom you. Jeremiah interprets all this more broadly.[10]

11. *And now many nations are assembled against you, saying: Let her be profaned.* What we read as "Let her be stoned" [11] you read more accurately as "Let her be profaned" *(profanetur).* You see, we have the same word also in Moses when he says that with their idolatry they profane the land.[12] The meaning, then, is this: "Your wickedness has deserved that you be led away as a captive. Your enemies will gather against you,[13] and they will think that you are absolutely at the end of your rope. They will cry out

10 Jer. 25:11-14.

11 The Vulgate has *lapidetur* or *lapidabitur.*

12 The reference to Moses has not been identified. Num. 35:33 speaks of profaning the land, but there is no reference to idolatry. In Jer. 3:1, 2, 9 and Ps. 106:38 the Hebrew word for "profane" (חָנֵף) is used as Luther here describes it.

13 We have read *te* for *de.*

against you. They will be completely confident that they are always going to hold dominion over you. But have faith! You will reduce them to nothing, not they you." This was a strange prophecy to the ears of the wicked.

And let our eyes gaze upon Zion. This is a Hebrew expression which occurs also in Ps. 54:7: "My eye has looked in triumph on my enemies." It means the same as our German expression *Ich sehe meine Lust dran.* You see, this is the way the hostile foes were baring their fangs against the people of God, for the hatreds of the nations living round about them were very bitter. The psalmist records their cries in Ps. 137:7: "Raze it! Down to its foundations!"

12. *But they do not know the thoughts of the Lord.* It is as if he were saying: "They are confident of their own victory. They feel secure because they have prevailed against you, but they do not understand the Lord's plan. The Lord will turn your grief into joy. You are going to have a King, who will rule over all nations."

That He has gathered them as sheaves to the threshing floor. Thus He makes the number of your enemies great so that their devastation may also be great, so that the Lord may be able to destroy more of them. You see, this is the Lord's practice, that whenever He intends to destroy the wicked in an extraordinary way, He first magnifies them and makes them glorious. He lifts them on high that they may fall with a greater crash. This is what happened to the very powerful ruler of the Assyrians, of the Romans, etc.

13. *Arise and thresh, O daughter of Zion.* These are metaphorical expressions with all of which the prophet wanted to express the power and efficacy of the Gospel. It is as if he were saying: "Through the Gospel you will make all nations your subjects. You will accomplish this without weapons, with the Word alone. But in the meantime they will dominate you for a little while."

And you shall devote their gain to the Lord. In the Hebrew it reads this way: "And you will make accursed their plunder (gain) and their power, etc." That is, by the preaching of the Gospel you will snatch the more select away from the wicked and transfer them to Christ as a votive offering. You will win them over for Christ. Thus the glory of this kingdom will always become greater through the effectiveness of the preaching of the Gospel. Christ also used this figure of speech in Luke 11:22: "But when one stronger than he assails him and overcomes him, he takes away all his armor in which he trusted and divides his spoil."

Then you will be destroyed, O daughter of the hireling.[14] This item also belongs with the preceding verses. People have taken this to refer to the wicked synagog that opposed the prophets and killed them. But I do not see by what reasoning their explanation hangs together with what has gone before. I shall be daring and make this interpretation: I think the prophet is still going on and continuing with his description of the coming vengeance against the heathen after the restoration of the kingdom of Judah. I think that he is calling Babylon the "daughter of the hireling." But our reading "daughter of the hireling" *(filia latronis)* is inappropriate. Jerome also reads this way everywhere in the sacred account when he translates "[daughter] of the hireling." It ought to have been translated "[daughter] of the soldier." Here, then, instead of "daughter of the hireling" we ought to read "daughter of the soldier." That is, "You, O Babylon, who have been equipped with arms and military forces, you who are so harsh in warfare,[15] you who make trouble for everyone, you whom no one can resist easily, you who attack everyone in battle array." I simply translate this entire passage from the Hebrew as follows: "Then we shall make war also on you, O daughter of the military, who set your siege against us." The sense, then, is this: The daughter of Zion will dedicate to the Lord all the wealth of the nations. Among that booty you also will be, O Babylon, who now are making war, a very powerful military force. You who are now laying siege to us, you who are now overthrowing Jerusalem, you will in turn be destroyed by us. What you are doing physically they will do spiritually through the Gospel.

With a rod they strike the cheeks of the rulers of Israel. That is, they consider them as very vile. They treat them completely without dignity. Jerome and other interpreters apply this to the Passion of Christ, but what they write is forced out of the text.

[14] In the usual reckoning this is verse 1 of chapter 5.

[15] *Studiisque asperrima belli,* borrowed from Vergil's description of Carthage, the bitter foe of Rome, in *Aeneid,* I, 14.

CHAPTER FIVE

2. *And you, O Bethlehem Ephrathah, who are little.* Up to this point, he has been discussing the great victory which will come to the people of God under Christ.[1] Now he is describing the Head or Leader of this kingdom, and he explains clearly the place from which this King is going to rise. You see, that faith might be made certain, a definite person, place, and time had to be designated for the newborn church. So here the prophet is describing the definite place, just as other prophets described the time when this King was going to come, namely, after the Babylonian captivity. The person, then, is Christ; the place, Bethlehem; the time, after the Babylonian captivity. But how Matt. 2:6 quoted this passage from Micah in a different way we have noted in sufficient detail in our postils, as they call them.[2]

Among the clans of Judah. This is a Hebrew expression taken from Moses. Moses established the clans, as we have this in Deuteronomy.[3] Among the clans of Judah was the clan of Bethlehem, which was in the tribe of Judah. Christ, therefore, was going to be born of the tribe of Judah and in the kingdom of Judah, just as he adds here:

From you will come forth for Me. The Spirit of this prophet was great. He was able to define very precisely the place where Christ would be born. This he could not have done without a very definite and clear divine revelation.

One who is to be Ruler in Israel. With this one word he takes

[1] Luther attached his commentary on v. 1 of this chapter to the previous chapter.

[2] Cf. Luther's *Kirchenpostille,* 1522, W, X-I-1, 555—728, but especially pp. 557 f.

[3] Cf. Deut. 1:15.

away whatever there is that belongs to a physical kingdom. He says that this King is going to be born from Judah, and yet He is going to rule also over Israel, although it was very certain that the kingdom of Israel would never be brought back. It was scattered throughout the entire world, and we never read that it was led back. This text, then, very clearly convinces that the kingdom of Christ would be a spiritual kingdom. This is something people could not understand, for this prophecy seemed impossible and contrary to itself. Israel had been led off and would never be brought back. Even Judah was going to be carried off. Yet Micah is prophesying that this Ruler would reign over both Judah and Israel. In this situation, Judah had to be saved also physically because of that King, who was being prophesied to be born from Judah.

Whose origin is from of old. That Ruler came forth at the time when the days of the world began. He was at the same time with the beginning of all creatures. He does not come forth first from Bethlehem after the Babylonian captivity but came forth a long time ago already. This is just the way John describes the divinity of Christ (John 1:1): "In the beginning was the Word." In his song, Ps. 90:2, Moses sings: "From everlasting to everlasting Thou art God." There Moses used the same expression that Micah uses here, that is: "You did not begin with the world, but, when the world began to be, You already were." Christ also says about Himself: "Before Abraham was, I am" (John 8:58). This passage, therefore, has a double meaning. First, that Ruler would come forth from Bethlehem. He came forth with the beginning of the world. That is, it had been determined that He came forth so that every merit of every person might fail. He was given purely out of mercy, not because we had deserved this or had wished for it, but because this is the way it had been predestined from eternity, as Paul has it.[4] The other meaning is this: His going out is from the beginning of the world. That is, He was born of the Father. I like the first meaning, because "going out" *(egressus)* echoes an external appearing rather than an internal birth: "I came from the Father, and have come into the world" (John 16:28).

3. *Therefore He shall give them up, etc.* Now that he has described the person of the Ruler, he follows with His office: how He

[4] Cf. Eph. 1:4 ff.

is going to rule, with what arms and forces He is going to rule; and that His kingdom will not be physical but spiritual. Moreover, he is speaking in the prophetic manner when he says "them," without naming those whom he intends to signify by name. Rather, from his prophet's state of mind he sets this before their eyes as if they were in the presence of the Lord. He means the synagog that is still remaining.

Until the time of her who is in travail. He means until the time when the church is born and established through the Gospel. A summary of the meaning, then, is this: "When that Leader will have been born from Bethlehem, He will save this kingdom. He will still reserve the remaining part of the synagog until the church is born, although that external kingdom will cease to exist."

And until the rest of His brethren shall return to the children of Israel. He does this in order that the rest of His brothers, having heard the Gospel, may also believe and be converted. The synagog will last, then, until the Gospel will be spread in part *(ex parte)* throughout the world. Consequently, the synagog must be preserved for a time. This occurred after the Passion of Christ. This is what is also said elsewhere (Mal. 4:6; Luke 1:17): "And He will turn the hearts of fathers to their children and the hearts of children to their fathers." Thus he is here saying clearly: "They shall return to the children of Israel," and by this he intends to show that this kingdom will be spiritual and not carnal or external. Otherwise he would have said, "They will return to Judah."

4. *And He shall stand and feed His flock in the strength of the Lord.* He proceeds to describe the remarkable kingdom and wonderful success of this kingdom. That King, who will hold all nations under His sway, will not do battle with force of arms and of soldiers. He will use no military force, no sword, but will "feed his flock." This will be a strange sight, a new kind of fighting, which the Jews were completely incapable of understanding. Even the disciples of Christ had not yet understood it after the death of Christ, Luke 24:21, when they said, "We kept hoping that He was the One to redeem Israel." The idea, then, is this: "That King Christ will stand and feed His flock. That is, He will declare the Word of the Gospel, and He will do this in the strength of the Lord, that is, with the Holy Spirit cooperating and adding His efficacy." That Gospel,

that humble-appearing Word, will set itself against all the gates of hell and powers of the air, for it is "the power of God," Romans 1:16. When those who do battle under this King will have heard and believed by the power of this Word, they will conquer death, sin, and hell.

And they shall return. According to the Hebrew you read this more accurately as "and they will dwell." With this single expression, he has embraced that entire security of peace from the Gospel. Because of this security, those who believe are safe against the assaults of all creatures. It is as if he were saying: "They will be safe in the great storm of the cross. No creature will prevail against them, not even the gates of hell." Cf. Rom. 8:31. This is how the prophets everywhere include also the cross.

5. *And this shall be peace when the Assyrian comes.* I think that the meaning of this passage is that He is attacking the false prophets about whom he has spoken at length before, who preach peace and bite with their teeth. So he is setting his preaching against theirs and says, as it were: "Your prophets say things that please you. They declare that peace and security will come, but I say that there will be no peace, because your kingdom will be destroyed and you will be taken into Assyria as captives. And yet there will be peace, but peace of another kind and in another way, a peace different from the kind for which you are hoping. Before that peace comes, you will suffer wretched affliction. You will first feel the powerful vengeance of the Assyrian, who will trample down our palaces. Furthermore, you are not acquainted with the way of peace. This is going to be a spiritual peace. I am prophesying an eternal Ruler for you, an eternal kingdom. You, however, nourish the vain hope that that King will come to you while you dwell in a physical kingdom, but you will first be led away."

And we will raise up against him seven shepherds. "Certainly the Assyrian will wreak his vengeance on you. He will cause you great affliction, but afterwards we will avenge ourselves against him; we will make him subject to us; we will send against him seven shepherds and eight ordinary overseers."[5] This prophecy appears remarkably foolish—that against so very powerful a king seven shepherds and eight ordinary, or plebeian, overseers are

[5] In the Zwickau text the German synonym *Amtleute* ("functionaries") is used.

sent. Obviously these are going to overthrow the kingdom of the Assyrians in turn. Everything, however, pertains to a spiritual kingdom. That is, we will overwhelm him not by force of arms, not with military forces, not with the assistance of the powerful princes of the world. Instead we will send them shepherds, some rustic overseers of the people, who will preach the Gospel and with their preaching subject to themselves that entire kingdom. That is, "I will send them apostles, poor and lowly men, not powerful ones." This is what he is saying, "eight plebeian leaders of men," that is, poor and lowly men. Other people take this to mean the leaders of the Persians and who knows what else, but that interpretation is worthless. I also think that the prophet is using a definite number for an indefinite one to indicate that it would be with a small handful, with a very few men—and those lowly and contemptible—that that very powerful kingdom of the Assyrians is going to be converted to the obedience of faith. The same expression also occurs elsewhere, as in Eccles. 11:2: "Give portions to seven, or even to eight," that is, "Just keep on giving."

6. *They shall rule the land of Assyria with the sword.* That means with the Word of God, "with the sword of the Spirit," as the apostle says (Eph. 6:17).

And the land of Nimrod with his sword. I prefer to translate the Hebrew word with the noun "sword." The meaning of this passage is the same as what Christ said in other words in Matt. 10:34-35: "I have not come to bring peace, but a sword. I have come to set a man against his father, etc." So he is here saying: "I will send them the Word, and when they believe it, they will convert each other. A father will assail his son, and a son his father. In this way 'he will be freed from the Assyrians.' That is, when we shall first have been led off into captivity by the Assyrians, where we shall be totally ruined, then the Assyrians in turn will be overcome when that new King has come and the new kingdom has been established. And there is no reason for us to hope that that King will come, unless you will first have been led off into captivity, etc."

7. *The remnant of Jacob shall be in the midst of many peoples.* Now that he has taken care of the vengeance which was going to occur against the kingdom of Assyria because of the captive kingdom of Israel, he specifies by what force it is going to come about

that that revenge will be fulfilled—namely, the remnant of Jacob. He describes the power and functions of the apostles and other early preachers of the Gospel and tells what kind of men they are going to be—first among the Jews from whom they had been taken, and then among all nations throughout the world.

In the midst of many peoples. To be sure, at that time the synagog was filled with people, for even many Gentiles had been converted to Judaism, as we can see from Acts 2. This prophecy certainly looks ahead to the Day of Pentecost, when the Holy Spirit was sent from heaven and the apostles spoke in different tongues, as the account in the Acts of the Apostles has it.

Like dew from the Lord. That is, the Holy Spirit, not men, will send them. This will be a heavenly act without the advice and concern of men. Enlivened by the Spirit, they will rain down the sweetness of the Gospel. As the dew comes down from heaven on the crops and flowers and waters and drenches the earth without our knowing, so also when the Holy Spirit has been sent from heaven, will they preach, etc. In 1 Cor. 3:6, 9 Paul interprets this as follows: "I planted, Apollos watered, but God gave the growth. For we are God's fellow workers; you are God's field, God's building." In this way the Gospel is heaven-sent dew. From the Gospel, which they declare, the apostles are called dew that waters the grass; that is, they shower the people with the preaching of the Word of the Gospel, etc.

Which tarry not for men. That is, the grass does not await the hands of men. The works and labors of men do not cause it. It comes spontaneously without any cultivation. The prophet means the effective power of the believed Gospel against the preachers of the Law, who know nothing else than to force and compel with their preaching. Such men can give neither the power to fulfill the Law nor a willing heart; in fact, they add to anger and sin because of that demanding. The same comparison we read here we also have in Ps. 72:16: "And men will blossom forth from the city like the grass of the field." That is, imbued with the Word alone and with the Holy Spirit, without the energetic cultivation of men, without the compulsion of the fear of punishment like that of the people of the Law, who are coerced by force and by laws, they will bear fruit voluntarily. Here the prophet is saying exactly the same thing: "The Gospel will be enough for them; the Holy Spirit will teach them all truth. It will not be necessary for them to be taught the doctrines and traditions of men, but they will voluntarily be good, as the remnants of Jacob shower them with dew. This is what happened on the Day of Pentecost as Peter and the other apostles preached. He is distinguishing the people of the Law from the people of the Gospel. The latter are a voluntary people who need not be compelled by laws or traditions but are moved to do good voluntarily by the power of the Holy Spirit, for they are led by the Spirit of God, as the apostle has it (cf. Rom. 8:14). In addition, there are going to be such men "among the Gentiles," that is, in the church of the Gentiles and not only among the Jews, as we have said before. This overwhelming of the Gentiles is a spiritual thing, accomplished through the power of the Gospel; for the apostles and other early preachers of the Gospel were taken from among the Jews and were established as the heads and foundations or princes over the earth, as the psalm says.[6] That is, they were the foundations of the church throughout the world among the Gentiles as well as among the Jews.

8. *Like a lion among the beasts of the forest.* This is metaphorical language with which he indicates the power of the Word and the might of the Spirit. It is as if he were saying: "As a lion puts to flight, knocks down, and seizes its catch when it attacks a herd, so also the Word of the Gospel will make all things its subjects." You see, the Gospel burst forth with such great force and might, it destroyed and overthrew the kingdoms of the Gentiles in such a way, that they could not escape its force and destruction. No matter how great they may have been, the most powerful and greatest kingdoms were converted, like those of the Assyrians, Romans, etc. This is in every way the same thing he said earlier in chapter 4:13: "I will make your horn iron and your hoofs bronze, etc." Thus the prophet often repeats the same things but in other words and with different prophetic figures, and this he does out of his abundance of the Spirit.

10. *And in that day, says the Lord, I will cut off your horses.* He is adding this to indicate that he is speaking not of a physical kingdom but of a spiritual one. Otherwise this would not agree with

[6] Ps. 18:43; 45:16.

what he said before, where he promises victory over all nations. We certainly do not take this to mean external powers and weapons but a spiritual thing accomplished through the preaching of the Gospel, which is the power of God (Rom. 1:16). Thus he is saying here: "You will be superior to all nations. You will make all men your subjects, but you will be a wanderer throughout the earth. You will have no weapons, no horses, no fortresses, no fortifications, no counselors whom you can trust. Yet you will overcome all nations through the Gospel, which is the strength and power of God, etc." But in the meantime the apostles were, as it were, destined to die, as we read in 1 Cor. 4:11: "We hunger and thirst, we are ill clad and buffeted, etc."; and in 2 Cor. 6:4-10: "Through great endurance, in afflictions, hardships, calamities, beatings, imprisonments, etc. . . . as poor, yet making many rich; as having nothing, yet possessing everything." The meaning of this passage, then, is this: "'I will take away your horses; I will take away your chariots.' That is, I will influence you in such a way that you will hold every pompous power of the flesh in contempt. I will give you another power and other weapons; and with these you will be superior to all nations. You will not be dependent on human powers, but I will send to you from heaven the power and might to make all things your subjects.

12. *And I will cut off sorceries from your house.*[7] In Hebrew there are many words for foretellers of the future. In Deut. 18:10-11 Moses has gathered together almost all of them. As much as we could we have made a distinction among them that we may be able to understand them. The Hebrew word (כְּשָׁפִים) which our Latin translation has rendered as *maleficia* ("sorceries") I translate with the word *augur*, which means those who divine and foretell the future from the flight of birds. Also, what we read as *divinationes* ("soothsayers") I translate as *coniectores* ("seers"), that is, those who interpret signs either in the skies or on the earth, such as preternatural births and things similar to these. Now, with these words he is quietly censuring and stinging the false prophets, and he says, as it were: "I will bring it to pass that you no longer employ the advice of men, which, to be sure, is vain, as the psalm says (cf. Ps. 94:11). I will take away from you that which has nothing definite,

[7] Both the Hebrew text and the Vulgate text have "from your hand."

nothing firm. They are merely guessing. They cannot establish anything for certain." Moreover, we must fulfill one responsibility: we must be very certain in our conscience about the Word which we teach or are taught, a thing human doctrines cannot achieve. You see, the conscience is still uncertain about the will of God, and teachers of human traditions cannot strengthen and uplift consciences that have been confused and terrified. In Ps. 14:3 we read: "They do not know the way of peace"; also in Ps. 14:5: "They were in great terror where there was no terror." [8] The Gospel makes a conscience certain and causes it to have peace. In this way all this is said by way of comparison, as if he were saying: "Now you depend on your fortresses, your walls, and the strength of your arms, likewise on idolatry and thoughts of the flesh. But I will take all these away from you, and I will raise up all very firm and definite things for you."

13. *And you shall bow down no more to the work of your hands*, that is, to idols. This manner of speaking is a common one also in Moses. Those also bow down to the work of their hands who trust in their own works and the righteousness of the flesh, for this, too, is to make idols. Otherwise, without that faith an idol is nothing, as the apostle says.[9] But what I trust in, what I depend on, and what I ascribe righteousness to—that is in the true place of a god for me, as we said earlier in sufficient detail regarding the fashioning of a god. In short, "I will destroy your sacred groves and wipe out that false worship and those false powers with which you abound and on which you rely. Then your worship will be valid and true through the Word and Spirit."

14. *And in anger and wrath I will execute vengeance.* He adds a warning and threatens the contemptuous with evil lest the magnitude of this great blessing be despised. It is as if he were saying: "Although this is the highest grace and eternal life, yet it is going to come to pass that few will believe and it will not be accepted. Although the Gospel is the power of God, yet it is 'a stumbling block to Jews, and folly to Gentiles' (1 Cor. 1:23). But I do not allow Myself to be despised in vain, for I will avenge Myself on

[8] These passages of Ps. 14 are in the Vulgate on the basis of the Septuagint. Cf. *Luther's Works*, 25, p. 29, n. 15.

[9] Cf. 1 Cor. 8:4.

those who despise Me." He has spoken these things, then, to terrify the wicked and says that those who despise and persecute the Word of the Gospel are going to be punished by Him. But he has also said this as a comfort to the preachers of the Word that they stand firm in their calling; that they pursue their ministry, no matter how much they see the world despise the Gospel; that they endure the persecutions at the hand of the wicked and allow God to avenge the contempt of His Word, thus following the example of Christ, who left vengeance to Him who judges justly, 1 Peter 2:23.

CHAPTER SIX

In the last two chapters he almost finished his prophecy about Christ and the kingdom of Christ through the Gospel. Now in the chapters that follow he returns to his task, namely, that of rebuking the wickedness of the people. Most of all he attacks their way of life. This is the custom of all the prophets, first to attack wickedness as the source and wellspring of evil works, and then to prescribe righteousness. Once they have learned and absorbed this, good works properly follow. This is the true order of the prophets and apostles, as we very clearly see in the Pauline letters. But this is something the false prophets do not do. They simply prescribe morals, rebuke sins, set out rewards, and omit the teaching of piety as regards the justification of the heart, etc.

1. *Hear what the Lord says.* As I have said, this entire chapter is devoted to censuring behavior and sins. But he declares with great boldness that the Lord has sent him out to do his task.

Contend in judgment before the mountains. "Plead your case before the mountains." This is a more accurate translation, as we also have it in Ps. 43:1, where it is translated "Defend my cause." The idea, then, is this: "Set yourself against the mountains, that is, against the rulers. Charge them with wickedness. Show them their wickedness and sin."

Let the hills [*hear your voice*]. The hills are the powerful and wealthy who stand above others, who outstrip others. As we see in various places in all Scripture, so also we see it here: the Word of God assails the proud, the lofty, the glorious, and the saintly in appearance—briefly, all that the world makes important. For God chose what is foolish in the world to shame the wise, and God chose what is weak in the world to shame the strong, etc. (1 Cor. 1:27).

2. *And you enduring foundations of the earth.* That is, "You princes, kings, priests, prophets—the ones on whom the people depend." He is using a fine epithet when he calls them "enduring," that is, the very strong and powerful people in the world.

For the Lord has a controversy with His people, and He will contend with Israel. He separates "His people" from "Israel." We see from this that the prophet is speaking while the kingdom of Israel is still standing and flourishing, so that we learn that the order of the chapters in the prophets is not always true. This is very clear to see from Jeremiah, where it happens very frequently. You see, these last two chapters may have come before the others, which speak about Israel as already led off into captivity. It has been useful to note this in the reading of the prophets.

3. *O My people, what have I done to you?* This is a complaint and a reminder of past blessings in which the Lord sets forth and presses His case, as if to say: "Why are you causing My name to have a bad sound among the nations? Given over as you are to wickedness, you provide the nations with an opportunity to blaspheme My name." He is imitating Moses, Deut. 32:6: "Do you thus requite the Lord, you foolish and senseless people? Is He not your Father, etc.?"

4. *For I brought you up from the land of Egypt.* He is now reminding them of past blessings—first, the rescue from the wretched slavery of Egypt, which is taught in various places in Scripture. He wanted to show them this external example as a sign to admonish them to remember divine goodness. They should not doubt that they were going to be freed from every peril and evil, however great, if they believed and remembered that exodus from Egypt. He has given us, too, those external signs of grace, Baptism and the Eucharist, by which He encourages us to remember those things which have happened to us through the Gospel and which never fail to happen to those who believe.

5. *O My people, remember what* [*Balak, king of Moab,*] *devised.* This is another blessing. With the preceding blessing He reminded them of their liberation from the violence and all the power of the pharaoh. With this second one, He reminds them of their deliverance from cunning and trickery—namely, that Balaam, who had come to curse them, was unable to harm them,

Num. 22 and 23. The Lord, however, had made the strength and might and power of the pharaoh weak and useless and of no significance. On the other hand, He had made the weakness of His people strong and powerful, and thus He turned also the curse of Balaam into a blessing. These are the blessings which He still offers to all the devout, and such blessings certainly are very great.

And what happened from Shittim to Gilgal. [1] Shittim is a place or field on the plains of Moab where the people of Israel built a camp. It stretches from Moab all the way to the Jordan, Num. 25:1; Joshua 3:1.

That you may know the saving acts of the Lord. The Hebrew has "for the sake of a knowledge of the saving acts of the Lord." This is said with ambiguous obscurity, so it can be taken in two ways: first, that you may know the saving acts of the Lord; second, that the saving act of the Lord may be known, may become known (yet this comes out to almost the same thing); that is, that you may know that you are saved not by your own works or virtues but by faith in Me, by My blessing, without man's merit or work. This saving act of the Lord, by which He justifies us, I explain passively, just as Paul did in several places in his letter to the Romans.

6. *With what shall I come before the Lord?* The prophet is explaining himself. The meaning is this: "With what shall I appease the Lord? With what shall I head off His wrath?" "It will come to pass that He will punish you and you will be eager to head Him off. But you are wrong; the worship you decide on is wicked. Your heart is unclean; therefore your works, no matter how great they are, are of no account."

And bow myself before God on high? This is a clear and evident text against the righteousness of works, an idea that Isaiah also has described in many words in chapter 1:11 f. He is manifestly condemning gestures and external works, however fine they may appear, if the heart is not pure. For works which come from an impure and wicked heart do not please God—not even those which He otherwise has commanded. One may see clearly both here and in Isaiah that even works commanded by the Law, like sacrifices,

[1] Contrary to all Bible versions, the Weimar and Erlangen texts read Gilead instead of Gilgal.

are condemned, because they were doing them with self-confidence and in the righteousness of the flesh. Because even those things which the law of God requires have no value without faith; how much less valuable will be the spurious works of our monks, etc.

7. *Shall I give my firstborn?* The heathen used to sacrifice their sons and daughters to the idol Moloch. Even the Jews lapsed into this wickedness, so that they thought they, like Abraham, were pleasing God by sacrificing their children. That is what the prophet is alluding to. See Deut. 12:31.

8. *I shall show you, O man, what is good.* This is a wonderful Teacher, that He not only reproves what is wicked and false but also shows what is right and good. The duty of prophets is to censure not merely external bad behavior but especially hypocrisy in order to humble and confound the proud hypocrites, who sorely offend God with their hypocrisy and in the meantime think that they are the only people who please God. God is looking for people who are truly righteous, truly holy, not for hypocrites, whom He hates very much. Here we see the same thing clearly. The prophet is calling the people back to their original, sincere, and good devotion, which he completely embraces with these three parts: "to do justice, to love mercy, and to walk humbly with God." Up to this point the prophet was assailing their wicked external morals. Here he is turning to the true worship of God or to the truly good behavior, which God requires of the devout.

To do justice. I have explained this phrase several times earlier in other prophets. It means to harm no one, to render to each person what is his own, to bother no one; on the other hand, to help others, to promote their welfare, to prevent damage and violence, so that the wealthy may not surround and oppress the needy, and so that the guilty may be punished and the innocent protected. This is what is said in Jer. 7:5: "If you execute judgment between a man and his neighbor," that is, if you restrain the wicked and protect the good. This, then, applies to all people, for the prophet wants them to be influenced in such a way that they be concerned about the public peace so that the state may be in good condition and each person may in peace enjoy what is his own. But he says clearly "to do" justice because he wants to see these things presented not merely with words but with the matter itself. With this one expression he has embraced the good part of Christian behavior or of Christian morals. You see, violence against one's neighbor is forbidden; then covetousness, that I should not covet my neighbor's goods, or wish him ill, but protect him, ward off danger from him, etc. Whoever does this will incur the hatred of many people against himself, for tyrants and others who strike out against the poor will be annoyed by resistance against themselves. Therefore whoever resists them can do so only with danger to his reputation and life. Persecution follows immediately, for Satan cannot do genuinely good works; but hypocrisy he is capable of to the highest degree. In fact, he establishes and promotes hypocrisy that by it he may lead men away from true godliness, from faith in God, to their own works and righteousness. The flesh gladly hears and says these words, but it does not do what the words say, nor can it, except it be renewed by the Spirit.

To love mercy. This means that it pleases us to be blessings to others, for the Hebrew word (חֶסֶד) properly means mercy that has been shown, as Christ also indicates in Matt. 9:13: "Go and learn what this means, 'I desire mercy and not sacrifice.'" Therefore God requires no good works from us for Himself; He wants everything to yield to the use and welfare of our neighbor. The glory of such works is enough for God. Faith is the beginning of justification, as all Scripture reveals. Being justified by faith, we neither can nor should offer anything to God other than the sacrifice of praise; that is, that we bear witness with our preaching of the grace we have received, that we magnify God, that we preach His glory, and do this preaching through the Gospel. These are the "fruits of our lips," Hos. 14:2. Then let us show mercy to our neighbor, that is, let it be our pleasure to help a neighbor, to seize every opportunity to help a neighbor. Let us also stir up others to perform the responsibilities of love, so that in this way our entire life yields to the good of our neighbor, since we owe nothing to anyone, except that we love him, Rom. 13:8.

And to walk humbly with your God. The prophet certainly is speaking about the good behavior which we practice toward our neighbor. All other works he condemns—even those which appear to be very holy—with which the wicked hypocrites think they please God, while in the meantime they wretchedly afflict and oppress and swallow up the poor with their rapacious taxes and wicked usuries. This third point which he is adding here is certainly an admonition especially necessary. In fact, there is a danger that after we have been justified we become lukewarm, that we become proud, that our gifts of the Spirit tickle us because in them we surpass others, that we please ourselves. It is as if he were saying: "When you have done what I say, when you have developed a concern for your neighbor, see to it that you do not become smug, that you do not have an eye for mischief, that you do not please yourself and go around looking for praise and glory that is owed to God alone." Even the most spiritual-minded cannot be without that very wicked φιλαυτία ("self-love"). As soon as they see that they are better than others, more learned than others, and that they have received more gifts of the Spirit, they please themselves and immediately despise others who are beneath them. For esteem and good works by their own nature please a man. Scripture sets forth for us a terrible example in Saul, who was renowned for his good works. There was no better man than he in all Israel, as Scripture says 1 Sam. 9:2. He was filled with the Spirit of the Lord, but he lacked what Micah requires here. Therefore he fell very badly, and God rejected him in a really terrible way. Altogether correct is the dictum of the holy fathers with which they generally made note of this malicious self-love (φιλαυτία): "No matter how you bend it, the head of the thistle always stands straight up." Thus this wicked state of mind always creeps into the hearts of the saints. They cannot be without it. This is the only evil which sets a snare for good works, as St. Augustine says in his rule. God oftens allows his saints to slip very badly, as did Peter and that holy man David. Thus they should be terrified and humbled by a rather serious fall, should always live in fear of becoming too proud, and should recognize the weakness that is still theirs. So David cries out in Ps. 51:3: "My sin is ever before me." In this way the saints should be humbled by looking at and recognizing their own weakness and sin and should cease from their pride in their own good works or gifts of the Spirit which they have received from God. This, too, is "to walk humbly with God," that is, to have a humble and lowly regard for oneself, to walk without guile, to want always to hide and to strive for no glory or honor by good works, and to seek to gain what that wicked self-esteem (φιλαυτία) and that malicious state of mind cannot attain. That self-love, you see, wants to be seen by all men; it wants everyone to notice what it does in order that it may procure glory and praise for itself, that it may have a good reputation before men, etc. To this is related exactly what Christ teaches in Matt. 6:3-5: "When you give alms, do not let your left hand know what your right hand is doing, so that your alms may be in secret, etc. And when you pray, you must not be like the hypocrites, etc." Thus with a lowly and guileless conscience we ought to give and do everything in such a way that we want no one to know it. Consequently, those are in a dangerous position who have a greater supply of God's gifts than others do and who have to be set over others in the ministry of the Word, which is not just every man's thing.[2] For even the most holy people have always complained about this evil, and they could not be rid of it, no matter how hard they tried to correct it. What we read in Ecclus. 3:20 applies here: "The greater you are, the more you must humble yourself in all things, etc."

9. *The voice of the Lord cries to the city.* This is clearly a new section, a new topic, or sermon. The prophets did not do all their prophesying at one time, but some at one time and some at another time, as I have mentioned earlier several times. The meaning, then, is this: "This is not my voice but the voice of the Lord with which I am speaking to you. He is preaching through me. He is using me merely as an instrument for preaching His Word, and this is not happening in vain, for those will be blessed who have feared the name of the Lord, and contrariwise, those will be cursed who have not feared it."

Sound wisdom. The Hebrew word (תּוּשִׁיָּה) which our translator[3] renders as *salus* ("sound wisdom") properly means, I believe, blessedness, success, and what turns out well and successfully. The same expression occurs in Prov. 8:14 in this way: "I have counsel and sound wisdom, I have insight," that is, "One counsels correctly through Me, or else one counsels badly without My counsel. Also, through Me, plans are carried out successfully. It is I who give the successful outcome so that what men plan turns out suc-

[2] Luther uses the Greek phrase όυκ ἔστι τυχόντων.

[3] The Vulgate.

cessfully." In this way I think we understand the meaning of the word. Then, when he says "to the city," the number is singular instead of plural, for He turns all cities to Himself, just as the text reads in the Hebrew: "The voice of the Lord cries in every town" *(oppidatim)*, that is, the Lord sends His Word throughout the kingdom of Israel. The apostle Paul has also expressed this phrase beautifully in his letter to Titus, chapter 1:5: "Appoint elders in every town."

And who will favor it? They translate the Hebrew here in different ways. The Septuagint translators rendered it "who will appoint"; Jerome, "who will favor"; and others in other ways. I do not at all understand what the prophet wants to say, and I am afraid that we are still ignorant of some of the Hebrew language, especially when special words of any kind, such as this is, occur in Scripture. Lest we completely bypass this passage, we will still say and translate it with others this way: "who will transfer, or go away," so that the meaning is: "He has been sent by God to the ministry of the Word; he has received a divine command to preach; therefore there is no reason why he can desert the responsibility assigned."

10. *There still is fire in the house of the wicked, treasures of wickedness.* Earlier he taught that the Lord requires that they do justice and love mercy. Here he is censuring them for doing neither: they do not do justice, even less do they love mercy. To mistreat the poor, from whom they enrich themselves and grow wealthy, certainly is not to do justice nor to love mercy, if they use scanter measures than is just. Those who use scant measures are a source of ill to the poor and needy, so do they draw off their possessions. The meaning, then, is this: "No matter how much we may cry out and censure you through the Word of God, yet we accomplish nothing. There are very few who have the Word in their heart, for the others continue in their wickedness." I still see fire in the house of the wicked; that is, I see many treasures taken through wickedness. These, I believe, are nothing else but a sort of fire which is going to consume the wicked who possess those treasures. Thus I interpret the fire as punishment. It is as if he were saying: "They are still struggling with their own wickedness; they are taking away the goods of others by greedy deceit, with false

scales, etc.; but all those goods are going to be a source of evil for them and will cause their destruction. The same phrase occurs this way earlier in Amos 5:6: "In that day He will break out like fire in the house of Joseph."

And the scant measure of wrath. The Hebrew language speaks elegantly. It speaks of a measure of scantiness, that is, a measure by which they impoverish others and squeeze out their substance which they take to enrich themselves and by which they themselves become wealthy. I interpret this phrase in the same way as I did the one above, so that the meaning is this: "There is still wrath in the house of the wicked – namely, the scant measure. They hoard up wrath for themselves while they devour and impoverish the poor with their unjust measures. Because of this they are now wealthy, but that very same thing will produce great evil and destruction for them."

11. *And with a bag of deceitful weights.* We have the same phrase in Prov. 16:11: "A just balance and scales are the Lord's; all the weights in the bag are His work," where our books have the inappropriate reading "in the age" [instead of "in the bag"].[4] Thus the Lord here is saying: "Should I approve of your false weights and unjust scales, with which you have enriched yourselves by your wicked usuries and thefts?" He very necessarily adds this, for He sees that they are acting wickedly, that they are getting around the poor and defrauding them with usuries and false scales. Yet they want to cure this wickedness with what they think are good works. They feign a sort of pious appearance while they perform their sacrifices and do the works of the Law like pious people. The Lord, however, rejects all that and condemns that perverse sanctity with which they kept thinking they were pleasing God while they were making the poor their wretched prey. Therefore He is saying all this against the wicked presumption and smugness of the perverse saints.

12. *Whose rich men.* Earlier I said that the singular was used for the plural – namely, of cities.[5] That is, the rich men went out with those false weights and measures and did a gross thing.

[4] That is, the Vulgate versions in use in Luther's time must have read *saeculi* for *sacculi*.

[5] Cf. p. 264 above.

Therefore, whatever goods they have they have obtained by doing harm.

And whose inhabitants spoke lies. That is, they confirm their deceits and wicked fraud with lying. They set a high price on their own merchandise and what they sell to others. With their deceitfulness they impose on their neighbors, just as is the custom of our own merchants, who have absolutely no concept of godliness, provided they make their sale.

13. *Therefore I have begun to smite.* We must read this in the present tense, as we also say in German: *Darum will ich auch anheben* ("Therefore I have a mind to begin"). The judgment of God is strange. At the very time that the wicked want to please God with their own worship which they establish, they provoke Him the more; and at the very time they want to gain success with their thieving, wicked tricks with which they impose on their neighbor, they are finally reduced to extreme poverty. This is what happens when God shows Himself perverse to a crooked man, as we read in Ps. 18:26. Thus no other outcome remains but that, no matter how many and how great may be those goods which they have obtained wickedly, they will suffer a bad fall, just as he said earlier in chapter 1:7: "For from the hire of a harlot she gathered them, and to the hire of a harlot they shall return." Our princes today should entertain no better hopes. They know nothing else but to squeeze out the substance of the poor and to collect great treasures. Although they could help many by giving a hundred or a thousand gold pieces for the poor to use, they give nothing. They have no consideration for the poor but are interested only in enriching themselves, and later on they will be forced to pour out many thousands of gold pieces on wicked soldiers when the judgment of God causes wars to begin. Then the mercenaries have the benefit of it. Some lose their goods to prostitutes, and even though most of their substance may go to their heirs, yet they will squander it very prodigally. This is the judgment of God, which does not deceive us; no one should have hopes for anything better. "Goods ill got must ill be lost." [6] The hire of a harlot will return to the hire of a harlot. God will not tell a lie. We have learned this from experience and are compelled to admit that it is true.

[6] Cf. p. 214, n. 4, above.

14. *You will eat but not be satisfied.* That is, "I will cause such a famine for you that, although you have eaten, it will not be enough to take away your hunger with food. What you do eat will come to you crumb by crumb, and you will never leave the table satisfied."

You will have hunger cramps in your inward parts. We have the same expression [7] in Ps. 38:6: "I am utterly bowed down and prostrate; all the day I go about mourning." The meaning is as if he were saying: "I will see to it that you are more and more oppressed every day, and I will cause a decrease and diminution of all your resources in your inward parts. All your goods will pass away in wretched fashion."

You will put away but not save. That is, "You will not be able to save your property and your children, whom you hope you will protect from destruction; in fact, all this will become the loot of the Assyrian. If there will be some thought of flight and escape, I will see to it that it perishes by the sword." This is the way God overthrows the wicked so that not even their name continues to exist, as we read in Ps. 37:10, 28, 35-36.

16. *You have kept the statutes of Omri.* He adds this that we may see that He is speaking about the kingdom of Israel, as I also said earlier.[8] Omri was the father of wicked King Ahab, under whom the kingdom of Israel first began to flourish. King Ahab was a very prosperous man, but he was also very wicked.

[*And you have walked*] *in their counsels.* That is, "You also gave your approval to whatever pleased them."

[7] Luther reads *incurvatio* here in Micah, and Ps. 38:6 has *curvatus sum* ("I am doubled up") in the Vulgate.

[8] Cf. p. 210 above.

CHAPTER SEVEN

In this last chapter he has brought together into one small package as it were his entire prophecy. He first rebukes the wicked way of life of the people and then passes over to the kingdom of Christ. Moreover, he presses his case for the people with great affection; he has a great thirst for the salvation of his people. With great exertion he urges and does everything to turn them away from their wickedness. He compares himself to a grape gatherer who goes into the vineyard he has very carefully cultivated; he looks for grapes to eat but finds nothing. This metaphor has been taken from Moses and also from other prophets here and there. It appears in the song in Deut. 32:32 as follows: "For their vine comes from the vine of Sodom and from the fields of Gomorrah; their grapes are grapes of poison, their clusters are bitter." We have the same idea in Is. 5, where the people of Israel are called the vineyard of the Lord. Here, then, the gatherer of the grapes or vintager is the prophet, who runs through his people seeking some good fruit, but he finds nothing except thorns, that is, a wicked people, who hold both God and His Word in contempt. "I have become like the master of an estate who goes to see his vineyard to look for the fruit of his labors. The vineyard at first encouraged great hopes for itself, but I find nothing in it except wild grapes and thorns. (Isaiah also speaks in exactly the same way in chapter 5:2: 'I looked for it to yield grapes, but it yielded wild grapes.') Not even a single cluster to eat do I find, much less will there be a crop of clusters from which to press out wine."

1. *The firstfruits.*[1] That is, "I do not even find enough to give the firstfruits to those to whom they are due, namely, the priests, etc." So he is speaking about the entire vine, about the branches

[1] Luther apparently reads *primitias* for the Vulgate's *praecoquas ficus* ("first-ripe figs").

which appear to be full of the developing clusters. That is, he is speaking about all the people, so that we must not take this to mean only the remnant, as some want it to be understood.

2. *The godly man has perished from the earth.* He himself explains the simile which he has used. Scripture calls him a godly man who is justified by grace, who has received mercy from God. The godly man of this kind he contrasts to the others—hypocrites and those who pretend to have what appears to be great sanctity. It is as if he were saying: "Although many people feign the name and appearance of godliness, yet they are wicked, they are not godly, just as Hosea said earlier" (cf. Hos. 4:1).

There is none upright among men; [2] *they all lie in wait for blood.* He states that he had accused them all of wickedness, as if to say: "Love is so dead, so does no one have any consideration for his neighbor, such mutual savagery rules, that they all are lying in wait for each other. They are all filled with hatred and envy, they are all ἄστοργοι ("inhuman"), as Paul says (Rom. 1:31; 2 Tim. 3:3).

Each hunts his brother to curse him. That is, he absolutely wants his brother killed, lest there be any mention of him or salvation for him in the future. You see, things devoted [3] were never redeemed, but they were killed in fulfillment of the vow, as we have it in Lev. 27:28.[4]

3. *The evil of their hands they call good.* The prophet does not mean to say that they are so terribly senseless as to call murder, theft, and wicked violence against their neighbor good things and to approve of them. Rather, he is censuring the hypocrites' attitude. Hypocrites do have certain pursuits, certain external good works, which are indeed evil before God as coming from an evil and wicked heart. Nevertheless, to them these works seem to be good. They flatter one another with them and boast about them, and yet they had to be censured because of them. So in the same sense Christ also said (Matt. 7:15): "They will come to you in sheep's clothing but inwardly are ravenous wolves." And we read in Is.

[2] In the Weimar text this first clause is added to the previous paragraph, as if it were the quotation from Hosea.

[3] We have read *anathemata* for *anathema,* as in the Zwickau text.

[4] The Altenburg text in the Weimar edition has *ut est in Numeris,* but the Zwickau text has the correct reference: *Levitic. ultimo.*

5:20: "Woe to you who call evil good and good evil, who put darkness for light, etc." Hypocrites, you see, can act in no other way.

The prince [*and the judge*] *ask for a bribe.* We can take this to mean two things: first, that this is connected to that which follows in this sense, that if the prince demands unbearable taxes, the judge is immediately ready to make it legal. That is, the judge approves that wicked taxation of the prince. The second meaning is this: All princes are heavy taxers; they all seek only their own gain, and this they do at their subjects' risk and loss. But the judge provides the legal warrant, that is, he receives gifts that corrupt him so that he perverts his judgments. If someone is an important man, he passes judgment in his favor, etc. In this way his opinion varies. Wicked princes and preachers cannot act differently; they merely seek their own interests, not those of the Lord, as the apostle says in Rom. 16:18; they swallow up and destroy the people physically and spiritually. This is also described beautifully by the psalm about the Antichrist.[5]

And the great man utters the evil desire of his soul. Our translator[6] renders this badly with the word "desire," for the Hebrew word means "punishment" and "fault," as when we say in German, *Er ringt nach Unglück* ("He is contriving trouble"), and also, *Er hat ein Unglück angerichtet* ("He has brought about a calamity"). Thus we indicate both punishment and fault with a single word. We have the same word in Ps. 91:3, where we read "from the harsh word."[7] In the Hebrew this is "from the deadly pestilence," that is, from an unfortunate situation. Thus the meaning here is this: The rich and powerful decree and decide anything at all in accordance with their own sinful will. They precipitate a calamity whenever it seems advantageous to them.

Thus they weave it together. The Hebrew word means a rope—something knotted. In Ps. 2:3 we read: "Let us . . . cast their cords from us"; and in Ps. 118:27: "Bind the festal procession with branches." The idea, then, is this: "Each man does as he wishes

[5] The Zwickau text adds "Psalm 11."

[6] The Vulgate. It is criticized for having *desiderium* for *pravitatem*.

[7] The Vulgate has *a verbo aspero* for the Hebrew הַוָּה.

according to his own evil desire. The people have no concern for God and the Law. Therefore everything is disturbed, and there is no order in the state."

4. *The best of them is like a brier.* David also used this simile in his last words (2 Sam. 23:6). Christ says in Matt. 7:16: "Are grapes gathered from thorns, or figs from thistles?" Also, the ram that was to be sacrificed instead of Isaac was caught in a thicket, as we have it in Gen. 22:13. Thus the wicked are here and there compared to thorns in Scripture. The meaning, then, is this: "Even their holiest men, who feign an outstanding show of saintliness, are nothing else but thorns and thistles. They look pretty, but they produce no fruit. They offer nothing else but pricks of conscience, with which they harm the people."

The day of your watchmen. "So I bid you farewell. I try in vain to turn you aside, I preach in vain; you produce no fruit. Therefore the watchmen of your visitation are coming, for the king of Assyria will come to punish the land as it deserves." This is the way the prophets generally use the word "watchmen" *(speculatio),* as Zeph. 1:12 used the same expression: "I will search Jerusalem with lamps," that is, "I will search Jerusalem very carefully and seek out all the wicked that I may find them and destroy those whom I have found."

5. *Put no trust in a friend; have no confidence in a ruler.* I take this passage to mean that the prophet is describing in general terms the faithlessness of the people; if we do not understand it in this way, everything will hang together poorly. As we say in German *Es ist kein treuer Mensch auf Erden,* ("There is no faithful man on earth"), so the prophet speaks here. It is as if he were saying: "The people trust neither their princes nor their priests nor their prophets, because they teach false doctrines," as he mentioned earlier. He is saying this, then, to humble the people, to take away their vain smugness, and to draw them away from the empty promises of the false prophets with which they were promising peace and tranquility, as he said earlier,[8] when there was no peace, as Jeremiah says.[9] I believe that this entire passage is proverbial, as if he were saying, "Do not be deceived by false promises

[8] Cf. p. 231 above.

[9] Jer. 6:14.

with which the false prophets are enticing you, because otherwise, too, there is no faith in men. Have faith in God alone, for He cannot lie and deceive."

6. *For the son treats the father with contempt.* The Hebrew word means what we express with "to disgrace." Today exactly the same faithlessness holds sway, and nowhere is there true faith, for the flesh is always the same. Gold and silver frequently are the cause of very bitter hatreds between brothers, regardless of how closely they otherwise might be related by common blood.

7. *But as for me, I will look to the Lord.* Now he is going over to giving comfort, and he leaves out the threats. The prophet is speaking in the person of all the rest of the devout, who nevertheless also were going to suffer wretched affliction for a time and were going to be led into captivity but afterwards were going to be glorified again because of the promises made to David. As we have said earlier several times, the threats pertain to the wicked, the comfort or promises to the devout.

I will look. That is, "I will watch carefully, I will prepare myself to see," for the Hebrew word includes all that. That is, "Even if we shall be punished thus along with the wicked, yet let us hope for better things. The Lord will redeem us."

8. *Rejoice not over me, O my enemy.* That is, "O Babylon, who will boast over my oppression, who will revile me, cease your boasting! For I shall again be glorified, so do not think that it is all over with me."

I will rise again. "My original vigor will return to me; in the meantime, even while I am not yet glorified, the Lord is my fortune while I am in the midst of darkness, that is, in afflictions, in wretched captivity. You see, in Scripture "darkness" means afflictions and doubtful times. We have it thus in the psalm (Ps. 112:4): "Light rises in the darkness for the upright." [10]

9. *I will bear the indignation of the Lord.* This entire passage is a beautiful one, filled with pious affection. The wicked cannot endure the hand of the Lord in affliction; they are forced to despair when they have fallen under the judgments of the Lord. The

[10] The Weimar editor suggest Ps. 97:11, but that passage does not contain the phrase "in the darkness."

righteous, on the other hand, confess their sin and patiently endure the hand of the Lord as they await their very certain freedom.

That I may behold His righteousness. That is, "That I may delight in His righteousness, that I may take pleasure in it." This same phrase has also appeared earlier. It also occurs in Ps. 91:8: "You will see the recompense of the wicked"; and in Ps. 54:7: "My eye has looked in triumph on my enemies." This is also the same expression as that which follows:

My eyes will gloat over her. That is, "I shall be delighted to see her, because I shall see what I have desired."

Like the mire of the streets, because Babylon as well as that entire realm finally was destroyed by the king of the Persians, as history recounts. This is the way God with His judgment confounds the wicked who flourish for a time and who alone seem to hold sway. Then He punishes their sin with sin, etc.

11. *That your walls may be built.* This was fulfilled when Cyrus, the king of the Persians, conquered the Babylonians and set free the Jews who at that time were being held captive to return to Jerusalem, as the account of Ezra shows. Then after they had returned, they rebuilt the temple and the old remains.

The Law. The Hebrew word (חֹק) does not mean the law of Moses but a statute or ordinance. We have this in Ps. 2:6-7: "On Zion, the holy hill, I will tell of His decree"; and in Prov. 8:27: "With a definite rule *(lege)* He drew a circle around the deep," that is, [He set] a measure or decree. Thus here:

Shall be far extended. That is, "The ordinance and statute—that yoke of the Assyrians—shall depart. You shall escape and be free. The Assyrian no longer shall have the right to pass ordinances against you, because the Lord will set you free." "He looses the belt of the kings," as we read in Job 12:18, that is, the well-founded kingdoms on which kings depend, etc.

12. *On that day they will come to you from Assyria and from the fortified cities, from Tyre, and from sea to sea and from mountain to mountain.* This is the way I think we must read this most accurately from the Hebrew. These are Hebraisms, just as we say "from one city to the next." That is, "I will again lift up Jerusalem, I will restore the temple. Very many peoples from different nations

will come together there, and the glory of the temple will be great." For the latter temple had greater glory than did the first one, as we have said earlier in great detail.[11] Thus he comforts the faithful that they may give to God the glory that He is truthful and that He will preserve forever the kingdom of David, even though they suffer captivity for a time.

13. *And the earth will be desolate.* We can take this to have a double meaning: that it refers to the Assyrians—an idea which does not please me. I connect it to the promise in this way: "Indeed, a great multitude of peoples will come to Jerusalem, and your glory will be great, but in the meantime, give careful consideration to your captivity, because your sins have earned it. Your land will be destroyed, but afterward it will be restored."

14. *Shepherd Thy people.* I apply this simply to the kingdom of Christ, for he is here describing that new realm because of which all things in the old happen and about which we spoke earlier in great detail.

Shepherd. That is, be the Shepherd.

Take up Thy staff. "This is the Gospel with which You will feed the sheep which are to be fattened." So Ps. 110:2 speaks of the staff: "The Lord will send forth from Zion the scepter of Thy might."

Who dwell in the forest, and shepherd Thy people in the midst of Carmel. This is how this passage must be construed correctly, for our translation hangs together poorly. He continues with his comparison of the flock and the shepherd, for he is comparing to a flock (which shepherds are accustomed to lead to pasture) the Jews who were scattered here and there among the wicked nations. They hope only in God, they are attached to no human protection, they have no leader or protector in the world on whom to depend. He says: "Thou, Lord, Thou, Shepherd Christ, have a concern for these. Feed them with Thy Word and be their Leader, for Thou hast promised, etc."

[11] This statement seems to contradict what Luther had said previously: "The latter temple was not as large and magnificent as was the former" (p. 237 above). But Luther stated the ultimate greater glory of the latter temple in words like these: "It was necessary that there be a first, external place for the Gospel to be preached. This happened through Christ and the apostles in the temple at Jerusalem. Cf. pp. 237—238 above.

In the midst of Carmel. Because of its fertility, this mountain is greatly renowned in both sacred and secular literature. Here the prophet is being completely contradictory, it appears, when he says that this Shepherd is going to feed the flock in the forest and immediately adds that it will be fed in the midst of Carmel. This inconsistency, then, clearly forces us to apply all this to a spiritual kingdom rather than to a physical or external one. The meaning, therefore, is this: "Feed Thy people in the forest; that is, in the danger of the world, where they are exposed to the attacks of beasts, where Satan, like a roaring lion, always lies in wait for them, eager to devour them, as Peter says.[12] "In the midst of Carmel," then, means the abundance of the promises of the Gospel, with which they are to be quickened and fattened.

Bashan and Gilead. These were in the kingdom of Israel and were never brought back from captivity, just as all Israel was not led back. We must therefore confess that he is speaking about a spiritual feeding through the Word. Consequently, I am moved to interpret all this about the kingdom of Christ through the Gospel.

I will show him marvelous things. As is the custom of the prophets, he changes the person. He is saying that He will do strange and marvelous things, just as He had done when He had led them out of the captivity of Egypt. This, too, just as the preceding points, cannot be taken to mean the new restoration of an external kingdom, but the spiritual kingdom.

16. *The nations shall see and be ashamed.* So great will be the course of the Gospel and of this new kingdom, so broadly will it extend, that it will even reach the heathen, who will see the miracles of Christ and of the apostles. They will see so great a power of the Spirit in those miracles that they will become ashamed and quickly cease to trust further in the arm of the flesh. No longer will they glory in their own strength and in the righteousnesses of the flesh in which they used to trust. Rather, they will glory in this, "that they have known Me," Jeremiah 9:24.

Their ears shall be deaf. That is, they will no longer boast of their own righteousness. After hearing of Christ's true righteous-

[12] 1 Peter 5:8.

ness, all their own righteousness will become filthy to them. They will want to hear Christ alone, etc.

17. *They shall lick the dust, etc., like the crawling things of the earth; they shall come trembling out of their strongholds; they shall turn in dread to the Lord our God.* There is a great error in the Latin Bible when it reads here: "They will not desire *(non desiderabunt)* the Lord our God." All this is said about the fruits of the Word preached among the Gentiles. Such will be the fruits when the Gentiles will have heard the Gospel. Furthermore, these are metaphors which indicate the humiliation of the Gentiles and their self-abasement when they have heard the Gospel. A humble confession has great significance, for when we have heard the Gospel, we condemn all our own activities and say that there is no righteousness, no wisdom, no strength—that the flesh has nothing—when this is compared with the great and beautiful righteousness of Christ. This is what he is saying here: "Like the crawling things of the earth, they will come trembling out of their strongholds." That is, they will feel very humble about themselves in the presence of the great magnificence of Christ. Therefore with great hustling and bustling they will come out of their hiding places (as grubs generally hurry very swiftly away from the presence of men), that is, from their own righteousness and traditions on which they used to depend before and in which they used to live. They will rejoice in and tremble at the righteousness of Christ. They will make all their own acts as nothing and will wonder at and take up all the acts of Christ alone.

Who pardons iniquity. "Not everyone will believe the Gospel, but only a remnant, chosen from eternity. From these You will take away their sins, for they cannot take them away with their own works, righteousnesses, and ceremonies. No works will save them, but this will be their salvation, that You take away their sins. Indeed, You alone are true God, who can take away sins."

He will not retain His anger forever. He will not hang on to His anger tightly but will let it go, since it pleases Him to be merciful. These are the very broad promises and comforts with which the heart can be quickened in every temptation, no matter how great, when that heart knows that God is the Father of mercies, who does not want the death of the sinner but that he live, as Ezekiel says,[13] and who wants to forgive sins, etc., just as he here adds:

Into the depths of the sea. That is, He will put our sins far away from us so that they never again trouble our conscience. He will give us peace of conscience and a very free conscience, for indeed, peace follows the forgiveness of sins—a peace where the heart feels the sweetness of divine goodness, now that its sin has been forgiven, etc.

20. *For Thou wilt show faithfulness to Jacob.* That is, "You will fulfill what You have promised to the fathers—namely, Your blessing and the Gospel of eternal salvation." Thus Scripture everywhere excludes all our own merit. For this reason God gives His grace, for this reason He forgives sins, for this reason He saves us—that He has made a promise, not that we have earned these, etc.

To Christ be praise and glory!
Wittenberg, April 7, 1525

[13] Ezek. 33:11.

LECTURES ON NAHUM

The Altenburg Text

Translated by
RICHARD J. DINDA

THE PREFACE AND HYPOTHESIS FOR THE PROPHET NAHUM

EVEN the name of the prophet fits the prophecy. You see, Nahum means "comforter," or "comforted," to the Jews. He does justice to his name in every respect through his prophecy, for there is nothing else in it than comfort for the remnant of the people of Judah, which had been preserved from the destruction of Israel. Earlier in the preceding prophets we saw the destruction of all Israel. Israel was so wretchedly afflicted and oppressed as it was carried off into captivity that it was never brought back. Earlier Jonah was sent to the Assyrian king as a prophet to reveal their wickedness to the Assyrians. That situation turned out well. After all, with his preaching he turned the entire kingdom of the Assyrians to repentance. Otherwise the Lord was planning to destroy that kingdom, unless they came to their senses. This we treated earlier in Jonah in considerable detail. Because they turned to repentance, the punishment was deferred; but such are the hearts of men that when the punishment ceased, so did the repentance. They slipped back into the same wickedness under which they had labored before. After all, in prosperity men cannot but conduct themselves more immoderately than is reasonable, for they are unable to use prosperity moderately, and this, a famous man has said, will undermine the good intentions even of the wise.[1] This has caused the ruin of all the kingdoms, because they used success in their affairs immoderately. This is why the Assyrians perished. So the Persians were destroyed at the hands of the Greeks, the Greeks at the hands of the Romans, and the Romans at the hands of the Goths. Also today the pope is being destroyed by the Word of God. Some wise men, although they were strangers to godliness, have even seen this when they said that the great do not last long.

[1] Cf. *Luther's Works,* 19, p. 114.

You see, it cannot happen that the minds of men restrain themselves within their limits in prosperity so that they do not become inflated. As I have said, the same thing also happened to the people of Nineveh. Because of their affluent wealth and great successes, they returned to their old way of thinking, even though Jonah had taught them otherwise. They were even beginning to threaten the destruction of Judah, just as they earlier had led all Israel into wretched captivity. They believed that they would accomplish this easily. After all, the people of Judah were few and weak—the smallest part of the kingdom. Thus the Assyrians had absolutely no doubt that they would easily swallow up that number. It was into this situation that the prophet Nahum was sent as well as that other prophet who followed him. They were to comfort and to encourage that weak and insignificant remnant—the lowest dregs—of the people of God not to despair as the Assyrians attacked them but to believe that God would step in to save them.

Accordingly, this prophet has briefly the following purpose: to keep in faith toward God the Judah which still survived the great destruction, to completely assure their hearts that this kingdom would remain firm in the Word and worship of God, that His divine promises would be fulfilled, and that the kingdom would not cease to exist but would last until the coming of Christ, who was to be born of Judah, as the prophecies declare. Thus there is nothing else here but the doctrine of faith. You see, he is teaching us to trust in God and especially when we despair of every human protection, every human power and planning, to believe that the Lord is close to His people and protects them against the assaults of every foe, no matter how powerful such foes may be, etc. But there is need here for a faith that believes that.

CHAPTER ONE

1. *The burden of Nineveh. The book of the vision of Nahum of Elkosh.* I like Jerome's idea when he says that Elkosh was the name of the district or country of Nahum. Just as Micah was of Moresheth, so Nahum came from Elkosh.

He begins his prophecy with a wonderful word of consolation when he says, "The burden of Nineveh." It is as if he were saying: "The burden which up to now has been crushing you will be removed from you. You will be free. It is far from the truth that you will perish—that in your oppression you will fall. In fact, the people of Nineveh, whom you have feared and still fear, are the ones who are going to be crushed." "The burden of Nineveh" is a Hebrew expression; in Latin we say "the burden upon Nineveh." You see, Nineveh, as we noted earlier in Jonah,[1] was the chief city of the Assyrian kingdom. The Latin-speaking people referred to it as a showplace.

2. *The Lord is a jealous God and avenging.* With many words he presses home his point about the wrath of Divine Majesty against the enemies of His people. If we examine the matter carefully, the words are very fiery. The people in the kingdom of Judah were weak. They feared the captivity which had occurred to their brothers, the Israelites. The fierce Assyrians were confident of their strength and resources and boasted about them. They thought they would easily swallow up a people so small and so weak. This is something which the blasphemies of Rabshakeh in Is. 36:8-9 clearly indicate: "Come now, make a wager with my master the king of Assyria: I will give you two thousand horses if you are able on your part to set riders upon them. How then can you repulse a single captain among the least of my master's servants, etc." "Do not let Hezekiah deceive you, for he will not be able to

[1] Cf. *Luther's Works,* 19, p. 4.

deliver you" (Is. 36:14). "The Lord said to me, 'Go up against this land, etc.'" (Is. 36:10). No matter how fierce the Assyrians were, no matter how sure they seemed of victory, in the face of all this, Nahum strengthens the hearts of Judah not to be afraid, no matter how powerful the Assyrians may be. He tells them that the Lord will take revenge on the enemies of His people, that the Lord will save them, just as the God of David had also foretold to their fathers. This prophecy seemed most foolish and ridiculous to the Assyrians. There undoubtedly were even some in the land of Judah who no more believed that that would happen than they believed what Nahum foretold here when the peril was already threatening. Assyria was already bestirring its very powerful army to destroy them, and Nahum orders them to be untroubled. He promises them freedom. He promises that the Lord will go to battle for them and will avenge Himself against their foes. They had need for a very great faith that would lay hold of those divine promises, a faith that would await the vengeance of the Lord against the Assyrians, a faith that would no more doubt that that vengeance would come than if it were already taking place. All the words and promises of God are of such a character that they clearly surpass all understanding and all reason, so that the flesh cannot but laugh at them and hold them in contempt. Faith alone believes all these things, and such faith only a very few had, such as pious King Hezekiah and a few others, who threw themselves on this kind of promise of the Lord. We, too, would rightly understand those promises if we would be in the same straits as they then were, straits for which those promises were made—if the pope and princes would rage against us and come with a very powerful army to destroy us, etc. Then we would understand the functions and power of these comforting words.

The Lord is . . . avenging, the Lord is avenging. He states this twice. This is an indication of both certainty and vehemence.

The Lord takes vengeance on His adversaries. It is the fullest consolation of the righteous when they hear that the Lord calls those who oppose the righteous, who persecute and kill them, His adversaries. The Lord makes the same promise in clear language in Ex. 23:22: [2] "I will be an enemy to your enemies and an adver-

[2] The Weimar text has "Deuteronomy."

sary to your adversaries." So He here calls the Assyrians, who were the enemies of Judah, His enemies. "What is it, then, that we should fear? So long as we believe, all the most powerful foes can accomplish nothing against us. After all, they are battling the Lord, not us; they are the Lord's enemies, not ours. That battle will bring them a terrible calamity, since they purpose to fight against our great and mighty God." Here, too, the prophet clearly strengthens the hearts of Judah in the same way. It is as if He were saying: "Take heart. They cannot harm you in the least. All the hairs of your head are numbered. The matter is not between them and you but between them and the Lord, against whom they will fight a losing battle." All the very powerful promises of this kind are aimed against the wicked blasphemies of the Assyrians as I mentioned earlier on the basis of Isaiah.[3] Their purpose is to lift up the hearts of the righteous, etc.

3. *The Lord is slow to anger.* This verse our exegetes have interpreted in different ways. We interpret it as Paul does in Rom. 2. You see, the prophet anticipates and turns aside their question and objection by which they had been able to make that objection as follows: "You promise us freedom and deliverance. You say that the Assyrian will accomplish nothing against us and, in fact, that the Lord will take vengeance on our enemies. In the meantime, however, they are secure. They vaunt their savageness against us and threaten us with destruction." The prophet answers, "This is the way of God. He is slow to anger. He does not punish immediately, just as Paul also says (Rom. 2:4): 'Do you presume upon the riches of His kindness . . . ? Do you not know that God's kindness is meant to lead you to repentance?' " Here, too, the prophet speaks with the same compassion, as if to say: "The Lord permitted the Assyrians to rage savagely against Israel. Even now He allows them to threaten you with evil. Thus God delays and postpones His punishment. He allows the power of the foe to increase. He permits it to increase to such an extent that they become violently enraged. But then, when it appears that nothing else can happen but that you will be overcome, when you become absolutely desperate about everything, when it is impossible for any human might to resist them, then the Lord is at hand. He

[3] Cf. p. 284 above.

resists them and scores a great victory. For God is great and omnipotent. He accomplishes great things. He exercises His strength against everything strong and powerful. Thus He allows the wicked to come right up to us, that they may fall with a greater crash." All these ideas describe beautifully the nature of God and of His works that we may not lose faith regardless of what great difficulty embraces us but may trust that God will the more quickly be at hand when we completely despair of being able to escape the peril that threatens us. He acts this way that we may believe that the Lord will finally take vengeance on our—no, on His—enemies, for that's what the Lord calls them. But it is a weakness of ours that we want the Lord to take vengeance right now. When His vengeance is not immediate, we think it's all over with us, etc.

And the Lord will by no means clear the guilty. He speaks in the Hebrew fashion. We ought to translate this differently. After all, we should omit the participle *mundans* ("purifying"). We have the same phrase in the psalm (Ps. 49:7): "Redeeming, a brother will not redeem." This we render in Latin *Frater non redimet* ("A brother will not redeem"). So here we translate it "He will not clear the guilty" [4] or "He will make no one guiltless." It is as if He were saying: "They are not innocent before the Lord, no matter how brightly men may shine, no matter how much they may boast of their righteousness and holiness. Those who feel most smug in their own righteousness, those He immediately treats as indicted for an offense, and He judges them guilty in the highest degree." In this way, too, the Assyrians used to boast about the fact that they had come against the people of God by order of the Lord to destroy Israel; that they had been forced and had not come of their own free will, as Rabshakeh said in Is. 36:10: "Go up against this land and destroy it." An opinion of this sort cannot but be nurtured in all who persecute the righteous, so that they think they are "offering service to God," as Christ says (John 16:2). This is what our mad princes think today when they persecute the Gospel of the glory of God Almighty and the preachers of that Gospel. God, however, ultimately has His revenge on them and passes the opposite judgment. Even today this is our comfort against the mad bishops and princes. Meanwhile we shall give them titles of righ-

[4] With the Zwickau manuscript, we have read *non innocentabit* for *non nocentabit*.

teousness. But the Lord finally will take vengeance for this insult to His Word and bring the whole matter into the clear. Let us in the meantime believe in God and allow ourselves to be oppressed innocently, so that no one but God alone knows this, etc.

The Lord is in whirlwind and storm. This is a marvelous description of divine vengeance against His enemies. You see, there is a far greater revenge than anything we may be able to plan or hope for. It is as if he were saying: "No force, no wisdom, no human ingenuity will be able to resist the vengeance of the Lord, because the Lord moves like a whirlwind and storm." He says all these things, as I mentioned earlier, to warn the great and very powerful kingdom of the Assyrians and to comfort small and weak Judah.

4. *He rebukes the sea and makes it dry.* These are descriptions of the Lord's powers. He takes up certain examples which were familiar to the Jews, like the crossing of the Red Sea and the Jordan and others. From these examples he draws some general descriptions, as if to say: "The Lord once made the Red Sea dry. He will be able to do the same thing and even more now. Don't be afraid, troubled little flock. If He could make a sea dry, He will also be able to provide [5] another sea to destroy the entire army of the Assyrians. What is there for us to fear, then, when the Lord who can cause a sea to dry up stands at our side?" Many prophets use this illustration, as we see clearly several times in the psalm where the prophet says that he will always remember the marvelous works of the Lord.[6]

He dries up all the rivers. Once He caused the Jordan to dry up. There is no river, therefore, which He cannot dry up. This is how great the power is of the Lord who will go to battle for us, whom all your foes will be unable to resist.

Bashan and Carmel wither, the bloom of Lebanon fades. Bashan has very fertile, very productive soil. It even derives its name from its fertility.[7] Carmel, too, had a rich and productive soil. The forest

[5] With the Erlangen edition we have read *adducere* for *abducere*.

[6] Cf. Ps. 77:11, 16-20.

[7] "Fertile" would be an extension of the basic meaning of בָּשָׁן, "smooth," as applied to terrain.

of Lebanon was full of trees. But ours is a God who makes all these things perish. That is, He reduces to nothing all powers, all wealth, all abundance, all the most powerful and strongest things. Let our enemies, then, cease their boasting, because our God is capable of destroying strength and the most powerful forces, etc.

7. *The Lord is good, a Comforter in the day of trouble.* Just as he earlier terrified our foes and adversaries with great threats, so here he strengthens with a very clear promise of comfort the godly people of Judah, a lowly handful. It is as if he were saying: "As far as your wicked foes are concerned, the Lord is a strong and terrible Avenger, but He is gentle and sweet to bring comfort in the day of trouble." In a marvelous way this is an outstanding statement, overflowing with consolation. We must relate and apply it not merely to that trial of Judah but to absolutely every day of our trials and adversities, so that we may learn to flee for refuge in any trial at all to this sweetness of the Lord as if to a holy anchorage. Many psalms are filled with statements of this sort. Thus Ps. 9:9 has "a stronghold in times of trouble." The Lord is a sweet Stronghold at the very time when we are greatly afflicted, when we hunger, when we suffer adversity, when our consciences trouble us, as He says elsewhere in the psalm (Ps. 50:15): "Call upon Me in the day of trouble; I will deliver you." He commands us to flee to Him for refuge, to call upon Him. Yet such is the weakness of the human heart that even if it is ordered to seek out and escape to this sweetness, it fears and loses faith in temptation. In this way, clearly, the Lord comforts in tribulation. That is, even when temptation presses us hard, yet He will not allow us to succumb. Paul says the same thing in every detail (1 Cor. 10:13): "God is faithful, and He will not let us be tempted . . . but with the temptation will also provide the way of escape."

He knows those who trust in Him. This, too, is a word overflowing with comfort—that the Lord knows His people, that He keeps an eye on them, protects and watches over them, that they are His concern, as David says in the psalm (Ps. 121:4): "Behold, He who keeps Israel will neither slumber nor sleep." What greater comfort can one have in every adversity, every temptation, both temporal and spiritual, than that the Lord keeps an eye on him, that he is the Lord's concern? A conviction of this character overcomes sin, death, hell, and every temptation. We, then, must have this sort of conviction in temptation, no matter how great it may be, so that we may have a conviction of glory in the greatest dishonor, a conviction of fullness in the midst of hunger, a conviction of life in the greatest despair over all things, etc. This is what Psalm 1:6 says: "The Lord knows the way of the righteous." But concerning the wicked, he adds:

8. *And when the flood will have passed over.* It is a Hebraism when he says, "When the flood will have passed over." It is similar also to Is. 28:15: "When the overwhelming scourge passes through, it will not come to us;" and to Ps. 32:6: "Yet in the rush of great waters they shall not reach you." That is, a flood certainly is at hand. It threatens evil. Many evils overwhelm the righteous, but all of this will soon pass over like some storm. They will soon cease. As we say in German, *Es ist nur ein Übergang* ("It is a mere transition"). No matter how much your enemies may rage, no matter how confident they may be that they will completely swallow you, yet they will accomplish nothing. They themselves will perish, and you will escape in safety. This is what Solomon says in Proverbs (Prov. 10:25): "The wicked pass like a tempest." We, too, have already experienced this to the full extent, and we shall experience it again in the case of our wicked princes, who along with the pope have raged against the Gospel of God but accomplish nothing to its harm, as he here says:

But He will make a full end of their place. Some interpret this as pertaining to the place where the army of Sennacherib, the king of the Assyrians, met its destruction, as the sacred accounts have it. I, however, think he is speaking in general, so that this is the sense: "Whenever a storm or flood will have taken place somewhere, there the Lord will cause it to pass over. The wicked will accomplish nothing against the faithful." You see, in that very place where they believe that they will easily swallow up the righteous, the righteous will remain in safety, and they themselves will succumb and perish. So also we and those who will come after us will see the wretched destruction of our princes, who madly rage against the glorious Gospel of God Almighty. Christ will show how powerful a Lord He is. He will avenge the insult of the wicked. He will take vengeance on them in that very place where they now savagely boast and rage against the righteous, as he adds here:

Darkness will pursue His enemies. In Scripture "light" signifies good fortune, success, as I have mentioned earlier several times in other prophets. We see this in Prov. 31:18: "Her lamp does not go out at night." [8] On the other hand, darkness indicates adversities, evil, failure of all things. The sense then is this: "The wicked will perish forever. Their evils will not pass away from them. In the meantime, the righteous whom they wanted to destroy will be saved, etc." So the prophet has interpreted, as I said, a verse of Ps. 1 [v. 6]: "The Lord knows the way of the righteous, but the way of the wicked will perish."

9. *What do you plot against the Lord?* In great certainty of the promise which he gives to the godly who have been strengthened and as a warning with which he terrifies the wicked, the prophet utters a kind of apostrophe against the wicked. It is as if he were saying: "Why is it that you wretched people decide to fight against the Lord? Why do you still rage with your might and power? You are resisting the Lord, against whom you will fight without success. The battle which you are plotting against the Lord will bring you no success." The wicked, however, believe that nothing is farther from the truth than that they oppose the Lord. They think they are offering service to God. This I indicated earlier [9] from Is. 36, where Rabshakeh says, "The Lord said to me, 'Go up against this land and destroy it.'"

No double distress will rise up. I translate it from the Hebrew this way: "Distress will not rise up once again." All the sophists have treated this passage, and they have all been tormented by it in a strange way. You see, it gave rise to countless questions for them. Even the Master of Sentences [10] treated it. All this, however, will not at all stand in our way. In short, I believe that the real

[8] The Weimar text has "Proverb. 28," but the passage quoted is as identified. The passage that fits the context best is Prov. 13:9: "The light of the righteous rejoices, but the lamp of the wicked will be put out." This is what the Zwickau manuscript has.

[9] Cf. p. 286 above.

[10] Peter Lombard, (1100—64), *Sententiae.* Cf *Luther's Works,* Companion Volume, p. 86.

sense is as if he were saying: "You have done enough, O king of the Assyrians. You have destroyed the kingdom of Israel. You have given enough orders now. You will not add any extra distress now. I shall not allow you to go on and devastate Judah, too. Indeed, the Lord will free Judah from the tribulation which now threatens it, but a second tribulation will not encompass it." To be sure, the prophet here is speaking about his own time, not about the entire time of the kingdom of Judah. After all, the kingdom of Judah also passed away afterward, as did that of Israel. There is a similar passage in the Books of Kings (2 Kings 6:23): "And the Syrians came no more on raids into the land of Israel." That is, at that time when war was going on between the kings of Syria and Samaria, they did not return, etc. There is also a general sense which we can relate to all our trials and adversities: Our enemy will not always prevail against us. The time will come finally when he will fall. There is a fine and wonderful prophecy in Isaiah, where the Spirit taunts the king of the Assyrians and says that he will return without glory to his own land without having gained a victory.[11] Today, too, let our princes, the enemies of the Word of God, read these verses. Let them learn here that they will accomplish nothing of what they have planned to do against the Word of God. They will perish in the midst of their attempt. Then their greatest fear will be that they will perish, just as we have already experienced the same judgment of God against the false prophets of our day. At the very time when they were in the middle of their job, at the very time when they were hoping to achieve what they had been planning for a long time, they perished by the miraculous plan of God. They were frustrated in their wicked hope. You see, they always have against them the divine judgment expressed in the psalm (Ps. 55:23): "Men of blood and treachery shall not live out half their days"; and again (Ps. 21:11): "They devised mischief against you and were unable, etc." These statements all await the wicked princes who battle against the Lord today. There is nothing better for which they may hope. Unless they turn back from their wickedness and violent cruelty, they will perish in the midst of their attempt.

10. *Because like thorns that are entangled.* I translate from the Hebrew as follows: "They will be swallowed up like very dry

[11] Cf. Is. 37:29-35.

stubble while the thorns are still entangled and while they are still drinking at their feast." The prophet used words which indicate the great contempt with which he demeans the great strength and auxiliary resources of the king of the Assyrians. He compares them to dry stubble. It is as if he were saying: "Just as some stubble that is tinder-dry can easily be consumed in the fire, so they themselves will easily perish no matter how great their power and number." The most powerful armies, therefore, accomplish nothing against the Lord. The Assyrian king had in his camp 185,000 armed men. That great multitude the prophet nevertheless here compares to stubble, and so it turned out to be, for in one night the angel of the Lord struck down that entire army, as the sacred account records in Is. 37:36. This clearly is the end of the wicked, as we also have seen in our own false prophets. Moreover, he calls them "entangled thorns." That is, they have united their forces, they have pledged allegiance like friends, they believe that they will come out as victors. They anticipate great things because they have "tangled together" their might. But they are thorns. They will perish at the same time that they have joined their might together. When they will abandon themselves to royal luxury and drink at their feasts, when they will be sure about their victory, then they will perish. As in the earlier verses, so also here we must apply this in a general way to every comfort. Thus we become confident in any persecution when the princes plot against us that they will accomplish nothing but will perish and be consumed by the fire like dry stubble.

11. *For will not one come out from you?* This is a Hebrew phrase similar to one in Is. 49:17: "Your builders [12] will outstrip your destroyers, and those who laid you waste will go forth from you." That is, they will depart, leave you, scamper off. Clearly it is the same expression here. It is as if he were saying: "When those thorns will have been thus consumed, then the counselor Belial, who plots against the Lord, will depart from you, then he will no longer go on to taunt you." To the Jews, Belial signifies one whom we call a worthless fellow, a good-for-nothing.

12. *Thus says the Lord, "Though they be strong."* A little earlier

[12] For the Weimar text's *destructores* we have read *structores,* as in the Vulgate.

the prophet was speaking to the Assyrian. To strike terror into his heart, he kept threatening him with destruction. Here he turns his words to afflicted Judah to comfort and uplift it. After all, the prophet made his prophecy in Jerusalem, in the kingdom of Judah, not in Nineveh. The sense here, then, is: "Don't be afraid, O kingdom of Judah. Imagine that your foes are very strong. Imagine that they are very well armed, that they are most resourceful and wise, so that they lack nothing that belongs to a well-equipped army. Then imagine this also, that they have many armies, all of which threaten you with destruction. Let none of these bother you at all. Let them cause you no fear, no matter how well-equipped and numerous they may be." This is what John says in his epistle (1 John 4:4): "He who is in you is greater than he who is in the world."

They will be cut off. He spoke in a Hebrew manner, and this is a prophetic word. Isaiah also used it when he said (Is. 7:20): "The Lord will shave with a sharp razor, etc." This is the shaving of the head which we have frequently in Moses and in the other prophets, as in Isaiah for instance (Is. 3:17): "The Lord will shave the heads of the daughters of Zion." Thus "to be cut off," as the prophet says here, is nothing else than that the people around the king will be killed. You see, the hair and beard signify the princes or courtiers of the king. The hairs of the feet are the king's subjects, the crowd, the worthless dregs of the *hoi polloi.* So with just this one word the prophet draws in and includes everything that was giving courage to the Assyrian. As Ovid says, "Now there's a cornfield where Troy used to stand, and all ready for harvest's sickle and cord is a land fertile with Phrygian blood." [13]

And thus will pass away. This happened on that night when the angel of the Lord cut off all the hair of Sennacherib, that is, when in the camp of the Assyrians he killed 185,000 men, so that Sennacherib was wakened and forced to flee in disgrace, Is. 37.

Though I have afflicted you, I will afflict you no more. That is: "Up to this time I have allowed you to be afflicted. Now the time has come when I shall free you so that your enemies no longer will

[13] Ovid, *Heroides,* I, 53—54. Cf. *Luther's Works,* 19, p. 126.

have a right to rage against you. I will not allow them to abuse you anymore, but I will turn every evil against their own head."

13. *I will break his yoke from off you [and will burst your bonds asunder]*. We have exactly the same words in Ps. 2:3: "Let us burst their bonds asunder and cast their cords from us." The power which up to this time has held sway over Judah he calls the "yoke." The "bonds" are the yoke with which the Assyrians had up to now oppressed Judah and held it captive, etc.

14. *But the Lord will give commandment against you.* Now the prophet again switches over from Judah to Sennacherib, the king of the Assyrians. As we read the prophets, we must note this change in the persons addressed. Furthermore, he again uses prophetic language when he says: "He will give commandment against you." To be sure, everything happens by the Word of God. "For He spoke, and it came to be; He commanded, and it stood forth," as we have in the psalm (Ps. 33:9). Therefore the meaning here is this: "The Lord will do something against you. He is going to command something against you, etc."

No more shall your name be perpetuated. There is a Hebraism in the word "perpetuate." Some have applied this verse to the posterity of Sennacherib. That is, they say that the Lord is threatening that Sennacherib would have absolutely no further descendant. However, I prefer to apply this to the rule of Sennacherib, so that the meaning is this: "You have oppressed the lands of all nations. You have harvested the labors of all peoples. All tribute has come back to you because you have had the ruling power over all people. But this now will no longer take place. Your authority, your tyranny, which you have used to oppress the peoples and make them your tributaries, will cease. Now you will no longer be king. "No more will your name be perpetuated, etc."

I will cut you off from the house of your god. That is, "Not only will you not be lord in Judea, but you will not even be lord among your own Assyrians. You will also amount to nothing in the house of your god." Surely the prophet saw that prophecy in spirit. Later it was fulfilled when Sennacherib's army was destroyed and he himself fled into the temple of his god, where he was killed by his own sons among the idols, 2 Kings 19.

Because you are vile [*I will make your grave*]. That is: "You will be considered unworthy of burial in the place for kings. Therefore you will be buried amid your idols." The Lord uses the same threat to warn the Jews in Moses when he says: (Lev. 26:30): "I will mingle your bodies with your graven images," obviously in such a way that one statue topples down on another, etc. Undoubtedly such contempt came on King Sennacherib, as some want this to mean, because he returned in flight to his land when he lost the campaign as well as his entire army. Thus he incurred the anger of his own sons. They also doubtless killed him so insultingly not without the consent of the people amid the idols in the temple of his god.

15. *Behold on the mountains the feet of him who brings good tidings, who proclaims peace!* In this way are we all convinced that there is not any one prophet who did not blend something of his prophecy with the coming of Christ and the grace to be revealed through Christ. Here I would gladly draw this passage toward Christ. There is no other passage in this prophet which we can take as related to Christ except this one. You see, we have the same words in Isaiah (Is. 52:7), and Paul also uses them in Romans (Rom. 10:15), where he brings out the point about the heralds of the Gospel that no one can preach the Gospel except he be sent. But in the name of the Gospel come not only spiritual promises and consolation for consciences but also all the joyful and good messages in which even temporal blessings are promised. Still, I am not quite sure that Paul intended to apply this passage of Isaiah to the Gospel of grace (that is, the Gospel which promises remission of sins and salvation in Christ), which the prophet Isaiah nevertheless did speak. So, too, in this prophet Nahum of ours, I believe that we must not only take this passage to refer to the Gospel of grace promised and revealed to us through Christ, by which believers become the sons of God and coheirs with Christ, but I think we must also understand it to apply to temporal promises such as to a vanquished and routed enemy, to the spoils gathered, to a hallowed peace, etc. I really think that he makes this as a general statement about temporal victory to which he still connects in a general way the grace of Christ and the Gospel.

Behold. This is the cry of one who rejoices over a victory. He is speaking in the manner of prophets, in the present tense, even though what he says is yet to come.

On the mountains. The land of the Jews was mountainous. So he is speaking here in the Hebrew mode. We would say it this way in German: *hin und wider auf den Bergen,* here and there in the various parts of the land. It is as if he were saying: "Everywhere some new report is published, the report of an evangelist. Luke 1:39 uses the same Hebraism: "Mary arose and went with haste into the hill country"; and also (Luke 1:65): "And all these things were talked about through all the hill country of Judea, etc."

The feet. You see, a report runs. It gathers strength as it goes.[14] Also, the "bringers of good tidings" run.

Who proclaims peace. This is a Hebraism. You see, the Hebrews say "You have peace" when we say "Your affairs are in good shape." There is peace. We are doing well.

Keep your feasts, O Judah. That is: "Feel secure now that the hostile king has been killed and his army destroyed. Now in safety you can celebrate your feasts, which you could not do before because of your involvement in warfare. Now those who belong to Judah will again gather to the temple of the Lord, as the law of Moses demands.

Fulfill your vows. What "fulfill your vows" is we have discussed in great detail earlier in other prophets.[15] It means to sacrifice to the Lord, to bring not only beasts but also thanks to God, to praise Him, etc. These are the "fruit of our lips," the only thing God asks for,[16] Hos. 14:2. As I have said, this entire passage can be applied in a general way to Christ as well as to the Gospel which is preached "on the mountains," that is, throughout every land, as the psalm has it (cf. Ps. 19:4). But he proclaims peace—that is, the remission of sins. He promises eternal righteousness in Christ through whom we become the lords of all creatures, etc. He en-

[14] Luther quotes Vergil, *Aeneid,* IV, 175.

[15] Cf. *Luther's Works,* 19, pp. 81—82.

[16] We have read *requirit* for *reliquit* with the Wittenberg edition in spite of the Weimar editor's note: "W[ittenberg] did not understand this word *reliquit* and reads *requirit* instead." The reading *reliquit* would probably mean: "We will render the fruit of our lips, the only thing God has left [us to give]." See Luther's comment in Hos. 14:2 above.

courages the Jews to receive this Gospel when he says, "Keep your feasts, O Judah, etc." That is, "Make your sacrifices now, fulfill now your vows which you made. Up to this time you have not really sanctified and kept your feast. But now praise your God; now sacrifice the fruits of your lips for the grace you have seen. You see, Belial will no longer come against you. No enemies, physical or spiritual, will exercise their tyranny on you anymore."

CHAPTER TWO

THE Jews mark the beginning of the second chapter at the point where Nahum turns to address Sennacherib and says, "No more shall your name be perpetuated." In this way they beautifully connect the king's death with the destruction and death of the city of Nineveh, which the prophet describes in this second chapter of Nahum.

1. *The shatterer has come up against you.* The beginning of this chapter seems difficult to us. Hebraisms give us great difficulty, so that the rationale of the grammatical structure delays us more than the sense of the prophet. The prophet is beginning to describe and, as if painting a picture, to set before the eyes of Judah the captivity and destruction of the city of Nineveh. You see, just as the prophet through the Spirit depicts that destruction of the Ninevites in his own heart, so also he reveals it to his hearers. The sense, then, is this: "O King of the Assyrians, you now sit in your city remarkably fearful and trembling. A little earlier you were rejoicing in your victory. As you celebrated that victory, you were raging fiercely. Now you are forced to see an [enemy's] army move about at random before you. Yet you do not dare to engage it in battle and send out your army to hold back that hostile army, although you still see how that opposing army rages freely against your men. Now you are being besieged and destroyed, but you dare not utter a complaint. You hide in sadness, you who used to vanquish everyone before, you who used to lay siege to other cities, and having besieged them, you used to overcome them and take them by force."

Watch the road. This is an allusion to the military custom that, even when there was no fighting on either side, yet they would generally keep guard, they would keep some at station to watch the approaches of the roads, lest an enemy attack them unexpectedly without their being prepared. So here he taunts the king of the Assyrians, as if to say: "[Watch the road], where your horsemen now ride to keep your highways safe and to set their ambushes. Come on, run out and push back your foes!" In this way he says everything sarcastically.

Gird your loins, that is, "Be brave."

Collect all your strength, that is, "Take courage. Recover your boldness and break out, if you dare."

2\. *For the Lord is restoring the majesty of Jacob as the majesty of Israel.* This is a very puzzling passage, especially in our Latin translation.[1] In Hebrew it is a little clearer. We can take it to have two meanings. First, the meaning may be this, one which others hold: "When you were so savage before, when everything turned out so successfully before, that happened because the Lord avenged the pride of Jacob, and He did this through you as His minister." Although I do not reject this meaning, yet I do not accept it. I think that it can be better understood imitatively (μιμητικῶς) in this way: "Before this time you repressed all nations and kept them in subjection to you, lest they become haughty. But now the time has come when the glory of the kingdoms of Jacob and Judah will return. No longer will Judah be afflicted, but it will become glorious." Thus *superbia* here means majesty—the pomp, splendor, and greatness or elegance of the kingdom. This is also shown in Ex. 15:1, where we have the same word in Hebrew:[2] "For He has triumphed gloriously," or "He has done proudly." You see, the prophet is mindful of the boast of the Assyrians with which they had taunted others as they triumphed over them. Now he directs that taunt against their own jugular veins and says, as it were: "Now finally you will cease taunting Judah."

Because destroyers have stripped them and ruined their branches. These are prophetic metaphors. It is as if he were saying: "There was no hope of recovering the kingdom. No semblance of the people of Judah remained anymore. That's how the Assyrians destroyed everything; that's how savagely you used to rage against

[1] The Vulgate.

[2] In Ex. 15 the verb גָּאָה ("be exalted"), here the noun גָּאוֹן ("majesty").

us and taunted us, O Sennacherib. Now you will taunt us no more. Indeed, evil now falls on your own head. Therefore you are now inglorious, and we are the glorious victors who triumph through the Lord. The glory of our kingdom has returned to us, and so has its honor and elegance, which you had taken away before." This is my interpretation of this passage. I like it better than other interpretations because of the Hebrew word which our translator [3] renders with the word *reddidit*, which appears to me to be completely foreign to the Hebrew intent. I translate it this way: "For just as the Lord has laid the pride of Jacob to rest *(quiescere fecit)*, or made it subside, etc." Why he says "branches" here or what this means we see from the psalm (Ps. 80:8, 11): "Thou didst bring a vine out of Egypt, . . . it sent out its branches to the sea, etc." It means that all Israel was destroyed, that not even a remnant was left on the earth.

3. *The shield of his mighty men is red.* Here he begins to describe and set before their eyes, as if it were already on its way, the army of the Chaldeans. But he says "red" and "scarlet" and "fiery" to terrify the Assyrians, as if to threaten them with bloodshed, as if he already sees them slain and bespattered with blood. But he describes this to comfort Judah, as I have mentioned several times earlier.

The chariots flash like flame on the day of readiness. That is, "Their chariots flash by just as burning torches emit a glittering flame," so that the word "readiness" is connected not with the chariots but with the flame, or fiery torch. Certainly he is not describing chariots which must still be made ready but chariots already drawn up and equipped with all their weapons and military men. He likens them as they are equipped to a flame, or torch, as if to say: "They have flaming chariots." You see, even the histories and the poets of the heathen are agreed that not only the Jews but all nations used to fight in chariots. These chariots were remarkably swift, and the prophet alludes to this here.

And his chargers prance. This, too, has been translated very badly in our Bible. To be sure, the Hebrew word בְּרוֹשִׁים signifies "javelins" made from the tallest trees as well as "lancers," as John

[3] The Vulgate.

Reuchlin[4] has translated it. The meaning then is: "While the chariots speed so fast, while the chariots careen on their headlong course, the lancers seated in their chariots shake and brandish their lances."

4. *The chariots rage in the streets.* In Hebrew this reads: "They rage on the plazas or on their circuits." These are clearly Hebrew expressions with which he is indicating that there is no order or formation among the chariots as the Chaldeans move against the Assyrian. It is as if he were saying: "They drive by in such hordes that no one knows which is last and which is first."

They clatter along together. That is, they just roar by, because they are so many. So great is the number of chariots that they come headlong without any reasonable order.

They gleam like torches. He said the same thing earlier (v. 3). With all these expressions he strikes terror among the Assyrians as he describes their foe, the Chaldeans, as very brave, very well prepared. It is as if he were saying: "They seem like flashes of lightning that strike one another, that do battle against one another and crash into one another, etc."

5. *He will summon his officers.* Here you see the practice of this prophet that he quickly switches from person to person, from one army to the other. In one context, he seems to speak now about the Chaldeans, and yet he switches his conversation and speaks about the Assyrians, whose frightened, fleeing army he describes as if to say: "As the Chaldeans now approach in their fiery chariots, the king of the Assyrians will summon his officers, his chiefs, that with them he may be able to move against the approaching Chaldeans." Thus he taunts the Assyrian with irony, just as everything which follows in this chapter is filled with his ironies. The Hebrew word here does not so much mean brave as pompous, pretentious, eager for glory, as if the prophet were saying: "You obviously have outstanding leaders and officers with you. Now you really ought to be using their efforts in restraining the foe, but you have only some ostentatious show-offs and Thrasos[5] with you."

[4] *De rudimentis Hebraicis* (1506) by John Reuchlin (1455—1522) was a combined grammar and dictionary that proved very useful to the Reformation scholars and translators.

[5] Thraso is the name of the braggart soldier in Terence's comedy *Eunuchus*. Cf. *Luther's Works,* 13, p. 182.

They will stumble as they go. That is, it is all over with them wherever they go and whatever they plan, they will stumble, for they also have God as their Adversary.

They will hasten to the walls. Because the Jews connect this with the preceding into a single verse, I, too, take it to refer to the Assyrians. The sense is this: "So great is their loss of hope, so great is their shock, that they do not even dare to go outside the city to face the Chaldeans. They dare not stand up against the foe. They place their safety in flight. They take to the walls on which they look for hidey-holes. There they protect themselves with certain ramparts which, nevertheless, are scarcely protecting ramparts or bulwarks." You see, that's what the Hebrew word means.

6. *For the river gates are opened.* We really are not sure why he says "river gates." It is, however, likely that he speaks of "river gates" because the city of Nineveh was watered by rivers and had rivers flowing by it. Great and famous cities generally were of this sort. What others say—that the gates of the rivers are the gates of the people—seems to me to be quite far-fetched and improper.

The palace is in dismay. In Hebrew this reads as follows: "The royal residence, or palace, is forsaken." He is not describing the destruction of the palace so much as its spontaneous destruction or, if I may speak this way, its spontaneous collapse. So, as I have said, all this is filled with ironies, as if the prophet were saying: "The river gates which otherwise are strong and which one cannot easily approach are now easily taken. They lie open. The palace falls by itself, even though it has not been destroyed." So very sure does the judgment of God against this city appear that anyone can conquer it with such ease.

7. *Its soldiery is taken prisoner and led away.* Here I shall follow the meaning Lyra[6] suggests. He translates the Hebrew correctly: "His wife or the princesses have gone up as captives." Indeed, we have the same expression also in Ps. 45:9: "At your right hand stands the queen." The prophet, therefore, sarcastically taunts the queens and consorts of the princes, as if to say: "Thus, indeed, the queen goes about, resplendent in her royal garb and elegance.

[6] Nicholas of Lyra (1270—1340), whose commentary on the Bible Luther studied carefully and often praised.

Until now she was sitting regally upon her lofty throne, but now she is taken prisoner and still sits on a throne, but an inglorious one. Indeed, she now receives the greatest dishonor in place of her previous honor."

And her maidens lament over their own hearts. You see, this is the way we must translate this correctly, not as our Bible reads, "moaning." We have the same word also in the psalm (Ps. 68:25), where it is correctly translated "in the midst of those who lament,[7] etc." Therefore, he taunts her handmaidens in the same way that he taunted their queen. They weep and are overcome with grief as they bemoan their captivity. It is as if he were saying: "What a beautiful dance they are presenting. Now that they are taken captive in this way, they are performing their drumming on their own breast. Surely this is a great "dance"; that is, they are now beating their breasts, etc." This is how the prophet compares their earlier delights and pleasant[8] dances with their captivity.

8. *Nineveh is like a pool whose waters run away.* He is now describing the city after it has been deserted. It is as if he were saying: "The city has been taken, the palace is deserted. The queen has been taken prisoner along with all her maidens. So now Nineveh appears to be nothing else than a pool without water. You see, just as a pool is desolate and dry when its dike is broken and the water drains out, so also is Nineveh now. Before, the city had been resplendent—filled with people. Now the Chaldeans had broken the dike, and everyone was in flight who still could run away. They do not keep waiting, even though they are ordered to stand firm. No matter how much parents cry out to their children and wives to their husbands, 'Stand firm! Stand firm!' they do not stop and look back but busy themselves with flight." This is the delight which the prophet takes in the desolation of Nineveh which he saw was going to come. Therefore he depicts this to an afflicted Judah as if it were already happening, obviously so that he might comfort and encourage Judah, as I have mentioned several times already.

9. *Plunder the silver, plunder the gold!* There is no end of

[7] The Vulgate has *tympanistriarum*, "maidens who play the tambourine."

[8] For *delicantes* we have read *delicientes*.

crafted goods, such as commonly serve as utensils—washing basins and various sorts of sacred vessels. You see, they had taken for themselves whatever was precious to all nations. Scripture calls cities of this sort "mountains of prey" (Ps. 76:4). So the prophet cries out to the Chaldeans that they should plunder everything of any value, since the inhabitants are fleeing and there is no end of very precious equipment. He follows with:

It is loaded with all its vases. Jerome omitted[9] this expression,[10] or perhaps a copyist's lack of care caused its omission. This phrase, too, is heavily freighted with irony, as if to say: "Since the supply of all things is so great, come on, you Chaldeans, empty it out a little bit, lest perchance they be further burdened as if with a heavy load. Do help lighten their load!"

10. *So it has been plundered.* This we ought to render "destroyed," for earlier he used the word "destroyers" (v. 2), and here we have the same word. Then Nineveh was evacuated; finally it was destroyed. First he says it was devastated and its citizens and queens carried off. Next, it was evacuated, and all its treasures robbed. Third, it was destroyed and its buildings razed.

Its heart faints. Obviously they remain safe nowhere. They have no place where they may dare to stand firm, even if they have run away.

Knees tremble. They are so afraid, they have no strength in their loins or backbone.

And all faces are like a black pot! We have also had a similar passage earlier in Joel 2:6, where the translator renders it this way: "All their faces are made as black as a pot." Here he translates it "like a black pot." Since there clearly is no agreement in these translations, I translate it this way: "Let them be gathered together in a pot." However, what the prophet intends with this Hebrew figure of speech I do not know. Generally this is the interpretation: "So great is their grief and sadness that they have become strained and pale, so that they appear similar to black pots." The metaphor is completely absurd. I do not believe the prophet intended this. The following pleases me more, but still I would not dare declare

[9] In the Vulgate text.

[10] The Latin word *gravis*, representing the Hebrew כָּבֵד, "loaded."

it a certainty that the prophet intended this: "They are going to be consumed and destroyed the way the chunks of meat thrown into the pot for cooking are generally eaten; like meat in the pot, they are cooked by external evils and persecutions. This is the way the prophet has described the captivity of Nineveh. Now he adds the boast with which he taunts them. You see, he is adding a song of triumph. He sings a little song about them, and thus he censures them for their earlier savagery.

11. *Where now is the lions' den?* That is, "Where is your strength now? What is Nineveh now, that very rich and large city in which used to live the most powerful princes for whom all nations were booty. Just as lions used to prey, certainly they had μοναρχία ("sole rule").

13. *I will burn your chariots in smoke.* "I will burn them—obviously through the Chaldeans. You who up to this time have been living in sunshine and in high honor will perish in smoke. You will die in shame."

The voice of your messengers. That is, "I will put an end to your kingdom. You will never again send out your messengers. Your rule is finished." You see, the chiefs and guards which the Assyrians had set up throughout the world he is calling "messengers." They were the people who carried out the royal mandates, who everywhere performed magisterial duties and exacted taxes and tributes. All these things, he says, are going to stop now. That is, the kingdom of the Assyrians will fall into ruin.

CHAPTER THREE

1. *Woe to the bloody city.* The prophet is still pressing home his prophecy about the ruin of Nineveh and the destruction of the kingdom of the Assyrians. You see, no matter how much he has mentioned all this in considerable detail earlier in the second chapter, he is still having his pleasure and, in the Spirit, uses a profusion of varied expressions and figures. As is the custom of the prophets, he repeats the same ones. The sense of this chapter, too, is easy, except that the grammatical scheme will slow us down.

He has called it a "city of blood" in the Hebrew custom for a bloody and cruel city, a city with a propensity for bloodshed.

All full of lies. More correctly, "a complete liar."

And full of booty. That is, "Violence holds control over you. There is no limit to your pillage. One plots against the goods of another, when and how he can." He notes three faults, as if to say: "The hour of your destruction has come. You have been very cruel and a great liar. There is no longer any trustworthiness, any dependability, in you. Finally, everything is full of plunder." This is the only thing that can happen to all the kingdoms of the world when they have reached their apex, when they have begun to flourish in the highest degree, etc.

No end to the plunder! "You are the very absorption of all good things. You devour all things, as beasts generally do one another."

2. *The crack of whip and rumble of wheel.* God's patience (μακροθυμία) is great, as all Scripture repeatedly indicates. He bears our sins with great tolerance so long as they are hidden. When, however, we have become so blind that even the people in the street are aware of them so that our sins seem to become part of us and we make a habit of them, then clearly He can no longer

bear them. He notes them and punishes them. Here, too, we see the same thing in every detail. He threatens the Ninevites with destruction and the wrath of God, because they knew no limit in their wickedness. I read all these things according to the Hebrew in the nominative as follows: "[The crack of whip] and rumble of wheel, galloping horse and bounding chariot! Horseman charging and flashing sword and glittering spear, etc." With all these, like a painter on canvas, he depicts and sets before their eyes the hostile army of the Chaldeans as they oppose the Assyrians and the misery of the Assyrians, just as he also did earlier in chapter 2. It is as if he were saying: "With great violence and enthusiasm, the charioteers urge on their horses and chariots. That is their noisy rumble. They are driven nearly headlong and rumble with their speed. The horsemen charge quickly on their horses, and their spears flash like lightning, etc." He is speaking about the war chariots in which the soldiers were seated, as the accounts of the heathen also record it.

3. *Hosts of wounded and widespread destruction.* This is the other part of the picture, as I have said, namely, the wretched calamity of the Assyrians. This he sets forth as if it were occurring in the present as he was seeing it by the Spirit in the future. By the way, the Hebrew word which our translator here renders "widespread" *(gravis)* occurs often in Scripture and is always translated this way, as in Genesis (Gen. 13:2): "Abraham was very rich in gold and silver." Also (Gen. 12:10): "For the famine was severe in the land," that is, a great or extensive famine. So also here. We have *gravis ruina* ("widespread destruction"), that is, a mass and heap of dead bodies. You see, what we here read as "destruction" is poorly translated. The same thing we also have in the psalm (Ps. 110:6): "He will bring judgment upon the nations. He will complete the destruction *(implebit ruinas).*" There we ought to translate it: "He will fill them with corpses." That's the way we must render it here.

4. *And all for the countless harlotries.* He gives the reason for this terrible disaster and describes it as if it were happening now in the present. I translate it from the Hebrew in this way: "Because of the harlotries of a comely harlot, of a wife of sorceries." This he obviously said in the Hebrew manner, as when they speak of

Beelzebub, that is "the man of the fly." And so we have "a man of storms," a "man of blood," etc., instead of a stormy man or a cruel man. So here we have "the wife of sorceries," that is, the sorceress.

She betrays nations with her harlotries. I believe that the prophet is speaking figuratively and metaphorically, so that in the custom of Scripture he calls wickedness and contempt of God "fornication" and "idolatry." Also, there is no nation so barbarous and so savage that it does not boast also about the name and worship of God. We see this in the Turk and in all other sects as well as in the pope. Therefore also the Assyrians used the name and worship of God as a pretext for their own wickedness and idolatry. Thus it happened that they drew many nations away with them into the same wickedness, as the prophet is saying here. It is as if he were saying: "So great is your wickedness, and so far have you promoted it, that you have allied many other nations with yourself in your wickedness." [1] Furthermore, Assyria had so many wicked teachers which it trained in this wickedness that they added to their own wickedness, etc. It is a Hebraism when he says "she betrays." It is a common expression in Scripture. Paul, too, uses it in Romans (Rom. 7:14): "sold under sin." So also here "she has betrayed nations." That is, she has seduced them and forced them to fall into the same wickedness so that they, too, might perish. He notes the greed of the false teachers who entice men and make a fortune at their expense.

5. *I will lift up your skirts over your face.* Here again it seems to me that the prophet is using poetic language as is his custom. You see, he is alluding to the mind's inclination to lust when it is inclined toward fornication. So he means a spiritual harlotry. It is as if he were saying: "Just as a fornicating harlot is prepared and set out for the lust of everyone, so also you have prostituted yourself to everyone with your idolatry. Therefore I will uncover your abominable evils; I will make your sins visible to you. I will confound you so that you become a spectacle for all nations." This is God's practice, that when He intends to destroy the wicked, He first reveals their wickedness to them. We have seen this today in the pope. His prostitution has been revealed through the Gospel.

[1] We have read this clause in the second person, as the context seems to demand. The Weimar text has it in the third person.

Thus all those things which used to be very pleasing and well thought of are now clearly sordid and abominable. After all, what is more abominable now than the wickedness of Masses! Yet, before the Gospel was revealed, all this seemed to be very holy and in conformity with the Word of God, etc.

And to kingdoms [I will reveal] your shame. He now places "shame" opposite that which he had said before, opposite "the comely harlot." It is as if he were saying: "Now you are pleasing, now you are comely, but the nations and kingdoms will become nauseated over you. I will see to it that your filthiness becomes obvious, because it will become quite clear to them how shameful you are. I will see to it that this happens," just as he here adds:

6. *I will throw filth at you.* Our translator renders this badly with the word "abomination" [*abominatio*]. We have the same [Hebrew] word in the psalm (Ps. 107:40) too: "He pours contempt on the princes," that is, He makes them a source of contempt. This He does beautifully with the light of the Word. So here, too, we must take this to mean: "I will cause you to be filth to everyone. You will be filthy to everyone."

I will treat you with contempt. This is an elegant expression in Hebrew, as if he were saying, "I will make you foolishness." The Germans, too, imitate this Hebrew expression. As they make a bitter remark against a person, they say *Du bist ein Narr.* "Contempt" is what he calls the foolishness which has been recognized, drawn out into the open, and made completely obvious.

Therefore he [who looks on you] will shrink from you. That is, "Whoever will have pity on you," as if he were saying: "Everyone will rejoice over your destruction. There will be no one to comfort you, etc."

8. *Are you better than Alexandria of the peoples?* This is one of the most difficult verses in the prophets. The Latin translator [2] has changed it strangely. He renders Jer. 46:25: "I will bring punishment upon the tumult of Alexandria." Here he translates "Alexandria of the peoples." We have the same word also in Ezekiel (Ezek. 30:14, 15). Now the question is what city the prophet is talking about, for there are various arguments about the matter.

[2] The Vulgate.

We are sure that the prophet makes the city of Nineveh inferior to that city about which he is speaking. You see, he is arguing from the greater to the lesser. This is very clear from the text. He has spoken then about some ancient, outstanding, very noble, and very powerful city—either about ancient Thebes, which they said had a hundred gates, or about the best fortified city of Ethiopia which they say was very strong and well known, located on the delta of the Nile. If it is neither of these, we can make no guess at all about this passage of the prophet. What our translator renders as "of the peoples" is also poorly translated. I translate this passage as follows: "Are you better than No, the city of craftsmen?" You see, the Hebrew word אָמוֹן means disciple, craftsman, artist.

9. *Ethiopia was her strength.* This is the point which moves me to feel that this city is the capital of the kingdom of Ethiopia. You see, that description fits in every detail that fortified city which Josephus describes.[3]

11. *You also will be drunken; you will be dazed.* It is as if he were saying: "There is never any human ingenuity, there is no wisdom against the Lord, there is no power strong enough, when the Lord is angry. Therefore if that city, so strong, so powerful, so wealthy, could not escape the judgment and vengeance of the Lord, so much the less will you escape. You also will be drunken, namely, with the cup of anger and wrath of the Lord." You see, the prophets had the custom of frequently speaking this way about "drinking the cup." We see it in Jer. 25:27: "Drink, be drunk and vomit[4] and fall"; and in Ps. 75:8: "In the hand of the Lord there is a cup with foaming wine well mixed." See also Is. 51:17.

You will seek a refuge from the enemy. That is, "The enemy press you hard, because they are so strong. You will look for some place of refuge, but you will not find one. It is all over for you. You have perished, etc."

12. *All your fortresses, etc.* I translate this from the Hebrew as

[3] In *Antiquities of the Jews,* II, ch. 10, 2, Josephus describes Saba, "the royal city of Ethiopia which Cambyses afterwards named Meroe after the name of his sister," as "very difficult to besiege." But the Ethiopian king's daughter, Josephus goes on to say, fell in love with Moses, the general at the head of the Egyptian army, and delivered the city into the enemy's hands.

[4] We have read *vomite* for *venite.*

follows: "All your fortresses are like fig trees with their first-ripe figs. If anyone should shake them, they will drop into the mouth of the eater." The prophet laughs at the efforts of those who still are left in the city, who think that they will not quickly be overwhelmed because they are surrounded by their walls. He says that they will be overcome very easily, just as a small effort will knock down ripe figs. You see, once the trees are shaken, the figs fall easily. So also the Chaldeans would be victorious without any trouble. It is as if he were saying: "The king of the Chaldeans will strike you down and vanquish you with a small band. Very small efforts will capture all your fortresses because your heart is terrified," as he will immediately add. In short, to the Assyrians he assigns hopeless strength and courage; to the Chaldeans, on the other hand, an easy victory, a strong and confident spirit.

13. *Behold, your troops are women in your midst.* He is explaining his simile of the ripe figs. To summarize this passage: "You no longer have any courage, confidence, or hope of a victory yet to come. So the entire situation is most desperate on your side. Indeed, the soldiers, whose nature it was to be courageous, whose service and power you should be using to hold off the foe, are now as timid as women. Divine judgment has taken the heart out of them." After all, not only the secular literature of the heathen but also sacred literature indicates that women have a weak spirit.

The gates of your land are wide open to your foes. He is speaking in the Hebrew fashion. You see, the Hebrew tongue speaks generally in this way: "Rejoicing, I shall rejoice. Exulting, I shall exult." So also here: "By opening, the gates will be open." That is, "Wherever your land has been closed, the enemy will enter. They will burst through. You will not be able to stand against them, etc."

14. *Draw water for the siege, etc.* I read this from the Hebrew as follows: "Draw water for the siege for yourself. Strengthen your forts. Go into the clay and tread the mortar or cement." The ideas which now follow all the way to the end of the chapter are full of the bitterest derision and sarcasm, which foes generally use to taunt the vanquished. It is as if he were saying: "Draw water, mix the mud with which to patch up the walls we are going to break down. Yes, yes, just plaster and patch it up again! You are great

warriors, hiding forever within your walls, trying everything like women, and daring to come out of your city not once to face the enemy. But in the meantime you are getting water ready and bricks and defense materials, with which you think you can hold back the might of the enemy." Thus he is alluding to a military custom. In addition, he calls this "water for the siege," as if to say: "The water which you need, now that you are already under siege."

Tread the mortar. We have the same expression in Gen. 14:10: "[The Valley of Siddim] was full of bitumen pits." Then, what we read as "take hold of the brick mold" we ought to render from the Hebrew as "make strong bricks," that is, "Go ahead, get bricks ready to repair what has been torn down and broken by that tumult of war. You will accomplish nothing. Whatever you try will be useless." To this he adds the following:

15. *There will the fire devour you. The sword will cut you off. It will devour you like the locust.* That is, "Your every effort is in vain. You prepare defenses for yourself, but it is no use, even though you hope to be safe in them. In fact, the army of the Chaldeans will burn down the entire city along with the brickyard. They will kill all of you. The Chaldean slayers will overwhelm you the way locusts sweep across an area, swarm by swarm." Such similes of locusts, grasshoppers, and all sorts of other such creatures occur frequently in Scripture.[5] These similes, however, are not very helpful to us who are not familiar with such creatures. Solomon describes the nature of grasshoppers in Prov. 30:27: "The grasshoppers have no king, yet all of them march in rank." But there are various kinds of these insects, and the Hebrew language has an individual name for every kind. Jerome says that the kind of locust *(bruchus)* about which the prophet speaks here creeps on the ground rather than flies, that it devours everything down to the roots, and that it clearly is a very harmful enemy to all crops. Jerome no doubt concludes this from the context of the passage, for that is about the way the prophet here describes it; and yet, in Moses, it is listed among the "clean" animals, that is, those which the Jews could eat.[6]

[5] See the discussion of these insects above, p. 81.

[6] Cf. Lev. 11:22.

So, multiply like the locust. Here we have the same word in the Hebrew as we had earlier at the very beginning of this chapter (v. 3): "widespread destruction," that is, a broad heaping up of the corpses of the slain, as I explained above, following an example of Scripture from Genesis (Gen. 12:10).[7] So here we ought to translate: "Spread out like the locust. Multiply like the grasshopper." In fact, the Latin translator's [8] translation with two words is an unnecessary waste, for in Hebrew it is just a single word.[9] These are, then, words of taunting and filled with derision, as I have said. The sense, then, is this: "Come on, spread out, multiply, receive great strength, expand, that you may rout the enemy, that you may harm them as the locusts and grasshoppers generally do their harm and swarm into the grasses and trees. But your attempts will be useless; you will be unable to multiply. In fact, you have been scattered just as the locusts and grasshoppers fly about and scatter. You have no strength. All your brave soldiers have lost heart. They have all become like women. Their minds are devoid of strategies and strength," as he mentioned earlier.

16. *Increase your business more than the stars of the heavens.* That is: "Be brave now, O Nineveh. Be haughty now. Hold back the foe." Obviously he means to say: "You have now been humbled, you who once had such great wealth and strength. You were enlarged and enriched by very great business enterprises. To you all cities dedicated to maritime business interests used to flock. But now you can do nothing. Your roads are deserted. Your plazas show only emptiness because of the scarcity of inhabitants, although you once used to be full of people." It is hyperbole when he says "more than the stars of the sky." This figure Scripture often uses when it wants to indicate the multitude or abundance or power of something. The Lord also spoke in similar fashion to Abraham in Gen. 13:16 regarding the dust of the earth and the stars of the sky.[10] He says that the seed of Abraham would be no less than these, that is, from Abraham would come great and countless descendants.

[7] Cf. p. 307 above.

[8] The Vulgate.

[9] כַּבֵּד.

[10] See also Gen. 15:5.

But the locust spreads its wings and flies away. That is, "You are locusts who fly away, who are only ready to flee, who scatter. But the Chaldeans are genuine locusts. Whenever they gather, you scatter." He explains himself as follows:

17. *Your guards are like grasshoppers, and your marshals are like clouds of locusts camping on the fences in a day of cold.* He explains what he intended to signify with the flying locust. It is as if he were saying: "I do not compare you to the locusts that fly in but with those which fly away. You do not fly in with great confidence in swarms and do your harm. That's what the Chaldeans are like. You see, you are crawling grasshoppers that are afraid that the cold will kill them. They hide whenever they can. They do not so much try to do harm as to find some heat to save themselves that they may live," as he next adds:

When the sun rises, they fly away. Jerome says that this is the kind which hides on the fences when it grows cold, but when the sun warms things up, they fly away, and one cannot tell where they are, etc. Finally there is great and very bitter irony in the word "camping." (You see, this is the way I translate it from the Hebrew instead of our translator's [11] "settling.") It is as if he were saying: "That is a fine camp when you camp on the fences and not against the enemy. This way you will obviously drive away the enemy. Will it be by flight or by strength? You are making a fortress of your fear!" Then he follows with:

18. *Your shepherds are sleeping, O king of Assyria. Your nobles slumber. Your people are scattered on the mountains with none to gather them.* He is giving them the reason why he compares them to grasshoppers that fly away. The meaning is this: "Your princes, whose business it would be to stand in the front ranks, are sleeping because of their terror. They do not even dare step out into the open. They hide in their hidey-holes. They creep away like grasshoppers on a fence, where they look for hiding places in which they could be safe. Therefore, you will fight without success on all sides, for there is fear everywhere. Your princes make plans to flee; your people are scattered as the wanderer without a leader, etc."

19. *There is no assuaging your hurt.* "The judgment of God

[11] The Vulgate.

against you is obvious. You have become a spectacle for all people. Indeed, as the whole world watches, you suffer your hurt. You will not be able to assuage this evil which has befallen you. You have suffered a stroke of evil which even the hand of Chiron [12] will be unable to mitigate. It's all over for you. That some should be disturbed and grieved because of that wretched calamity of yours is so far removed from reality that 'all who hear the news of you will clap their hands over you.' They will rejoice that you have been overthrown. For you, O king of Assyria, and you, O Nineveh and the whole realm of the Assyrians, used to strike terror into all nations; you overran everyone. But now, because you are being overrun in your turn, they will rejoice. They will congratulate you on this destruction and judgment of God which has come upon you."

Here we see how everything in this prophet is filled with the comfort with which God Almighty comforts His godly people against the mighty taunting of the enemy. These consolations ought also to fill us all with courage in any need, so that we may have confidence and trust absolutely that the Lord will not allow foes of God's Word to prevail against us. You see, He had promised Judah freedom and a safe kingdom from which Christ was to be born. He stood by His promises. He did make them superior to all their foes, which the prophet has very clearly shown here in the case of the very powerful and wealthy realm of the Assyrians. In the same way, may we also have no doubts that He will be near us in every need, physical or spiritual. Indeed, our God is still the same One who redeemed Judah, who said that a hair of our head would not fall without His will.

Wittenberg, July 4, 1525

[12] One of the Centaurs, distinguished for his medical knowledge.

LECTURES ON ZEPHANIAH

The Altenburg Text

Translated by
RICHARD J. DINDA

THIS prophet [1] is quite simple and clear, since he himself indicates the purpose and time of his prophecy. Among the minor prophets, he makes the clearest prophecies about the kingdom of Christ. He does this quite copiously, in very clear detail and in rich words. His goal is like that of all the prophets: the kingdom of Judah was going to be destroyed by the Chaldeans; those of the tribe of Judah who still survived were going to be led into captivity; yet, some trace of Judah would be revived and saved for the sake of Christ and of the very glorious kingdom of Christ, who would be born of Judah and would rise in the kingdom of Judah, just as the promises say. But here there was a need for a very great faith to accept that discrepancy of the prophets, to believe that this people would be glorified and preserved—a people being led captive out of their land into Babylon after losing homeland, temple, and all sacred ordinances in a situation where everyone was in despair. After all, who would believe in freedom in captivity, etc.? This prophet is totally involved in that. He prophesied before the time of the Babylonian captivity. The title verse of the prophet indicates this when he says that he prophesied "in the days of Josiah, the son of Amon, king of Judah." You see, under Zedekiah, who was surrogate for the sons of Josiah, the entire nation was carried off into Babylon.

[1] The Altenburg text has the following title: "The Commentary of Dr. Martin Luther on the Prophet Zephaniah. Wittenberg, August 13, 1525."

CHAPTER ONE

1. *The word of the Lord which came.* I am spending no time on the question of Jerome on which he wastes much time and many words here and elsewhere – namely, that all those whom Zephaniah lists here as antecedents were prophets. The Jews have some strange dreams in matters of this sort, and this has become a great superstition of theirs. I concede that they belonged to the prophetic order. You see, among the Jews there were three orders (as we noted above).[1] The first order was that of the prophets, the second that of the priests, and the third that of the wise men. Jeremiah belonged to all three. The prophets had their own group or their own *collegium*, in which those gathered who were learning from the prophets. Those people did not all have the Spirit of God. Rather they would listen to and follow the prophets. The Book of Kings calls these people "the sons of the prophets" (2 Kings 4:1).

2. *I will utterly sweep away everything from the face of the earth,* that is, from Judea. He is speaking in clear fashion about the Babylonian captivity. But it is strange that He says (v. 3) He is going to sweep away, or uproot, even the animals, birds, and fish. But He is accustomed to speak by synecdoche in this way, as when He says that all the people of Judah were carried off into Babylon, although the poor did remain in the land, as the account relates (2 Kings 24:14). However, inasmuch as the greatest part was carried off, He says that all were led away. So also here. The people are carried away, the cities in the land burned, and so even the birds and fishes are taken away, that is, there is not going to be so great a purpose for birds and fishes now that the people to buy and sell them have been removed. So he is speaking about an established

[1] Cf. p. 129 above.

kingdom, in which there is an abundance of and function for animals. This abundance and function ceases when the inhabitants of the land have been taken away. Also, the Hebrew word אָסֵף does not really mean *congregare*, that is, "gather together," but rather what the Germans otherwise express with *wegraffen* ("sweep away"). This is what it is in Ps. 26:9: "O God, sweep my soul not away with sinners."

3. *I will overthrow the wicked.* Jerome's translation does not please me as much as that of the Septuagint, which translates this as follows: "I will overthrow the stumbling blocks along with the wicked." Thus the sense is this: "In this way will I at some time make an end of the stumbling blocks, that is, of idolatry and of evil worship with which they alienated from Me the people who ought to be serving Me."

Because I will cut off mankind from the face of the earth. The "face of the earth" here is Judah. Thus at the very beginning of the prophet he describes in detail and in threatening words a summary of the entire Babylonian captivity.

4. *I will extend My hand against Judah.* He is now explaining and describing the stumbling blocks which He says He is going to remove from the earth. The summary of the sense is as if He were saying: "I will summon the king of the Babylonians to come here. Through him I will exercise My hand and might and wrath and declare them against Judah."

And I will cut off from this place the remnant of Baal. This is one part of the stumbling blocks. The worship of God which the Law prescribed was preserved under King Josiah. The doctrine of the Law was pure, just as this king was very deeply concerned with piety. The Books of Kings bear witness of this. However, he could by no means achieve the total abolition of the wicked worship of Baal. There always remained in some of the wicked an interest in impious idolatry. The pious king accomplished this, that idolatry did not hold sway, but there always remained some remnants of it. And there is no reason why we should hope that we will thus eradicate all wickedness so that all men may be righteous. After all, if this could have been done, surely that king, so concerned with the Law and divine worship, would have accomplished it. Therefore a greater proportion of the people at that time were following after the Law. They were worshiping God with the worship which the Law prescribed. In the meantime, many others who were wicked continued their idolatry. Balaam spoke in this manner in Numbers, when he preached piety and the true worship of God among the people of Israel, Num. 23:23: "For there is no enchantment against Jacob, no divination against Israel." On the other hand, however, Stephen in Acts 7 charges with wickedness and idolatry all the fathers of the Jews who set out through the wilderness. He says (Acts 7:42-43): "Did you offer to Me slain beasts and sacrifices, forty years in the wilderness, O house of Israel? And you took up the tent of Moloch, and the star of your god Rephan, etc." Yet there is a harmony here. Scripture generally speaks by synecdoche so that it takes the part for the whole and the whole for the part, as I said just a little earlier. This is what they call the one key for understanding Scripture.

And the names of the idolatrous priests with the priests, that is, so that even their names will no longer exist. After all, to take away one's name is to make him unknown and without reputation. We have this at various places in the Psalms: "I will blot out their name under heaven."[2] Today, now that the Gospel has been revealed through the grace of God, the name of the pope has perished, that is, it is not held in honor, it is no longer respected. Furthermore, the same word which our translator[3] renders with the expression "idolatrous priests" we also have in the Books of Kings (2 Kings 23:5). Moreover, there was a singular kind of man trained in that wicked and idolatrous worship. You see, they had a name which was derived from ardent, burning devotion.[4] So the prophet here clearly says "the names of the idolatrous priests," as if to say: "They enjoyed greater respect among the people than all the rest of the priests. They had greater esteem. They used to suggest to the people that they were more deeply interested in religion and the worship of God than all the rest." I really think that this kind of person was of the sort we today have in the monks

[2] Cf. Ps. 9:5; 34:16; 83:4; 109:13.

[3] The Vulgate.

[4] Luther apparently connects the Hebrew word for "idol priests," כְּמָרִים, with כָּמַר, "to grow warm."

who call themselves "brothers of observance." [5] So there was even that wicked remnant under the very pious King Josiah. Clearly it is impossible for us to wipe out every wickedness and ferment. We should, however, see to this, that the kingdom of sin has no home in us, lest we yield our members as instruments of sin, as the apostle says.[6] In this zealous use of the Word, we always need to stand firm, reprove, correct, censure, lest the kingdom of sin overpower, etc.

5. *Those who bow down on the roofs to the host of the heavens.* This is another stumbling block against which the prophet Jeremiah frequently rails with many words, inasmuch as he often mentions the queen of heaven.[7] They used to worship the moon and the stars of heaven, which Moses forbade with a clear law in Deut. 17:3. Therefore that religious practice and wicked worship was an old thing. They had taken it over from their ancestors who had lived under Moses. In addition, to this wickedness they used to add the veneer of this splendor of piety, that they were worshiping the presence of God, which nowhere declared itself more clearly than in the sun, moon, and stars. Then that foolish mob began to worship God not only under or in the sun but even worshiped the very sun and moon themselves. No doubt many of our people do the same thing today. They were very much interested in idolatry and even worshiped the actual wooden statues of the saints.

On the roofs, that is, in a higher place, under the open sky. You see, they had flat roofs on which they used to eat or walk around.

Those who bow down and swear to the Lord and yet swear by Milcom. Some think that Milcom is an idol of the sons of Ammon; others want it to mean "king," for that is the meaning of the Hebrew word. I don't know which we must take, but both readings can stand. To swear by the Lord is a pious, holy thing, as is also to bow down to the Lord. But the Lord does not want this, that we swear by anyone else except Him alone, that we bow down to anything

[5] Perhaps Luther is thinking especially of those Franciscan monks who prided themselves on their strict observance of the earliest rule of St. Francis. But there were "observants" in other orders as well. Luther's own monastery at Erfurt was an observantine chapter of Augustinians.

[6] Cf. Rom. 6:13.

[7] Cf. Jer. 7:18; 44:17-19.

else except to Him alone. He cannot endure that we limp along on the other side too, as Scripture says.[8] After all, He clearly says in the Law: "You shall worship the Lord your God, and Him only shall you serve." [9] Here the prophet is reproaching such "limping." Yet we are no less serving God when we obey our public officials according to the will of God. Indeed, this is God-pleasing, as Paul says in Rom. 13:5: "Not only to avoid God's wrath but also for the sake of conscience." Also, Solomon says (cf. Prov. 24:21): "Honor . . . the king." The Jews used to swear by Milcom, or by the king. That is, they would trust in the king, and this we owe to God alone. The Lord used to rebuke them in this matter when they had chosen a king, contrary to the Lord. They would trust the king that he would see to it that they would be safer under his guard and protection than under the protection of the Lord. They were not entrusting themselves to God alone. They were putting their trust in the king, just as other nations did, as Scripture says clearly in 1 Sam. 8:19-20: "We will have a king over us, that we also may be like all the nations and that our king may govern us and go out before us and fight our battles, etc." So also here the prophet says that the people were giving the king the honor of swearing by him, which was due God alone. But here he also gives us the opportunity to ask many questions. We often read in Scripture that the saints swore by the life of their kings, for instance: "As your soul lives, etc." [10] And the apostle Paul swears (1 Cor. 15:31), saying: "By my pride in you, I die every day for you." Nevertheless, we must swear by God alone, just as we must also serve God alone. I do not have time to treat these ideas in detail, nor is it important to be repetitious here. I have mentioned it in sufficient detail in my commentary on Deuteronomy.[11] Although we owe to God alone honor and worship, or service, yet we must be subject to our brothers in love, so that one "outdoes the other in showing honor," as Paul says in Rom. 12:10. Yet, that service becomes the worship of God, especially when one for God's sake subjects himself to another in love. But that distinction which separates the service

[8] Cf. 1 Kings 18:21. Luther uses the figure *altero umero claudicare.* The Vulgate has *in duas partes claudicare.*

[9] Cf. Deut. 6:13.

[10] 1 Sam. 17:55.

[11] Cf. *Luther's Works,* 9, pp. 72—74.

of the righteous from that of the wicked lies in the heart, not in external matters. Certainly the Jews sinned, and the prophet here charges with wickedness because they swore by the king without faith. After all, both the good man and the wicked swear the same oath; the latter, however, with a faithless heart, for he certainly does not give honor and fear to God alone, but the latter with a faithful heart. This is how the good man uses gold, but he places no faith in gold the way the wicked trust in things made and in the abundance of property. He recognizes that this is God's creation, and that everything he has received belongs to God. But if anyone does not like this idea about the king, let him pursue the other about the idol.

6. *Those who have turned back from following the Lord, who do not seek the Lord nor care for Him.* What I am here rendering with the words "care for" is the same expression as in Ps. 14:4 "who do not call upon God." The sense then is this: "I shall also gather and destroy all the rest of the wicked who do not follow the Lord, who do not keep the law of the Lord and who do not seek the Lord, who are not interested in hearing the Word of the Lord, and who, after hearing it, do not recognize their ungodliness and do not come to their senses." Like this are those righteous men in the Gospel parable who say (Luke 14:18-20): "I have bought a yoke of oxen, I have taken a wife, I cannot come, etc." Those who are immersed in and given to the pleasures and concerns of this life neglect godliness.

7. *Be silent before the Lord God.* This is an exhortation. It is as if he were saying: "Since the Lord will cut you off in this way, be silent. Give place to preaching and correction. Hear the Word. Don't cry out against it, etc."

For the Lord has prepared a sacrifice. The prophet is playing with figures of speech, as the prophets do so often. It is as if he were saying: "The time for slaying the sacrifice is here. The Lord will slay a sacrifice for Himself, namely, you wicked people."

He has consecrated those whom He has invited. "He will get the Chaldeans ready to be prepared to devour that sacrifice, to destroy and ruin you." You see, the Lord has called them as His guests at that banquet of His. So the prophet is alluding to the ritual of sacrifice. When the sacrifices used to be made, then those who were going to eat of the sacrifice were cleansed or expiated. Thus here he is saying the same thing, and thereby he announces the captivity and destruction of the people: that the Lord had summoned the Chaldeans to be His guests who would eat that sacrifice of His. So he is laughing at their wicked offerings and sacrifices and external cleansing practices with which they were purifying themselves as they sacrificed. Meanwhile, their hearts did not believe, and were idolatrous, etc.

8. *On the day of the Lord's sacrifice I will punish.* The prophet continues with his threat just as he began. We shall follow the plan and sense of the prophet more easily when we look with one eye at the zealous ardor of the prophet and with the other at the inflexible obstinacy of the princes, priests, false prophets, and wicked people. Against these the prophet burns with threats of evil and of the wrath of the Lord to come. In fact, this is the nature of the Word, that it battles against the powerful, the wise, and the holy. That is an eternal battle, as all Scripture indicates. We see the same thing here. The prophet had stubborn hearers, who were infected with false beliefs and who kept laughing at the prophet. There were false teachers who kept calling the people away from the true Word of God, who kept teaching the opposite, who kept persuading the princes in another direction. They were saying that it would not come to pass that God would destroy His people, His city, and His temple. After all, God had promised that He would be near them there and that the king, who had been divinely established, would not perish, as the prophet here threatens when he says, "I will punish the king's sons." After all, no one hoped that this would ever happen, for this kingdom had been established and confirmed by divine word. Furthermore, they had the very clear promises of David that there would never fail to be a Son from his loins who would sit upon his throne, etc.[12] The prophet Zephaniah here is prophesying contrary to such clear promises. Therefore his prophecy appeared to them to be impossible, a lie. You see, they kept crying out against the prophets, as we have it in Jeremiah (Jer. 7:4): "The house of the Lord, the house of the Lord, etc.; Jerusalem, Jerusalem; the people of God"; and other cries of this kind. But

[12] Cf. 1 Kings 8:25.

these are the marvelous works of God (as we have said several times in the other prophets), who deposes the kings He has established, who lets go those who have been captured. For instance, Jehoiachin, the son of Josiah, was carried off into Babylon. Yet God preserved miraculously the kingdom and the kings, as He had promised to preserve them. You see, although Jehoiachin had been carried off into Babylon, although he had been thrown into prison, yet after Nebuchadnezzar died, he was exalted above the kings of Babylon, as the sacred account has it (cf. Jer. 28:4). Thus God in His own way was able to save the king in the midst of his enemies, in the midst of despair, when it appeared that nothing else would happen there but that the kingdom would fall and the king perish. But because this seemed impossible to reason and to the wicked people of Judah, they easily kept accusing all the prophets of lying.

In foreign attire. Here interpreters trouble themselves in various ways. Some think that the prophet here is calling attention to their imitation of the idolatrous worship of the heathen and is saying that even their priests wore clothes similar to those of the heathen priests. Since this, however, does not fit with either the preceding or following context, of what significance is it to so wretchedly tear up the sense of the prophet? It is clear that he is speaking about the princes and the sons of the king. Therefore I think that the prophet is speaking here also about the aristocrats or nobles of the king, who imitated foreign customs and attire as well as the rituals of these foreign nations who lived all around them. They abandoned the rituals, attire, and customs of their own country. So also today, the Germans are the "monkeys see, monkeys do" of almost all other nations, so that they dress in the fashion of all nations, now French, now Spanish, etc. This is an indication of great levity and of inconsistent minds, such as we find in the French and in us Germans who follow the French in this. The poet Ennius says very accurately, "The Roman state stands by virtue of its ancient morals and men." [13]

9. *And I will punish everyone who leaps proudly over the threshold.* The Latin translator [14] renders this quite well. You see,

[13] Ennius, *Annales,* 492. See Luther's earlier use of this quotation in *Luther's Works,* 10, p. 357.

[14] The Vulgate.

he respects the sense, if not the words. In the Hebrew it goes this way: "anyone jumping over the threshold on that day." We have the same expression also in the Song of Solomon (Song of Sol. 2:8): "Behold, my beloved comes leaping upon the mountains, bounding over the hills." Also here the interpreters are again looking for another meaning. They take this passage to refer to the priests of Dagon, who would not tread on the threshold of the temple of Dagon after their statue of Dagon had toppled, as we have it in 1 Sam. 5:1-5. However, as I said earlier, it is not my practice here to tear up the prophets as they are in the habit of doing who look for new meanings in almost every single clause and for whom all of it hangs together very poorly. The sense I get is this: Just as he had a little earlier rebuked the wicked princes and had threatened them and the sons of the king with captivity, so here he attacks the sycophants and servants of the princes, people who agree with their masters and their wicked acts and fawn over them. You see, the translator has rendered this poorly,[15] since it reads as follows in the Hebrew: "Who fill the house of their masters with their violence and fraud." Furthermore, he calls them "leapers." That is, they are just too smug and impudent. They are people who trust their masters, whom they are eager to please. At the same time they impose false measures and merchandise on their wretched subjects. They also oppress others unjustly and with open violence. And all the while their masters grow richer. So also today we see at various places in all the courts and halls of the princes prefects and commissioners to whom all authority has been delegated. They are more ferocious and exercise greater violence in their demands and oppression of subjects than the princes themselves. They are nothing but a plague upon the whole world, even under good princes, just as they were here under the very good king.[16] the world is full of examples, if we would only look at all the courts of all the princes.

Over the threshold. He speaks of leaping over the threshold. That is, they are servants, not heirs. They do their work merely by going out and coming in, as do those who today serve in a house-

[15] The Vulgate has "who fill the house of the Lord God with their violence and fraud."

[16] The Wittenberg text adds the name Josiah.

hold and tomorrow again are cast out. This clearly is what God wanted when He ordered the servant's ear to be pierced with an awl, Deut. 15:17.

10. *A cry will be heard from the Fish Gate.* For the layout of Jerusalem, see Nehemiah and Ezra. Nehemiah has described it very carefully (cf. Neh. 3). Jerusalem had two hills. The taller one they called Zion, on which was David's citadel. The lower one they called Mount Moriah, where the patriarch Jacob slept [17] and where the temple was erected.[18] The Fish Gate was the gate on the western side facing the Mediterranean Sea. All who sail to Jerusalem must enter at the Fish Gate. Jerome, then, is correct in saying that the Fish Gate is the one which leads to Joppa. Then the prophet says:

A wail from the Second Quarter. We must understand this as follows. There was an outer wall at Jerusalem which also had homes [under its shelter]. Then, inside there was a second wall which was called the Second Quarter. This is also well known in Scripture, as when we read about Huldah the prophetess, who lived in the Second Quarter, as we have it in the Books of Kings (2 Kings 22:14). From that area they used to call the gate the Second Gate. After that the hills are the center of the city—the citadel on Zion and the temple, as I have said. The summary of the sense, then, is this: "The whole city will be filled with your crying and wailing. After all, it will be completely destroyed. You all will be terribly distressed and carried off into captivity, so that nothing will remain."

11. *Wail, O inhabitants of the Mortar.* From a purpose yet to come he gives them a name when he calls them "inhabitants of the Mortar." Here again we have some strange variations. Jerome thinks that Jerusalem is called the Mortar from the descent or from the valley of Siloah. Lyra also has a different idea. He thinks the name comes from Tiberias, which is located in a valley, etc. I disagree with them completely. First, we must warn that there is an ambiguity in our reading where we have "inhabitants of the Mortar." We have to show this lest we employ the ambiguity when

[17] Cf. *Luther's Works,* 5, pp. 242 f.

[18] Cf. 2 Chron. 3:1.

we translate. This, we see, has been done here. *Pila* does not mean a ball which we use in play, but a mortar—ὅλμος, as Jerome translates it.[19] Therefore the prophet has taken his metaphor from the function of a mortar. The sense is this: "So great a grinding disaster will come to pass in the city that they will be ground down and reduced to dust as we grind down herbs and other things which we mash in a mortar. So also Jerusalem will become like a mortar for you. In it you will be ground down and reduced to nothing." Now, if this sense does not please you, follow the other which Solomon explains in Proverbs (Prov. 27:22) "If you crush a fool in a mortar, etc." Then the meaning is: "Jerusalem is like the mortar of the Lord, in which the Lord crushes you through the prophets whom He sends to censure and correct you, but He accomplishes nothing. Although you may be crushed daily, yet your foolishness does not depart from you. Therefore He will crush you once by the king of Babylon." He adds:

Since all the people of Canaan are silent. This expression is frequent in the minor prophets. Therefore we must take notice whenever they speak about silence and keeping quiet. To be silent means to be reduced to nothing. In this way the prophets mark a silence not so much of the mouth as of property—that there is no longer a use for property; that everything lies unused and in contempt. This is what we said above at the beginning of this prophet in the matter of the fish and birds being swept away.[20] Then, when he says "Canaan," we are uncertain whether this signifies a common noun or a proper noun. As a common noun it means a merchant. There is no doubt that the prophet takes Canaan to mean the people of Judah. Thus the metaphor is left, showing why he calls them Canaan. Certainly, if this is a common noun, the prophet is censuring the greed and evil tricks of the merchants in Judah, who achieved their success by defrauding others. But if this is a proper noun, the sense seems to me to be as if he were saying: "You surely are no Judah now but Canaan. Indeed, the Lord will treat you in no other way than the way He treated the Canaanites when He drove them out of their land and destroyed them." This is the sense I find more pleasing. Ezekiel

19 In Latin the two words *pĭla* ("ball") and *pīla* ("mortar") could be confused.

20 Cf. p. 320 above.

speaks in a similar way (Ezek. 16:3): "Your father was an Amorite, and your mother a Hittite, etc." Also, Daniel[21] says, "The seed of Canaan, not of Judah."

For all who weigh out silver are cut off. These are the rich who devote themselves to greed, who burn with a desire to acquire.

12. *I will search Jerusalem with lamps.* He continues to exaggerate their destruction. It is as if he were saying: "So great will be your destruction, so carefully will I search all the deepest and best hiding places in Jerusalem that no one will be able to escape My wrath. I will grind down all of you in that mortar from which they shall not escape." Furthermore, one who is lying in a mortar will not easily escape in the mortar, as the saying goes: "He is so smart that you couldn't strike his head in a mortar."

I will punish the men who are thickening upon their lees. These are the fat, those who stiffen in their own lees. This is a prophetic figure of speech of this prophet. This passage, too, can be understood to have two meanings. First, he uses lees—a very disgraceful and contemptible word—for their false righteousnesses and beliefs. While they place their confidence in these, they befoul themselves. They turn the true Word of God and His promises into the foulest ideas which they have invented. While they feel secure, they do not hear the prophets warning them of destruction, but they protect their own wickedness and support their own error, their own frigid, foolish ideas which they have learned from their own false prophets. The other meaning is this: As the last dregs are the lowest thing in the pot, so also this people is the last and the closest to destruction. Captivity threatens them. This is similar to Is. 7:4, where with great contempt he calls the two kings "two smoldering stumps of firebrands." It is as if he were saying: "There is no strength left in them. They will shortly be put out, no matter how much they are still smoking." Because this prophetic figurative language is unclear and ambiguous, we can also make no definite decision regarding its meaning. Nevertheless, I am more favorably inclined to the first meaning about their dogmas or beliefs with which they defend their errors to avoid hearing the prophets. In fact, the following passage explains the same thing.

Those who say in their hearts: The Lord will not do good. It is

[21] Susanna 56.

as if he were saying: "Among them I am considered nothing but an insane fool. After all, they do not believe that I am speaking about the true God when I threaten them with the wrath of God. Therefore they ridicule me. They mock me. You see, they are boasting of the promises God made to their fathers about preserving them, about an eternal kingdom, about possessing the land forever. But because I am making a prophecy against their ideas, they laugh at me and at my God whom I thus boast of and whose wrath I preach. They say: 'Our God has promised us salvation and a kingdom, but you threaten us with a destruction and captivity at His hands. Away with you and with your God! That evil which you threaten us will not come to pass. Your god will do well to leave us in peace, for our God will protect and save us as He has promised, etc.'" This obviously is the real sense of this passage—not that anyone should think that the Jews were so insane as to deny that God takes care of all things, etc. Rather, they were denying that the God who Zephaniah was saying was threatening them with evil, etc., was the true God. Even today they deny that it is the true Christ and the Gospel of Christ which we preach.

13. *And their strength will be plundered.* He is now describing the visitation with which He is going to visit the men stiffened over their own lees and about whom He had already spoken, saying that all their property would perish. You see, the prophet here is calling their resources, substance, and wealth their "strength."

For though they build houses. That is, "They are sitting secure and thinking that nothing like this will happen, no matter how much I cry out that their destruction is coming. The more I warn them of anger and judgment, the more insane they become. So, in their feeling of safety and having no fear, they build houses. They plant as if they were going to stay in their land forever. They charge me with lying, etc. Therefore the calamity will come upon them unexpectedly. So Christ also says (Luke 17:27 f.) that it will come to pass that before the day of the final judgment men will build, plant, take wives, etc. Also Paul says (1 Thess. 5:3): "When people say, 'There is peace and safety,' then sudden destruction will come upon them, etc." You see, it always happens and has happened in this way, that when kingdoms are the greatest and most powerful, immediate death and destruction follow. For this is God's game in human affairs, as the psalmist says (cf. Ps. 73:18): "You have set them in derision. You have cast them down because they were lifted up." The writings of nearly all the poets are full of this idea. Thus that well-known man has said most beautifully: "The great are not permitted to remain long." [22]

14. *For the great day of the Lord is near.* He is always opposed to the proud who contradict him, against the smug people who hold him in contempt, who kept on accusing the prophet of lying. They kept saying that the Lord would do them no ill, etc. Therefore, the prophet keeps on pressing home the coming calamity in great detail and with great vehemence. You see, as we have said before, they felt smug, they had no fear for themselves, they were confirmed in their false idea. But so it happens with the wicked. When they reach full flower and have complete control, when nothing seems less possible than their destruction, then sudden destruction comes to them. As the prophet says in the psalm, they will not live out half their days (Ps. 55:23). And Christ also says in His Gospel parable of the unjust servant (Luke 12:46) that the master will come when the servant is not thinking it. You see, because they remain stubborn, the threats of the Lord move them not at all. Therefore destruction comes to them suddenly and unexpectedly. After all, human nature cannot but be inflated by favorable circumstances. It cannot solve the enigma how far the greatest of misfortune is removed from the greatest joy, as the saying goes. You see, it cannot fear adversities in good circumstances, etc. The prophet here is saying the same thing, as if to say: "You are confident in that success of yours, but don't think that the Lord will tell you a lie when He predicts captivity for you. It is already threatening you."

The sound of the day of the Lord is bitter, that is, the sound of those who cry and grieve on the day of the Lord. He places the calamity before their eyes as if it were already present. You see, he is imagining that the people are in captivity, that their homes

22 Luther also quotes this passage without identification of the author in his sermon for the Visitation of Mary in the *Hauspostille*: *Magnisque negatum stare diu.* There he goes on to say: "Why is this so? When men become great and become conscious of it, it follows that they become proud; and then our Lord God must come and humble them and make the great small." W, LII, 695, 9—12.

have been destroyed, that they are crying, weeping, and wailing. He is calling the day of the Babylonian captivity "the great day of the Lord", not the Last Day. The latter is what Jerome thought, who, in accordance with his custom, regularly attaches individual meanings to almost every warning of the prophets.

The mighty man will be afflicted there. I do not have full grasp of the Hebrew word which the prophet has used here. You see, the Latin translator went over the letter ה quickly and thought it was a ח.[23] The lexicons of more recent men say that this word means "to cry loudly." Because we have nothing better and cannot make a firm decision about the force of the word, we shall follow them. Those more recent grammarians have been and still are more careful in comparing points of language than were the older ones, whenever an outstanding word of this kind occurs. Consequently, I translate it from the Hebrew as follows: "There the strong man will cry out loudly," so that we have a singular instead of the plural. That is, the courageous war-lovers, who had to be feared most among the people, and all the very powerful would cry out more and would fear more for themselves than would the rest of the people, etc.

15. *For a day of wrath is that day.* This passage has been used frequently in all the churches, whenever the priests chanted funeral Masses, and they have applied it to the day of the Last Judgment.[24] But here we very clearly see that they have very badly distorted it. After all, the prophet is speaking about the Babylonian captivity. However, what we read as "a day of ruin" has been poorly translated from the Hebrew. It ought to have been translated in the same way as the evangelist Luke did in ch. 21:25: "At the roaring of the sea and the waves"; and as we have it in Prov. 3:25: "Do not be afraid of the sudden storm of the wicked"; and in Ps. 65:7: "Who dost still the roaring of the seas, the roaring of their waves." Therefore it should have been translated "a day of a roaring attack." The prophet is showing that the Babylonians will come with a very

[23] Luther suggests that the Vulgate, in translating *tribulabitur* ("will be afflicted") instead of *clamabit* ("will cry loudly"), confused the Hebrew verbs צָרָה and צָרַח.

[24] This passage in the Vulgate forms the first line of the medieval sequence *Dies irae.*

great attack; they will roar against the people of Judah as the sea is accustomed to thunder and roar when strong winds stir it.

A day of darkness and gloom. The prophet imagines for himself some storm by which he signifies and describes the very violent and fierce attack of the Chaldeans. That is, the Jews are by no means going to resist. They will go down to ruin.

16. *A day of trumpet blast and battle cry.* Obviously, the day of the Chaldeans is meant, as if the Chaldeans, certain of their victory, will shout triumphantly and jubilantly, so that one could die from so terrible and great a noise.

Against the fortified cities. That is, "The Lord will lead the army of the Chaldeans against you so that you will perish, so that you will be carried off into captivity. You will be unable to resist. Your very stoutly fortified cities will do you no good. Not even Jerusalem or any fortress, no matter how firmly and strongly you fortify it, will be strong enough for you to be able to resist them. Therefore, there is no strategy, no wisdom, no strength against the Lord.

17. *And I will bring distress on men.* I do not understand that Hebrew word either. For it does not mean "to bring distress," as our translator renders it.[25] I say it this way: "I will resound among men. I will be heard from too. I will set up a hue and cry among you. That is, I will strike terror in you that you may realize that I am waging war, that I am fighting against you." You see, this is the way God wages war. He takes heart and courage away from those He intends to destroy, as I have mentioned several times earlier in other prophets. So it happens that they will very easily be put to flight without all the effort of the foe, yes, even by the leaf of a tree. Then they fight with absolutely no success. That sense he expresses when he adds:

So that they will walk like the blind. It is as if He were saying: "With that terror of their hearts, I will cause them to be deprived of all their strategies. They will be unable to recover their senses. They will be awestruck, and they will have no idea whether to flee, resist the enemy, or offer conditions for peace. They will be so confused, so devoid of plans, that they will walk like blind men."

Because they have sinned against the Lord. Everything fits very well with the meaning I have taken. You see, He here gives the

[25] *Tribulare.* Cf. n. 23 above.

reason for the earlier statements, as if to say: "I will give them a sense of sin. This sense, or revelation, of sin in their hearts will confuse them. Now, you see, they do not recognize their sin. In fact, they are even defending the sin with which they have sinned against the Lord. But there will be no remedy then. They will become powerless in their sins."

Their blood will be poured out like dust. We must not read this "like smoke." You see, the Hebrew word means earth that has been dug up and can be scattered like ash or dust. From this, also, God created Adam, the first man. Therefore it is often translated with the word "dust," as: "Remember, O man, you are dust, and to dust you will return" (Gen. 3:19).

And their flesh like dung. I read this very accurately from the Hebrew as "their bread like dung." Also, this is a Hebrew phrase, for foods or things to eat come under the word "bread" for the Jews. Thus we ought to translate this in this way: "and their food like dung." This is the way Paul spoke to the Philippians about their righteousness of the Law (Phil. 3:8): "I count all things as refuse." Perhaps Paul was looking back to this verse of the prophet. The sense then is this: "Even if they try to please God with flesh and blood, that is, of animals they have offered, even if they really want to sacrifice to the Lord, yet their sacrifices will not be pleasing. The enemy will come and scatter all their sacrifices, blood, and bread like dust." So we often find sacrifices called "food" in Leviticus, because they would be given to the priests. Certainly the Hebrew word means what Latins call "edibles" with their general word *esca*. But the evangelists followed the Hebraism and translated it with the word "bread." In similar fashion and in this sense, Hosea spoke earlier in chapter 9:4: "Their bread shall be like mourners' bread, and Israel will eat of it and be defiled." That is, their sacrifices are mournful—sacrifices which the Lord does not want. You see, this was taken care of in the Law; see Deut. 26:14. This, then, is a marvelous and elegant passage, for it rejects all the righteousness of the flesh and calls it dung, even as the apostle Paul calls it that. So he is indicating that one requires nothing for true righteousness except faith in the Word of God.

18. *Neither their silver nor their gold.* He says that all of this will not help them. First, he rejects their righteousness, their

religion, their worship, and their sacrifices. He says that these will not please the Lord so that He saves them from the enemy. After all, all these will be considered dung. Even they will feel their sin against the Lord in their own consciences. They are going to lose hope, and thus their tribulation will give them understanding, as Isaiah says (Is. 28:19). In addition he adds that not even in external things like wealth, silver, gold, will they find a remedy for this evil. That is, they will be unable to redeem themselves with gold or silver from being either killed or taken into captivity, because the Chaldeans will kill or carry off all of them.

In the fire of His jealous wrath. Once the wrath of the Lord has been kindled, it cannot be diminished. The Lord will not allow the Chaldeans to accept the gold or silver with which they want to redeem themselves, even though otherwise they generally did this in wars. Therefore nothing is left other than that the entire land of Judah is going to be consumed by the fire of the jealous wrath of the Lord. The sudden completion of this will take place for all who live in the land, so that neither their own righteousness nor any price will redeem them from that Babylonian captivity, etc.

CHAPTER TWO

In the first chapter we saw the prophetic warning about the coming Babylonian captivity. Now, after threatening the evil (as is the custom of all the prophets), he exhorts them to repent, if they could somehow be hidden on the day of the wrath of the Lord, so that they may please the Lord with their public assemblies and prayers, so that, if all the people were going to perish, yet a handful, a remnant, might be saved, etc. That is a summary of this chapter.

1. *Come together and hold assembly.* The first and second verbs are almost the same in Hebrew. In German we would correctly translate them *Sammelt euch und kommet her.*

O shameless nation. That is, "you hostile people, who are worthy of hatred, not of love."

2. *Before an order gives birth.* In the Latin Bible they have also added "and legal case" *(et visio)*, but a careless scribe inserted what another had noted to show a variant reading. The Hebrew signifies neither a command nor a legal case but a decree, a sentence, some thing defined, as in Ps. 2:6-7: "I have been set up as king on Zion, His holy hill. I will tell of His decree." There we clearly have the same expression in Hebrew. Moses also uses almost the same word for the ceremonial laws, as we noted somewhere earlier.[1] A summary of the sense, then, is this: "The sentence has been defined and already has been made against you. The only thing left is that it has not yet given birth; that is, it is not yet fulfilled. The effect of the threat still stands."

To a day that passes away like chaff. The Jews develop great difficulties for themselves in this passage. They think that this is ecliptic speech. I do not think that must necessarily be. I read it

[1] Cf. p. 273 above. The Hebrew word in question is חק.

simply and understand it this way: "Before a decree produces the day that will be like passing chaff; that is, like chaff taken violently as if by whirlwind." This method of speaking occurs frequently in Scripture. In Ps. 1:4 we have "which the wind drives from the face of the earth"; and in Job 21:18 "like chaff that the storm carries away." The sense, then, is this: "On that day you will be scattered the way chaff or dust is scattered by the force of the winds or assault of a storm."

Before there comes upon you. In the Hebrew this is stated negatively: "Before there should not come." This, however, is a custom of the Hebrew language, to express the affirmative at times by the negative. Furthermore, there is an omission in our Bible [2] of the word "day." You see, we must read it this way: "Before the day of the wrath of the Lord comes upon you."

3. *Seek the Lord, [all you gentle of the land]*. That is, "See to it that you do not come together in vain. See to it that this assembly of yours is not useless. Rather, by prayer and preaching summon each other back to come to your senses, all you gentle of the land." I translate the Hebrew word "gentle" as *elend,* humble, oppressed, those cast down before the world, whom few respect, the ἄφατοι, those who lack honor and wealth. Thus Christ came as a humble King, as Matthew quotes from Zechariah (Matt. 21:5); that is, humble, with no royal regalia, pomp, and glory, in whom all things appear most contemptible, etc. So also Mary sings about herself in her own song (Luke 1:48): ". . . for He has regarded the low estate, the humility, of His handmaiden."

Who do His commands. That is, "If there are still some among you whose heart holds on to righteousness and the Word of God; if there are still some of you who seek the Lord, who are humble; let them seek the Lord to see if they can somehow be reconciled, so that a very few may be saved, even though almost all the rest of the people perish."

Seek a just man, seek a gentle man. We must read this according to the Hebrew as "seek righteousness, seek humility." Here the prophet urges to humility ahead of everything else. After all, he

[2] The Vulgate.

knows that the humble please God, and that the proud and haughty and harsh despisers do not.

Perhaps you may be hidden on the day of the wrath of the Lord. That is, "Perhaps you may be protected from perishing when the wrath of the Lord comes." You see, the prophet does not say this to indicate that the captivity which he has threatened is avoidable. But he is commanding them to pray to the Lord that He be willing to protect and save them until the heat of His wrath pass, lest they, too, perish along with the rest. Job prays the same way (Job 14: 13): "Oh, that Thou wouldst conceal me until Thy wrath be past."

4. *For Gaza shall be deserted.* He argues from the strength of Gaza and of other cities whose overthrow and destruction he will threaten here. After all, it was a great miracle—it still is as far as I am concerned—that a nation as small as the Philistines, so insignificant that it had only five cities, could always very bitterly resist the Jews, and resist in such a way that under no king could they ever be subdued and that Israel could never control them except under David. The sense, then, of the prophet is this: "You, O tribe of Judah, still are left along with the tribe of Benjamin, now that Israel has been taken away and is lost. Now your misfortune, too, is giving birth. A great and burdensome captivity also threatens you. It is going to be so great that it will destroy not only you but also all the neighboring nations, no matter how strong they may be." Of course, the Latin translator could not render the beautiful verbal allusion which is in the Hebrew. You see, "Gaza" means strength. This is the meaning: "Gaza, which is strong and powerful, shall be deserted, and Ashkelon shall become a desolation."

Ashdod's people shall be driven out at noon. Because I have no other meaning to suggest here, I follow Jerome, although I have doubts about his interpretation: "They will be driven out at noon, that is, out on the open field of battle, without any tricks, without any deceit."

And Ekron shall be uprooted. Here, too, there is an allusion involved in the name. It is as if he were saying: "As your name is, so also will be your experience in actual fact. You will become a real uprooting, etc."

5. *Woe to you inhabitants of the cord of the sea.* This is a

Hebraism. You see, the "cord" [3] indicates distribution and measure, as we see from Joshua, when he writes that the land was divided by twelve cords (Joshua 17:15; 19:9). Also Moses says (Deut. 32:9): "Jacob is the cord of the Lord." The "cord," then, is the part, or portion, allotted. Here he calls the Philistines the "boundary of the sea," that is, those located along the seacoast. You see, they lived near the Mediterranean Sea, near which today is still the well-known port of Joppa.

You nation of the destroyed. Again we have a Hebraism. This is a nation which is going to be destroyed, cut down. They do a poor job of interpreting who say that this refers to the Cretans.

The Word of the Lord is against you, O Canaan. On this side of the Jordan were the Canaanites. There the Philistines also used to live. These he threatens with death and such great destruction that there will be no one to inhabit their land.

6. *And the seacoast will be habitations for the shepherds and their flocks.* We have the same word here which we translated earlier in Joel and Amos as "empty wilderness." [4] There we said it had the force of a common noun. Therefore we render it more accurately as "habitations of the wilderness." The sense, then, is this: "Up to now, the nation of the Philistines has always gone unconquered. The Jews could never overpower them. They resisted the Jews very bitterly. But now the end is threatening them. They will be so ravaged that none of them will remain as inhabitants. Everything will become a wilderness." You see, after the Babylonian captivity neither they nor the rest of the neighboring peoples were restored. They were scattered in such miraculous fashion and were distressed in such different ways that they never returned to their own places.

Now they bear the common name "Arabs," a nation of people gathered from all those nations. But they have lost their previous names. Those very noble cities of the Philistines have been so destroyed, so leveled with the ground, that no one has been able to rebuild them. Only traces of ruins still remain, like heaps of stones, as Jerome often mentioned, for he saw them. Then he follows with:

[3] The Hebrew word חֶבֶל means cord, tape measure, and area measured.

[4] For Luther's comment on the Hebrew word נְאוֹת, see pp. 86 and 131 above.

7. *The seacoast shall become the possession of the remnant of the house of Judah, on which they will pasture, and in the houses of Ashkelon they shall lie down at evening.* That is, everywhere there will be only folds for the sheep. The destruction of the Philistines will be so great that if the Jews return from Babylon, they will not find any trace of the Philistines' earlier might, power, and splendor. They will find only sheepfolds to which they will be able to bring their sheep back from the pastures at evening.

Because the Lord will visit them. That is, at some time they are going to return from their captivity. Then the Lord will redeem them. Their captivity will not last forever. Thus the prophets everywhere very diligently exercise care that they do not cast out the people of Judah completely, as if they were never to be restored. You see, no matter how hard they press the captivity and whatever is still come upon the people, yet the prophets still have their eyes fixed on the kingdom of Christ which is to come. They knew that kingdom would come from that people. They have the promises. We have mentioned this many times before. Therefore it was necessary that, if not all, then a few, be saved. So then, by the counsel of God, many were led back out of Babylon into their land. Also, by the miraculous plan of God, Jehoiachin was saved in prison lest the light of the house of Jacob be extinguished, as the promise says.

8. *I have heard the taunts of Moab.* Now the prophet has turned his face toward the east, and he threatens the Moabites and Ammonites with destruction, and also the Ethiopians, as follows below. But we know the history: that those two tribes always were very hostile to the Jews. They always assailed the Jews with very bitter hatred. Whenever they could, they resisted and struck back. Then they would rejoice and dance if anything bad happened to the people of God and would taunt them in their wretchedness. When God's people were being led off into captivity, the Moabites and Ammonites kept crying out to the enemies of the Jews to destroy and kill them all. This we see from the psalm (Ps. 137:7): "Remember, O Lord, against the Edomites the day of Jerusalem, how they said, 'Raze it! Raze it! Down to its foundations.'" Also, Jeremiah says (Lam. 2:15): "Is this the holy city, etc.?" That is, "This is the land of Judah, the people of God, whom up to now no

one has been able to overpower. It's all over for them now." Here he is clearly saying the same thing Amos also said earlier.

They have made boasts against their territory. That is, "They have boasted with puffed-out cheeks and great words. They thought that it was all over for My people. But they will not escape from being totally destroyed. You just keep holding up My hand. Don't lose hope."

9. *Moab shall become like Sodom.* It will not be destroyed like Sodom in every detail nor become exactly like it. But in this way the destruction of the people of Sodom is used as an example in almost all the prophets. Thus we have it in Jeremiah (Jer. 23:14): "They have become like Sodom and Gomorrah." Also Isaiah says (Is. 1:9): "If the Lord had not left us a few survivors, we should have become like Sodom and Gomorrah." The meaning of the prophet, then, is this: "So great will be the destruction of the Moabites that nothing safe will be left for them. Everything will be destroyed, so that they will not manage to rescue anything at all." You see, that's how all those neighboring nations were scattered and overthrown by the Romans, Persians, etc. They did not even keep their original names. As I said a little earlier, they all came together into a single nation.

A land possessed by nettles and salt pits, that is, salty places or areas, as we read in another place (Ps. 107:34): "He turns a fruitful land into a salty waste." To summarize: "The Lord will reduce everything to barrenness, so that nothing except nettles and thorns will grow on the ground. The soil will be sterile."

The remnant of My people shall plunder them. These clearly are the ones who are going to return from the Babylonian captivity. "They will be reduced to absolutely nothing so that what up to now have been very strong nations will be plundered by the little remnant of My people. This will happen in spite of the fact that previously My entire people were never able to subdue them completely." And yet, they have not taken away their entire kingdom but some of their cities here and there. The Persians, the Egyptians, and the Romans took some away too. So Jerome is worrying himself uselessly and in strange ways in regard to this passage, but then that is customary for him, etc.

11. *And to Him shall bow down men in their own places, etc.* After the return from the Babylonian captivity, the Lord will make the temple at Jerusalem more renowned than it was under Solomon, when some kings offered gifts to Solomon. But the religion and worship of God never grew as much and it was never spread so far among other nations as when they returned from Babylon. Luke shows this in Acts 2:5 when he says: "Now there were dwelling in Jerusalem Jews, devout men from every nation under heaven." You see, this was, as it were, a sort of prelude for the coming kingdom of Christ, which was going to spread not merely among the Jews but into the whole world, throughout all nations. Afterwards the apostles established and spread that kingdom, so that it then began to shine almost everywhere, even among the heathen. Therefore Christ brought it about that people everywhere worshiped the Lord, not just in Jerusalem but among all nations. That is what the prophet is saying here about the worship of God being spread even among the heathen: "All the islands of the nations" will bow down to Him. That is, they will offer their gifts in the temple at Jerusalem. Even the heathen will bear witness that this is the worship of the true God, etc.

12. *You, too, O Ethiopians, shall be killed by My sword.* This is obviously the sword which the Babylonian king will wield. Now the prophet has turned toward the south and is threatening the Ethiopians also with destruction. Thus he seems to want to preach absolutely the same thing and in the same order or method as did Jeremiah when the Lord commanded him to pledge the cup of the wrath of the Lord to all nations. It is as if Jeremiah were saying (Jer. 25:15): "If the Lord does not spare the people of Israel, whom He has chosen as His own, much less will He spare the other neighboring nations, which do not belong to the people of God." The prophet Zephaniah says exactly the same thing here. You see, he is subjecting all nations to the wrath of God and to the captivity, lest they think that only the people of God have merited captivity. Yet the Lord does begin first of all with His own people, as Peter says in 1 Peter 4:17: "For the time has come for judgment to begin with the household of God; and if it begins with us, what will be the end of those who do not believe [5] the Gospel of God?" You see,

[5] Luther translates the Vulgate's *credunt.*

after He has sent out His Word, He first crucifies His own martyrs and preachers of the Word. He makes His own people suffer many trials. Then, after He has afflicted the righteous for some time, the terrible wrath and punishment of God soon comes against the enemies of the Word and of the people of God. This is what we, too, are experiencing today.

13. *And He will make the Splendid a desolation.* I have already said earlier about this word that it is obviously a common noun, "the splendid." [6] But here it certainly is a proper noun rather than a descriptive one. Therefore, instead of "the Splendid" we must translate it "Nineveh." Then there is great confusion connected with the words which follow. I translate them from the Hebrew as follows: "And the fleet of ships like a wilderness." To be sure, the Hebrew word means pathless and waterless. But how can a wilderness become pathless, when it already is pathless? This absurdity, then, moves me to translate it the way I do. The sense, then, is this: "I will make Nineveh a desolation; where ships abound, that is, the coastal cities, which are near the waves or touch the sea and which are famous for their wares, I will reduce to nothing."

14. *Herds shall lie down in the midst of her.* It is every kind of animal of this nation, that is, of this area about which I am now speaking, not of all the nations, as our translator renders it.[7] It is as if he were saying: "After I have killed all the men and destroyed all their cities, those places will be nothing else but pastures for animals of every kind, tame ones as well as wild ones. All the inhabitants will have been carried away. So everything will be turned into a desert.

The pelican and the hedgehog also. Up to this very day grammarians of the Hebrew language argue about the names of things, as important men have argued also about this matter. Because the Hebrew language is, to a great extent, lost to us, so that we can make no certain decision about many words, we follow that uncertain light whenever we can find nothing better. The pelican

[6] Cf. *Luther's Works,* 19, p. 97.

[7] Luther reads *gentis,* meaning *regionis,* for the Vulgate's *gentium,* meaning "of the nations."

is a bird known in the Latin language. It puts its beak into the water and utters a loud cry. Man has not domesticated it nor does he have practical use for it, etc.

A voice of something singing shall be in the window. If I were allowed, here, too, I would place the proper name for a bird. Where our translator puts "of something singing," I would render it with the word for a crow or of another singing bird. But because I have no other example, I would not dare put it in. Certainly, one correctly translates the etymology of the word, if he translates it "of something singing." There are, however, many words of this sort in this language which, although they seem to be descriptive, nevertheless are proper nouns. I also could have translated the earlier word which our translator rendered "pelican" as "vulture." After all, the etymology of the word would allow this. You see, Pliny [8] writes many things about the gullet of the pelican. He says that it has, as it were, another kind of stomach and that it gathers there what it later slowly chews up and lets go into its belly, etc. But if one reads this descriptively with the Latin translator, the sense will be as if he were saying: "Night owls and other wild birds will hoot safely there in the windows where young men and girls used to sing before, etc."

We must take this entire passage to mean Babylon rather than Nineveh. You see, Nineveh had already been destroyed, and the kingdom had been transferred to the Babylonians. Therefore I am almost sure that this was the one kingdom and one jurisdiction of the Chaldeans and Assyrians. Yet they did have different kings who lived in different places to the extent that each wanted to, just as the different kings of Israel also lived in different cities, as the sacred accounts indicate. So here he is calling the kingdom which already had been transferred to the Assyrians Nineveh—I say he is calling it by its ancient name. This was the greatest and most important city of this kingdom, the capital of the kingdom. Scripture often has a change of this sort, of the names of even the kings, etc.

[8] Pliny, the elder, in his *Natural History,* X, 47, 66. The Wittenberg edition quotes Pliny more exactly: "Pelicans are similar to swans, and one would not think them distinguishable at all if the former did not have in their gullets a kind of second stomach. Here the insatiable creature accumulates everything, so that its capacity is remarkable. Once all the booty has been collected, it is gradually returned to the bill, and the bird sends it on to its true stomach the way a ruminating animal does."

15. *This is the exultant city.* The prophet mocks as he rebukes the pride and disdain, or insolence, of the kingdom. It is as if he were saying: "Here is that Nineveh, the most powerful city of the realm. Up to now it was boasting of its power, its abundance, its wealth, etc." You see, this is what the Hebrew word means which our translator [9] renders "exultant." This is what we mean when we speak of an exultant soldier,[10] not that he has glory, or one whom men admire because of his courage, but one who keeps offering himself for sale, etc. So also the prophet adds here: "I am, and there is none else."

What a desolation she has become, a lair for wild beasts. That is, "What desolation she has become! To what a wilderness she has been reduced, so that what once was the seat of empire has now become a lair for animals and wild beasts."

[9] The Vulgate.

[10] The *miles gloriosus* ("the braggart, swashbuckling soldier") was a stock comic character throughout the history of drama. Cf. p. 301, n. 5, above.

CHAPTER THREE

THIS third chapter prophesies[1] about the city of Jerusalem and the people of God who lived in Jerusalem after their return from captivity. They had again established their princes, priests, and scribes whom the Gospel frequently mentions. Thus I have the firm feeling, unlike others, that he is describing the condition of the people who had been led back to Jerusalem from the Babylonian captivity; of the people who had reestablished their religion and sacrifices just the way the Lord had commanded them through Moses. Next, the prophet again threatens destruction to the world after he has first described, as I have said, the wicked people to whom Christ was going to come. After all, this is the first thing he mentions at the beginning of the chapter. Then too, namely, when Christ came, there again were many wicked people who had deserved destruction. All this the prophet sees here as if it were present. Indeed, this is the course of the world which will last until the end just as it has endured from its beginning. When the Word of God spreads by the grace of God, there are those who despise and persecute it, just as happened before the Babylonian captivity. But because the Lord was a just Judge, He could not bear the contempt of His Word without taking revenge. He punished this with a wretched captivity.

When they had again been brought back from captivity and the sincere Word had been reestablished along with the true worship of God, they again had no shortage of false prophets to corrupt the sincere Word and to call the people away from true piety to wickedness, as all the gospel accounts indicate. So it finally came to pass that the judgment of the Lord wiped out and rejected the entire wretched nation.

[1] With the Wittenberg edition we have read *prophetat* for *prophetavit*.

We, too, shall experience exactly the same thing. We have the clear and abundant Word of God. It brings light to many. The rest, however, despise and persecute it. For these the wrath of God remains. After all, it is impossible for the Lord not to avenge the contempt of His Word. Accordingly, we can declare with the greatest certainty that a terrible evil will come upon those who despise the Word. You see, we cannot be deceived in this point. Furthermore, even when the sincere Word is restored, those will never be lacking who are going to corrupt the Word and that pure wine until Christ comes and puts an end to this evil and destroys them all. These are the points with which I wanted to preface this chapter.

1. *Woe to her that is rebellious and a redeemed city.* With the very word when he calls the city "redeemed," he indicates almost the entire argument of this chapter. It is as if he were saying: "You have been led back out of captivity. The Lord has restored you to your original position of dignity. Yet you do not cease irritating God with your wickedness and faithlessness." You see, he is starting with those worst vices which are the roots and wellsprings of all external shameful acts. These are the things God hates the most. They are the faults with which we make God angry: namely, when we ascribe righteousness to our own powers and works; when we argue with God; when we want to be righteous; and when we do not allow Him to condemn those abominable works of ours but protect them by snapping against the Word of God, etc.

Dove. We must try to figure out why he would call Jerusalem a "dove." We have the same thing in the Song of Solomon (Song of Sol. 6:9): "My dove is only one." So here he is calling Jerusalem "the dove of the Lord," that is, His beloved, whom He had selected as His own, as Isaiah calls her "the faithful city" (Is. 1:21). The prophet is secretly indicating that the Holy Spirit is in Jerusalem, for the Holy Spirit is God's "Dove," etc.

2. *She listens to no voice, she accepts no correction.* We must read all the words in the present tense, indicative mood.[2] Then the meaning will become clearer. Here he is listing the sins with

[2] The Vulgate text has the perfect tense.

which she is going to provoke the Lord. It is as if he were saying: "She does not listen to the voice of the Lord. She does not obey the voice of the Lord or the Word of God." You see, immediately after the Babylonian captivity they despised the true prophets. As substitutes for these, they took the Pharisees, Sadducees, and other sects of this sort. These tore the people apart in different ways and corrupted them with their depraved ideas. As a result, it came to pass that the Word of God cooled off, etc.

She accepts no correction. That is, she will not accept rebuke, she will not accept condemnation, as I said a little earlier. You see, she is so far from giving up on her own ability that she thinks that piety and the true worship of God belong to her alone. Therefore she lets no one tell her anything.

She does not trust in the Lord. That is, she teaches the righteousness of the flesh. She does not teach a faith that teaches one to fear and trust in God.

She does not draw near to her God. One draws near to God by acquiring knowledge of Him. This happens by faith, not by works, not by hands or feet but by zealous practice and daily exercise. This is what Paul calls "from faith to faith" (Rom. 1:17), from virtue to virtue, "from one degree of glory of the Lord to another" (2 Cor. 3:18), until we come out as perfected people, as we have it in Ephesians (cf. Eph. 4:13).

3. *Her princes.* He is not speaking about kings. It is as if he were saying: "They are not going to have kings any longer but savage tyrants who will swallow up all their resources. They will burn with such a desire for acquiring, they will work with such a strange greed, that they will make their own wealth stand firm." You see, here we have the first fruit of wickedness, greed. It is followed by violence, luxury, lusts, sloth, etc.

Her judges are evening wolves. We had the same expression earlier in Hab. 1:8: "more fierce than the evening wolves." There I said we had to translate it as "wolves of the desert." [3] But I am still not sure in those two places which of the two is the more accurate. He calls them "evening wolves" here. He says that we must thus render it with this antithesis as he says "that leave noth-

[3] Cf. *Luther's Works,* 19, pp. 112 and 170.

ing till the morning." This is the sense: "Such is the madness of their officials, so great is their greed, that they are insatiable. You see, so great a zeal for acquiring has swept over them that they want to swallow up the entire population and at the same time have all the resources and property of that people.

4. *Her prophets are wanton.* I would translate this in German with *Es sind lose Buben, leichtfertige Leute* ("They are dissolute rogues, irresponsible people"). The Septuagint translates, not badly, πνευματοφόροι ("spirit bearers," "windbags"). We have the same expression in Gen. 49:4: "As unstable as water." Paul has rendered it properly when he said (Eph. 4:14) "that you not be carried about by every wind of doctrine." They are turned by every whim of the mind, as water flows in no order when one spills it. We have the same expression in Jer. 23:32, where the translator, according to his custom, renders it with various detail "they have led My people astray by their lies and their miracles." Obviously there is extraordinary agreement with this noun with which the Latin translator here has rendered the same word. For what harmony is there between the word "wanton" and "miracle?" Therefore he should have translated it more accurately in Jeremiah as "in their recklessness," that is, "with their nonsense." We have the same expression in the Book of Judges (Judg. 11:3), when the writer writes that worthless robbers gathered around Zephthah, that is, unreliable men, who took nothing seriously. This is the way I translate it here: "Her prophets are unreliable." That is, they do not think. They have no deep insights and take nothing seriously. In the assembly they blabber out everything that comes to mind. They do not determine the intrinsic value and weight which lies in God's words. Whatever they think is human, etc. He thus adds:

Faithless men, more accurately, "men who despise." They consider the Word worthless. They do not have the rationale of the Word. In the psalm (cf. Ps. 25:3; 119:158) I translated it in German as *Verächter.*

Her priests profane what is sacred, that is, sacred things. They were treating sacred matters without dignity. After all, it is a profaning of sacred matters when one ascribes righteousness to them, when we teach people to trust in holy things, as those people were teaching trust in works. Thus they profaned the temple and the sacrifices divinely appointed, but not for this, etc.

They do violence to the Law. That is, they have corrupted the Law. They have interpreted it carnally, not spiritually, as they ought to have interpreted it. After all, it is spiritual, as the apostle says (Rom. 7:14). Thus, then, they have profaned both what is holy and the Law when they kept trusting in their worship, in their sacrifices and works which the Law required. Their profaning did not lie in the fact that they did not observe the Law or that they despised the temple and other sacred things. This is perhaps what our translator thinks. He is connected with the courts.[4]

5. *The Lord within her is righteous.* He is speaking about Christ Jesus, the Savior, who, unlike them, teaches true righteousness. You see, the greatest wickedness was again in control when Christ came. Therefore He set Himself against their wickedness, etc.

Every morning He shows forth His justice, that is, immediately and very quickly. This is the way the prophets generally use the word "morning," as in the psalm (Ps. 46:5): "God will help her right early." The sense of the prophet, then, is this: "No matter how much wickedness may rule when Christ Himself comes; no matter how much the Pharisees are going to blaspheme against the true righteousness which He will teach; and no matter how much they are going to despise it as worthless, yet it will continue to stand. He will bring forth His own righteousness as a light. His case against the wicked will continue safely." You see, nothing will help them, because they want to repress that righteousness by joining forces against it. He will crush it. He will move His own case forward to great glory. Then he follows with:

But the unjust knows no shame. That is, He will not approve of the shameful iniquity of others who will be promoting a different thing. This is what Ps. 1:6 says: "For the Lord knows the way of the righteous," that is, He approves of it. The way of the righteous is well-pleasing to Him. Also, Christ will tell the wicked (Matt. 25:12): "I don't know you." To summarize; He will allow others

[4] The text has *iudiciarius.* It may be that *iusticiarius* ("work-righteous") is meant. The criticism may be aimed at St. Jerome, "our translator," that is, the original compiler of the Vulgate.

to be carried away in their wickedness. He will have no truck with the wickedness He has censured.

6. *I have cut off nations; their battlements are in ruins;* This is a new paragraph from the previous ones. You see, the prophet began in this chapter to turn his prophecy to the people who had been led back from Babylon. This I have treated in sufficient detail earlier. Now he begins to make the past blessings which they had received from the Lord a reason for reproach. It is as if he were saying: "I brought you back from the Babylonian captivity. I destroyed many very powerful nations because of you. With My mighty hand I led you out of Egypt and drowned Pharaoh with all his army. I overthrew and destroyed the powerful realms of the Babylonians and the Assyrians. Yet you are forgetting all these things. They all grow old in your mind. You never, or, at best, only once, recall those miracles I have done for you." You see, this is how it happens, not just in human matters but in sacred ones as well, that nothing grows old more quickly in the hearts of men than gratitude and the remembrance of a blessing received. Also in spiritual matters we immediately forget all the things that have happened to us by the grace of Christ. After all, how very few there are today who consider from what great burdens and bonds of the pope the Gospel of Christ, now revealed to us, has freed us. The prophet is rebuking the Jews here for the same forgetfulness.

Their battlements, that is, their princes or chiefs. This means: "I have destroyed the sovereignty in those nations. I have killed their kings and princes." You see, this is the way Scripture commonly calls princes or leaders of kingdoms. Elsewhere it calls them "heads" or "hair" or "beard" or "mountains" or "battlements," etc.

I have laid waste their streets. It is as if He were saying: "Their kingdoms now are thronged with people. Their boys and girls crowd and run back and forth in the streets. But I will carry them all off, I will reduce them to a wilderness, I will take away the crowd of inhabitants."

7. *For I said: Surely you will fear Me, you will accept correction.* That is, "I have sent you My prophets. They have preached to you. They have taught you to fear Me and to accept correction.

In other words, they have taught you to fear Me through the reminder of those miraculous works I performed for you. They taught you so that you would not commit sins similar to your earlier ones. Thus I would not be forced again to destroy your habitations as I destroyed you before and led you off into captivity. You see, unless you learn fear and discipline, I will not spare your dwelling." And He didn't spare them, for the Romans laid terrible waste to everything, etc. In these few words the prophet has included whatever the life of a true Christian involves. The fear of God brings with it faith and humility of heart, so that we have reverence for the majesty of the Lord. "Correction" involves external behavior, that we behave among ourselves honorably without offending our brothers, that we live temperately, that we serve one another in love. This is the sum and scope of all the prophets and of all Scripture.

But they rose up early and made all their deeds corrupt. It is as if he were saying: "No matter how much the prophets may have taught fear, they have done it all in vain. You are still going on with your wickedness. You are persevering in the wickedness you inherited from your fathers. And you do this very eagerly and with all your might." You see, "early" indicates, as I mentioned a little earlier, immediately and quickly, as in Ps. 78:34: "They were coming to Him early," that is, those who intended to reconcile the Lord were coming quickly to find favor, etc. Thus we have here: "They rose up early and made all their deeds corrupt." That is, not only did they not listen to the warnings of the prophets, who taught the fear of God and discipline, they also were eager and energetic to increase their wickedness, to corrupt their faith and external behavior. Indeed, they are detestable, without faith, and useless for every good work, as Paul says (cf. Titus 1:16). Obviously then, we are found to be more interested in and eager for wickedness than for goodness. Also, Christ says that the "sons of this world are wiser in their own generation than the sons of light" (Luke 16:8). We have almost the same words in Ps. 14:1 as we have here: "They are corrupt, they do abominable deeds."

8. *Therefore wait for Me, says the Lord, for the day when I arise as a witness.* That is, "Because they do not have the Word of God in their hearts, because I warn them in vain through My prophets,

I despise them, even though they have now returned from captivity and have felt My wrath more than enough. I will go about throughout the world and will seek another people for Myself, because I have rejected you. I will finally bring matters to a conclusion with you. In a short time it will come to pass that your kingdom will be taken away from you and will be given to a nation that produces fruit, etc. (Matt. 21:43). I will stir you to jealousy in a foolish nation, one which is not a nation, etc.," as we have it in Hosea.[5] This will continue to happen until the day "of My resurrection." This sense does not displease me, but I approve of it because they interpret this passage as related to the resurrection of Christ. It is as if He were saying: "By virtue of My resurrection, when I shall rise from death, it will come to pass that a new people will come into being." There is the other meaning, that "rising of of the Lord" be taken, as Scripture generally takes it, for the vengeance and preparation of oneself against the enemy. We have this in the psalm (Ps. 44:23): "Rise! Why sleepest Thou, O Lord?" The meaning is this: "I will reject you. I will select a new people for Myself when I rise—obviously, through the Romans, whom I will send against you to destroy you and lay waste all that is yours." Moses says this, too (cf. Ex. 33:5): "I will go up once, and I will destroy you" from all the earth. Next, because He is speaking of the future,[6] Jerome troubles himself strangely. But the meaning is very simple, that is: "As for the rest *(de cetero)*, if I once arise."

For My decision is to gather nations. The prophet explains about what rising he has been speaking, namely, the resurrection of Christ. I have said that this sense pleases me more than the other. After all, after Christ was raised from the dead, He ascended into heaven and became the Judge of all the world, as we have it in the psalm (Ps. 110:6): "He will execute judgment among the nations." Here, then, the judgment means not so much the execution of wrath as it means the office and power of ruling, as we have it in more than one psalm. Furthermore, that gathering of kingdoms and nations took place through the Word of the Gospel which has been spread throughout the world.

[5] Hos. 1:9 may have been in mind, but Deut. 32:21 is much closer, and so we might read "Moses" for "Hosea."

[6] The Vulgate text reads *in die resurrectionis meae in futurum.*

To pour out upon them My indignation. The apostle Paul has interpreted this elegantly in Rom. 1:18: "The wrath of God is revealed from heaven against all ungodliness and wickedness of men, etc." You see, the message of the Gospel is (Matt. 3:2; 4:17): "Repent, for the kingdom of heaven is at hand." Also, Christ says in the last chapter of Luke [7] that repentance must be preached in His name. The Gospel first declares the outpouring of the wrath and anger of the Lord, just as He says here "to pour out upon them My indignation, all the heat of My anger." For so He says (Mark 16:16): "He who does not believe will be condemned"; What is more (John 3:18): "He is condemned already."

9. *Yea, at that time I will change the speech of the peoples to a pure speech.* The prophet selects all his words in such a way that we can have no doubt that we must take them all to mean the Gospel. Thus he here is describing the invocation of the name of the Lord and the single-hearted worship of God as "pure speech." Therefore the meaning is: "I will remove those who corrupt their own deeds, who adulterate the Word of God, who use impure speech. I will establish a holy people for Myself. I will give them pure speech. They will teach My Word in purity and will call upon My name." So He says, "I will change (or transform)," as if to say: "Your lips are unclean," as we read in Is. 6:5. "Therefore, I will change the speech for the peoples to a pure speech. They will teach the sound and blameless Word of faith. Because of this, they are going to receive very much fruit. For they will call upon My name, which they could not do otherwise, unless they taught pure speech, that is, the pure Gospel." You see, when they mix works and confidence in works with the doctrine of faith, they cannot invoke the name of the Lord. For how will they call upon Him in whom they have not believed? (Rom. 10:14)

And serve Him with one accord. That is, in harmony with one another, singleheartedly. They will not limp on both sides, as Elijah says in 1 Kings 18:21: "How long will you go limping with two different opinions?" All will be of one mind.

10. *From beyond the rivers of Ethiopia.* He means the fruit of the Gospel. That is, that people of His will be holy and of pure speech not only among the neighboring nations but even among

[7] Cf. Luke 24:47.

those which are very far away. You see, His suppliants are going to be beyond the rivers of Ethiopia, not only in the temple in Jerusalem. Their sound has gone out into every land.[8] Also, Christ says (cf. John 4:21-23): "The hour is coming and now is when you will worship neither in Jerusalem nor on this mountain, but the true worshipers will worship in spirit and in truth." Likewise, "My dispersed ones will offer Me gifts everywhere, not only in the temple at Jerusalem." Therefore whatever is to come will be new—a new way to pray, a new method of making sacrifice, and a new people. Surely, this is a very beautiful text. With very clear words it teaches the abrogation of the Law. After all, the Law forbids one to sacrifice and pray in any way except in the designated fashion and in a definite place, the temple at Jerusalem. But Christians daily offer spiritual sacrifices to God, as Paul says in Rom. 12:1: "Offer your bodies as a living sacrifice, holy, etc." He calls them "sons of My dispersion." This is what Peter writes too when he addresses his epistle to the chosen exiles of the dispersion in Galatia, etc. (cf. 1 Peter 1:1). You see, the Christians have been scattered throughout the world. They do not come together to a single place the way the Jews had to.

11. *On that day you shall not be put to shame by all your deeds.* That is, "I will cleanse My people for Myself. I will have true saints. Among them will be no hypocrisy, no impurity of impure doctrines, which contaminate souls. Rather, I will sanctify them all with the Holy Spirit, which I will give them in their hearts." Then he adds the explanation:

For then I will remove from your midst your proudly exultant ones. It is as if He were saying: "Up to now you have always been charged with having had false teachers with impure speech, officials with itching ears. The prophets always blamed you because of 'your proudly exultant ones,' that is, those who kept boasting of the righteousness of the flesh and of their works. But these I will remove from your midst. You see, I teach something different—that men must despair completely of their strength, their wisdom, and the righteousness of their flesh; that all men are guilty of damnation; that there is nothing in which the flesh can boast of itself, as the apostle says in Rom. 3:27: 'Then what becomes of our

[8] Rom. 10:18; Ps. 19:4.

boasting? It is excluded, etc.' Also (Rom. 3:19): 'That every mouth be shut and the whole world become accountable to God,' so that 'whoever glories, let him glory in the Lord.'" Cf. Jer. 9:24.

12. *A people humble.* These are the apostles and scanty remnant in Israel. "The most powerful, the wisest, the choicest part of the people, such as the priests and princes, will perish. But I will leave in the midst of you a poor and needy people who will hope in the name of the Lord." In few but very beautiful words he is describing the church of Christ, that it is a poor, needy, and oppressed people who call on the Lord and hope in the Lord. This is the greatest righteousness; this is the highest worship of God.

13. *Those who are left in Israel shall do no wrong.* He means the virtues or power and efficacy of faith. So also John says in 1 John 3:9: "No one born of God commits sin, for God's nature abides in him, and he cannot sin, because he is born of God." But we are born of God through faith. John 1:12-13.

A deceitful tongue, that is, one which with its good appearance seduces souls. It promises them something other than it can deliver. You see, it teaches and promises righteousness and gives death, etc.

For they shall pasture, namely, on the Word of the Gospel.

They shall lie down, namely, in peace, in a good conscience. With consciences at peace they will be in the presence of God, so that there is nothing which can frighten them. Rom. 5:1: "Since we are justified by faith, we have peace with God, etc." Also, Rom. 8:31: "If God is for us, who is against us?" You see, it is the glory of the kingdom of Christ that we are joyful and at peace through Christ, who has reconciled us to God; not that the cross will no longer be there in the future, not that the world and Satan are not going to set their traps for us; but that against all these the conscience is strengthened and secure, so that all these trouble it not at all. This is the work of the power of God in us, as the apostle Paul says.

14. *Praise, O daughter of Zion.* He has described the kingdom of Christ. In all this which follows the prophet with exuberant affection wishes joy to Israel and the daughter of Zion, that is, that such a kingdom has come to those who believe. This is what Paul does. He congratulates the Romans on their knowledge of Christ,

Rom. 1:8: "I thank my God through Jesus Christ for all of you, etc." "Praise" means "give thanks, be joyful in the Lord."

Rejoice, O Israel. From this it comes out very clearly that the prophet is not speaking about a temporal kingdom when he brings in a rejoicing Israel, for, as we see from Hosea, after the captivity Israel was never brought back or restored. Therefore he is clearly indicating that kingdom of grace through Christ which has been spread very broadly throughout the world and has gathered together all nations and kingdoms, as he said earlier, from the Jews as well as from the Gentiles.

15. *The Lord has taken away the judgments against you.* There is an ambiguity in this speech. We have the same phrase in Job (Job 34:5): "The Lord has taken away my right." That is, "He does not plead my case for me; He does not make a decision in my favor." But here the meaning is the exact opposite. Here the prophet has used the word "judgments" in the same way Paul used it in 1 Corinthians 11:31: "If we should judge ourselves, we would not be judged" by the Lord. That is, if we were to rebuke ourselves. Also, Rom. 13:2: "Those who resist will incur judgment." So also here: "The Lord has taken away the judgments against you." That is, "He does not want you to rebuke yourself anymore. He does not want you to hate yourself anymore. Rather He loves you like a beloved daughter. You now have a God who is a very gentle Father and no longer a Judge who wants to terrify your conscience with the Law." This is what the prophet calls "judgments," that is, the wrath of God threatened through the Law. That, he says, the Lord has taken away.

He has cast out your enemies. "He has done this so that your enemies no longer can harm you, no matter how much they attack you, no matter how much they rage against you. You see, there will be no lack of those who want to destroy you, but be confident! It is the Lord who causes you not to fear so that you may lie down and not be terrified." This is what the prophet says (Ps. 118:18): "The Lord has chastened me sorely, but He has not given me over to death." Also, we read in Ps. 105:14: [9] "He allowed no one to oppress them."

[9] The Weimar text has "Ps. 103."

The King of Israel, the Lord, is in your midst. That is, "The very Lord Himself is now your King. He is in your midst. Now you no longer have any men to give you orders, only the Lord Himself." John 14:23: "We will come to him and make Our home with him." You see, God is present in the hearts of the faithful, which He calls His temple, etc.

You shall fear evil no more. This is what he said earlier about safety and about the removal of their enemies. It is one thing to endure evil and another to fear evil, just as it is one thing to die and another to see or taste death, as Christ says in John (John 8:51). Thus the Law is dead as far as we are concerned when it has lost its power and sting. Then it can no longer frighten us; it no longer has the right to condemn us. In the same way, although death may come upon a just man, yet it cannot terrify him, nor can it exercise its tyranny against or upon him. Therefore to him death is more correctly a sleep. Here, too, the prophet is speaking about one's fear of his enemies, as we also have it in the psalm (Ps. 64:1): "Preserve my life from dread of the enemy." After all, to the extent that one worries over evil, to that extent does he feel it. Evils sadden and cast down the wicked, and the fear of evils sweeps over them. That is, within they are terrified in conscience by death and by sin, because the power of God has not strengthened them. That peace and security of faith are not in their hearts, etc.

16. *On that day it shall be said to Jerusalem: Do not fear.* This is what we have in the psalm (Ps. 118:15): "Hark, glad songs of victory in the tents of the righteous." It is as if the prophet were saying: "This is all you will hear, this is all that will be preached to you: 'Do not fear, O daughter of Zion, because you have God in your midst, and He is your King.' Whom then will you fear? 'If God is for us, who is against us?' (Rom. 8:31)" Thus even in the greatest statements of comfort, he still always hints that the cross will come and foes will oppose, but the power of the Spirit will be at hand. It will strengthen them from being broken by evils, from succumbing to them—in short, from fearing their enemies. You see, Satan never ceases attacking the saints. No matter how much they may resist, yet at times weariness and the length of the struggle overcome them, as some of the fathers have

said. After all, Satan is always tireless; he is always pressing to completion what he has begun. Therefore he adds:

Let not your hands grow weak. That is, "Persist! Don't stop! Persevere, etc."

17. *He will rejoice over you with gladness.* All these things signify that their consciences would experience that fatherly sweetness of the kingdom of the Lord. The sense is this: "You will feel joy. You will feel in your conscience that the Lord is kindly disposed toward you, that He surely is a kind Father to you in all things." You see, the Lord is said to rejoice over us when He causes us to sense His favor, τὴν αὐτοῦ χρηστότητα ("His kindness"). He has expressed the nature of the kingdom of Christ very aptly and emphatically. For thus it happens for the righteous that He allows them to be attacked, to be molested in various ways, and to be troubled by many evils, so that they be conformed to their King. Yet He adds that feeling of joy, that security of heart, so that all things may become sweeter, so that nothing can separate them from the love of God, Rom. 8:39.

He will be silent in His love. Not in "your" love, as we read.[10] That is, "He will cause you to be silent so that you may have in the secret places of your heart a very quiet peace and a peaceful silence. There will be no sound of rumbling and shouting such as is in the hearts of the wicked when evils oppress them and they lack that security of heart."

He will exult over you with loud singing. That is, "You will realize that He is kindly disposed. That sense of the goodness and kindness of God will cause you to exult in praise. Daily you will give thanks; you will bless and exult in God, your Salvation.

18. *I will gather together the worthless who had departed from the Law.* This is how Jerome has translated this.[11] He has his reasons which have led him to such a translation. He thinks that *nugas* ("the worthless") was a Latin word taken over from the Hebrew as from the source of all other languages. But it is a wonder

[10] The edition of the Vulgate current in Luther's time must have read *tua* for *sua*.

[11] The Vulgate text has *Nugas, qui a lege recesserant, congregabo.*

to me why God has allowed such great men to err so extraordinarily, as here Jerome, a very great man, has made a monumental mistake in a philological matter. For this is not a Hebrew word, as he suggests. The real word would be נוּגִים ("the grieved"). Furthermore, where we read "who had departed from the Law," the Hebrew word properly means "the established time," as becomes very evident from many other passages in Scripture. Gen. 1:14: "And let them be . . . for seasons." There we clearly have the same word.[12] Also in the psalm (Ps. 104:19): "Thou hast made the moon to mark the seasons." Also in the Book of Judges (cf. Judg. 20:38): "We shall give you a sign," or a definite time. In the Psalms this is translated as "feast days," as we have St. Michael's, Walpurgis,[13] Christmas, and all sorts of other days. Consequently, I translate it from the Hebrew as follows: "I will gather together those of you who are temporarily (or for a time) oppressed with grief." The sense is this: "The kingdom of Christ will be of such character that it will assemble the sad, who for a time are oppressed with grief, that is, those who have fallen into some sin because of weakness. As Paul says in Galatians (Gal. 6:1): "If a man is overtaken in any trespass, you who are spiritual should restore him in a spirit of gentleness, etc." To summarize: Christ bears those who are weak in their faith and character in order to correct and encourage them and hold them up until they grow up. He means, therefore, in this passage the motherly mercy of Christ, because He fosters and holds us just as a mother fosters and fondles her little son. This is just like Is. 49:15: "Can a woman forget her sucking child, that she should have no compassion on the son of her womb? Even these may forget, yet I will not forget you." Also Is. 46:3-4: "You who have been borne by Me from your birth, carried from the womb; even to your old age I am He, and to gray hairs I will carry you. I have made, and I will bear; I will carry and will save." That gentleness of Christ sees to it that weakness either of faith or of character cannot harm us, provided that we remain firm in the purity of the Word, provided that we do not fall out of that womb of

[12] מוֹעֵד.

[13] St. Walpurga's feast was held on May Day. She was thought to have influence against magic and evil spirits. The night before her feast, Walpurgis Night, was a night of revelry, when the power of witches was thought to be at its highest point.

God from which He gives us birth. When this happens, our kind Father easily closes His eyes to all other sins.

So that you will not bear reproach for it. Because the Gospel is very pure, it teaches a very pure faith and a genuine love for the neighbor, the greatest modesty, and purity. Reason, therefore, immediately finds fault with the life and character of the preachers of the Word if it ever sees that these do not square in every detail with the very pure doctrine which they teach. You see, reason judges their life on the basis of their doctrine and thus also despises their doctrine. So, too, the enemies of the Gospel today make the objection that they always hear the Gospel from us and see nothing evangelical. Clearly they are saying that we teach one thing and live another. They should remember what man is, a rational animal who has a divine mandate to rule over all creatures, Gen. 1. But look at a baby! Nothing of such a powerful ruler appears in it, since it is by far the most disaster-prone of all creatures. It is completely incapable of helping itself. It depends entirely on help from someone else. Otherwise it must die. Clearly, one who lies in a cradle and can do nothing but cry—how he would rule over every creature and animal! Pliny writes about this in detail. Yet, the infant still retains dominion over every creature, even though this may not be apparent. It still lives in that hope. It is nourished in that hope and fostered in that hope, so that it finally receives all its strength and takes possession of its position of command when it grows up. The same thing takes place in all creatures, in trees, grains, plants, fruits. Because this is necessary in little things, much more must it happen in very great matters and divine ones, so that from day to day we grow from faith to faith until we grow up and meet the Lord as perfect men, as Paul says in Ephesians (Eph. 4:13). Nevertheless, in the meantime, God, our kind Father, overlooks our weakness and condones all things easily, lest we bear reproach on that account, if only we keep the Word safe and sincere, if only we remain in the womb and bosom of God, in which He always carries us, etc.

19. *Behold, I will kill all your oppressors.* In the Hebrew this reads: "Behold, I will make." This is a Mosaic word. You see, Moses has the habit of speaking this way: "He will make a burnt offering for sin." That is, "he will offer, or kill." Vergil, too, speaks

this way: "When I make [an offering] of a heifer for the fruits, etc." [14] Our translator,[15] therefore, has rendered the sense correctly. It is as if he were saying: "For a time God allows the wicked to rule and triumph, to rage against the pious until their wickednesses are fulfilled. Then He destroys them irrevocably; then He takes revenge on them."

I will save the lame. This is taken almost word for word from Micah 4:6. He means the very people who had been troubled in different ways by various evil tribulations.

I will gather, namely, through the Word.

And I will change their shame into praise. That is, "When they will have glorified Me through the cross, when they will lift up My hand, the time will come that their judgment again will be brought to light (cf. Ps. 37:6); the time will come that they again are going to be glorified." Christ speaks in the same way (Matt. 10:32): "So everyone who acknowledges Me before men I also will acknowledge before My Father." Thus the apostles and martyrs finally were glorified before God and before the whole world. These the world before had regarded as most contemptible people, as Paul says (1 Cor. 4:13), "the refuse of the world." Now they are remembered with benediction, like John Hus and all those who suffered persecution and death for the glory of God. Their memory, which for a long time had been in the shadows, has now been revived. The memory of the wicked decays. They perish in the greatest disgrace and confusion. In disgrace also do they stay, etc.

20. *For I will make you renowned.* With a particular statement he embraces a universal one. It is as if He were saying: "You have suffered the Babylonian captivity and have been afflicted in various ways. However, I will redeem you – not only from this captivity but much more also from death, Satan, and hell." Amen.

To Christ be praise and glory!

[14] *Cum faciam vitula pro frugibus.* Vergil, *Eclogues,* III, 77.

[15] The Vulgate.

LECTURES ON HAGGAI

The Altenburg Text

Translated by
RICHARD J. DINDA

PREFACE TO HAGGAI[1]

HAGGAI is the easiest of all the prophets. If we should consider the subject matter unsympathetically, the prophet will seem quite trivial on the surface, especially in our day. Everything about which he prophesies, especially about rebuilding the temple, has ceased. As a consequence, we must consider the subject matter correctly, so that we look not so much at it as at the Word of God. To observe this principle is of significant importance both in this prophet and in many other parts of Scripture where we read of similar subjects. The subject matter *(res materialis)* is the temple. Yet, the Divine Majesty bends down so low that He speaks at great length about rebuilding the temple, as if that were the matter of great significance. With this admonition in mind, let us learn in Scripture to look at and evaluate not so much the subject matter *(res)* as the spirit *(adfectus)* and the words. In this way we evaluate the works of God according to the will of God, for all of these works are very good, no matter how insignificant and contemptible they may appear on the surface. Hypocrisy uses a different approach, for it holds God's Word in contempt. In a completely different attitude, it looks, with gaping mouth, as it were, at those works which are commanded to see whether they are small works or large works. But one ought not judge a work according to its greatness or smallness. Rather, we must judge a work according to the will of Him who commands such a work. This is what faith does, faith which knows that both are the work of the same God. It judges a work as great or small according to God's Word; and looking to this alone, it makes the will of God of great importance. After all, the Word by which the Jews were commanded to rebuild the

[1] The Altenburg text also has the following titled above this preface: "The Commentary on the Prophet Haggai by M. Luther. Wittenberg, September 11, 1525."

temple and that by which God from the beginning created every creature in heaven and on earth were one and the same Word. We have to apply the same principle here. Then this prophecy will be most useful to us, etc.

The time when the prophet Haggai prophesied is clear from the superscription, for he says that he prophesied under Darius the king.[2] But the accounts of the Greeks as well as those of the Romans regarding this matter are strangely different, so that we can make no certain decision. You see, historiographers argue in various ways about the number of Persian kings. With as much clarity as I could, I pulled together their order and their years on a table, which I believe is now known to everyone, because it has been published.[3] Whoever will want to know the order in which one king succeeded another, etc., will be able to find such information there. The difficulty is brought about only by the fact that one and the same king had two, or even three, names. You see, in the Book of Judith, Cambyses[4] or Artaxerxes is called Nebuchadnezzar. He was the son of Cyrus,[5] the most powerful king, whom Darius Longimanus[6] succeeded[7] on the throne as the fourth [king].[8] It was under Cyrus, then, that the Jews returned from captivity and began to rebuild the temple. Hindered, however, by neighboring tribes, they were unable to pursue the work they had begun, for even with great exertion they could hardly fight off the hostile nations. Then Xerxes[9] published an edict forbidding the rebuilding of the temple. Through Cyrus, therefore, nothing else was accomplished except that the Jews

[2] Darius I, king of Persia 521—486 B. C.

[3] Cf. *Luther's Works,* 20, p. 6, n. 1.

[4] Cambyses (II), king of Persia 529—522 B. C.

[5] King of Persia 550—529 B. C.; founded Persian Empire.

[6] Luther's sources for identifying Darius as "Longimanus" were historical lists attributed to Metasthenes and to Philo. Cf. W. LIII, pp. 18, 20, 107, and 109.

[7] That is, indirectly. Cyrus was succeeded by Cambyses (II), who was followed by the usurper Gautama ("False Smerdis"), who was defeated by Darius.

[8] Cf. *Luther's Works,* 20, p. 6.

[9] That is, Cambyses (II). The Zwickau manuscript says: "Cambyses. The Greeks call him Xerxes; Scripture calls him Artaxerxes." See also n. 3 above.

were led back from captivity. The temple could not be rebuilt, even though Cyrus had firmly commanded its rebuilding. You see, they did not yet have God's word. The recommendation and command were merely human. I say this lest anyone think there is some contradiction here.

ON THE SPIRIT AND MOOD OF THE PROPHET

The Word of God has this character that it is made known and comes when man is most desperate over everything, when he thinks that nothing is less likely to happen than what the Word of God says most certainly will happen. You see, it does not come to the lazy or the pleasure-seekers. To them it is a source of laughter. Rather it comes to the weak and the oppressed, to those in need. These also finally receive it in such a way that all human boasting vanishes and nothing is credited to our own strength and energies, but all to God alone. Through the lowest dregs of mankind divine goodness causes things clearly impossible to the judgment of reason to become reality, just as we see here most clearly. You see, here the rebuilding of the temple is ordered against very powerful, very bitter foes. The command is given, I say, to a weak people, few in number, a people against whom stand powerful princes and powerful nations, which lived round about and daily threatened imminent destruction, as one may see in Ezra. For the violence of the neighboring peoples was such that the Jews were forced to build with one hand and to fight with the other to ward off the hostile nations. Yet, against all these fierce and powerful foes this one weak prophet here dares to rise up and prophesy about rebuilding the temple. So he orders this handful of people, who had just recently been snatched from a most burdensome captivity, to stand up against a mad and inflated king who didn't want them to rebuild the temple. His army was so large that he could not count it but could only estimate his countless soldiers by groups of ten thousands. This power of mind and spirit we must take into consideration, even though in a very small matter. In this instance minds are stirred up against a very powerful king and the strongest nations, which preferred that all the Jews be wiped out rather than that they rebuild the temple. Yet it is the Word of God which commands such things, and to it we must listen even though the whole world resists it, as the Jews also did listen. You see, when we thus attribute to God the glory of truth, then it happens that everything which first was opposed to us now is compelled to promote and help us in our plans. This is what happened here, where all the very heavy burdens and bitter hindrances were changed into peaceful allies. After all, as the account shows, the king ordered the princes to help the people, whereas before that they had been ordered to resist and oppose them. So, what appeared impossible earlier became very easy because of God's plan. Obviously, this is the way divine mercy, working wonderfully, turns all things into good for those who believe; judgment is turned into salvation for them, sin into righteousness, etc., enemies into friends and subjects. For God, who is the παντοκράτωρ ("The Almighty"), holds all things in His hand. The whole world, kings and princes, too, must obey Him. You see, He allows no man to harm His Christians but "rebukes kings on their account," as Ps. 105:14 expresses so beautifully. Then, "if God is for us, who is against us?" as we read in Rom. 8:31. Clearly this is the point and scope of the subject and the message, or spirit, that we must observe in this prophecy. In this way all things will become sweet.

CHAPTER ONE

1. *In the sixth month.* This prophet was a contemporary of Zechariah, for both prophesied under King Darius (namely, the fourth king, who was Cambyses' immediate[1] successor to the throne). Haggai, however, began two months before Zechariah, as the first sentence of both indicates. Haggai began to prophesy in the sixth month, the other in the eighth, as history also shows.

On the first day. The Hebrew uses the same word for "one" and "first," as Gen. 1:5 also reveals: "And it became, with the evening and the morning, day one." But here we had to render it "on the first day."

In the hand. That is, by Haggai.

2. *This people say the time has not yet come.* He begins with a reproach, as is the custom of all the prophets. You see, first of all they set forth a rebuke, threaten the wrath of God, and then they add sweet and gentle promises. This is something Satan does not do. He first attracts with his enticements souls which he lures into error with those enticements, wounds mortally, and destroys. So also the heralds of Satan do the same thing with their teachings. God first leads souls to hell; then He brings them back, humbles them, lifts them up; He confounds them with dishonor and finally glorifies them.

The rebuke of the people here, then, begins with the negligence of those who delayed and were lax in the rebuilding of the house of the Lord. Here is the feeling of the people. It is as if they were saying: "Under Cyrus we began to build the temple; however, the neighboring peoples prevented us from pressing on with the task we had begun. This development, consequently, leads

[1] Cf. p. 368, n. 7 above.

us to the opinion that it is not the Lord's will that the temple be rebuilt at our hands." To this idea the prophet—or rather, the Lord through the prophet—stands in opposition. He wants us to pursue the work initiated; He wants us to overcome every foe, every power; He wants us to consider His will, lest we be overcome by evils and succumb to weariness, and that we thus persevere and be saved. And indeed, we must carry the work to completion, no matter how much the world rages against us.

No one in the service of God, therefore, is excused because he is attacked, because the world is opposed to him, even though Satan or the princes of the world or, for that matter, anyone might be his foes. After all, if a man is the servant of God and believes, he is not unaware that his Lord is more powerful than every might and power and superior to it. He knows that all the world's wisdom, power, glory, and strength are nothing else before God but the dust of the earth which the force and violence of a whirlwind hurl here and there. So also he knows that if they will ever be brought into judgment before kings and princes, God has promised to give His servants both an ability and a wisdom to speak that no one can resist. Jeremiah also mentioned the promise (Jer. 1:18): "I make you . . . a fortified city, an iron pillar, etc."

4. *Is it a time for you, etc.* The prophet carefully describes the unbelief of the people, that all they saw was the power and greatness of the king of Persia and the violent wrath of the neighboring peoples. But divine might was not before their eyes in the same way. Thus they could not but be fearful and succumb. So we must die and must be overcome if we who are about to die concentrate on death and sin, which cannot but declare our conscience guilty, confound it, and having done so, condemn it. Instead, we must do this: we must turn our faces away from sin, from death, from Satan, from foes, in short, from every evil that is burdensome to us; we must joyfully and eagerly be confident, as if those burdens were nothing, as if they had nothing to do with us, as the prophet says in the psalm (Ps. 3:6): "I am not afraid of ten thousands of people who have set themselves against me round about." Here the prophet does exactly the same thing when he wants to call the people back from lack of faith to faith, as if he were saying: "If this is not the time to rebuild the house of the Lord, how is it the time for rebuilding your own homes? So, it is pure lack of faith

in you as well as greed when in this situation you become totally involved in building your own homes but neglect the work of the Lord. Your only concern is your own comfort, not the Lord's." In addition, he says:

In your paneled houses. I don't know whether he is saying this in praise or in criticism of their houses. I take it to refer simply to their roofed houses. You see, I don't believe that they had houses which were constructed with beautiful vaults and arches. The meaning is simply this: "You neglect My house. You abandon and desert it. Yet you take care of your own homes; you build your own, etc."

5. *Place your hearts above your ways.* This is a Hebraism. That is: "Consider your ways and your inclinations, or works. Place the success of your affairs before your eyes. Consider how things are going for you." It is as if he were saying: "From the punishment itself you can determine that you have sinned; when everything turns out so badly for you, when no success is connected with any effort, when the land gives back without interest only the seed it has taken, when the vines produce poor grapes, etc. You have eaten, and you were left unfilled. You had few things with which to nourish yourselves. You had nothing else to put your wages into except a torn bag, full of holes." By "bag" He means the place we put our coins. This, then, is a proverbial figure of speech: "You have put your coins in a purse that is full of holes." That is, "Everything slips through your fingers; you have no success with your business, etc." But look at God's marvelous plan. He had brought this people out of slavery in Egypt with His great miracles and mighty hand. For forty years He had fed them in the wilderness. He had killed many nations and kings who had fought against this people. Finally He brought them into the land He had promised to their fathers. But what does He do now? Now that He has brought into the land a people that has the very wonderful promises made both to them and to their fathers, He allows them to be attacked and sorely afflicted by their neighboring peoples. The land does not return to them seed with interest accrued. They sow in vain; they reap in vain. They hunger; they thirst. Is this a way to stand by promises? Here it kept appearing that nothing was farther from the truth than that

God would be faithful and that what He had promised would come to pass. But no, clearly the opposite was happening, for the people were being hard pressed by great poverty and massive ills. Divine goodness does this, however, in accordance with its own custom to make us foolish and to bring our plans to naught. In this way we learn that by our own planning or enthusiasm we can accomplish nothing, that all things are nothing, and that nothing succeeds. We learn rather that the Lord alone does everything, so that we leave all things to Him. Then the storms which break upon us are changed to a pleasant calm. Afterwards, that the Jews might not boast or ascribe anything to their own powers, they were forced by necessity or taught by experience itself to acknowledge that the Lord had encouraged them in their absolute desperation over their situation and that the Lord had supplied them with both the strength of mind and success of efforts to thus rebuild the temple, etc.

7. *Place your hearts above your ways.* This is a repetition of what he said earlier (v. 5). It is as if He were saying: "It is not the time that is at fault. Rather, you cannot press on and complete what you began because you do not deserve it. After all, the time has long been ripe for you to have been able to go on, etc."

8. *Go up to the hills and bring wood.* This is the other part of his prophetic discourse. You see, after his threats and rebukes he here adds promises, lest he appear to have forgotten his duty as a prophet. Here finally a clear and obvious Word of God is added to the human work. He openly gives a command to rebuild the temple. No work, no matter how good and splendid in appearance, has worth before God, unless the Word of God approves of it or unless the Word of God had confirmed that that work is based on a Word of God. You see, consciences can never be certain without a Word that declares to us the will of God toward us. However, when conscience has in this way been strengthened through the Word and been made sure that God approves a work of the kind that it has initiated at God's command, then it dares anything. It rushes ahead with it, always looking toward the will of God. Then it happens that everything becomes pleasing to God, no matter how much some weakness of our flesh may hinder, as we see in the apostle Paul.

To the hills. I take "hills" here as the place where they had first built the temple and where they were going to rebuild it again. Here we have to remember what I said above at the very beginning,[2] that we must consider the subject matter from the vantage point of the Word of God. Then this will appear to be a very great work, namely, one which the Word of God has commanded and established.

That I may take pleasure in it. Here is another promise—and certainly a great one. By divine authority the Word of God has so strengthened their hearts that they have no doubt that the work which they have begun is pleasing to God. This phrase ("pleasing to me"), furthermore, is one which the evangelists have used, for instance (Matt. 3:17): "This is My beloved Son, with whom I am well pleased, etc." The mountain *per se* was clearly unimportant. After all, it was only earth, as the basis of the whole earth is. But when God picks that place for Himself with His own Word, when He declares that He takes pleasure in that place and is going to glory in that place, then that mountain stands ahead of all the rest of the mountains. This happens by virtue of the Word of God. Certainly this passage alone gave the Jews great opportunity for venting their savage rage against the Christians and against the prophets who were speaking against the temple. We have an example of this revealed in Acts in the account of Stephen.[3] The kingdom of Christ had been promised to the Jews. To this kingdom everything that happened before it came, words as well as works, had to be applied, as all things were also looking toward it. Therefore, all works should have been directed toward Christ. But because the hypocrites were not doing this, they misled both themselves and others. Surely this promise was a very lovely one for the Jews. By this promise about an external sign concerning a physical temple, the Word of God informed them about God's good pleasure, just as our sacraments are most pleasing to us. Christ wants them to be signs of the grace He has promised and presented to us, etc.

And that I may appear in My glory. The first temple was very renowned, everyone agrees. They had built it at very great expense

[3] Acts 6 and 7.

[2] Cf. p. 367 above.

and with many resources. A great supply of gold, silver, and precious stones was poured out for it, as one can see from 1 Chronicles. Nevertheless, no less was the glory of this latter temple, although it would not be rebuilt so splendidly. You see, that structure was not going to be compared with the earlier one. Yet the worship of God in the latter temple was much more crowded. Indeed, at that time all the nations which had been very dangerous to the Jews before the captivity finally came up into this latter temple along with the Jews to worship God, as I also mentioned earlier in Zeph. 3. This is something that did not take place in the earlier temple, into which the Jews alone used to come to worship God.

9. *I blew it away.* The prophet entangles his discourse strangely here. You see, he goes back again to his earlier rebuke, in which he had said: "Place your hearts, etc." (v. 7). Now, the Hebrew word [4] means "to breathe," as is also obvious in Genesis (Gen. 2:7), "to breathe into something," to emit a breath. This expression means that God very easily reduces the present forces to nothing; that when God curses, nothing succeeds; that forces, no matter how great, vanish. Conversely, He can send the greatest blessing into abject poverty, as it is God's nature to make all things out of nothing, to make out of total need the greatest wealth and most felicitous outcome and success of all things. Many psalms are full of such things, as are also the Gospel accounts.

You busy yourselves, that is, "You are too intent on your own affairs."

11. *Therefore I have called for a drought upon the earth.* Our translations read poorly, that He called for it upon the wheat. More correctly it would read "upon the grain, etc." We have said it all above.

12. *And the people feared before the Lord.* The prophet here adds what fruit the preached Word produced, for the Word of God is of such character that when someone preaches it, it never returns void. It cannot but produce fruit in some of the people to whom it goes out, as we read in Is. 55:11. Thus here, when they had heard the Word of God, they took up the Word by faith, they

[4] נָפַח .

believed the Word. They became aroused and eager to complete the work which God had commanded. This is work which they would not have done had not divine goodness first offered the sweetest and fullest promises of consolation. Once these promises had strengthened them, they did not doubt that they would please God by rebuilding the temple.

13. *With the Lord's message.* I would prefer to read "among the angels *(inter angelos)* of the Lord" to retain the Greek word (ἄγγελος), as we read also in Mal. 3:1: "Behold, I send my angel, etc." Also we read elsewhere (Mal. 2:7): "He is the angel of the Lord of hosts." The evangelist Matthew also retains this word (Matt. 11:10): "Behold, I send my angel, etc." The word "messenger" *(nuntius)* does not have the same lofty significance. The spirit (which we call "angel") ought not be distinguished from a man by means of the word "angel." After all, all those who bring the Word of God, all who are preachers or ministers of the Word, are called "angels of God," just as those who hire out to do the work of Satan, who preach the doctrine of Satan, are "angels of Satan," and that is what the apostle Paul called them too.[5] Surely it is a great glory for a wretched little human being to be called an ambassador of God and to have a name in common with the heavenly spirits. Paul at various places calls himself the ambassador *(legatus)* of the Lord,[6] and here Haggai calls himself the "angel of the Lord" because of the authority of the Word, etc.

I am with you, says the Lord. I think that he is beginning a new discourse here. You see, Haggai does not complete his entire prophecy with one speech. Also it is the custom of several prophets that often with only the briefest discourses they bring out the greatest and most magnificent promises, just as here the unspeakable mercy of God is promised in words that appear to be sparse and brief. If God, then, is for us, who can be against us? Much less [7] will an enemy be able to harm us, for he cannot harm God. Here all creatures must yield. If we have God as our Protector

[5] Cf. 2 Cor. 11:12-15; 12:7.

[6] Luther apparently equates *legatus, angelus,* and *apostolus.* Paul claims the title *apostolus,* usually at the beginning of his epistles.

[7] For *non minus* we have read *multo minus* to produce a reading that fits the context. The Zwickau text has *nemo potest vobis nocere quia nemo deo potest nocere.*

(for this is what he calls God being with us), no evil, no pestilence, no persecution, no temptation either physical or spiritual can be so great as to cause us to fall. How could creatures overcome their Creator? See Rom. 8:38 f. These points the prophets undoubtedly explained with very copious words when he preached.

14. *And the Lord stirred up the spirit of Zerubbabel.* The prophet also adds the fruit of this discourse. It was not enough to have heard the Word, if the Lord had not also added His power to the Word so that it would be effective in their hearts. After all, we must follow God the Worker after we have heard the Word, as Christ also says (cf. John 6:65): "No one comes to Me unless My Father has drawn him, etc." You see, the Spirit,[8] who stirs up the heart, must go along as Companion to the Word, as here the spirit of Zerubbabel and of the rest is said to have been stirred up. This passage opposes the insane prophets of our times who hold the hearing of the Word in contempt, in fact, completely reject it, even though here it is clearer than daylight that the Holy Spirit inscribes in their hearts that very thing which Haggai had declared, etc.

The spirit. This is enthusiasm, *Mut.* The Germans use this word in various ways. *Er hat einen Mut;* that is, he is proud; he is also full of life. He is endowed with a certain strength of mind to endure adverse situations bravely. This God the Spirit stirs up in us when God breathes upon us with His Spirit, when He causes in us through the Spirit the courage or confidence to finish something we have begun and to which we otherwise would scarcely aspire in our timidity. To be sure, the Holy Spirit is like that because we tremble in God's business. The flesh cannot by itself believe in God. It cannot but fear the world and its enemies. We have, therefore, a need for the Spirit as our Strengthener and Encourager. When He comes, He so encourages us that we shun nothing for the sake of the glory of God, we dare all things. We even draw near to God.

[8] We follow the Weimar editor's suggestion to read *spiritus* for *verbum.*

CHAPTER TWO

On the twenty-fourth day of the month. There appears to be a discrepancy here—namely, a difference of days in what was said previously.[1] You see, in the first chapter the prophet says that he began his prophecy on the first day of the month. Among the Jews, March is the first month. This, then, was the month of August. The prophet preached for three weeks and, during that time, he also added some other men who helped him with his preaching. Lyra's explanation here pleases me. He wants this small part of the second chapter to apply to and connect with the end of the first chapter, so that we finally begin the second chapter after the part "of Darius the king." Thus Haggai preached for three weeks and three days before Zechariah began his prophecy.

1. *In the seventh month, etc.* Here the new chapter and a new discourse begin. In the Hebrew the verses are separated here. The Hebrew separations, however, do not agree in all places with the Latin chapters. With this passage the prophet begins a third discourse, in which he comforts the people as he describes the kingdom of Christ which was coming and which was, in fact, imminent and had to be declared immediately. Here, you see, the prophet is describing the kingdom of Christ in such a way that it appears as if it were standing at the door (as we commonly say). He declares it as so near that there is hardly another of the prophets who achieves the same thing. He gives himself completely over to a description of the kingdom of Christ so that the people most certainly should believe the truth of His promises.

3. *Is it not in your sight as nothing?* He begins his comfort[2]

[1] For *in octo* we have read *in dicto.*

[2] The Weimar text does not begin a new paragraph here, nor does it quote the text commented on, but the comment points to verses 2-4.

by means of a concession. He concedes that God's words do seem impossible to them. After all, the captivity had lasted for 70 years. Many little children had been carried away into captivity, like Daniel, who lived almost until the return from the captivity. Here, too, this text indicates that there were still some survivors who had seen God's earlier house which had been so magnificently and beautifully constructed. So it did seem impossible to them that the temple could be restored. We have had the same experience. In the beginning, the preaching of the Gospel seemed foolish to us, but this is the way God declares His power. You see, at the time when we expect nothing less, when we think that everything is going to pieces, that's when the Lord is near, as we mentioned in the preface at the beginning. After all, our reason cannot look into the Word of God. It has its eyes fixed only on present things, as our text here clearly demonstrates. God, however, whose nature it is to make all things out of nothing, clearly gives His Word contrary to a present need that we may learn to be more intent on His Word than on present things. You see, when the priests and the people were looking at the job of rebuilding the temple, the task clearly appeared impossible. Their frightened minds trembled at the magnitude and difficulty of the job. The Lord, therefore, is strengthening the people with His sweetest promises: "Let all the people take courage, for I am with you, says the Lord of hosts."

5. *Fear not, etc.* These surely are fiery words to stir up the heart of the people. You see, he is repeating the same words from his last discourse (ch. 1:3) to indicate how beautiful his preaching is, how very full of comfort, because the Lord is promising to be with us, etc. It is as if he were saying: "If you are afraid of Satan, death, sin, opposing nations, I, your God, who am far more powerful than all those, am with you, and I am going to keep the promised covenant which I made with you in Egypt." Today we do not have a promise of the sort that the Jews once had, where all the people were called God's people. Now, however, the kingdom is a spiritual one, and promises of this sort apply only to the righteous, whether they be Jews or Gentiles. God has preserved the Jews—the righteous as well as the wicked—because of Christ's coming kingdom. And although He may sometime spare this or that region today because of a number of righteous men, yet we do not have the promise of God as the Jews once did.

My Spirit will abide among you. That is, "He will be fixed on you. That means that you will have a daring and confident heart."

6. *Once again, in a little while, I will shake.* You see why He tolerates the wicked and preserves the promise. He is giving consideration to neither merits nor faults. He looks only at the coming kingdom of Christ. Because of Him—that is, Christ the King—he tolerates all men alike, since indeed Christ was going to be born of one of them. This passage very clearly and very obviously convinces all the Jews so that they are unable to contradict it. You see, it clearly indicates that this first people (that is, the Jews) would endure in the flesh up to the coming of Christ. It could not perish before Christ's birth. Because of Christ the external people were being preserved, and God was calling them His people, separate and select from all the nations of the earth. But now the Jews are not a people of this kind, for they have neither a kingdom nor a priesthood. So, if the text here is true—as it cannot but be very true—the Jews cannot deny that the Christ promised to their fathers has come. Today, you see, they have no king, no priests, no prophets. Before Christ's birth they never lacked these, not even in captivity. After all, in the captivity they had Daniel and Jeremiah as proclaimers of the Word, who by the Word of God kept sustaining and encouraging them, lest they lose their faith, etc.

And the dry land. Theologians of the church give various explanations here concerning the Lord's birth, about which the prophets do not say much. We, however, must take this to refer to the ministry of John, as Christ says (Luke 16:16): ". . . the Law and the prophets were until John." The kingdom of Christ began with the baptism and preaching of Christ, not with His nativity. That is, it began when Christ was baptized and the voice of the heavenly Father was heard saying: "This is My beloved Son, etc." In this way He became Teacher, Master, Leader, King. Thus almost all the passages of the prophets look forward to the kingdom of Christ. A few look to His nativity, as that passage in Isaiah (Is. 7:14): "Behold, a virgin shall conceive and bear a Son, etc." So by the kingdom of Christ everything has now become changed. The Law and the prophets have lasted until the time of John. We have become new men through the Gospel. Now the earth has been changed for us, because we no longer cling to the elements of this world. The pope is nothing, for hearts have been changed, and the pope's realm displeases them; that is why it will not be able to last. Today also God moves all things in this way because He has changed hearts which do not give a care for the madness of the world and its princes, etc.

7. *So that the treasures of all nations shall come in.* Read "treasure" or "what is treasureable"[3] among all nations. We can take it as a passive or an active. I take it in the form that befits all nations, that is, as a treasure that had to be published through the Gospel. So he speaks of a most pleasing treasure, of which the Gentiles were so unaware that they were unable to desire it. In this way he indicates that the kingdom has to be spread throughout the world to all nations, as Christ also says in the last chapter of Luke (Luke 24:47): "And that repentance and forgiveness of sins should be preached in His name to all nations, etc." We have spoken in great detail about this matter earlier in other prophets. I ask, what will the Jews be able to mutter under their breath against this passage? Let them tell us what this desirable treasure, spread to the heathen in so short a time, is, as is here stated. Surely we have received from them nothing other than the preaching of the Gospel, which is the noblest treasure and desirable good.

And I shall fill this house with splendor. He spreads the word of this treasure more widely that the people may know that they are going to worship the Lord in the new temple along with the Gentiles. The splendor of that latter temple was that Christ adorned it with His presence and preaching, even though it was enough splendor that also the Gentiles gathered together to that latter temple as they were converted to the faith.

8. *The silver is Mine and the gold is Mine.* This is an ambiguous statement in Hebrew which we can explain in two ways. The first sense is this: It is if he were saying: "You think that there is no great supply of gold and silver as there was in the earlier temple. It cannot happen, then, that this latter temple is going to be so splendid. Yet I am rich in all things. I am quite wealthy. Mine are all the things on the earth. Don't be concerned, therefore, about gold, etc." The other sense is this: "You don't need gold or silver for this splendor. All these things are products of My hand, as you

3 Instead of the Vulgate's *desideratus* ("desired"), Luther suggests *desiderium* ("desire") or *desiderabile* ("what is desirable").

read in the last chapter of Isaiah (Is. 66:2) and in Ps. 49:11-13: 'For every beast of the forest is mine . . . If I were hungry, I would not tell you . . . I will not eat the flesh of bulls, etc.'" So there is a transfer from the splendor of the flesh to the splendor of the spirit. That is why this sense pleases me. It is as if He were saying: "There will be no splendor in gold, silver, or any external things, but in My Christ, who will bring peace," as now follows. With this he shows that the Gospel must be spread in Jerusalem, as Isaiah also says (cf. Is. 2:3): "The Law has come forth from Zion, and the Word of the Lord from Jerusalem"; and in that last chapter of Luke (Luke 24:47): "Beginning from Jerusalem." Here again let them answer us as to when this will finally happen, when the Gospel will have to be spread from Jerusalem, etc. This then is also a very obvious passage against the Jews. It is indeed worthy of our observation, not so much because of the Jews, that we may close their mouths when they deny that Christ has been born, as for our own sakes that our consciences may be strengthened. You see, in all Scripture there is hardly so strong an argument against the Jews. Now, however, since they have been so confounded by and ashamed of their mistake, they are contriving some trifling ideas and dreaming up their third temple. But the text clearly is speaking about this last temple. You see, now that Haggai was prophesying, they were beginning to see that the splendor of this temple would be far greater than that of the first one. This splendor could not lie in gold or silver or other precious objects, since that first temple had been built much more richly and splendidly. Rather, this is a spiritual splendor, which comes through the preaching of the Gospel. All these things have been fulfilled in Christ, etc.

10. *On the twenty-fourth day of the ninth month.* Up to now we have explained three discourses of Haggai which he delivered to the people at various times. Here a fourth follows. In it the Spirit in the prophet exhorts them not only as people who are afraid but also as the weary. The first temptation [to be afraid] commonly occurs when we are enthusiastic about divine matters and the things which the Word of God commanded, because Satan does not cease besetting us with various adversities. Then, when he sees that that hope is failing him and that he can establish nothing at the left hand, he turns to the right hand to call us away from the works of God with an ignoble laziness and lack of concern. You

see, it is with a sort of smugness that he attacks us when we are not careful and cautious enough. Surely this is not a minimal temptation. In fact, it demands a greater warning than when we are openly evil. This entire discourse, then, addresses itself against the smugness of the people. For this purpose the prophet goes into the question of holy flesh, as the text says, in which question the prophet rebukes their negligence and carelessness and sets up penalties. God wants us to press on with what we have begun that our work may come to a boil. If this does not happen, if we do not energetically perform our job in a matter which God has commanded us, this displeases God, no matter how good the work may otherwise be. Furthermore, here he uses a kind of exhortation different from what he used earlier, as we see.

12. *In the skirt*, that is, "at the edge or fringe of the garment."

If one carries holy flesh, etc. This question has two parts: whether a cloak makes unclean flesh holy, and whether an unclean person makes something unclean. Because this does not occur naturally, he asks the priests to make a decision according to the Law. After all, according to nature, all things are clean because they are the good creation of God. But the Law makes a distinction between clean and unclean things and says that an unclean person makes all things unclean, as we read in Leviticus (cf. Lev. 19:8). How things are made clean again we also read there. Therefore, the priests could give an answer easily. In short, with this question the prophet did this: he roused and stirred a people who had become tired and careless, as I mentioned earlier. So he is using a new type of speech in order to get their attention. Good teachers generally do this to stir up their listeners with some new propositions to make their hearers sharp and attentive to the subject, etc. He attaches a last question.

14. *So it is with this people, etc.* It is as if He were saying: "Whatever the people have touched is unclean in My presence." Thus he is obviously exhorting a sluggish people that seemed to be holy to itself. Yet they were unclean so long as the temple remained unfinished. It is as if he were saying: "If you want to be pure, hurry to rebuild the temple. Complete the temple. Otherwise you cannot be made holy by a sacred task. In fact, because you are unclean, you pollute everything, even the temple, which is holy

in itself." Thus also the apostle Paul in his Epistle to the Corinthians gathers together wonderful arguments—very highly and carefully polished ones—to cut out of their hearts their smug carelessness. So also here Haggai quite carefully and scrupulously investigates his subject. Yet he splendidly weaves in the purity of faith with legalistic purity. Otherwise the promises given without our faith are not promises, etc.

And all the things which they offered, etc. This includes not only what they do that is not connected with religion but also those very things which they do in their worship of God, with which they believe they are pleasing God. They are not pleasing God, because they lack faith and because they want to make satisfaction with the righteousness of the Law. This God does not approve of. After all, to neglect faith and judgment is much worse than omitting matters of the Law, as Christ also says (Matt. 9:13): "I desire mercy and not sacrifice." Judgment, mercy, and faith are more significant than the Law. We must do the former and not omit the latter. The sense, then, of this section is this: "You are unclean even if you are clean according to the Law." Here we see that works do not cleanse one; also, that works without faith are nothing before God, because "whatever does not proceed from faith is sin" (Rom. 14:23)." This is a harsh statement against all the self-righteous, who perform as the heralds of their own works and righteousness.

15. *Pray now, consider what will come to pass from this day onward, etc.* He repeats the same thing he mentioned earlier in the first chapter (vv. 5, 7). He also reminds them of the loss they have suffered and of past evil, so that they may thus become more mindful of their previous wickedness and may more easily believe the prophet. This passage is completely proverbial, as we commonly say, "Fools must be deloused with a club." [4] You see, it is so ignoble a crowd that it does its work by force and blows. So also Christ says (Luke 7:32): "We piped to you, and you did not dance, etc." The prophet here is saying, as it were: "If you don't want to learn from promises, you will learn from blows." Yet, the wicked blindness of human nature is such that not even blows stir it to return from error. Isaiah says (Is. 9:13): "[The people] did not

[4] *Narren muss man mit Kolben lausen,* that is, "We must treat fools as they deserve." Luther uses this adage frequently. Cf. *Luther's Works,* 6, p. 63; 14, p. 113; 46, p. 167.

return to Him who struck them." In fact, the more one reproaches human nature, so much the more does it harden itself. This we see very clearly today in the Jews, who tenaciously protect their vain hope and belief. Their stubbornness makes them insuperable. They do not recognize their own blame, just as the papists, too, are stirred by neither blows nor signs to believe the Gospel of God Almighty.

18. *Consider from this day onward.* He repeats the same thing which he has said before (v. 15). You see, this is a custom of the Hebrew language to repeat the same thing frequently. We have seen this done very frequently in Moses. Here our interpreters bring up the question about the month, but I don't know whether this is of any importance to our subject. Haggai began to prophesy on the first day of the sixth month,[5] as the title of the prophecy indicates. At that time they laid the foundation of the temple. Therefore he orders them to hurry the task, to press forward with the work they had begun. He says that it is time for them to produce results.

Of the ninth month. This would be in January for us, because they begin the year with March. Also they call September the beginning of the year, as we see in Exodus (cf. Ex. 12:2). Therefore this discourse lasted until April or May.[6]

21. *Speak to Zerubbabel, the governor.* At the end he adds a promise regarding Zerubbabel. The Lord declares this to comfort both the king and the people. He clearly announces here the same change which he had earlier declared about a change of all things. This occurs through the Word of the Gospel in the hearts and consciences of men.

23. *Like a signet ring,* that is, "like a ring that bears the signer's identification."

For I have chosen you. This applies not so much to the person of the king as it does to the person of Christ, who was born out of his loins, because "salvation is from the Jews," as John writes (John

[5] The text reads *mense primo,* but in Hag. 1:1 we read *in mense sexto, in die una mensis.* We should therefore read here: *mense [sexto], primo [die].*

[6] The reckoning in this paragraph is obviously only approximate. Luther considers the time element immaterial.

4:22). Therefore, Christ, who came from the Jews, changed everything with His coming, namely, through the preaching of the Gospel. You see, as long as Zerubbabel lived that change did not occur. It came after his death when the new King, Christ, was born. To Him be praise and glory. Amen.

LECTURES ON MALACHI

The Wittenberg Text

Translated by
RICHARD J. DINDA

CHAPTER ONE

1. *The burden of the word of the Lord* [*to Israel by Malachi*]. A summary of this prophet is that he makes the synagog passé and describes it as a thing of contempt—like an old woman now about to be deserted. Therefore almost all the words which are here spoken in the name of the Lord echo a sort of disgust. The Lord has had enough and is, as it were, nauseated by their ceremonies which He wanted to preserve up to the time of Elijah. But they themselves preserved them for their own gain and profit, not with a sincere heart but with a greedy one, giving no glory to God. This, then, is his entire case—that the people as well as the priests have defiled the ceremonies of God. The stomach is the greatest idol in every religion. Unbelief is the cause for greed. This is what the prophet especially treats here. At that time Israel was to some extent gathered together from the remainders and was led back to Jerusalem, although the kingdom of Israel was not restored, and all the tribes were then mixed up.

2. *I have loved you.* He begins with a reproach as if to bid farewell to a people that complains and does not recognize the grace of God. That's the kind of hearers the prophets had. To be sure, among His own people God always appears weak, caring little for them. Thus He wants our virtue to be hidden in Himself. The weaker we are, so much the more powerful does He want to be in us. So Paul says in 2 Cor. 12:10: "When I am weak, then I am strong." It is as if he were saying: "I am throwing my own virtue off onto God, so that I succumb in weakness and triumph in weakness." This is something the spirit rather than the flesh

realizes, for the flesh believes that the world is more the victor. This is how the prophets told the people that they had a propitious God. On the other hand, when the people saw their own reverses and how dejected those reverses made them, they believed that God was very far away from them. The flesh then believes that God is far away when blessings do not come. Conversely, it does not recognize the will of God toward it, nor does it endure temptation, but it loses hope. God, however, does allow His people to sink but not to drown. He says (Ps. 55:22): "He will never permit the righteous to be moved." Again we read in Prov. 11:8: "The righteous is delivered from trouble, and the wicked gets into it instead." These, then, are words of faith and of the Spirit when God says: "I love you. I am favorably inclined to you, I am a propitious Father to you." These are the things we must look for, not the things in front of our eyes. But both the unfaithful and the saints also say in their long-lasting temptation: "Where are Your mercies which were of old, etc.?" And they considered the prophets liars.

Was not Esau Jacob's brother? By example he proves the love of God for His people. He says: "You will remember how I preserved you in the midst of the tribulations which the Assyrians, Babylonians, and others stirred up against you. But I neither loved nor saved Esau, who had the same reason to be loved, because he was Jacob's brother. But I have loved Jacob from the beginning, and I still love him today. From this argument you surely ought to have been aware that I do love you, even though the love is mixed in and involved with the cross." If you would look only at the external situation, you would believe that God loved Esau more, because Esau held the throne and was more powerful than Jacob. Nevertheless, all the works of God begin in weakness and are completed in strength. If you have been weak, wait! That weakness is the test of faith, whether you wish to trust in God or in your own strength. Esau fell and was not restored. Even though Jacob fell, he nevertheless was finally lifted up again, and that is the sign of My love to him. And it was his own adversaries who lifted him up, the kings of the heathen, Cyrus, Darius, etc. This did not happen to Esau. His end is near. Jerusalem was not built as a nest for vipers like Edom. After all, the remnants of this impoverished people remained in the land of Judah to cultivate it, lest it be turned into a desert; their kings and priests were preserved.

4. *They will build.* "They should entertain no hope that they are going to be restored as you were restored, although you had been destroyed earlier. This is how you may see that I love you rather than the children of Esau. The kings of Persia will hold them back, but they are favorably inclined to you, just as they favored you in restoring the sacred vessels, of sending you away, of building with you according to My will. Yet because of an insignificant persecution, you say that I don't love you."

And they will be called the wicked country. There will be no end to the devastation of Edom. To be sure, it is an ill-starred structure which the Lord destroys, whether it be physical or spiritual. Christ says (Matt. 15:13): "Every plant, etc." Furthermore, it is called a destruction of the kingdom when everything is upset and there is no order, when only the dregs of the people are left and everything is in a wretched state. So, even if people will be living in Edom, yet God will not be with them. Sin rather than the worship of God will be with them. Wickedness and the wrath of God will rest upon them. Ps. 137:7 says, "Remember, O Lord, against the Edomites the day of Jerusalem," that is, "as they did to Jerusalem, etc." On the other hand, the Lord was magnified in the borders of Israel. He lived there, and His worship was there. They were the borders of godliness which the Lord loved. This is where the temple, the priests, and the prophets were. He is saying, "You see, then, that the Lord is still glorious in your midst." The sign of the presence of God is the presence of the pure Word and the pure use of God's sacraments.

6. *A son honors his father.* Now he begins to censure their ingratitude, their contempt for and neglect of a God who loves them. He especially censures the greed of the priests, by which they did harm to the glory of God, which lies in the acknowledgment of Him and in obedience to His Word. Now, he is arguing on the basis of a comparison: "In nature it is normal for a son to respect his father and for a servant to respect his master. But if nature does this and if it happens thus among men, how much the more necessary is it that this be done toward Me, the Lord God and your Father, the most powerful and indulgent One of all?" This is also

an argument from the lesser to the greater: "A son honors," that is, "he is accustomed to honor and ought to honor." Then, "if I am אֲדוֹנִים," that is, "if I am Lords" (plural). This is the way it appears in the Hebrew. It indicates the mystery of the Holy Trinity and it is used for the sake of reverence, because God is Lord of all lords.

To you, O priests, who despise My name. Paul says (Rom. 2:24): "The name of God is blasphemed . . . because of you." This occurs in two ways, in doctrine and in life. But the greater blasphemy lies in ungodly doctrine, where the name of God is added to a lie. Here the prophet is speaking carefully and says "you despise" when he speaks about doctrine. The other blasphemy occurs in life and works when we attack each other, when we are proud, when we are given to greed, etc. Surely the whole world has the name of God in its mouth, namely, the filthy drivel of blasphemy. That's when this prayer "Hallowed be Thy Name" ought to make this life a bitter plague for us. He is saying: "You priests, then, who should be foremost among all in glorifying Me, despise My name more than others. With your false doctrine you cause My name to be blasphemed. Yet you still want to defend yourselves and not be considered unjust. After all, you are saying:

How have we despised Thy name? Certainly it is a terribly dangerous situation that, when someone is holding a wrong idea, he not only blasphemes the name of the Lord, but he does not want to cease his blasphemy and even defends his sect. The instigator of a sect is converted to the truth either with the greatest difficulty or not at all. This is how they wish to avoid being accused of contempt of God, as men who have taught the glory of God and have very diligently worshiped Him—yes, of course, their god, which is their own belly. But He answers: "This is how you have despised My name":

7. *You offer polluted bread upon My altar.* Regarding the showbread, they had the command in Lev. 24:8 and Ex. 25:30 [1] to change it every sabbath. They also had a command about the offerings of foods. These would at times become unclean because of the ingredients involved and at other times because of trickery

[1] The Weimar text reads "Levitic. 24, et 26.," but the latter chapter contains nothing regarding the showbread.

or theft.[2] Also, the priests were teaching that whatever was offered was clean, no matter what its quality was. He says, "You are saying that the table of the Lord is despised." Now this is not what the priests were actually saying, but they did give that impression. After all, to teach and believe that whatever is sacrificed is clean is certainly as if they were saying: "The table of the Lord is worthless and despicable." You see, they would say for the sake of their own gain: "It does not matter what sort of things you offer. After all, the Lord has given His command: 'None shall appear before Me empty-handed, etc.' in Ex. 23:15." The people then would pretend poverty and use the words of Haggai (cf. Hag. 1:6): "We have sown much, etc." The surest method of becoming rich is to seek first the kingdom of God and His righteousness. "Then," He says (Matt. 6:33), "all these things will be added unto you." We, however, turn things around and seek money and possessions first. Then we add the kingdom of God. But Christ first must be a beggar. First the Word of God must go forth, and those things which are of God. Incidentally, what Christ does not get, the state treasury will.[3] And if God does not tolerate deceit in ceremonies, much less will He tolerate it in love. He says, "You even say to the people:

If you offer a blind animal, etc. This is what it means to blaspheme God and the Law.

Present that to your governor. This is an argument from the lesser to the greater. A merchant is unwilling to accept a coin that has been damaged too much, but will God accept what does not please Him? Or is this the way we fear and honor God, as a stupid idol? Present such a thing to your governor and see if he will be appeased or if you please him! And now you are praying to God for

[2] The Halle manuscript adds: "The showbread became unclean . . . sometimes because of faulty ingredients of the bread or because it was acquired through theft or trickery on the part of the priests, who said that there was no sin if someone made an offering of things acquired by fraud, as the pope also accepted what was derived from usury." W, XIII, 679, n. 20.

[3] In his *Army Sermon Against the Turk* of 1529, Luther quotes the same maxim *Quod non tollit Christus, tollit fiscus,* in support of his statement: "What the people have saved, stolen, and scraped together, what they have withheld from their preachers and pastors, they will now have gathered for Brother Veit, the mercenary, and have no thanks for it. The princes will take it from them without mercy and hire soldiers with it." W, XXX-2, 181—182.

mercy through those terrible sacrifices of yours. Besides, you are defending your own iniquity. So that's how you will please God! Even now we certainly see everything in the world filled with deceit and greed.

10. *Who is there among you who would shut, etc.?* That is, "Would that there were one among you who would shut the doors of the temple, and would that you did not offer such vain sacrifices." Thus Is. 1:12, "When you come to appear before Me, who requires this of you, etc." It would be preferable to abstain from prayer than to pray in an evil manner. It is a bad thing merely to take on the appearance of worshiping. In the presence of divine majesty everything should be done seriously.

11. *For from the rising of the sun to its setting.* He is saying: "I will begin something else which pleases Me." The name of the Lord is great, not in terms of capital letters but in terms of celebration and confession and praise, because the Lord is merciful, etc., that is, when it is valued highly and preached with splendor. He is saying this over against the contempt of the name of God about which He said earlier: "You Jews are despising My name, but the Gentiles will make a great thing of it." Indeed, what glorifies the name of the Lord is not our works but the preaching of the grace and mercy and goodness of God.

In every place incense is offered to My name. This sacrifice Paul explains in Rom. 15:16 when he says: "To be a minister of Jesus to the Gentiles in the priestly service of the Gospel of God, so that the offering of the Gentiles may be acceptable, etc." Therefore through the Gospel, as if through a priestly tool, he offers the Gentiles. That is, he offers and shows them to God as people who are pure of sin, who are mortified in the body and in the flesh. Also through the Gospel their old mistakes are wiped out. In their heart the Gospel stirs up the truth which confesses God, which believes in Him, which praises Him, and which finally mortifies the flesh. The Mass, then, is not this sacrifice about which he here speaks, whether you imagine it is *ex opere operantis* or *ex opere operato*.[4] Otherwise even fornication *ex opere operato* would not be sin,

[4] *Ex opere operato* is the Roman formula used in speaking about the efficacy of the sacraments "by the act completed," that is, without reference to the doer. *Ex opere operantis* speaks of that efficacy "by the act of the doer," that is, with reference to the doer. Luther expressed himself more fully on this subject in his 1519 treatise *On the Blessed Sacrament, etc.* See *Luther's Works*, 35, pp. 62—65.

because a woman is a good creation of God, just as they say a sacrament is. Nevertheless, all the commandments have regard for the work of the doer. One does not ask how good the thing is but whether one uses it well or badly. Also a pure sacrifice requires a pure sacrificer. This is what God intended when He prohibited the blind, the lame, and those having any defect at all from ministering at the altar, etc.[5] This is a new kingdom which God is promising to establish here. The people in it are not of the flesh, but they are spiritual. "But anyone who does not have the Spirit of Christ does not belong to Him" (Rom. 8:9). The weak, therefore, are tolerated in this kingdom, but only those who are not completely without the Spirit. Those, then, who have the Spirit of Christ, even if they are few, are nevertheless scattered through every land, and because of the Gospel, which is everywhere, they shine like lights everywhere in the world as they keep the Word of life.[6] Burning incense and sacrificing food were very popular among the Jews. They practiced these as their best works for the worship of idols in every valley and under every leafy tree. Incense we take as prayer. Word and prayer, therefore, are the two sacrifices of Christians. Prayer takes place along with thanksgiving and praise. The sacrifice of Christians is clean, because they themselves are without fault, because they have been washed by the blood of Christ, etc. Unbelievers offer no sacrifice. Christians do not offer a worthless, blind, lame, or false sacrifice but a faithful and pleasing one. If their heart is faithful, then their sin is not counted against them. Also, we cannot take this sacrifice to refer to the legal, Mosaic sacrifice. And they were not allowed to make this sacrifice anywhere else. But he says here "in every place" and "among all nations." All these certainly could not come to Jerusalem, nor would there be enough Levitical priests for every place.

12. *But you profane it* [*when you say that the Lord's table is polluted*]. Since he mentions "table," he is particularly speaking about the bread.

And what is placed upon it [*may be despised*]. More correctly, "and its offshoot (or fruit) be derided with its food." The table is like a tree, food like fruit. Under the Law, the table would sprout with fresh bread every sabbath. The first loaves were the food for

[5] Cf. Lev. 21:16-23.

[6] Cf. Phil. 2:15-16.

the priests. It is as if He were saying: "You priests are saying that the fresh bread as well as the old is contemptible. Because you speak—that is, teach—this way, you therefore pollute the sacrifice." There was no fire on the table, nor is the phrase "with fire" in the Hebrew.[7] The table was defiled by a fault in the bread or by a fault of those who ate it, but most of all by a fault that lay in the doctrine of those who did not distinguish the profane from what was not profane.

13. *What a weariness this is.* "Even with great effort we barely got these loaves. If we had better ones, we certainly would offer them." Indeed, God is patient and merciful, but He cannot endure a tempting or, in fact, a contempt of Himself. Greed always has its own little effort and disguise. Likewise, God has patience in life and conversation, but He has none in the case of corruption of doctrine.

You sniff at that sacrifice. "You have been working for your own convenience. You have been sacrificing to yourselves, not to Me. You pretend that you labor under poverty. It is your fault, not Mine, for you are not seeking first My glory but your own gain."

You bring in what has been taken by violence or is lame or sick. The prophet here is speaking about other offerings in which they have sinned in similar fashion. Nowhere did they keep the teaching of God, and yet they never recognized that they had sinned. Whenever a false idea slips in, false works follow in the same area. They pretended that they were poor, and yet they were robbers. To be sure, this may not have been a public thing, but they were deceivers. Behold, this is a double sin: to make a spurious sacrifice and to say that it is not false.

14. *Cursed be the cheat* [*who has a male in his flock*]. This is an exclamatory summary.

A male, that is, something good, whole, brave, etc.

Something blemished, that is, defiled, faulty. Among the Jews the name of the Lord has ruled exclusively, but the Gentiles have revered it more than did the Jews. Therefore the rejection of the Jews is not far off.

[7] The Vulgate text has *et quod superponitur contemptibile est cum igne qui illud devorat.*

CHAPTER TWO

1. *And now, O priests, this command is for you.* In addition to their greed, they pretended to him that they were impoverished. So God is here threatening that He really will send them poverty. You see, what the wicked man fears will come upon him. Moreover, all power lies in the administration of the Word. Therefore He addresses this discourse especially to the priests. After all, if the leaders err, how much will those who are to be led err? Priests are called shepherds and watchmen, because Satan is always in the midst of the children of God. He is always stirring up the greedy and those who corrupt the Word. Therefore we too must always watch in the Word.

2. *To give glory.* To teach false doctrine in the name of the Lord is to blaspheme God. Paul says in 1 Cor. 15:15: "We are found to be false witnesses, etc." Every teaching of conscience comes in the name of the Lord. To glorify the name of the Lord, therefore, is to teach what is true, what pleases God, and what is the true will of God.

I will send upon you the curse, or wasting. In Scripture gifts which we have under the benediction of God are called blessings. Those priests, then, called it a blessing when they had filled their homes with plunder. "But," He says, "this is a curse, and I will turn it into a curse. I will reduce you to poverty."

Because you do not lay it to heart. "You have not recognized your sin. You have ignored it. In fact, you have defended it as righteousness."

3. *Behold, I will rebuke your offspring.* This reads more accurately: "I will rebuke your arm"; that is, "Your power, your administration, your honor of making sacrifice and of teaching I will

take away from you." The prophet had in mind the rule that gives the priests a right shoulder of the peace offerings.[1] But manure they used to carry outside the camp. "This," He says, "I will turn around. I will take your shoulder away from you and throw the dung in your face. You appear pure to yourselves, as if you were not sinning against Me. You clean the outside of the vessels, but inside you are full of filth, deceit, greed. You are interested in your bellies, etc. Therefore I will not merely take the priesthood away from you, but I will also add confusion—a filth that you will not wash away." On festive occasions the priests were outwardly absolutely clean. Within, however, they were terribly befouled, filled with greed. "The dung will carry you off with itself. That is, I will put you out along with the dung, or I will put you out just as you throw the dung out."

4. *And you shall know.* That is: "You shall find out from experience that it was My command that you should not do anything of the kind."

With Levi, that is, the covenant made with the whole tribe of Levi, the command handed down through Moses that they teach rightly and deceive no man.

5. *My covenant.* This is the commendation of the good priests to the disgrace of the wicked ones. Aaron was the first righteous priest.

Of life and peace, of happiness and safety. These God gives to those who fear Him—people like Aaron and the other saints who did not dare utter a single syllable beyond the Word of God. Heretics do not fear God. The fear of God is not a property of human strength, but He says, "I gave him fear, etc."

6. *The law of truth* [*was in his mouth*]. If the teacher has not been corrupted, the Word of God remains pure. Conversely, hypocrites teach what is corrupt and defiled. That righteous priest, then, taught the Law with purity and truth. He did not create hypocrites. He took away the showy works of outward holiness and vain faith, because the Law teaches one to recognize sins. "You priests now have the law of falsity in your mouth."

[1] Ecclus. 7:31.

No wrong was [*found on his lips*]. That is: "He did not corrupt the Word. He did not twist it. He did not add to it or detract from it."

In peace and uprightness. Here He is speaking about life-style and good example. Good works follow good teaching. They are the good fruits of a good tree.

[*He walked*] *with Me,* that is, "in My presence. He offended no one. He was a blessing to all. He paid back what he owed. He did not seek his own gain. He shared what he had." See, the prophet here includes all that is Christianity—faith, peace, uprightness. *And he turned many away* [*from iniquity*]. The fruit and effectiveness of the preached Word follow a priest who conducts his ministry in this way. You see, that is where the Holy Spirit is. From iniquity he turns away many, if not all.

7. *For the lips of a priest guard knowledge.* Certainly God could with His Spirit instruct and justify those whom He would, but it has pleased His wisdom more to instruct and save those who believe through the foolishness of preaching. The Word is the channel through which the Holy Spirit is given. This is a passage against those who hold the spoken Word in contempt. The lips are the public reservoirs of the church. In them alone is kept the Word of God. You see, unless the Word is preached publicly, it slips away. The more it is preached, the more firmly it is retained. Reading it is not as profitable as hearing it, for the live voice teaches, exhorts, defends, and resists the spirit of error. Satan does not care a hoot for the written Word of God, but He flees at the speaking of the Word. You see, this penetrates hearts and leads back those who stray. Paul says in Gal. 4:20: "I could wish to be present with you now and to change my tone, etc." The live voice is the guardian of both the Law and knowledge. It teaches the ignorant, it corrects those who err, it condemns those who corrupt it. Written words are more likely to produce trickery.

Knowledge, that is, the correct representation and recognition of things, practical judgment. Therefore, the lips of a priest are instruments for salvation to others. They guard knowledge, not in his own heart, but in the hearts of those whom he teaches and who are perfected. Such people will seek and look for the Law and will

of God from priests. You see, God has sent such a priest not as a scribe but as an angel and apostle to explain in words the business of God. A mouth and lips of this kind, then, are instruments of God. Books keep the Law privately; lips preserve it publicly. Also open lips, not closed ones, preserve it; that is, when they preach it.

8. *But you have turned away.* It is as if He were saying: "You degenerate sons of such great and important fathers ought to be ashamed. You do all things contrary to them."

From the way, that is, from the fathers' way.

You have caused [*many*] *to stumble.* "You set up stumbling blocks for your hearers so that they stray and fall away from the way. You also err and cause others to err with you. You do not convey the true sense, but your own, an alien one, even though you go over words clearly. Thus under the pretense of the Word of God you pour out poison for your people, and that is a very serious sin. You void and corrupt the covenant of Levi to whom God promised, ahead of the other tribes, the priesthood forever. From priests you have turned into wolves, thieves, pirates. You are unworthy, therefore, of conducting this office further." He says: "Because you have cast Me aside, I will also cast you aside, etc. Just as you have despised My name, so also will I make you despised and abased among all nations. I will not lift up your faces, just as you did not lift up the face of My law. There is no esteeming of a person before Me, as there is before you and all who do not teach purely."

10. *Have we not all one Father?* This passage treats some matters about divorce. At the same time it also deals with the example of marrying a foreign wife. This it censures as a sin, but most of all because this was sanctioned by their teaching as something correct. They said, "Didn't Abraham, the father of us all, marry a foreign woman? Why aren't we allowed to do this? Also, isn't our God the God of the Gentiles? Why, then, do we hold each other in contempt? Why don't we do as our father Abraham, Judah, and others did?" The Jews kept looking for relationship with the Gentiles in order to have peace; for otherwise the Gentiles had despised them. Also, the Gentiles used to give rich dowries to their daughters. Because of this, their daughters held

dominion over their husbands, contrary to God's command, but this is what usually happens when they bring a large dowry. But we may better understand this to be the words of a prophet who is urging them not to marry foreigners and despise their own kin and Jewish women; of a prophet stirring their sympathy with their unity of blood: "Have we not all one Father, etc."; and with their unity in the worship of God: "Has not one God created us?" These are also two outstanding statements for correcting the cruelty of husbands, namely, if they look at their wives as God's creation and as women who have a God in common with them. This is what Peter is saying in 1 Peter 3:7: "Let husbands live considerately with their wives, etc." Here he also lifts their eyes to God and indicates that they honor God when they honor their wives as God's creation.

Why then are we faithless to one another? Faithless in that one does not wish to marry another's daughter or sister, etc. בָּגַד means two things: to hold in contempt and to disregard it as if it were nothing. When the conviction is added to a wrong that someone thinks it is right, then he not only holds it in contempt but also disregards it. Thus the Jews held their brothers in contempt, and thus violated the covenant of the fathers. This was not a covenant which the fathers had set up, but one which came through the fathers to their descendants. That covenant is the law of God. This is therefore a notorious disregard of the divine law (it is also called an abomination) not only among the common people and out in the country but also in Jerusalem, where the leaders and priests live who hold in contempt the command of God about not marrying foreign women.

11. [*For Judah has profaned*] *the sanctuary of the Lord,* that is, the Law. With a careful eye, then, the prophet takes a look at those who corrupt the Law. You see, as long as the teaching remains pure, there is hope for easily correcting one's life. The rays of the sun remain pure even when they fall and shine on manure. And God keeps something holy in our midst through which we may be sanctified, even if we have fallen. This is His Word, by which we quickly condemn a sin that has been committed. The Lord magnifies this.

Which He loves. "Obviously it is the Lord who loves it. But you have no pangs of conscience over this because you have corrupted it so."

He had the daughter of a foreign god. That is, he married the daughter of a foreign god and behaved as a husband to her. He knew this woman, a foreigner, an ungodly woman.

12. *The Lord will destroy the man.* Or, "The Lord will cut off the man," so great a sin is it to corrupt the Word. Against such we must show no moderation. But in an evil deed, we must deal with brothers in patience and must instruct them gently. עֵר indicates a teacher or "one who rouses." It means princes. Some explain these two (עֵר וְעֹנֶה) as opponent and respondent; others, as instigator and executor. The Lord will cut off those who cut off His Law, whoever they may be: princes, people, priest.

13. *You were covering* [*the altar of the Lord*] *with tears.* The Lord wanted people to serve and worship Him not in sadness but in joy. "Rejoice before the Lord," He says (cf. Deut. 26:11). Grief was polluting the priests. But here everything was filled with grieving mourners—obviously the Jewish women, because the Jews despised them and were marrying foreign women. From the Jewish women the priests received offerings of grief contrary to the Law. Thus one improper thing begets more. He is saying: "All your sacrifices are corrupt. I have no way of regarding highly either you or your offerings, which you, nevertheless, think are acceptable and pleasing to Me." Whoever offends his neighbor worships God in vain, for He says, "I want mercy and not sacrifice" (Hos. 6:6; Matt. 9:13).

14. *You ask: Why does He not?* See how they hold Him in contempt and ignore Him! They do not acknowledge their sin. In fact, they defend it.

Because the Lord was witness. He is saying, "The Lord has sanctified your marriage and said, 'Therefore a man will leave his father, etc. (Gen. 2:24).' He has called the wife a helpmeet. That is, behold the witness and decree of God. A wife is a gift of God. Therefore she is her husband's helper. A man should cling to her with all his heart." This is no small comfort for spouses, that they have a divine witness. They must note especially this, that the prophet is saying this against divorce.

And she is your companion. He is explaining what sort of helper a wife is: a companion for life, a wife by covenant and pact which God has made between spouses and which they have made with each other.

15. *And the one did not do it.* This is a confutation against citing the example of Abraham. It is as if he were saying: "What you say is meaningless: 'One did it, Abraham; he married a foreigner. Therefore we may also do this. Also, he later divorced her. Therefore we may also do this.'" To imitate an act of the fathers contrary to God's call is very unhealthy. The teaching of this act is most harmful. Rather we must imitate their faith and obedience to the Word of God. God wants one person to do and perform one thing, another to do and perform something else. This man should be an eye, that one a foot, etc. Let each person see what command God has given him, and not what someone else has done. But they want to emulate Abraham. They say: "That holy man, our father, did this. His spirit has not died. We who are his seed have the same spirit." The negative here should be applied to both propositions, as the Hebrews commonly do.[2] The prophet answers: "There is no good reason for you to raise this objection against me. Investigate the history, and you will see that it is not what you think. For Abraham did not follow the lust of the flesh and riches, as you want to do, but he was forced to act to look for the seed that God had promised him. After all, he saw that Sarah was barren. At Sarah's bidding he took another, not a wealthy woman, not because of her relationship, not for lust's sake, not a foreigner but a servant from his household. He thought that perhaps through her would come to pass what God had promised. This was before God expressed Himself about Sarah as the future mother. He did not do, then, what had been forbidden, as you do, but he carried out a command under the authority of God. Also, Abraham did not leave his spirit to you, because you follow your flesh, you seek riches.

[2] The Halle manuscript has: This verse I would quote as follows: *Et non unus fecit et residuum spiritus eius.* For the Hebrews one negative applies to both statements, as in the psalm (Ps. 44:18): "Our heart has not turned back, nor have You let our steps depart from Your way" *(Et non recessit retro cor nostrum; et declinasti semitas nostras a via tua).* The meaning therefore is: "And it does not follow, or don't bring up the objection, that one, namely, Abraham, did it and the remainder of his spirit, that is Abraham's spirit (we), will not do it."

Therefore guard your spirit; stand firm on what you have been told: 'A man will cleave to his wife (Gen. 2:24).' You have the command to marry the daughters of Judah. Remain firm in the Word of promise, through which the Spirit comes. God is seeking your seed, not a Gentile seed."

[*Let none be faithless to*] *the wife of his youth,* that is, "the wife you married when you were a young man." Some explain this according to the Latin text this way: "Didn't God make us all? Even foreign women are the remnant of His Spirit. God wanted us to be His remnant and handful after the captivity. What does this one God ask for but the seed of God? That is, we should multiply ourselves by any women whatsoever."

16. *Because you hate her.* This is another objection, namely, to be allowed to divorce wives by authority of the Law. The prophet answers as does Christ (Matt. 19:3-10), that one should not abandon his wife; that the flesh should not be separated but joined together. The text of Moses does not say "because you hate her" but "if she finds no favor in your eyes because you have found some indecency in her" (cf. Deut. 24:1). But if anyone wants to divorce his wife, the Lord says, "Iniquity will cover him." It is as if he were saying: "If you wish to do this according to this law which is given to and borne by the wicked, the hard-hearted, and the cruel, well and good. Then you must bear the name of being evil and wicked rascals. After all, whoever divorces his wife because he hates her is revealed as a violator, a hurter, a promise-breaker, a violator of his pledge, a man who lacks honesty and honor, one who has not done what he should but what he should not. That iniquitous stain he will carry on his coat. He will be marked, so that he is recognized, with this name: that is, 'He couldn't bear his wife's behavior.' This stain covers him like a cloak. It is as clear and noticeable as a cloak. Thus Christ says 'for hardness of heart, etc.' (Matt. 19:8). You are hard-headed, stiffnecked, and peevish. No one can handle you." Also, "cloak" everywhere also signifies outward behavior. The sense then is this: "Outwardly you want to appear to be a saintly man, a good man. You have a fine coat. But I am going to mark it and show that you are wicked, cruel, ἄστοργος ("lacking natural affection"),[3] etc. None of the saints divorced his

[3] Cf. *Luther's Works,* 6, pp. 252—256.

wife, nor do we read this about others of the people of God, so that also in that account God declares that that law was given only for hardened murderers and haters of men. Yet the prophet is especially treating that matter which they not only did badly but also defended by example and by the Law. Yet the Law most of all ought to teach the knowledge of sin. They, however, wanted to excuse their sin through the Law, and that is a doctrine of the devil. Abraham was deeply grieved that he had to divorce his concubine Hagar.

17. *You have wearied the Lord.* That is, you have caused the Lord to be angry with you and ashamed of you. When the wicked see themselves flourish and grow but those who worship God suffer many adversities, they say that there is no God or that He is unfair or a liar. They even rebuke Him in regard to His promises. Why, even the saints in a similar zeal have often murmured against God. It seems right that the just should rule and that the wicked should serve, but the opposite is occurring. The kingdom of God, however, rests on faith. It demands faith. Also, in the midst of their tribulation, God comforts His people. In the midst of death, He gives them life. These, then, are the words of wicked men: "Where now is the judgment of God, etc.?" He is saying: "With such words you grieve the Lord." Reason has a false idea about God. That is why Christ says in John 16:8: "The Holy Spirit will convince the world concerning judgment."

CHAPTER THREE

1. *Behold, I will send My messenger.* The people are tired. The preacher, the prophet, is tired. They say: "Wait. Wait again, etc. No matter how much we serve the Lord, yet the Gentiles have it better than we." But He says: "Have confidence. Behold, your salvation is now at the door and that kingdom will be changed. Your murmurings and the complaints of the prophets will cease, who believe that they are preaching in vain. The righteous will be separated from the wicked, and the wicked will no longer be more powerful, more fortunate." But He is saying all this in a spiritual sense and especially in regard to His teaching and accomplishment. Where the pure Gospel is, there Christ rules. There are excluded the heretics, the antichrists, the wicked, the hypocrites, those who remain in sin and death. In the old synagog there were more wicked teachers than good ones. Two men who teach contrary doctrines cannot stay at the same time. The people want one true and steadfast teacher whom they can trust. Here the Lord promises one who would give his hearers a sound and secure mind in all their tribulations. He says, "I will send you the genuine Malachi,[1] that is, a messenger, who is John the Baptist."

[*To prepare*] *My way.* These are Christ's words, even though He Himself quotes them differently.[2] A prince who is about to enter a city sends messengers ahead to prepare for him whatever is necessary as well as others to clear a path for him lest he be hindered by thronging people. פִּנָּה means to empty, to make room, or even to provide a reputation. John, therefore, will see to it that the appearance of the way would look beautiful and unencum-

[1] The meaning of the Hebrew name Malachi (מַלְאָכִי), "My Angel," is emphasized.

[2] Cf. Matt. 11:10; Mark 1:2; Luke 7:27.

bered. After all, there are many things which hinder the "way," that is, the work of the Lord. Those things must be removed, especially human reason, self-love, one's own wisdom, one's own righteousness, etc. That preparing, then, is to make humble and to arrange things so as to allow God to work in one. You see, the way of the Lord is where He Himself walks. The prophet mentions nothing about our ways except that we should abstain from them. After all, our works lie in His way, so that Christ cannot work or enter. John told all the Jews and those doing very fine works "Repent!" as if he were speaking to sinners. He is saying: "Let the Lord enter. He Himself will justify you and will do the will of the Lord. Neither you nor your works will do this." This is what it means to convince the world of sin, of righteousness, etc. Those who believe, then, are those who are prepared to meet the Lord and to receive Him. In them He is able to work, that is, in those who have been brought back to a knowledge of their sins.

And the Lord will come suddenly. He will come suddenly, unexpectedly, immediately after His messenger. He says in John 1:26-30: "Among you stands One whom you do not know . . . even He who ranks before me." That is, He was ordained to preach and to save.

To His temple. This is that physical or spiritual temple, the church.

The Lord whom you seek. "You seek Him to free you from the wicked, to be both your Priest and your protecting King, the Messenger of the covenant, that is, the Messenger of the agreement and the glorious King. Unlike David, He will not rule physically but in the preaching of the Word. He is the Messenger, the Minister of the living Word." The covenant is the promises of God, which all point to Christ, even the temporal promises. The covenant required death. Therefore, He is here identified not only as God but also as the Man who suffered, died, and even now rules. The distribution of the [inheritance of the] covenant is eternal life.

Behold, He comes! The repetition indicates certainty.

2. *But who can endure the day of His coming?* In Hebrew this reads: "Who will regulate or control the day, etc.?" or, "Who will provide?" It is as if he were saying: "Remain in your fear, then.

Stay humble. Let that Messenger prepare you. You see, He will not come in royal garb, as the kings of the world do. He will come before any man will be able to foresee when and how He will come. He will fulfill all things, and no one will know that He is the Christ." With this the prophet reveals the very great humiliation of the Word and of the Son of God. Still today His coming is like this, unexpected.

And who will stand when He appears? With this the prophet is speaking about the stumbling block which is in Christ. "He will appear to be of such lowly character that, unless you will have listened to the voice of that previous messenger and will have followed his pointing finger, none of you is going to receive Him. None of you will believe in Him. Rather you are going to say, 'Ah, here is a king who has no place to lay his head, who is crucified and dies.'" Because of this, Christ Himself says (Matt. 11:6): "Blessed is he who takes no offense at Me," that is, "Blessed is the man who does not measure Me according to his reason." Therefore His messenger also is sent ahead so that the light of reason may be extinguished and the carpenter's Son may be recognized as the Messiah. Many who were looking were not seeing, for who will stand firm in the faith?

For He is like a blazing fire. Blazing, or purifying. That is, "He will condemn all your works and enthusiasms. All your attitudes will have to be mortified, just as a fire melts and purifies silver and separates it from all impurities." בֹּרִית means a sharp cleaning agent or soap that washes great stains out of garments. This is how Christ will condemn all things and demand only spiritual qualities. In spite of his scales, Satan has a very difficult time enduring this. The Jews kept puffing themselves up with their own righteousness. From this it is very difficult to pull them away to follow Christ. The kingdom of Christ is a mystical smelting furnace that purges out the impurity of the old Adam. Here the prophet seems to be speaking about the white linen cloaks which eastern people wore most commonly. These are washed with soap. Christ is not merely the Purifier but also the purifying Agent. He is not only the Blacksmith but also the Fire; not only the Cleaner but also the Soap. He does not sit indolently at the right hand of His Father. Rather He is always working among us vitally, effectively, and uninterruptedly as He is spread abroad over His mystical body, as fire is applied to metal. So He is elsewhere called Salvation, and not just Savior. That is, He is Salvation itself and the Laboratory of salvation. This is what Christians sense. They have less affection for wealth; they are less afraid of death; they disregard everything secular. The power to do this is the "fire" and the "soap."

3. *He will sit as a blazing fire.* The "seat" has the force of teaching and of judgment. This, then, is a strange kingdom, established not on external armor but on the cleansing of people, on the renewing of souls which are then brought back to salvation and eternal life. To be sure, this is a magnificent situation. It is, however, a spiritual kingdom. Outwardly it offends all flesh.

And purifier of silver. In Ps. 12:6 we have this: "The promises of the Lord are promises that are pure, [silver refined in a furnace on the ground, purified seven times]." To be sure, the Word of God is completely pure in itself, but it is purified in us daily because it purifies us. Scripture is a very bright light, but to a wicked man it is pure darkness. God is very well known, but if you don't know Him, that is your fault. These words are light. Christ is the Purifier; [3] He is Righteousness, Redemption, Life, etc. I say, these words are light which we never look at enough and which becomes clearer every day. The matter lies not in the sound of the words but in the inmost depths of the heart. The sun is darkness to the blind. That is not the fault of the sun but of blind or closed eyes.

And He will purify the sons of Levi. He is now explaining what that purifying of silver is, namely, the purifying of Holy Writ, for our sake. You see, here is where all the wise men of the world do battle and want to make this obscure. Yet, while their dung keeps smelling, the Word of God always becomes more clear. Finally "their folly will be plain to all." [4] Furthermore, the prophet is indicating that the kingdom of Christ will be totally sacerdotal, and that there will be no distinction or respect of persons. Everyone in this kingdom is Christ's brother. Through Christ, each can come to God and pray and teach. There will be other, true Levites, namely,

[3] For *emendator* we have read *emundator* to agree with the Vulgate *text emundans argentum.*

[4] With 1 Tim. 3:9 we have read *omnibus* for *omnium.*

purified ones, and the old ones will have been rejected, for they were only purified outwardly but within were wicked and impure.

And He will refine them. "He will purify, elevate, cleanse them. He will remove the dross of false doctrine to reveal the light of divine truth through the Word by which they themselves will be led. The kingdom of Christ is the exercise of Word and faith because of the perpetual harm of the wicked. Whoever, therefore, wishes to become a Christian must give himself over to being purified.

Offerings in righteousness. A sacrifice in righteousness is a sacrifice of the new covenant. After all, what need would there have been to promise sacrifices that they were already making? The things they were doing then, however, were all impure because impure priests were making the sacrifices. Moreover, the sacrifices of Christians are pure and right, because they themselves are pure and right, as we read in Ps. 132:9: "Let Thy priests be clothed with righteousness, etc." In this way, then, the prophet describes first the justification of the person, and then the righteous work. Our sacrifice is the mortification of the flesh, signified by the tearing away and destruction of that old flesh. But by the fire of the Spirit and of love a fragrance very sweet to the Lord is kindled.

4. *And the offering . . . will be pleasing to the Lord.* When the persons are pleasant and pleasing, their sacrifices, too, are pleasant and pleasing.

As in the days of old and as in former years, that is, as in the days before the Law had been given. You see, all this has been said in reproach of the Law. After all, hypocrites started when the Law was given. Before the Law, sacrifices were sanctioned through faith. But the same faith, the same Spirit, the same grace which existed in the days before the Law will be in the kingdom of Christ. Faith makes voluntary offerings, while the Law compels them against the will.

5. *Then I will draw near to you [for judgment].* After the prophet has described how it will be with the saints in the kingdom of Christ, he now reveals what will become of the wicked, who will be separated[5] from the righteous. Purity of doctrine will

[5] We have read *separabuntur* for *superabuntur.*

remain with the righteous. Those who are befouled with manifest wickedness will not be tolerated in that new kingdom. He says: "I will come through the Word for judgment. I will excommunicate, condemn, cut off."

And I will be a witness, "one who blames, censures. I will not leave anything hidden. Poisoners and evildoers abuse the Word of God. Therefore they will be excluded."

And those who oppress widows, that is, who rob them.

6. *For I the Lord do not change.* "I do not lie. I do not revoke the promises I have made through so many prophets. So, have no doubt! Your unworthiness will not hold back My truth. I have promised freely. I will redeem those promises freely. It is for this that I brought you back out of captivity, to fulfill My promises. The entire matter, therefore, must be credited to divine goodness and not to any [6] merits of any men, for you have always sinned against Me." That He says "From the days of your fathers" (v. 7) corresponds to that earlier statement (Mal. 2:17): "Everyone who does evil is a good man, etc." He turns the blame back onto them. It is mercy, then, that they have not been destroyed.

7. *Return to Me, and I will return to you.* These words seem to support the free will of man. They are, however, words of the Law, upon which the ability to obey does not immediately follow. After all, He has already said that they had never kept the Law, even if they were eager to keep it. To be sure, God is a good Lawgiver, but we are lazy doers of it. The Law tells us what we should do. He says, "Return to obey Me, and I will return to you to bless you. I will be your kind Father of mercies."

How shall we return? The prophet has to deal with holy hypocrites, who are unwilling to accept rebuke and who are unaware of any sin or turning away from God.

8. *If a man will rob God.* "Will man attack or rob God? Because you have robbed Me." This is a Hebraism. There is a similar passage in Jer. 2:10: "Cross to the coasts of Cyprus and see, etc." Here God is challenging the behavior of the entire human race. Everywhere they worship their gods with great care and

[6] We have read *ullis* for *ullus.*

never steal anything from an idol, except that among the Jews things are stolen from the true God. Furthermore, He reproaches their behavior no more than their doctrine, because they have been defending their sins, and that is the unforgivable sin against the Holy Spirit. That is when one cultivates a lie for the sake of piety. Reason, which controls the heathen, teaches that something sacrilegious is wicked, but the Jews even defended this as right. So also the papists worship their idols more diligently than the true God. Now, although we ought to be giving to ministers of the Word and to the poor, we are more eager to get and to take away. Formerly we were very quick in our giving. But we then gave not a few things to misleaders and to the outright worthless.

In your tithes and offerings. There were two rituals connected with offerings. One consisted of a simple elevation. These were called תְּרוּמָה. The other would be done with a gesture to the four points of the compass. These they called תְּנוּפָה. He says: "In regard to those things which you ought to be giving to feed the priests, you inflict violence and theft on Me." Certainly God does not say this as if He really cared about tithes, etc. Rather He says it to preserve the ministry of the Word.

9. *In your poverty you are cursed.* "You have been cursed with a curse, a wasting away. Because you have committed sacrilege against Me, I will see to it that all your possessions waste away. You will not rejoice in your possessions,[7] because there is no benediction there; or, more accurately, because you suffer poverty and put the blame back on Me, you are stealing from Me what belongs to Me."

10. *Bring* [*in the full tithe*]. An exhortation follows the reproach. He is saying: "Let there be food in My house. See to it that My priests may stay. 'Seek first the kingdom of God, etc.' First satisfy Me and see whether or not I am going to satisfy you also." God is the kind of Physician who tears away to repair, who becomes angry to show mercy, who cuts to heal. Against Satan He only wounds and does not heal again. We have here also the Hebrew phrase "to open heaven." This means to rain. For heaven to be closed means not to rain.

[7] We have read *possessione* for *professione.*

11. *I will rebuke the devourer for you.* This [devourer] is a singular for the plural: caterpillars, gnawing worms, and destroyers of grain and fruit, etc. After all, what would the situation be if there were an abundance in the fields and the worms were eating everything? Ah, where is faith here? God grants and preserves all things, and He destroys them again when He wishes.

12. *For you will be a land of delight.* "All nations will want to have such a land as you have, fertile and protected from worms." This, then, is a rebuke and an exhortation for those who neglect the ministers of God. Furthermore, no one gives enough consideration to what great loss would follow, should preachers of God's Word be neglected.

13. *Your words have been stout against Me.* Here we have another discourse and another rebuke (about which also chapter 2:17 above spoke)[8] of the sin of the murmuring of the Jews over the good fortune of the Gentiles and over their own misfortune, for they were the people of God and preserved the Law, whereas the Gentiles, on the other hand, did none of these things. And yet, here the complaint is directed more at the murmuring against those who were living among the Jews, in fact, against their own brothers. You see, because the Holy Spirit had not yet been given and the mystery of Christ had not yet been revealed, therefore when the prophets preached the promises of God, those who always saw the opposite happening would become angry. The muttering of the flesh against God is a fault very difficult to overcome. He says, then: "[Your words] have been stout," that is, "your words have been harsh, bitter, strong against Me. I can no longer endure your murmurs and blasphemies." They were sacrilegious in their work, blasphemous in their words. In addition to this, they defended their sins. They said, "What have we spoken against You? We have walked in blackness and darkness; we have been defiled; our souls, bodies and lives have been afflicted, and He gave us no answer. God does not freely bless. Yet we see the proud, the stubborn, the presumptuous, the licentious, the insolent, the rash, the savage leading a sweet life and having good fortune, and we are forced to deem them blessed" (v. 15).

[8] The text reads "chapter 3, above, at the beginning," but the last verse of chapter 2 was thought to be the first verse of chapter 3.

15. *Indeed, they have prospered.* "They have prospered in family, in flocks, in property."

They have been saved. "They are not chastised, they are not punished as are we who worship the true God."

16. *Then those* [*who feared the Lord*] *spoke with one another.* He is saying that they have not been forgotten in the presence of God. He Himself is writing in a book of remembrance what they are saying to each other, those who comfort each other, who fear God, who do not murmur, who do not become upset because of the good fortune of the wicked.

Who thought on the name of God. That is, they persevered in their worship and piety, even though they were suffering persecution.

17. *On the day when I make them My possession.* That is: "When I shall make an end, namely, of their murmurings and blasphemy, they shall become My possession, or property. That is, they will be revealed as people who belong to Me and already are Mine." This seems to be spoken about the kingdom of the New Testament. After all, the people who were under the Law always murmured and blasphemed.

And I will spare them as a man spares [*his son who serves him*]. Here He promises that He is going to be a Father who is kindly disposed to those who fear and serve Him, that is, to the believers. When He says "I will spare," He indicates that that kingdom would come not without sin. Therefore, it would be a kingdom of grace and forgiveness of sins, a kingdom of sparing. He says, "At that time you shall see clearly what a great difference there is between the righteous and the wicked, etc." (v. 18).

CHAPTER FOUR

1. *For behold, the day will come.* All this is being said about Christ. Those who fear God are comforting each other and are saying these things to each other. At the time when they trust in His Word, the righteous certainly have everything opposing them. On the other hand, the wicked have everything going well for them. This is not the way it will always be for both groups, but only until the hour came, etc. "The day will come," namely, the day of Christ's kingdom.

Nor offshoot, that is, "branch." You see, the light of the Gospel has burned and devoured the entire synagog. Now it has neither root nor branch, neither kingdom nor priesthood. The day of the revelation of the Gospel has consumed all these, so that nothing of them remains.

2. *And [the Sun of righteousness] will rise for you who fear.* In the Mosaic kingdom there is pure darkness. All things are hidden in mystery [1] and are confused. Then the wicked will be separated from the righteous by something shining—obviously, by the open truth of God through the Gospel of Christ. Here you see the kingdom of Christ again described in such a way that it is the ministry of the Word. He is saying: "Indeed, a new Sun will shine, and it is not that sun which also animals see. It is the Sun of righteousness, who justifies, who sends out the sort of rays that make men righteous and free from their sins, who drives out every harmful attitude of fleshly lust. Those rays are the Word of the Gospel, which penetrates hearts and is seen as that Sun only by the eyes of the heart, that is, by faith. It is closer to the righteous than is that visible, physical sun. You see, it shines by the Holy

[1] For *in ministerio* we have read *in mysterio*.

Spirit. It shines day and night. Clouds do not hinder it. It is always rising. 'It will rise for those of you who fear'—who fear the name of God, obviously; that is, the humble, those who are not presumptuous, those who do not trust in their own works but recognize that they are sinners."

With healing in His wings. Here you clearly see that we cannot explain this as the Last Day, when judgment will come. But now there will be salvation and protection under the shadow of Christ. Such, then, is the rule of Christ that He Himself is the Mediator and Protector, the way a hen protects her chicks from the hawk. Therefore, let everyone who wants to be safe from the wrath and judgment of God seek refuge under the wings of Christ. This is what the Law urges. Under the Law there is weakness and condemnation; under the wings of Christ, under the Gospel, there is strength and salvation. The Sun rises when the Gospel is preached. One hides under the wings when he believes. Therefore, although you may be a sinner, yet you will be safe when you flee for refuge under His wings. You will not fear death. The lust of the flesh will not overpower you.

You shall go forth like calves leaping from the stall. Here is the fruit of faith and of the kingdom of Christ, a happy conscience, a public confession of faith, thanksgiving, joy in affliction, preaching and the conversion of others to salvation.

Leaping. More accurately: "You shall be poured out, you shall be increased." This is a property of joy. Sadness, on the other hand, confines. The Christian believes that the world is his. He goes out into the open. He does not head for the corners.

Like calves leaping from the stall. He says: "This is the way you will be corralled in the righteousness of faith. You will be active. Your fodder is Christ."

3. *You shall tread down the wicked.* There are always enemies of the church, tyrants or heretics or false brothers. Heretics keep the righteous busy, and they [the heretics] finally are reduced to nothing, to ashes, to dust, etc. "The faithfulness of the Lord endures forever."[2] The fire of Christ will reduce them to ashes.

[2] *Veritas Domini manet in eternum* (Ps. 117:2).

Therefore, you will tread them down easily. Yet, they first tread us down. But finally the wheel turns, and nothing grows from ashes.

4. *Remember the law of My servant Moses.* Malachi has now prophesied about the kingdom of Christ, but it has not yet come. He says: "In the meantime, be included under the Law until that Sun shines. The Law will last until the time of Him who will not come without first sending ahead His messenger, who will say that He is there. Therefore neither neglect Moses nor put him aside. He bears witness to you about Christ; he holds you back from evil. When the time comes for Me to free you, I will send you My messenger in the spirit and courage of Elijah, etc." This passage, then, is the closing of Holy Scripture, the end of the Old Testament. Here the prophet stops and waits for the messenger Elijah, who is John the Baptist, who is going to perform the function of Elijah, "to turn the hearts of fathers to their children." Thus they will recognize the wisdom and faith of their fathers, they will all together be in harmony about Christ. They have already been separated into sects, as John discovered when he preached the baptism of repentance and saw the many Pharisees and Sadducees, etc., in short, that this one people had one heart, one faith, etc. The time of the Gospel is the day. All the rest is night and darkness. You see, Christ Himself is the Sun.

Terrible. It will blind the proud, illumine the humble.

Great. It will magnify; it will give life, justify, save, etc.

6. *Lest I come and smite the earth with a curse,* that is: "Lest I reduce it to absolutely nothing." This is the way Scripture uses the word חֵרֶם, anathema, that which may not be redeemed but must be consumed. "Lest this happen among My people and that at least a remnant be saved, I will send John, etc."

The End of Malachi

By LUTHER POELLOT

INDEX TO SCRIPTURE PASSAGES